Microsoft

Office 2000 Visual Basic for Applications

Fundamentals

David Boctor

D1604683

Microsoft Press

PUBLISHED BY
Microsoft Press
A Division of Microsoft Corporation
One Microsoft Way
Redmond, Washington 98052-6399

Library of Congress Cataloging-in-Publication Data
Boctor, David S., 1972-
    Microsoft Office 2000/Visual Basic for Applications Fundamentals /
  David Boctor.
      p. cm.
   ISBN 0-7356-0594-7
   1. Microsoft Office. 2. Business--Computer programs.
 I. Microsoft Press. II. Title
 HF5548.4.M525B628 1999
 005.369--dc21   99-20167
                                                CIP

Printed and bound in the United States of America.

1 2 3 4 5 6 7 8 9 WCWC   4 3 2 1 0 9

Distributed in Canada by Penguin Books Canada Limited.

A CIP catalogue record for this book is available from the British Library.

Microsoft Press books are available through booksellers and distributors worldwide. For further information about international editions, contact your local Microsoft Corporation office or contact Microsoft Press International directly at fax (425) 936-7329. Visit our Web site at mspress.microsoft.com.

TrueType fonts is a registered trademark of Apple Computer, Inc. ActiveX, FrontPage, Microsoft, the Microsoft Internet Explorer logo, Microsoft Press, the Microsoft Press logo, MSDN, MS-DOS, the Office logo, Outlook, PowerPoint, Visual Basic, the Visual Basic logo, Visual C++, Visual J++, Visual Studio, Windows, and Windows NT are either registered trademarks or trademarks of Microsoft Corporation in the United States and/or other countries. Other product and company names mentioned herein may be the trademarks of their respective owners.

The example companies, organizations, products, people, and events depicted herein are fictitious. No association with any real company, organization, product, person, or event is intended or should be inferred.

Acquisitions Editor: Eric Stroo
Project Editor: Rebecca McKay

For nSight, Inc.

Project Editor: Peter Whitmer
Manuscript Editor: Joseph Gustaitis
Technical Editor: Mannie White (Pioneer Training)

Contents

Part 1

Learning Microsoft Visual Basic for Applications

Part 2

Managing Documents and Files and Manipulating Document Content

Part 3

Working Across Applications

Chapter 7
Communicating Across Microsoft Office   **233**

Chapter 8
Developing an Integrated Office Solution   **257**

Part 4

Working with Active Window Content

Part 6

Developing COM Add-Ins for Office

Acknowledgments

I would like to thank Rebecca McKay, project editor at Microsoft Press, for her encouragement and understanding, and Peter Whitmer, project manager at nSight, Inc., for his contributions.

I would also like to thank my friends Noah Edelstein, for his perspectives, and being one of the funniest people I know; and Christopher Konrad, for his encouragement, and being one of the craziest people I know. And to Cynthia, for the balance she gave to me.

Introduction

Creating documents, building databases, and writing e-mail are just some of the things you can do with Microsoft Office 2000. But Office 2000 also gives you a way to do these and other tasks, as well as extend built-in functionality, through Microsoft Visual Basic programming. This book shows you how to develop the Visual Basic code that will let your Visual Basic programs automate tasks, tie content together, extend existing functionality, and develop new functionality for Office applications through COM add-ins. You'll learn how to take features beyond their original design in order to meet the needs of your customers or your company.

Microsoft Office 2000 Visual Basic for Applications Fundamentals is organized by *task* rather than by *application*. For example, the task of retrieving the current selection in the Microsoft Word, Microsoft Excel, Microsoft PowerPoint, and Microsoft Outlook applications is discussed in one place. The same goes for saving Word, Excel, or PowerPoint documents. Whether you need to develop code that accomplishes a task in any single application or in all of them, you will understand the similarities and differences among the applications. The side-by-side comparisons and code samples give you a way of learning how to write code to accomplish the same task in several Office applications.

The side-by-side comparisons are grouped in the following ways:

- How to insert and manipulate content such as text, tables, shapes, cells, values, and anything else that makes up a document. (Chapter 6)

- How to create and manipulate a document (the content's container). (Chapters 4 and 5)

- How to start one application from another to allow your programs to share and use content from one document source in another. (Chapters 7 and 8)

- How to retrieve and set the selection of content in a document window. (Chapters 9 and 10)

This book also describes how to do the following in any Office 2000 Professional application:

- Manipulate menus and toolbars.

- Set up event procedures.

- Develop COM add-ins so that you can tie all tasks and functionality together into a redistributable solution for you and your customers.

Important   This book is designed for use with Word, Excel, PowerPoint, Microsoft Access, and Outlook in Microsoft Office 2000 Professional, Premium, or Developer for the Microsoft Windows 95, Windows 98, Windows NT 4.0, and Windows 2000 operating systems. This book is also designed for use with Microsoft Visual Basic 6.0 Professional Edition in order to build COM add-ins for Office 2000. The COM add-in examples in this book, however, can also be used to build COM add-ins with Microsoft Office 2000 Developer. To find out what version of the software you're running, you can check the product package, or you can start Word, Excel, PowerPoint, Access, or Outlook, click the Help menu, and click About Microsoft <product> (where <product> represents the application you started). If the version of your software isn't compatible with this book, a Microsoft Press book for your software is probably available. Please visit our World Wide Web site at *http://mspress.microsoft.com/* or call 1-800-MSPRESS for more information.

Finding Your Best Starting Point

This book is designed for Office users who are learning to program with the Visual Basic language and for programmers who have experience with Visual Basic programming but who want to understand the services and objects provided by Office in order to integrate Office with, for example, a larger software solution. This book is also designed for the experienced Office developer who needs a reference to the new programming functionality that Office now provides, including the new COM add-in and event support.

To find your best starting point in this book (and get the information you need to build your custom Visual Basic programs), consult the section entitled "The Fundamentals Roadmap" towards the beginning of Chapter 1. The Fundamentals Roadmap diagram will give you a quick look at the elements in the user interface or the content in a document that you might want to manipulate through Visual Basic code. The diagram will direct you to the chapter that contains the descriptions and samples you'll need to manipulate elements of the user interface, documents, and content. Chapter 1 also contains a description of this book's six parts, along with a list of sample scenarios to help you find the information you need.

Installing and Using the Practice Files

The CD inside this book's back cover contains practice files that you can reference as you perform the exercises in the book. By using these practice files, you won't need to spend time creating the samples used in the chapters—instead, you can concentrate on learning how to become proficient at using Visual Basic for Applications in Office. With the files and the samples in the chapters, you'll also learn by doing, which is an easy and effective way to acquire and remember new skills.

Installing the Practice Files on Your Computer

To install the practice files on your computer's hard disk so that you can use them with the exercises in this book, complete the following steps:

1. Remove the CD from the package inside the back cover and insert it into your CD-ROM drive.

2. On the taskbar at the bottom of your screen, click the Start button, and then click Run.

    The Run dialog box appears.

3. In the Open box, type **d:setup** (if your CD-ROM drive uses a drive letter other than "d," substitute the correct drive letter).

4. Click OK, and then follow the directions on the screen.

    The setup program window appears with recommended options preselected for you. For best results using the practice files with this book, accept these preselected settings.

5. After the files have been installed, remove the CD from your drive and replace it in the package inside the back cover of the book.

    A folder called Office VBA Fundamentals has been created on your hard disk, and the practice files have been placed in that folder.

Using the Practice Files

Each chapter in this book explains when and how to use any practice files for that chapter. When it's time to use a practice file, the book will give you instructions on how to open it. You should always save the practice file with a new name (as directed in the chapter). That way the original practice file will be available if you want to go back and redo any of the chapters.

Here's a list of the practice files included on the practice CD, along with where each file is used:

Chapter	Filename	Description
2	Basics.ppt	Reveals the fundamentals of the Visual Basic programming language.
3	UserForm.xls	Provides a set of custom UserForms showing the use of buttons, list boxes, drop-down lists, and other common controls in dialog boxes.
	frmBasic.frm, frmAsst.frm, frmSubwy.frm, FullWizd.frm	Each file provides a UserForm template for the different stages of creating an Office wizard.

(continued)

(continued)

Chapter	Filename	Description
	modAsst.bas, Assistnt.bmp	Contains code to display tips in the Assistant balloon, as well as to close it when necessary. The code is reusable in any Office application. The file Assistnt.bmp is a bitmap file you can use on a button on a custom dialog box. The button gives your users a way to display the Office Assistant and access help for your solution.
	modBrwse.bas, modFlDlg.bas	Show how to use Windows application programming interfaces (APIs) to display the Browse for Folder and File dialog boxes provided by the Windows operating system.
4	DocMgtWd.bas, DocMgtXl.bas, DocMgtPp.bas	Show how to use the Add and Open methods on the Documents, Workbooks, and Presentations collection objects to create and open documents. They also show how to use the *Print, Close, SaveAs,* and related save methods in Word, Excel, and PowerPoint.
	FileMgmt.bas	Contains code that uses built-in functions in the Visual Basic for Applications language to parse filenames. The code also tells you how to display Windows system dialog boxes that allow the user to specify a file or folder.
	FileSys.bas	Contains code that uses the Microsoft Scripting Runtime object library, which provides objects, methods, and properties you can use to access the file system where your program is executed. Before you use this code in your program, you need to reference the Microsoft Scripting Runtime object library in the References dialog box of your Visual Basic development environment.
	OutlItem.bas	Contains code to create an Outlook e-mail item from any Office application.
	SHGetFdr.bas	This module contains the definition of the Windows application programming interface (API) named SHGetSpecialFolderLocation, which is used to get folders like the Desktop, Application Data, and Favorites on the user's machine.
	ShellExc.bas	Shows how to use the ShellExecute Windows application programming interface (API) to load or print any file or load an application on your machine. The ShellExecute API is used to display a Web page saved from Word, Excel, or PowerPoint in the Web browser installed on your machine.

(continued)

(continued)

Chapter	Filename	Description
5	WdEvents.cls, WdInit.bas, XlEvents.cls, XlInit.bas, PpEvents.cls, PpInit.bas	The combination of the two files for Word, Excel, and PowerPoint shows the event procedures that are called in your programs when any one of the following commands or their programmatic equivalents (as described in Chapter 4) are invoked through the File menu or through Visual Basic code: New, Open, Close, Save, Save As, Save as Web Page, and Print.
6	WdContnt.bas, XlContnt.bas, PpContnt.bas	Show how to insert content such as text, tables, shapes, and cell values and how to manipulate content, including text and shape formatting. You can use the code to search for specific content in a document.
7	CreatePP.doc	Creates a PowerPoint presentation from the headings in a Word document.
	AppObjs.bas	The procedures in this standard code module create instances of Office applications using the CreateObject and GetObject functions and the New keyword that is built into the Visual Basic for Applications language.
8	Energy.mdb	This Access database file contains data used to automatically generate a Word document based on a prebuilt template (EnerRpt.dot), an Excel workbook, a PowerPoint presentation, and an Outlook e-mail message.
	LabEnerg.txt	A text file containing data generated by a hypothetical digital meter connected to a computer.
	EnerRpt.dot	A template that determines what the report that Energy.mdb creates will look like.
9	WdSelect.bas, XlSelect.bas, PpSelect.bas, OlSelect.bas	Provides the code required to develop programs that need to retrieve, set, or act upon the active document or current selection.
10	WdEvents.cls, WdInit.bas, XlEvents.cls, XlInit.bas, PpEvents.cls, PpInit.bas	The combination of the two files for Word, Excel, and PowerPoint shows the event procedures that are called in your programs when the user changes the selection of content or double-clicks or right-clicks any content item.
	WndMenu2.xls	Shows how you can use a combination of events, such as window activate, window deactivate, and command bar control clicks to build your own custom window menu similar to the Windows menu in Word, Excel, and PowerPoint.

(continued)

(continued)

Chapter	Filename	Description
	OlEvents.cls, frmPreview.frm	Provide code that allows you to display a modeless custom dialog box that displays the body text of the first item in a selection of items in your Outlook Mailbox. The behavior of the custom dialog box mimics the behavior of the Preview Pane in Outlook.
11	CmdBars.bas, Class1.cls	Contains Visual Basic code to customize, add, or delete menu commands and toolbars in any Office application.
	TgglEvnt.cls	This class module provides an event procedure that reveals how to toggle the up-down state and caption of a menu item or toolbar button.
	CmboCtrl.bas, ChngEvnt.cls	CmboCtrl.bas shows you how to create a combo box drop-down list similar to the built-in *Zoom* control on the Standard toolbar in Word, Excel, and PowerPoint. ChngEvnt.cls shows you how to write code in the Change event of a combo box control that determines if a numerical value along with a percent sign is entered in the combo box. The code in the event procedure allows you to add a custom combo box control that mimics the behavior of the *Zoom* control.
	DropCtrl.bas, DropEvnt.cls	The combination of the standard code module and the class module shows how to add a drop-down list control and determine which item is selected in the list.
	ChngMPtr.bas, ChngMPtr.cls	The combination of the two files shows how to use the Windows application programming interfaces (APIs) LoadCursor and SetCursor to change the mouse pointer to an hourglass (or wait) cursor. The toolbar button *Click* event procedure also uses the Windows API Sleep to delay the execution of code.
	FindCtrl.bas	Contains code that uses the new *FindControls* method on the *CommandBars* collection object. The *FindControls* method allows you to write code that searches for a specific control and returns a subcollection of all the controls in the command bar set that match the search criteria.

(continued)

(continued)

Chapter	Filename	Description
12	FileSrch.xls	Displays a custom file search UserForm to search for specified files on your system.
	modMenu.bas	Reusable code to add or remove menu items in any Office application.
	modAssnt.bas	Reusable code that allows you to create custom Office Assistant balloons. The samples show you how to create balloons with formatted text such as bold, underlined, and colored. The code also shows how to add check boxes and labels and to specify the buttons to be displayed in the Assistant's balloon.
13	BascAddn.vbp, CnntWord.Dsr, CnntExcl.Dsr, WrdEvnts.cls, XclEvnts.cls, Dialog.frm, CmbInit.bas, CmbEvnts.cls	The Visual Basic 6.0 project, BascAddn.vbp, provides the basics for creating a COM add-in for any Office 2000 application. The project files CnntWord.dsr and CnntExcl.dsr allow the add-in to target Word and Excel. The remaining class module files, along with the standard code module files, show how to set up an Office application event procedure and a command bar control event procedure in a COM add-in. You use the project file Dialog.frm to show how a Visual Basic 6.0 form can be displayed in an Office application.
14	AppStart	The Visual Basic 6.0 project in this subfolder provides the code in a COM add-in that is used to determine how an Office application was started. For example, was the application started by a user through the Windows Start menu? Or was it started through Automation code using the *CreateObject* function built into the Visual Basic for Applications language?
	AutoList	The Visual Basic 6.0 project in this subfolder references each of the Office 2000 applications for which the COM add-in is targeted in order to take advantage of the Auto List Members feature in Visual Basic while writing code.
	Commncte	The two Visual Basic 6.0 projects in this subfolder provide the code that enables one COM add-in to communicate with another. The first COM add-in communicates with the second through the use of the *COMAddIn* object defined in the Office 9.0 Object Library.

(continued)

(continued)

Chapter	Filename	Description
	Distngsh	The Visual Basic 6.0 project in this subfolder provides the code used to tell which application has loaded the COM add-in. If you develop a COM add-in that's loaded in more than one Office application, you'll often need to write code that is specific to one application. Therefore, by using the Name property on the Application object in each Office application, you can write Select Case statements to determine the application that the COM add-in is loaded into.
	DmndLoad	The Visual Basic 6.0 project in this subfolder provides the code used to create a COM add-in that is loaded on demand. You can create a COM add-in that needs to be loaded only after a user clicks on a specific menu item, toolbar button, or combo box.
	NoDsgnr	The Visual Basic 6.0 project in this subfolder shows you how to develop a COM add-in that doesn't use the add-in designer. Instead, it uses a class module in Visual Basic that implements the IDTExtensibility2 interface. This project also requires you to use a Windows Registry file with the file extension .reg to register your COM add-in.

Uninstalling the Practice Files

Use the following steps to delete the practice files that the Setup program added to your hard disk:

1. Click the Start button, point to Settings, and then click Control Panel.

2. Double-click the Add/Remove Programs icon.

3. Select Microsoft Office 2000 Visual Basic for Applications Fundamentals from the list, and then click Add/Remove.

4. Click Yes when the confirmation message appears.
   The practice files are uninstalled.

5. Click OK to close the Add/Remove Programs Properties dialog box.

6. Close the Control Panel window.

Conventions and Features Used in This Book

Before you start going through the chapters in this book, you'll save time by learning how the book portrays the instructions, the keys to press, and other items. Please take a moment to read the following list, which also points out other helpful features.

Conventions

- Hands-on exercises for you to follow are given in numbered lists of steps (1, 2, and so on).

- Text that you are to type appears in **boldface**.

- New terms and book titles appear in *italic*.

- Names of keyboard keys for you to press appear in SMALL CAPITAL LETTERS. A plus sign (+) between two key names means that you must press those keys at the same time. For example, "Press ALT+TAB" means that you hold down the ALT key while you press TAB.

- Program code appears in monospace type (`monospace type`).

- The Note, Tip, and Important labels identify the different types of supplementary material that include additional information, alternative programming practices, or essential information that you should be aware of before continuing with the chapter.

Other Features of This Book

- You can perform many operations in Office by clicking a button on a toolbar or a tool in a toolbox. When the instructions in this book tell you to click a toolbar button, you'll see a picture of the button in the margin next to the instructions. The Run Macro button in the margin next to this paragraph is an example.

Run Macro

- Screen capture illustrations show sample user interfaces and the results of your completed steps.

- Sidebars—short sections printed on a shaded background—introduce background information or features related to the information being discussed.

- You can get a quick reminder of how to perform the tasks you learned by reading the Chapter Summary at the end of a chapter.

Corrections, Comments, and Help

Every effort has been made to ensure the accuracy of both this book and the contents of the practice files CD. Microsoft Press provides comments and corrections for its books through the World Wide Web at:

http://mspress.microsoft.com/support/

In your browser, use the search string "Office & comments and corrections" in the Knowledge Base Search section of the support Web site. If you have comments, questions, or ideas regarding this book or the practice files CD, please send them to us.

Send e-mail to:

mspinput@microsoft.com

Send postal mail to:

Microsoft Press
Attn: Fundamentals Series Editor
One Microsoft Way
Redmond, WA 98052-6399

Please note that support for the Office software products is not offered through the above addresses. For help using Office and Visual Basic for Applications, you can call Microsoft Technical Support Services at (800) 936-5700 or visit Microsoft Support Online on the Web at

http://support.microsoft.com/support

Visit Our World Wide Web Site

We invite you to visit the Microsoft Press World Wide Web site at the following location:

http://mspress.microsoft.com/

You'll find descriptions of our books, information about ordering, notice of special features and events, additional content for Microsoft Press books, and much more.

You can also find out the latest in software developments and news from Microsoft Corporation by visiting the following World Wide Web site:

http://www.microsoft.com/

Part 1

Learning Microsoft Visual Basic for Applications

Chapter 1

Microsoft Office/Visual Basic for Applications Overview

Estimated time: 45 minutes

- Use the Fundamentals Roadmap to find out where to go in this book for the information you need.

- Learn what Microsoft Visual Basic for Applications means and how you can benefit from its use.

- Work with the Visual Basic Editor to write code.

- Work with properties, methods, and events and learn how they form an object model.

- Use the Macro Recorder, the Object Browser, and the Auto List Members tool to learn and use Microsoft Office objects in your Visual Basic for Applications programs.

Microsoft Office allows people to create, organize, communicate, and collaborate on ideas and information, serving a wide range of customers from the desktop to the World Wide Web. To allow developers to extend how people work with information, Office includes the built-in programming language Visual Basic for Applications, or VBA.

Visual Basic for Applications provides a programming environment and a language for you to build custom programs that extend Office's capabilities, integrate Office with other software applications, and incorporate Office into a set of business processes. Building custom programs with Visual Basic for Applications lets you take full advantage of the functionality and services provided by Office applications.

To help you develop custom programs with Office, this book provides information for the following types of developers:

- The beginning developer who is familiar with Office but not with Visual Basic programming and wants to learn how to program with VBA

- The developer who has some experience with Visual Basic but who wants to understand the services and objects provided by Office in order to integrate Office with, for example, a larger software solution

- The experienced Office developer who needs a reference to the new programming tools and functionality provided by Office, including the new COM add-in and event support

Because developers often write and segment programming code based on specific tasks, code samples and descriptions in this book are organized by task rather than by application. Throughout this book, you'll find side-by-side comparisons of tasks such as saving a document or determining the current selection, so that you'll learn how to write code to accomplish the same task in more than one Office application.

The Fundamentals Roadmap

Before you start building your solution, you need a general plan of what you want to accomplish, one that takes into consideration where to start, what tools are required, and what your customer scenarios are. Once you know the job you need to accomplish, the following Fundamentals Roadmap diagram, the description of this book's six parts, and a list of sample scenarios should help you find the information you need to build your custom programs.

Finding Your Starting Point

This book has six parts, described below. Depending on what you need to learn, you can begin with any one of them.

Part 1: Learning Microsoft Visual Basic for Applications

This part includes a description of the Visual Basic Editor and explains how to use it to write code. It will familiarize you with the Visual Basic for Applications language; teach you about objects, methods, properties, and events; and show you how to create custom dialog boxes and wizards. It will also introduce you to the concepts of Visual Basic in Office applications and show you how to use the Visual Basic for Applications programming language and development environment to write code.

Part 2: Managing Documents and Files and Manipulating Document Content

This part describes how to use code to create new documents; to open, save, print and close them; and to find where they are on a file system. It also tells you how to write code to trap events when a document is created, opened, saved, printed, or closed. Finally, it discusses how to insert and manipulate content in a document once it's loaded into an Office application.

Scenarios

- Find files to open and folders where you can save files.

- Create content invisibly and then display it to the user on-screen.

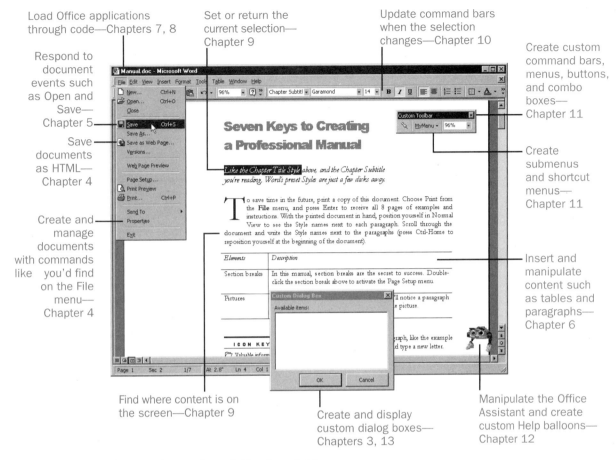

Load Office applications through code—Chapters 7, 8

Respond to document events such as Open and Save—Chapter 5

Save documents as HTML—Chapter 4

Create and manage documents with commands like you'd find on the File menu—Chapter 4

Set or return the current selection—Chapter 9

Update command bars when the selection changes—Chapter 10

Create custom command bars, menus, buttons, and combo boxes—Chapter 11

Create submenus and shortcut menus—Chapter 11

Insert and manipulate content such as tables and paragraphs—Chapter 6

Find where content is on the screen—Chapter 9

Create and display custom dialog boxes—Chapters 3, 13

Manipulate the Office Assistant and create custom Help balloons—Chapter 12

- Batch print from selected files in a folder.

- Set and retrieve document properties, like Author and Title, as well as determine if a specific document property is set before a document is saved, printed, or closed.

- Add header and footer information to documents that are opened, closed, or saved to a specific file location.

- Insert content—like text, tables, shapes—into a document and manipulate it.

- Insert or remove a sheet in a workbook or a slide in a presentation.

- Find and replace text.

Part 3: Working Across Applications

If you need to retrieve content from one source for use in creating a new Office document, this part describes how you can do that. Your code can start any Office application and create documents based on content from another data source. For example, you can create a report in Word along with a supporting presentation in PowerPoint, which is based on data retrieved from a Microsoft Access database or any other database.

Scenarios

- Use Visual Basic code to start an application or access an instance of an application already running.

- Use an Office application invisibly to create documents and content.

- Exchange information between Office applications.

- Create a custom form in Access that provides options to create a Word report, an Excel worksheet for data analysis, a PowerPoint presentation for meetings, and to send documents attached to an e-mail message sent using Microsoft Outlook.

Part 4: Working with Active Window Content

When you select a word in a document and click a toolbar button to apply formatting, the Office application determines the selection's content type and applies the appropriate formatting. This part describes how to determine the type of content in a selection and apply formatting based on the selection. It also tells you how to update menus and toolbars based on the content type and how to find content on the user's screen.

Scenarios

- Retrieve content or the active selection and format it.

- Trap double-click or right-click events and display your own dialog box or shortcut menu.

- Position a dialog box specifically around a text selection.

- Navigate to a specific content item like a slide in a presentation, a sheet in a workbook, and a paragraph in a document, or find specific text.

Part 5: Customizing the User Interface

This part describes how to create custom menus and toolbars. You'll learn how to use the CommandBars object model to mimic the state and behavior of built-in controls such as the Bold, Zoom, and Ruler commands. You'll also learn how to create custom balloons for the Office Assistant. You can use a custom balloon to display a list of choices, gather information from a user, or display a message to a user.

Scenarios

- Click a toolbar button to display a dialog box and format the current selection.

- Create a zoom drop-down list or a menu drop-down list.

- Create a top-level menu or a submenu like the Macro submenu on the Tools menu.

- Create a depressed button (like the Bold button) or add a check mark beside a menu item like the Ruler menu item on the View menu in Word and PowerPoint.

- Change an icon or caption of a button to toggle the state of the button.

- Display another toolbar when a button is clicked—for example, click the Drawing button on the Standard toolbar in Word and Excel and have it display the Drawing toolbar.

- Based on the visible state of the Office Assistant, determine when to display information to the user through the Office Assistant or a standard message box.

Part 6: Developing COM Add-Ins for Office

The last section has two chapters on the COM add-in model, which is introduced in Office 2000 as Office's first consistent add-in model. This model allows you to create a single add-in file targeted for more than one Office application. It also gives you the ability to create add-ins in any Microsoft development environment (although only the use of Microsoft Visual Basic 6.0 is discussed). Chapter 13 provides detailed instructions on how to create a COM add-in as well as a pointer to finding the COM add-in template for getting started in minutes. The last chapter describes the COM add-in model in-depth.

Scenarios

- Find a menu or toolbar control when an add-in is loaded and add commands as necessary.

- Remove a control when an add-in unloads.

- Load an add-in when the Office application starts.

Quick Guide

The following table lists the common tasks involved when you are first learning to program with Visual Basic for Applications in Office.

Task	Description
Open the Visual Basic Editor	On the Tools menu, point to Macro, and then click Visual Basic Editor; or press ALT+F11.
Record a macro	On the Tools menu, point to Macro, click Record New Macro, type a name for the macro, click OK, and perform the actions you want to record.
Stop recording a macro	On the Stop Recording toolbar, click the Stop Recording button.
Run a macro	On the Tools menu, point to Macro, click Macros, select the macro name, and click the Run button.

(continued)

Quick Guide *(continued)*

Task	Description

Traverse the branches of an object hierarchy tree	Use a period (.). For example:
	`Application.Presentations(1).Slides(1). _`
	`Shapes(1).TextFrame.TextRange = "Some Text"`

Turn on the Auto List Members feature	In the Visual Basic Editor, on the Tools menu, click Options, click the Editor tab, and select the Auto List Members check box.
Display an Auto List Members list of enumeration values	Type an equal sign (=) immediately after a property name (or type a comma after a method) to which a list applies.
Display the Object Browser	In the Visual Basic Editor, on the View menu, click Object Browser; or press F2.
Search for information about an object in the Object Browser	Select a library in the Project/Library drop-down list, type a name (such as a class or member) in the Search text box, and click the Search button.
Set the value of a property	Type an equal sign after the property name followed by the value you want to assign.
Run a method	Type the object name followed by a period, the name of the method, and any required or optional arguments. For example: `ActivePresentation.SaveAs "MyPresentation"`
Specify a particular object in a collection	Use the object's index position in the collection or the name of the object. For example: `Sheets(2) or Sheets("Sales")`
Declare an object variable	Type **Dim** followed by the variable name, **As**, and the object type. For example: `Dim sldSlide As Slide`

Where Code Can Be Written

When writing Visual Basic code for a business solution that incorporates Office, you can store your code in one of three general types of Office projects: a document, a template, or an add-in or wizard. How do you know which one to use? The first thing to decide is what type of solution you want to deliver, based on the projects' characteristics.

Document Projects

Document is a collective term used to represent all types of Office documents: Word documents, Excel workbooks, PowerPoint presentations, and Access databases. The Visual Basic code you write in the Visual Basic for Applications project of a document commonly provides customizations specific to the document's contents.

Code in a document project is stored within the same file as all other content of the document. Thus, when the document file location changes, the project moves with the file. In an example in Chapter 8, the code that drives the automatic generation of the Office documents is added to an Access database. In this case, you create a document project since the code is stored in the Access database and should move with the database if its file location changes.

Templates

Template is a collective term used for all types of Office templates, including Word, Excel, and PowerPoint templates. Writing code in a template is essentially the same as writing code in a document project because the code provides customizations to a document. The difference is that when you apply a template in Excel or PowerPoint, the code is copied into the workbook or the presentation. In Word, when you attach a template to a document, you make the code, along with other Word-specific content such as text styles and AutoText, readily available to the Word document.

Add-Ins and Wizards

Add-ins are tools that you can create to customize and extend the functionality of Word, Excel, PowerPoint, or Access themselves. An add-in is a supplemental program that adds custom commands and specialized features to any Office application. For example, you can write an add-in program for Word, Excel, and PowerPoint that displays a list of contacts retrieved from your Outlook Contacts folder. You can create an add-in in the form of a wizard that steps a user through a series of tasks. Most add-ins are accessed through a menu command or toolbar button. Chapter 3 shows you how to create a custom wizard. Chapters 13 and 14 describe how to develop add-ins for any Office application.

The Office/Visual Basic Relationship

Visual Basic for Applications is a combination of an integrated programming environment (the Visual Basic Editor) and the Visual Basic programming language. This combination allows you to easily design and develop Visual Basic programs. The term "for Applications" refers to the fact that the Visual Basic programming language and the development tools in the Visual Basic Editor are seamlessly integrated with all Office applications so that you can develop custom functionality and feature solutions using these applications.

How Does Visual Basic for Applications Relate to Visual Basic?

Visual Basic for Applications (also known as Visual Basic, Applications Edition) isn't the same as—and shouldn't be confused with—Microsoft Visual Basic. Office features the Visual Basic language and exposes the ability to control Office functionality through a set of programmable objects. Using the Visual Basic Editor and the different objects exposed by Office (which are integrated with all Office applications) you can create specialized programs for Office. You can store these programs in an Office document or in a separate file called an *add-in*. In Chapters 13 and 14, you'll learn how to build add-ins (called COM add-ins) using Microsoft Visual Basic 6.0.

The tools and graphical user interface provided by the Editor are consistent with the Microsoft Visual Basic version 6.0 development environment. Visual Basic 6.0, however, provides much more advanced programming tools and functionality, so you can create complex programs for the Microsoft Windows operating system and components for other Windows programs. You can develop self-contained executables (.exe files) as well as application extensions (.dll files) for Office using the tools in the Visual Basic 6.0 programming system.

The Visual Basic Editor

Each document, workbook, presentation, or database you open in Word, Excel, PowerPoint, or Access respectively has an associated Visual Basic for Applications project. When you open a workbook in Excel, for example, an associated Visual Basic project is listed in the Project Explorer window of the Visual Basic Editor. To write Visual Basic code in the Excel workbook's Visual Basic for Applications project, you must display the Visual Basic Editor. One way to display it is to point to Macro on the Tools menu, and then click Visual Basic Editor on the submenu.

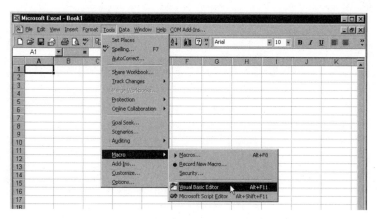

All the applications in Office provide the same integrated development environment. The Visual Basic Editor contains all the programming tools you need to write Visual Basic code and create custom solutions. For example, you can switch to the Visual Basic Editor window from PowerPoint the same way you do from Excel (from the Tools menu, point to Macro, and then click Visual Basic Editor).

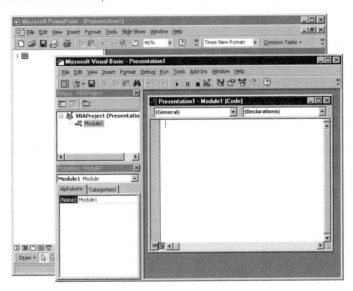

Although the Editor is a separate window in all Office applications, it looks and functions identically in each one. Thus, you can potentially have three Visual Basic Editor windows open at one time, each one associated with a separate application. When you close a given application, its associated Visual Basic Editor window closes automatically.

Examining the Elements of the Visual Basic Editor

The Visual Basic Editor provides a number of advanced programming and development tools that were once found only in development programs like Microsoft Visual C++.

- **Project Explorer** This window displays a hierarchical list of the projects and all of the items contained in and referenced by each of them. When you open a document in Word, for example, a Visual Basic for Applications project is associated with it in the Project Explorer. The items in a Visual Basic for Applications project can be any number of code modules or UserForms.

- **Properties Window** This displays an alphabetical or categorized property list of an *ActiveX* control in a UserForm, a UserForm itself, or a code module. An item's list of properties is on the left side of the window and its list of corresponding values is on the right.

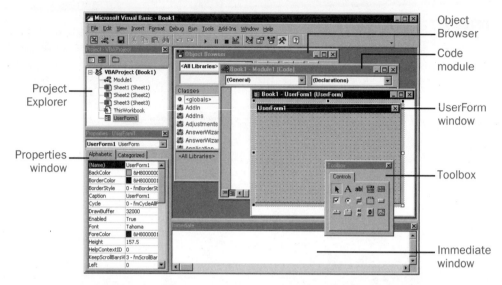

- **Object Browser** Think of this as a map for navigating through the objects, methods, properties, and events provided by an *ActiveX* control or an application such as Word, Excel, PowerPoint, Access, or Outlook. As you'll learn later in this chapter, the Object Browser will be an invaluable tool for determining how you can program a specific object provided by Office.

- **Code Module** This is where you write all of your Visual Basic code. (You see the code in a code module through the Code window.) There are three types of code modules: standard, class, and form; each type serves a specific purpose. Code modules allow you to group together code with common functionality.

- **UserForm Window** This window contains a UserForm that allows you to create custom dialog boxes for use in your Visual Basic for Applications programs. With a UserForm (and the *ActiveX* controls in the Toolbox), you can re-create any dialog box you've interacted with in Office and add your own customizations. You can also create your own dialog boxes to suit the needs of your Visual Basic for Applications program.

- **Toolbox** Listed here you'll find a set of *ActiveX* controls. Like the Control Toolbox in the Word, Excel, and PowerPoint windows, controls in the Visual Basic Toolbox can be dragged and dropped. However, in the Visual Basic Editor, you can drag and drop controls only onto a UserForm.

- **Immediate Window** Here you can enter and execute one line of Visual Basic code and immediately see its results. You commonly use the Immediate window when you debug Visual Basic code.

To debug means to find and correct errors in your code. Chapter 2 describes writing code and debugging in the Visual Basic Editor.

Microsoft Office Objects

We're all surrounded by objects that we perceive by vision or touch. We distinguish things by their properties, how they are related to other objects, and how they are affected by an action. Most objects have some sort of functional or aesthetic purpose, and many are collections of objects grouped together. An obvious example would be your computer. It consists of a monitor, a keyboard, speakers, a processor, disk drives, a mouse, and perhaps other components. Each component is further composed of objects—until you finally reach a fundamental element.

Software provides a similar ordering of objects. You can't, of course, put them on your mantel, but you can distinguish them by their properties and the relationships they have with one another. In Office, almost all the functionality you work with and all the viewable content you create is represented by an equivalent object in Visual Basic for Applications. Because these objects are programmable, you can develop a Visual Basic program that manipulates the properties that an object exposes. The collections of Office objects are categorized by either Word, Excel, PowerPoint, Access, Outlook, or Office, and they allow you to navigate down to the smallest detail of information in any of your documents.

The Object Model

Most objects are described in relation to another object. For example, a key on your keyboard doesn't stand on its own; it's a functioning part of the whole keyboard, which in turn is part of your computer. It's the relationship of objects that forms the basis of an object model in Office; the model is the hierarchy of objects in relation to each other.

All Office applications have the same general hierarchy model of objects, with the *Application* object residing at the top. Each *object* represents an element of an application, such as a shape on a slide, a cell in a worksheet, a word in a document, or a table in a database. Navigating up and down the object model hierarchy is similar to using a road map, which displays the routes you might take to reach certain destinations.

The *Application* object represents the starting point. From the *Application* object, you travel down a branched highway, selecting objects to pass through until you reach the object you want. If you want to change the color of a shape in a PowerPoint slide, you start with the *Application* object (PowerPoint), indicate which presentation the slide belongs to, and then find the slide that contains the shape. Finally, you reach your destination by selecting the shape on the slide.

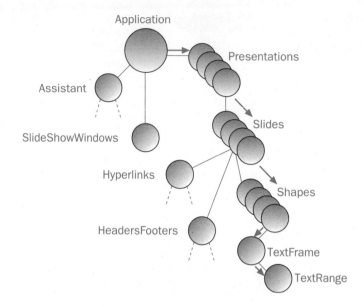

Representing the Object Model in Code

To manipulate an object's property, such as the text of the first shape on the first slide in a PowerPoint presentation, you have to traverse down the branches of the PowerPoint object model hierarchy tree. In Visual Basic programming, each branch in the object model diagram is represented by the dot operator (.), which is accessed by the period key on your keyboard.

Tip The verbal translation of Visual Basic code uses "dot" instead of "period." It's used in the same way as when you hear "dot" used to distinguish the extension of a filename in the Windows operating system. For example, for a file named MyFile.xls, you'll usually hear "MyFile dot X-L-S."

---

1. Start PowerPoint. In the opening PowerPoint dialog box, select Blank Presentation and click OK.

2. In the New Slide dialog box, select the second slide layout (Bulleted List) and click OK.

3. On the Tools menu, point to Macro, and then click Visual Basic Editor on the submenu.

4. In the Editor, on the Insert menu, click Module.

5. In the inserted module, type **Sub ChangingText** and press ENTER.

6. Insert the following line of code just after the line Sub ChangingText() and before End Sub:

```
Application.Presentations(1).Slides(1).Shapes(1) _
    .TextFrame.TextRange = "Some text."
```

In the above line of code, you don't need to type "Application" and the subsequent period. When you're writing Visual Basic code in the PowerPoint Visual Basic Editor window, the *Application* object, which in this case represents the PowerPoint application, is implied. Likewise, if you're writing Visual Basic code in Excel, when you access a *Workbook* object you don't need to specify the *Excel* application object (though it never hurts to be explicit about which application you're using). However, if you want to access a PowerPoint object while writing code in Excel, you need to make an explicit reference to the *PowerPoint* application object. In Chapter 7, "Communicating Across Microsoft Office," you'll learn how to drive other applications from one specific application.

7. Place the cursor within the *Sub ChangingText* procedure and press F5. Switch to PowerPoint and examine the new text on the slide.

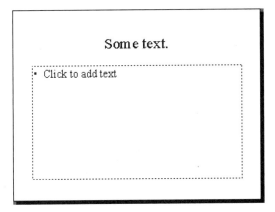

With this procedure you added text to the first shape of the first slide in the first presentation in PowerPoint.

Important   The text in the line of Visual Basic code in step 6 of this example parallels the objects being manipulated. However, as you'll see in the "Object Browser" section of this chapter, in a number of cases what you type in code doesn't map directly to the object name in the hierarchy tree.

---

8. Exit PowerPoint without saving your changes.

Collections and Objects

In Office, you'll find that although a number of objects are of the same type, each is distinguished by a unique name or index value. Together, these objects form a *collection*. Think back to the computer metaphor. Your keyboard has a set of keys that represent a *collection* of keys. Each key is uniquely distinguished by an index value in the collection of keys, but many keys are used for the same purpose (entering text) and thus are of the same object type. The names of collections are always plural, such as *Sections* in Word, *Worksheets* in Excel, and *Shapes* in PowerPoint.

In PowerPoint, the *Presentations* collection object represents a collection of all the presentations currently open in PowerPoint. The objects within the *Presentations* collection are *Presentation* objects, and each *Presentation* object in the collection contains a collection of *Slide* objects. To access a single object item in a Visual Basic collection, you refer to it in one of two ways. The first is to type the collection name followed by a period (.), and then type **Item(*<index>*)**, where *<index>* represents either the name of the specific item in the collection or its index value (position) in the collection. Pressing F5 runs the procedure you're currently working on. Using this method, the code sample used in step 6 in the preceding example would look like this:

```
Application.Presentations.Item(1).Slides.Item(1) _
    .Shapes.Item(1).TextFrame.TextRange = "Some text."
```

Or, as shown in step 6, you can remove the keyword *Item* and the preceding period and just type in the collection name followed immediately by the index value. Either syntax works, but the abbreviated version requires less typing and usually produces more readable code.

In Excel, the *Workbooks* collection is the equivalent of the *Presentations* collection in PowerPoint. The *Workbooks* collection object represents all workbooks currently open in Excel. Each Workbook object has a collection of Worksheet objects. In Word, the equivalent to the *Presentations* or *Workbooks* collection is the *Documents* collection, which represents all documents currently open in Word. Within each *Document* object in the collection, a *Sections* collection represents all sections in the document.

Count the Number of Objects in a Collection

Every collection in Office allows you to access each item in the collection as well as the number of objects in the collection.

1. Start Excel. On the Tools menu, point to Macro, and then click Visual Basic Editor on the submenu.

2. In the Visual Basic Editor, on the Insert menu, click Module.

3. In the inserted module, type **Sub NumberOfShapes** and press ENTER.

4. Insert the following line of code just after the line Sub NumberOfShapes() and before End Sub:

```
MsgBox ActiveSheet.Shapes.Count
```

ActiveSheet refers to the worksheet currently displayed in the Excel application window. Each worksheet has a collection of Shape objects. A *shape* in Excel is any object in the worksheet that floats above the cells. The Count property in the line of code you just inserted returns the number of shapes in the current active worksheet.

5. Place the cursor in the line `SubNumberOfShapes()` and press F5. You should see a message box showing the value 0 (zero). Currently, the *Shapes* collection of the active worksheet object has no shapes.

6. Click OK to close the message box, and then switch to Excel.

7. If the Drawing toolbar isn't displayed, on the View menu, point to Toolbars, and then click Drawing on the submenu.

8. On the Drawing toolbar, click any of the shape buttons (oval, rectangle, and so on), and add any AutoShape to the worksheet.

9. On the Tools menu, point to Macro, and then click Macros on the submenu. Select NumberOfShapes and click Run.

10. Click OK to close the message box.

11. Repeat steps 8 through 10 several times.
    Notice that each time you add shapes to the active worksheet, the value displayed in the message box is incremented by the number of shapes you added. Try deleting shapes from the active worksheet as well. When you run the macro, you'll see the number of shapes in the *Shapes* collection decrease by an equivalent amount.

12. Exit Excel without saving changes.

Understanding Properties, Methods, and Events

Each object that's part of a computer contains components with specific characteristics. For example, the keyboard is made up of a collection of keys, and each has properties that distinguish it from the others. Each key has a different label, such as "A," "ESC," or "F1," and is uniquely positioned on the keyboard. The SPACEBAR is usually much bigger than the other keys, and it doesn't have a label. The label and position are *properties* of a key. In addition, the keys provide a method of entering data into the computer by allowing the user to perform the action of pressing them. Thus, "press" is a *method* of a key.

When you press a key such as "A," you trigger an *event*. The Windows operating system, working with another program, *handles* the event in a number of ways, depending on the conditions. If the computer is turned off, nothing happens. If the computer is on and the current, active application is a word processor such as Word, the letter "a" is displayed on the screen at the position of the cursor.

Each Office object contains one of three types of members: a property, a method, or an event.

Object Member Type	Description
Property	A characteristic attribute, such as size, position, or shape, that defines or describes an object. (Adjective)
Method	An action, such as save, close, or delete, that you can perform on or with an object. (Verb)
Event	Something that takes place, such as a click, a press, or a change, that causes an object to react. (Noun)

Properties

In most cases, you can retrieve the value of a property or you can set a property to a specific value. However, you'll find a number of instances where a property is read-only. This means you can retrieve the property value but you can't set it. When you can set a value to a property, the range of values you can assign often has restrictions. For example, the size of a font used in text in a Word document must be a number between 1 and 1638.

In addition, you can only set a property to a specific type of value (although there are some cases where you can set a property to multiple types of values). For example, to set the characteristics of a font used in text, you can use the Name, Size, and Bold properties. You can only assign an integer value to the Size property (which sets the size of the font used in text). On the other hand, you can only assign a string value to the Name property (which indicates the name of a font, such as Times New Roman). Finally, you can only assign to the Bold property one of the two Boolean values, True or False.

Set a Property Value

To set a property, you equate a value to the property with an equal sign. To retrieve a property value, you just specify the property and, in most cases, assign it to a temporary variable.

1. Start PowerPoint. In the opening PowerPoint dialog box, select Blank Presentation and click OK.

2. In the New Slide dialog box, select the second slide layout (Bulleted List) and click OK.

3. If the PowerPoint window is maximized or minimized, restore the window so that it can be moved or resized.

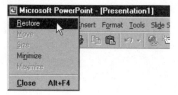

4. Open the Visual Basic Editor and insert a new code module. In the module, type **Sub MoveWindow** and press ENTER to create a new procedure.

To insert a new code module, click Module on the Insert menu in the Visual Basic Editor.

5. Add the following code:

```
MsgBox Application.Left
Application.Left = 50
MsgBox Application.Left
```

6. Place the cursor in the *MoveWindow* procedure and press F5. Click OK to close the message boxes.

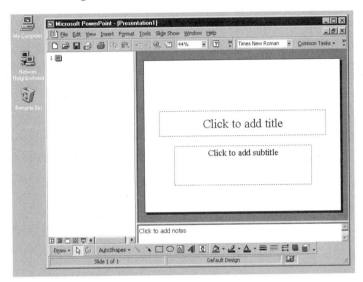

The procedure moves the PowerPoint application window to approximately position 50 (near the left side of your screen). The first line of code sets the Left property value of the application window and displays the property value in a message box. The second line sets the property value to 50, and the third displays the resulting value.

Enumerations

Throughout an Office object model, whether that's Word, Excel, PowerPoint, or Access, you often set object properties to an integer value within a range specified by the specific application. But in order to set a property value to a valid integer you need to know the valid range of integers and understand what each value represents. The enumeration value is a label that represents an integer, but you don't necessarily have to know what the integer is. In order to provide a convenient way to select a value from a known number of choices—and to make your code more readable and understandable—each object model provides a list of enumeration values. An *enumeration* represents a finite list of unique integers, each of which has a specific name and special meaning in the context in which it's used.

An integer is a positive or negative whole number or the number zero.

Note   Each application in Office provides a set of enumeration values. Each enumeration value in a specific application has a name with a two-letter prefix. In Word, Excel, PowerPoint, Access, and Outlook, enumeration names are prefixed with *wd*, *xl*, *pp*, *ac*, and *ol*, respectively.

Use Enumeration Values to Select a Slide Layout

When you create a new slide in PowerPoint, you can select a slide layout from the list in the New Slide dialog box. Each layout is different and displays a title, text, chart, clip art, and a few other placeholders in a unique combination and position. Layout is a property of a Slide object, and through Visual Basic you can determine the current slide layout or set the layout you want.

1. In the Visual Basic Editor of PowerPoint, move the cursor beneath the procedure you created earlier (*MoveWindow*) and create a new procedure called *EnumList*.

2. Add the following line of code:

    ```
    ActivePresentation.Slides(1).Layout=
    ```

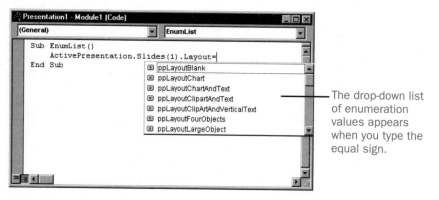

The drop-down list of enumeration values appears when you type the equal sign.

When you type the equal sign, the program displays a drop-down list showing all the possible values to which the Layout property can be equated. As you'll see later in the "Object Browser" section of this chapter, these are enumeration values and are really integers.

Tip   If you don't see the drop-down list of enumeration values, the Auto List Members feature isn't currently selected. On the Tools menu in the Visual Basic Editor window, click Options. In the Editor tab, select the Auto List Members check box in the Code Settings group and click OK.

---

3. Select an item from the drop-down list and press the TAB key.

4. Place the cursor in the *EnumList* procedure and press F5 to run it. In the PowerPoint application window, the layout of the first slide in the active presentation is set to the value you selected in step 3.

5. Go back to step 2, remove the enumeration value and the equal sign, and then retype the equal sign and set the Layout property to a different enumeration value in the drop-down list.

6. Run the procedure again, and then switch to the PowerPoint application window to see the new layout of the slide.

Notice how the name of the enumeration value describes the actual property setting. For example, ppLayoutBlank represents a slide with a blank layout.

Tip   Each Office application provides a set of enumerations that represent predefined integer values. For example, ppLayoutBlank represents the number 12. You should use the enumeration instead of the integer value because it makes your code more understandable when other developers read it or when you come back to read it later.

Methods

When you work with an object's properties, you use an equal sign; when you work with an object's methods, you don't. With some methods, you just type the method name, but in a number of cases you can send information, or pass *arguments*, to a method.

Pass Arguments to the SaveAs Method in PowerPoint

1. In the Visual Basic Editor, place the cursor below the last line of code in the Code window. Type **Sub SavePres** and press ENTER.

2. Add the following line of code just after the line Sub SavePres():

```
ActivePresentation.SaveAs
```

3. Press the SPACEBAR just after the word SaveAs, and in the Auto Quick Info window you'll see a list of arguments you can pass to the *SaveAs* method.

The list of arguments appears in the Auto Quick Info window when you press the SPACEBAR after SaveAs.

Note   If the Auto Quick Info window isn't displayed, click Options on the Tools menu in the Visual Basic Editor. In the Editor tab of the Options dialog box, select Auto Quick Info and click OK.

For now, you just need to pass the first argument to the *SaveAs* method. This argument is the filename under which you want to save the presentation. The other arguments in the list are optional.

As you'll see in the section of this chapter entitled "Learning the Members of the Object Model," Auto Quick Info and Auto List Members are Visual Basic Editor features that make it unnecessary for you to memorize the syntax of every member in an object model.

4. Type "**MyPresentation**" (including the quotation marks) and press ENTER.

5. Press F5. Notice that the title bar changes, showing that you saved the presentation with a new name. The title appears in both PowerPoint and the Visual Basic Editor.

The title bar changes when you save the presentation with a new name.

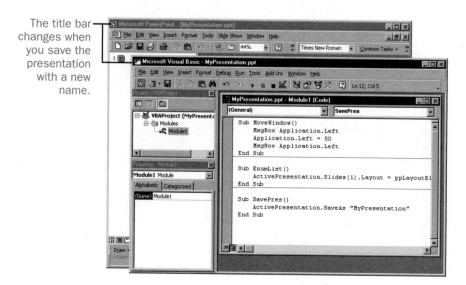

6. Exit PowerPoint. Your changes are already saved.

Events

In the context of Visual Basic programming, when an event such as saving a document takes place, you can set up your code (procedures) to respond to it. These procedures have specific names and are referred to as *event procedures*. An event procedure contains code that you write to perform some action to handle the event when it's triggered. Event procedures have a syntax like that shown in the following table.

Note   Chapter 5 describes how to handle events that occur when creating, opening, saving, printing, or closing any Word, Excel, or PowerPoint document. Chapter 10 shows you how to handle such events as the user changing the selection of content or double-clicking or right-clicking on content in the same three applications.

Application	Event Procedure Example
Excel	Sub Workbook_Open()
	Sub Workbook_NewSheet (ByVal Sh As Object)
Word	Sub Document_Open
	Sub Document_Close

In some cases the application passes an argument to the event procedure. In one of the preceding cases, when you open a new worksheet in Excel, Excel passes the newly created sheet to the *NewSheet* event procedure so that you can start working with the new worksheet right away.

Work with Properties, Methods, and Events in Word

A Word Document object exposes properties, methods, and events. The *Document* object represents an open document in Word and allows you to access every word, table, shape, or other element in the document.

1. Start Word. On the Tools menu, point to Macro, and then click Visual Basic Editor on the submenu.

2. In the Editor, if the Project Explorer window isn't open, click Project Explorer on the View menu. Double-click the ThisDocument item.

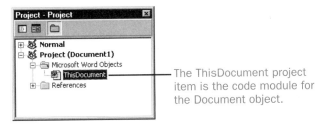

The ThisDocument project item is the code module for the Document object.

The ThisDocument project item is often referred to as the code module "behind" the Document object. When you insert *ActiveX* controls into a document, the controls are listed in the code module belonging to the document in which they reside. In Excel, controls reside on a worksheet and are listed in the code module for the *Worksheet* object. In PowerPoint, controls on a slide are listed in the code module for the Slide object.

Note   By default, PowerPoint doesn't display the code module for each *Slide* object in the Project Explorer. When you insert the first *ActiveX* control into a slide, the Project Explorer lists the code module for the *Slide* object. Excel lists code modules for each *Worksheet* object by default.

---

3. In the ThisDocument module, type **Sub WordDoc** and press ENTER.

4. In the *WordDoc* procedure, add the following line of code:

```
MsgBox ActiveDocument.Name
```

This line displays the name of the active document. Name is a read-only property of the *Document* object, and it returns a string value representing the document's filename. If you haven't saved the document yet, the Name property represents the default name that was given to the document when you created it. (The default name for the document is displayed in the Word application window's title bar.) The Name property behaves the same way for both the *Workbook* object in Excel and for the *Presentation* object in PowerPoint.

5. Now add the following two lines:

```
ActiveDocument.SaveAs "C:\Temp\MyDoc.doc"
MsgBox ActiveDocument.Name
```

The *Document* object supports a *SaveAs* method that represents the act of saving the document with a specified filename. The complete procedure looks like this:

```
Sub WordDoc()
    MsgBox ActiveDocument.Name
    ActiveDocument.SaveAs "C:\Temp\MyDoc.doc"
    MsgBox ActiveDocument.Name
End Sub
```

Important   Make sure that the folder "C:\Temp" is a valid folder on your machine. If it's not, either create C:\Temp or change the line above to indicate a folder where the document can be saved. Once the document is saved, the line above displays a message box with the text: "MyDoc.doc." The Name property of the *Document* object now represents the filename, without the path.

---

6. Place the cursor in the *WordDoc* procedure and press F5. You'll see a message box showing the default name of the active document (Document1). Then the document is saved, and the filename, without the path, is displayed in another message box.

7. Click OK to close each message box.

8. In the Object drop-down list of the ThisDocument code module, select Document.

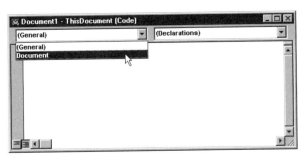

9. In the Procedure drop-down list of the ThisDocument code module, select Close.

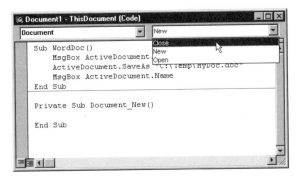

The items in the Procedure drop-down list represent the list of exposed events that the *Document* object can react to. The *Document* object provides three separate event procedures: *Document_Close*, *Document_New*, and *Document_Open*. If a placeholder was created for the *New* event procedure, you can ignore it.

10. In the Document_Close event handler, type the following line:

```
MsgBox "This document is now CLOSING."
```

When the document closes, it's an event. When this event occurs and there's code in the event handler for the Close event of the document, the event handler runs. In this case, a message box saying "This document is now CLOSING." is displayed just before the document is closed and removed from memory.

11. In the Procedure drop-down list of the ThisDocument code module, select Open and add the following line in the Document_Open event handler:

```
MsgBox "This document is now OPEN!"
```

When the document opens, it's an event. When this event occurs and there's code in the event handler, the event handler runs. In this case, a message box displaying the text "This document is now OPEN!" is displayed just after the document is opened and loaded into memory.

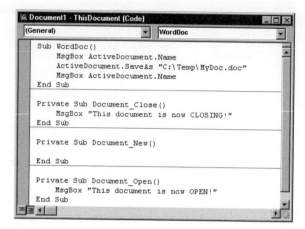

12. Switch to Word, and then, on the File menu, click Close.

13. Click OK to close the message box, and then click Yes to save changes.

14. On the File menu, click *1 C:\Temp\MyDoc.doc* (the recently opened file list) to open the document again.

    You can open and close the document several times. Each time you do, you trigger the Open and Close events, and the code you wrote in the event procedures runs.

15. Click OK and then exit Word.

Learning the Members of the Object Model

Just as an application is rich in features and functionality, the equivalent object model is filled with members that represent the same features and functionality. An average object model in Office contains hundreds of members, including collections, objects, properties, methods, and events. To learn all of the members of a model, you may have to switch frequently between the corresponding Visual Basic Help file and the Visual Basic Editor window.

Visual Basic for Applications provides four tools that simplify the search for the list of properties, methods, or events that an object supports. They are the Macro Recorder, the Object Browser, Auto List Members, and Auto Quick Info.

Macro Recorder

Word, Excel, and PowerPoint provide a macro recorder that helps you quickly learn the object model of the application. (Access and Outlook don't provide a macro recorder.) Macro recording provides the equivalent Visual Basic code of an action that you conduct through an application's graphical interface.

For example, to change the color of a shape on a PowerPoint slide, you se-lect the shape, click AutoShape on the Format menu, and then select a fill color from the Color drop-down list (in the Color And Lines tab). The equivalent macro-recorded code is as follows:

```
Sub Macro1()" Macro recorded 1/1/99 by David Boctor'
    ActiveWindow.Selection.SlideRange.Shapes _
        .AddShape(msoShapeRectangle, 246, _
            288, 138, 132).Select
    With ActiveWindow.Selection.ShapeRange
        .Fill.Visible = msoTrue
        .Fill.Solid
        .Fill.ForeColor.RGB = RGB(128, 0, 0)
    End With
End Sub
```

Note   Macro recording is selection-based. This means that the Macro Recorder will record actions on selected objects in an active window.

The macro-recorded code gives you a good start on whatever you might want to do or create with Visual Basic code. Look at the first working line of code in the macro above and you'll see how to add a shape to a slide. If you want to add a shape to a specific slide (for example, the second one) rather than the slide in the active window, you can replace the code in the *Macro1* procedure with the following code in *Macro2*:

```
Sub Macro2()
    Dim NewShape As Shape
    Set NewShape = ActivePresentation.Slides(2). _
        Shapes.AddShape(msoShapeRectangle, 246, _
        288, 138, 132)
End Sub
```

Make sure you have at least two slides in the active presentation. The code above adds a rectangle to the second slide. This line closely resembles the first line of the recorded macro. You just replaced ActiveWindow.Selection.SlideRange with ActivePresentation.Slides(2) so that your code works on a specific slide; you don't have to have the slide displayed in the active window. This macro also demonstrates how to declare a variable (*NewShape*) that represents the new shape that's added to the slide. You'll learn more about declaring variables and work-ing with shapes and other objects later in this book.

Although most macro-recorded code doesn't provide the exact code you need for your solution, it does provide the exact syntax you need to manipu-late many objects within Word, Excel, and PowerPoint. It also helps you write Visual Basic code without constantly searching through the Help file.

Recording Macros

A macro is a Visual Basic for Applications program that automates a series of actions. These can range from a simple procedure you conduct with your document content and application tools to complex solutions that manipulate your document content and interact with other Office features. A macro resides within the Visual Basic project of a Word document, an Excel workbook, a PowerPoint presentation, or an Access database. Because macros are usually actions grouped together, they enable you to accomplish a series of common, often repetitive, tasks automatically with a single command. You often create simple macros to make editing and formatting tasks readily available through a dialog box.

Word, Excel, and PowerPoint each offer an easy way to create a simple macro: with the Macro Recorder. Access and Outlook don't provide a macro recorder. You can see a recorded macro's contents in the Visual Basic Editor, where you can easily modify the macro. Recording a macro is like recording music or video. When you play it back, it automatically repeats recorded actions.

Each macro you record is stored in a Visual Basic code module that's attached to the open document, workbook, presentation, or template. Using the Visual Basic Editor, you can edit macros or move macros from one code module to another in any open Visual Basic project.

Record a Macro that Sets the Same Formatting to Multiple Shapes

Imagine that you want to manually change the color of a shape on a PowerPoint slide. To do that you have to select the shape, choose AutoShape from the Format menu, and then select a color from the Fill Color drop-down list (in the Color And Lines tab in the Format AutoShape dialog box). To determine the equivalent functionality in Visual Basic syntax isn't necessarily a straightforward task for a beginner or even an experienced Visual Basic programmer. Fortunately, macro recording provides what you need without much effort.

1. Start PowerPoint. In the opening PowerPoint dialog box, select Blank Presentation and click OK.

2. In the New Slide dialog box, select the second slide AutoLayout (Bulleted List) and click OK.

3. On the Tools menu, point to Macro, and then click Record New Macro.

The Record Macro dialog box is displayed. Notice the default macro name in the Macro Name box and the presentation name in which the recorded macro will be stored.

4. Click OK to accept the default names.

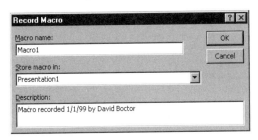

Macro recording has started, and the Stop Recording toolbar is displayed on your screen.

Until macro recording is stopped, the equivalent Visual Basic code of most of the actions you conduct is recorded in a code module in the Visual Basic Editor.

5. On the Drawing toolbar, which is the same for Word, Excel, and PowerPoint, click the Rectangle button.

Rectangle

6. Drag a rectangle anywhere on the slide.

7. On the Format menu, click AutoShape to display the Format AutoShape dialog box.

8. In the Colors And Lines tab, click the Color drop-down list and select a color from the color grid. Click OK.

9. Stop the macro recording by clicking the Stop Recording button on the Stop Recording toolbar.

Stop Recording

10. Start the Visual Basic Editor by pressing ALT+F11 and, in the Project Explorer window, open Presentation1 by clicking the plus sign next to it.

This is the presentation that you selected to store the recorded macro.

11. If necessary, open the Modules folder by clicking the plus sign next to it.

12. Double-click Module1. This displays the Code window.

The following code was recorded:

```
Sub Macro1()
'
' Macro recorded 1/1/99 by David Boctor
'     ActiveWindow.Selection.SlideRange.Shapes _
          .AddShape(msoShapeRectangle, 246, _
          288, 138, 132).Select
```

```
With ActiveWindow.Selection.ShapeRange
    .Fill.Visible = msoTrue
    .Fill.Solid
    .Fill.ForeColor.RGB = RGB(128, 0, 0)
End With
End Sub
```

Your recorded code may be slightly different. This macro is currently stored in the Visual Basic project of the active presentation.

Run the Recorded Macro to Create a Shape on Another Slide

View Microsoft PowerPoint

1. Switch to PowerPoint by clicking the View Microsoft PowerPoint button on the Standard toolbar in the Editor.

2. On the Insert menu, click New Slide.

3. Select the second slide icon (Bulleted List) in the AutoLayout dialog box and then click OK.

4. On the Tools menu, point to Macro, and then click Macros.

5. In the Macro dialog box, select Macro1 from the list, and then click Run.

On the new slide, Visual Basic automatically re-creates the same shape in the same color that you previously created manually.

Object Browser

Many road maps have an index that lists all the locations on the map. To give the Visual Basic programmer a similar guide for navigating through an object model, the Visual Basic Editor provides a tool window called the Object Browser. By learning to use it effectively you'll save a lot of time.

Look at the Object Browser

1. Start PowerPoint. In the opening PowerPoint dialog box, click Blank Presentation and then click OK.

2. In the New Slide dialog box, select any slide layout and click OK.

3. On the Tools menu, point to Macro, and then click Visual Basic Editor on the submenu.

4. In the Editor, on the View menu, click Object Browser. (You can also press F2.)

The Object Browser's window contains five main elements: the Project/Library drop-down list, a Search text box with Search Results box, the Classes list, the Members Of list, and the Details pane.

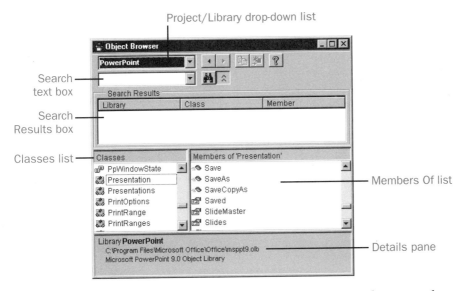

Project/Library drop-down list

Search text box

Search Results box

Classes list

Members Of list

Details pane

- **Project/Library drop-down list** This list displays the currently referenced libraries for the active Visual Basic project. By default, <All Libraries> is selected in the text box, which allows all of the libraries to be displayed in the Object Browser at one time.

  You'll find the object model definition for each application in Office (and for any other application that supports an object model) in a file referred to as an *object library*. An object library's filename usually contains the extension .olb. However, sometimes an object library is contained within a dynamic-link library (.dll) file. Generally, the object library file is just an information file for whatever objects, properties, methods, events, and enumerations an application exposes. By providing an object library, Visual Basic can search for the objects an application exposes without having to load the entire application itself and then ask it for a list of exposed objects.

  In Part 2 of this book, you'll see that referencing an object library is important when you program Office using objects and functionality from multiple applications. That's because you can do it all from within one Visual Basic Editor window.

- **Search text box with Search Results box** The Search Results box displays a list of libraries, classes, or members matching the criteria you specify in the Search text box. You'll learn more about these boxes in the next example.

- **Classes list** This list displays all the objects exposed in a given object library. When you select <All Libraries> in the Project/Library drop-down list, all objects in all libraries are listed. However, if you select a specific library in the Project/Library drop-down list, only the objects in the specified library are listed.

For example, you can start PowerPoint, display its Visual Basic Editor, and press F2 for the Object Browser. In the Project/Library drop-down list, select PowerPoint. In the Classes list, you'll see only the objects that PowerPoint exposes. The list has a number of objects, including familiar ones such as Presentation, Slide, and Shape.

- **Members Of list** This list displays all the properties, methods, and events that are supported by a selected item in the Classes list.

  If you select PowerPoint from the Project/Library drop-down list and then select Presentation from the Classes list, in the Members Of *Presentation* list you'll see the methods and properties that you might know from the PowerPoint menus and toolbars. Familiar methods include *Close, Save, SaveAs,* and *PrintOut*, while common properties include Name, Path, and FullName.

- **Details pane** When you select an item in the Members Of list, the contents of the Details pane reveal detailed information about the selected member.

If you select Presentation from the Classes list and then PageSetup in the Members Of list, the Details pane displays the following information:

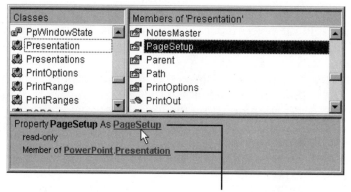

Words that are underlined and green are links to other items in the Object Browser.

Note that the last word in the first line in the Details pane, "PageSetup," is underlined and green. This indicates two things: (1) the PageSetup property returns an object called *PageSetup*, and (2) you can navigate to the *PageSetup* object by clicking the link.

Search for Information About an Object

The Search Results box gives you a quick way to determine which members in an object library support certain properties, methods, or events. After searching through the specified object library or libraries, it lists members that match the criteria you specified in the Search text box. If you select <All Libraries> in the Project/Library box, the search is conducted in all the libraries in the Project/Library list; if you select a specific library, the search scans that library only.

1. In the Object Browser, in the Project/Library box, select PowerPoint.

2. Right-click anywhere in the Object Browser window. This displays the shortcut menu for the Object Browser.

3. Select Find Whole Word Only.

4. In the Search text box, type **name**.

5. Click the Search button next to the Search text box.

Search button

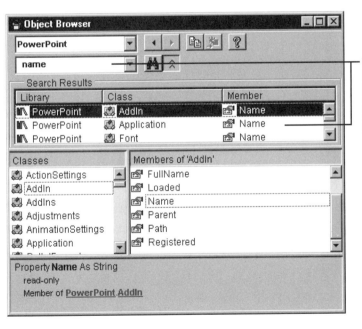

The Search Results box reveals all instances of the property Name in the Microsoft PowerPoint 8.0 object library.

The first column in the Search Results list is the Library; the second column is the Class, or object; and the third is the Member property. Selecting any row in the Search Results list refreshes the contents of the Classes list and the Members Of list, so you can navigate to the exact location of the search result item in the object library.

Auto List Members

One of the Visual Basic Editor's newest and most exciting additions is the Auto List Members drop-down list, which you saw briefly in a previous example. Because of it, you never have to memorize the methods or properties of an object again. All you need to do is start typing, and once you type a period (.) after a valid object name, Auto List Members automatically displays a drop-down list of all the properties and methods supported by the object. You can scroll down the list with the mouse, or you can continue typing the method or property name. If you continue typing, Auto List Members selects an item in the list that matches your typing.

Enter Properties the Hard Way

Imagine that you want to define a name of an object within one of your procedures.

1. In the Visual Basic Editor, insert a code module, type **Sub WithoutDeclaration**, and press ENTER.

2. Between the lines Sub WithoutDeclaration and End Sub, add the following line of code:

```
MsgBox sldSlide.Name
```

When you start to use a term or variable that the Editor doesn't recognize, you have to do all of the work yourself. In this case, you must already know that sldSlide is the name of a slide and that a Name property applies to slides.

Enter Properties the Easy Way with Auto List Members

When you declare an object variable, you also take advantage of the Auto List Members tool. The Auto List Members drop-down list displays information that would logically complete the statement at the current insertion point.

1. Add the following declaration and Set statements above the line of code you've already typed:

```
Dim sldSlide As Slide
Set sldSlide = ActivePresentation.Slides(1)
```

You've now declared the *sldSlide* variable as representing a PowerPoint Slide object, and the Visual Basic Editor now knows what type of object this variable references. Your procedure should look like this:

```
Sub WithoutDeclaration()
    Dim sldSlide As Slide
    Set sldSlide = ActivePresentation.Slides(1)
    MsgBox sldSlide.Name
End Sub
```

2. Now delete the line you previously typed, `MsgBox sldSlide.Name`, and then type it again. (Yes, this is the same line that you typed before, but something different should happen.)

```
MsgBox sldSlide.Name
```

When you start typing the line above and get to the point where you type a period (.) after sldSlide, the Auto List Members drop-down list appears.

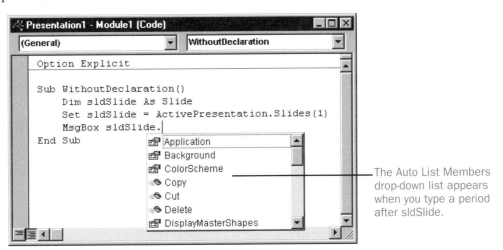

The Auto List Members drop-down list appears when you type a period after sldSlide.

At this point, you can scroll down the list and select the property or method item, or you can continue to type the name of the property or method if you know it. As you continue to type, the list automatically scrolls down to find a match for the text you started to type. If the property or method name is long and the item is selected in the Auto List Members drop-down list, you can press TAB to insert the item in your line of code.

3. Select Name in the list and press TAB.

4. Press F5 to run the macro.

5. Exit PowerPoint without saving changes.

When Auto List Members Doesn't Appear

When you type the dot ('.') as you enter code in the Visual Basic Editor in Word, Excel, PowerPoint, Access, and Outlook, the Auto List Members drop-down list sometimes won't appear. For example, start Excel, display the Visual Basic Editor, click Module on the Insert menu, and then type in the following procedure.

```
Sub ParentProperty()
    Dim sh As Worksheet, shNew As Worksheet
    For Each sh In ActiveWorkbook.Worksheets
        If sh.Name = "Sheet3" Then
            Set shNew = sh.Parent.Worksheets.Add(Before:=sh)
            shNew.Name = "New Sheet"
            Exit For
        End If
    Next sh
End Sub
```

The Parent property allows you to return the object from which you access another object.

In this procedure, sh.Parent returns the Workbook object. The parent of a worksheet isn't the *Worksheets* collection, it's the workbook. In all cases in Word, Excel, and PowerPoint, the parent of an *item* in a collection isn't the collection but the parent of the collection itself. In a number of cases, the Parent property of an object returns an object defined as the generic Object type. When you type the dot ('.') after the code sh.parent in the first line in the If…Then block in the preceding procedure, the Auto List Members drop-down list doesn't appear. You can create a new variable, such as *wb*, declare it as a Workbook, and assign *wb* to sh.Parent.

```
Sub ParentPropertyWithAutoListMembers()
    Dim sh As Worksheet, shNew As Worksheet
    Dim wb As Workbook
    For Each sh In ActiveWorkbook.Worksheets
        If sh.Name = "Sheet3" Then
            Set wb = sh.Parent
            Set shNew = wb.Worksheets.Add(Before:=sh)
            shNew.Name = "New Sheet"
            Exit For
        End If
    Next sh
End Sub
```

In the new procedure, you declare the variable *wb* as a Workbook and assign it to the return value of sh.Parent, which is always a Workbook object. You then use the variable *wb* in the line that adds a new worksheet. When you type in the dot after the variable *wb*, the Auto

(continued)

When Auto List Members Doesn't Appear (*continued*)

List Members drop-down list appears. If you executed the procedure *ParentProperty* before the new procedure *ParentPropertyWithAutoList-Members*, make sure you switch back to Excel and delete the worksheet "New Sheet." If you don't, the above procedure will fail to rename the new worksheet.

Auto Quick Info

As you write your code, you have a number of ways to determine the exact syntax of the object, methods, and properties you use. One of the easiest is to display the Auto Quick Info window, which shows function information and parameters as you type. The Auto Quick Info window is similar to the ToolTip you see when the cursor is over a toolbar button.

In the "Pass Arguments to the *SaveAs* Method in PowerPoint" section of this chapter, when you pressed the SPACEBAR after typing the SaveAs method name, the Auto Quick Info window appeared as follows:

You can see in the Auto Quick Info window that the *SaveAs* method of the *Presentation* object in PowerPoint takes three arguments. Each argument in the Auto Quick Info window is separated by a comma (,); as you type a comma, the next argument in the window becomes bold. Some arguments are encased in square brackets, which indicate that specifying the argument is optional. In the *SaveAs* method above, the first argument is required and the second and third are optional. If the argument is optional, the application defines a default value for it.

In the *SaveAs* method, the second argument, *FileFormat*, defaults to the current version of a PowerPoint presentation. You can also see in the case of the second argument that when you type a comma, both the Auto Quick Info window and the Auto List Members drop-down list are displayed. The Auto List Members drop-down list is displayed because the *FileFormat* argument is one of the enumeration values (PpSaveAsFileType) in the list.

Tip   When both the Auto Quick Info window and the Auto List Members drop-down list are displayed, you can toggle between them by clicking either one to put it in front of the other.

Chapter Summary

This chapter introduces you to the outline of this book and starts you down the path of using Visual Basic for Applications. Using the Fundamentals RoadMap figure, you can determine where to find the information you need. As a new user to Visual Basic programming and the Visual Basic language, you will find that the concepts described here will help you throughout this book.

Chapter 2

The Fundamentals of Writing Visual Basic Code

Estimated time: 50 minutes

- Create a procedure in which you write Microsoft Visual Basic code.

- Declare variables and constants.

- Control program flow using Visual Basic decision-making statements.

- Repeat a series of steps with looping structures.

- Debug the values of variables and constants.

This chapter describes the fundamentals of the Visual Basic programming language. With them you'll be able to exploit all of Visual Basic's features when writing programs for Microsoft Office. Although the Visual Basic programming language is based on the same principles as most other programming languages, it's much easier to learn than most.

Quick Guide

The following table lists a common set of tasks when writing Visual Basic code.

Task	Description
Open a new module in which you can type Visual Basic code	In the Visual Basic Editor, on the Insert menu, click Module. This opens the Code window.
Create a Visual Basic procedure	In the Code window, type **Sub** followed by the procedure name and press ENTER.

(continued)

Quick Guide *(continued)*

Task	Description
Add comments to code	Type a single quotation mark (') followed by the comment, either on a line by itself or at the end of a line of Visual Basic code.
Declare a variable to contain a specific type of data	At the beginning of a procedure or module, type **Dim**, the variable name, **As**, and the data type. For example: `Dim iCount As Integer`
Have your Visual Basic application run certain code based on a condition	Use an If...Then...Else or Select Case statement.
Declare the scope of a variable	For procedure-level variables, declare the variable within the procedure. For module-level variables, declare the variable at the top of the module. For public variables, declare the variable at the top of the module using the keyword *Public*.
Repeat the same block of code several times	Use a For...Next, Do...Loop, or While...Wend loop structure.
Determine the length of a string variable	Use the *Len* function.
Retrieve characters from a string variable	Use the *Mid$*, *Left$*, or *Right$* string variable functions
Have your code pause at a particular place	Set a breakpoint by placing the cursor in the line of code and pressing F9; or click Toggle Breakpoint on the Debug menu.
Determine the value of the variable while in break mode	Place the cursor over the variable name in Code window (this displays the Data Tips window); or drag the variable name to the Watch window; or display the Locals window; or in the Immediate window, type **Print** and the variable name, and then press ENTER.
Run a line of code immediately	Type the code in the Immediate window and press ENTER.

Beginning to Write Code

When you write a report, you use the rules and symbols of your spoken language to tie words, sentences, and paragraphs together. The report is organized into elements such as sections and paragraphs. Each section presents a specific point, but all are tied together to support the report's main purpose. In Visual Basic programs, these elements are represented by modules and procedures—elements that you create to organize your code into logical tasks, each of which serves a specific function.

Opening a Blank Code Module

In Visual Basic for Applications, the Visual Basic Editor is your development environment, and your written code lies within a *code module*. You can insert as many code modules as you need to organize your code into manageable pieces that can be used in other programs or by other users. Opening a blank module is one of the first steps in writing Visual Basic code.

1. Start Microsoft PowerPoint. In the opening PowerPoint dialog box, select Blank Presentation and click OK.

2. In the New Slide dialog box, select the second slide layout (Bulleted List) and click OK. (The actual slide layout you select makes no difference.)

3. On the Tools menu, point to Macro, and then click Visual Basic Editor on the submenu. (Or press ALT+F11 as a shortcut to display the Visual Basic Editor.)

4. In the Editor, click Module on the Insert menu.

Creating a Procedure

You can create two common types of procedures in Visual Basic: *Sub* and *Function*. A *Sub* procedure performs actions but doesn't return a value; a *Function* procedure, however, returns a value. You can use a third type, the *Property* procedure, to create and manipulate custom properties, but the *Property* procedure is beyond the scope of this book.

Sub procedures start with the keyword *Sub,* followed by the name of the procedure, and end with the keywords *End Sub*. To create a procedure, give it a unique name or header.

1. In the Code window of the module you just opened, type **Sub MyNewProcedure** and press ENTER.

   Visual Basic automatically inserts the keywords *End Sub* two lines below. End Sub indicates where the procedure ends, just as a paragraph ends with a "return" in a word processor. Generally, procedures within a code module have common features that logically tie them together.

2. Add the following lines between the line `Sub MyNewProcedure` and `End Sub`:

```
MsgBox "This text is displayed in a " & _
    "message box"
```

Visual Basic treats the two separate lines as one. The space and underscore (_) at the end of the first line indicate that you want to continue a line of code onto the next line. This is analogous to what you do in text when you add a hyphen to continue a word from one line to the next. You use the ampersand (&) here to concatenate (join sequentially) two pieces of text. You complete each line of code by pressing ENTER at the end of the line.

The procedure should look like the following:

```
Sub MyNewProcedure
  MsgBox "This text is displayed in a " & _
      "message box"
End Sub
```

3. Make sure you place the cursor within the *MyNewProcedure* procedure and press F5 to run it.

Note   When you press the F5 key, Visual Basic runs the code starting from the first line of the procedure in which the cursor is placed. Pressing F5 is equivalent to clicking Run Sub/UserForm on the Run menu in the Visual Basic Editor.

You'll see a message box like this:

4. Click OK to close the message box.

By creating individual procedures, you break your code into distinct elements so that if your program doesn't work right, you can systematically track down problems. In addition, if you encapsulate a specific programming task in a procedure, you can more readily copy the procedure and paste it into another program with few or no changes. As you'll see in Chapter 13, "Developing COM Add-Ins," procedures that you create to add or remove menus and toolbars can be used in any Visual Basic program for Office.

Add Comments to Code

When you write Visual Basic code, you may want to include comments for a couple of reasons:

- To remind yourself (or tell others) why you structured your code the way you did.

- To flag work items that are still outstanding.

In a word processor like Microsoft Word, you usually add a comment by clicking Comment on the Insert menu. In Visual Basic, you add comments to your code by adding a single quotation mark (') at the beginning of the sentence. Visual Basic doesn't read or run anything in this line.

1. In the same procedure you just created, move to the end of the first line `Sub MyNewProcedure` and press ENTER.

2. On the new blank line, press TAB and add the following text:

```
' The line below will display a message box
```

Once you type this line and press ENTER, Visual Basic colors this line of code green for easier reading. You can also add comments at the end of a line of code just by adding a single quotation mark. Unless you specify another color, green text in a code module indicates comments.

Tip   To customize the color of text in a code module, click Options on the Tools menu in the Visual Basic Editor. In the Editor Format tab, select any item in the Code Colors list box and select a new color in the Foreground drop-down list.

---

3. Click at the end of the line that reads "`message box`" and add the following text:

```
' This line is continued
```

The procedure should look like the following:

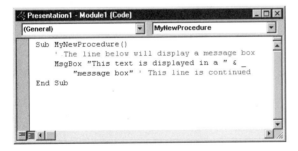

4. Finally, press F5.

Once again you'll see a message box. Visual Basic ignored both the comment line above the message box code and the comment attached to the end of the line of code.

5. Click OK to close the message box.

Tip   In Visual Basic programming you commonly indent code by inserting a tab at the beginning of each line of code, between the lines `Sub <Procedure>` and `End Sub`, as shown in the preceding illustration. This greatly improves readability. To insert a tab, just press the TAB key on your keyboard.

Categorizing Data in Visual Basic

You work every day with many kinds of data, including text and numbers. Where you store information on your computer depends on what kind of information it is. If it's text, you probably store it in a Word document; if it's numerical values or mathematical formulas, you probably store it in a Microsoft Excel workbook or Microsoft Access database; and if it's graphics, you most likely store it in a PowerPoint presentation. By storing information in a file of an Office application, you're telling the recipient of that file what type of data it contains.

Variables and Constants

Visual Basic, like most other programming languages, uses a variable or constant to represent and temporarily store data that you use in your program. A *variable*, on the one hand, represents data that changes—its value varies within a program. A *constant*, on the other hand, represents data that stays the same throughout your program. The syntax for defining variables and constants has two parts: a name and a corresponding value. These two parts are joined by an equal sign. The name of the variable or constant is stated on the left side of the equal sign, and the value is stated on the right. In the section "Specifying Declaration Statements" later in this chapter, you'll learn how to use variables and constants in code.

Determining the Data Type

When you assign a value to a variable or constant, it's of a specific type. In Visual Basic, you can explicitly categorize your data, or information, type. For example, if you're working with text, the equivalent Visual Basic data type category is String. If you're working with whole numbers less than 32,767, the data type is Integer. The table below lists more details on other numerical data types, as well as listing the Boolean, String, and Object data types.

Data type	Range
Integer	−32,768 to 32,767
Long (long integer)	−2,147,483,648 to 2,147,483,647
Single (single-precision floating-point)	−3.402823E38 to −1.401298E-45 for negative values; 1.401298E-45 to 3.402823E38 for positive values
Double (double-precision floating-point)	−1.79769313486232E308 to −4.94065645841247E-324 for negative values; 4.94065645841247E-324 to 1.79769313486232E308 for positive values
Boolean	True or False
Object	(Any property or method in an object library that returns a reference to an object.)
String (fixed-length)	1 to approximately 65,400

Note The preceding table isn't comprehensive; there are many other data types. For more information, in the Visual Basic Editor ask the Assistant for help using the words *data type summary*.

Examine User Input

1. In the Code window, move the cursor beneath the End Sub line of the procedure you created earlier (MyNewProcedure) and create a new procedure by typing **Sub InputType** and pressing ENTER.

2. Between the lines Sub InputType and End Sub, add the following line:

```
sInput = InputBox("Enter text or a number.")
```

   InputBox is a function built into the Visual Basic programming language. This function displays a dialog box containing a text box in which you can type. If you enter text and click the OK button in the dialog box, the function returns the value you entered. In this case, the returned value is stored in the variable *sInput*.

3. After the line containing the *InputBox* function, enter the following If...Then...Else statement:

```
If IsNumeric(sInput) Then
    sType = "number"
Else
    sType = "string"
End If
```

   In this code segment, you use the built-in Visual Basic function *IsNumeric* to determine whether the value the user enters, which is stored in the variable *sInput*, is numeric. If it's numeric, Visual Basic stores the string value "number" in the variable *sType*. If the input value isn't numeric, Visual Basic stores the string value "string" in the variable *sType*.

4. Finally, add the following message box statement as the last line (above End Sub) in the *InputType* procedure:

```
MsgBox "The data you entered was a " & sType
```

5. If Visual Basic displays a "Variable not defined" error, remove the Option Explicit statement at the top of the module. Place the cursor anywhere within the *InputType* procedure and press F5.

   You'll see a dialog box prompting you to enter text or a number. You can also enter a combination of text and numbers, although this combination is always considered a String data type in Visual Basic.

6. Click OK to close the dialog box.

Tip Visual Basic provides a convenient function called *TypeName* that performs a more robust version of the operation you performed in *MyNewProcedure*. *TypeName* returns a string indicating the type of information within a variable you specify. The MyNewProcedure only determines if the variable is a number or string. TypeName can determine if a variable is of any data type listed in the Data Type table. For more information, ask the Assistant for help using the word *typename*.

Specifying Declaration Statements

As you just learned, data is often of a specific type. For example, the whole number 12 is an Integer data type, and the text *Hello there* is a String data type. When you assign data to a variable, you'll want to tell Visual Basic what type of data you're using. To formally indicate this, you need to use a declaration statement.

Declaration statements for variables usually start with the keyword *Dim,* followed by the variable name and the type of data the variable should hold. The common syntax appears as:

```
Dim VariableName As DataType
```

The variable name must begin with a letter, can't be more than 255 characters long or contain any periods or mathematical operators, and must not be the name of a Visual Basic keyword. The data type can be any of the types discussed in the section of this chapter titled "Determining the Data Type" or any other types provided by Visual Basic.

You can specify more than one declaration at a time in a declaration statement, but you must specify the exact type for each variable. Visual Basic doesn't assume that the second variable is declared the same type as the first or any other declaration on the same line. By default, Visual Basic assigns the declaration without a specified type to the data type Variant. The following illustration shows variable declarations of several types.

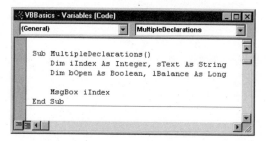

Declaration statements for constants start with the keyword *Const,* followed by the constant name, the type of data the constant should hold, and the value assigned to the constant. The common syntax appears as:

```
Const ConstantName As DataType = Value
```

The naming convention for a constant follows that of a variable name, as explained above. The data type can also be any of the types specified by Visual Basic. The value set to the constant must be a valid value within the range of the data type. The following simple procedure shows how to use the *Dim* and *Const* statements in your code:

```
Sub VariablesAndConstants()
    Dim iMyVariable As Integer
    Const iMyConstant As Integer = 10
    iMyVariable = 4
    MsgBox iMyVariable & ", " & iMyConstant
End Sub
```

Declaring variables and constants helps you reduce coding errors such as assigning an incorrect value or misspelling a name. As a good programming practice, you should place the keywords *Option Explicit* at the top of your code module. If you do, when Visual Basic runs your code it ensures that you explicitly declare and set a valid type of value to any variables and constants in your code. To have Visual Basic automatically add the keywords *Option Explicit* to every new code module you insert, in the Visual Basic Editor, click Options on the Tools menu, click the Editor tab, and then select the Require Variable Declaration check box.

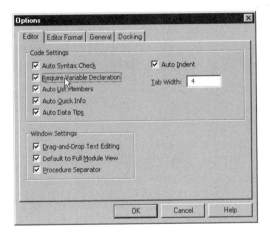

Tip   In programming you commonly prefix the name of each variable and constant with a letter that indicates the data type. This helps you and others reduce the time spent reading and debugging code because you can easily distinguish what type of data a variable or a constant should contain. For Visual Basic data types, a common syntax is to prefix each variable or constant as shown: *s* or *str* for String data type, *i* for Integer, *bln* or *b* for Boolean, *lng* or *l* for Long, *sng* or *sg* for Single, and *vnt* or *v* for Variant.

Declare the Scope of Variables and Constants

When you declare variables and constants, you also have to think about the scope in which they'll be available. *Scope* refers to the availability of a variable, constant, or procedure for use by another procedure. You can declare variables and constants at three levels: procedure-level, module-level, and public.

- **Procedure-level** As the name suggests, these variables and constants are available only within the procedure in which they're declared. You declare them at the beginning of a Visual Basic procedure.

- **Module-level** The top of a code module is referred to as the Declarations section. You can't declare module-level variables and constants anywhere in a code module except the Declarations section. They're available to all procedures within the code module containing the declaration. If you make declarations between procedures or at the end of a code module, Visual Basic displays an error when it tries to run the code.

- **Public** You also declare these variables and constants at the top of a code module, in the Declarations section. However, the declaration statement is prefixed with the keyword *Public,* indicating that the variable or constant is available to all procedures in all code modules in your program.

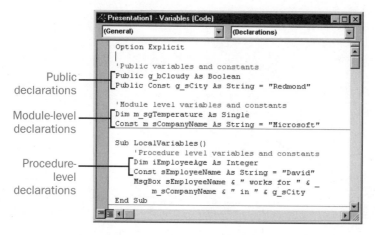

Tip In addition to prefixing variables and constants with letters that indicate the data type, it's a good idea to include letters that indicate scope. This also helps you and others reduce the amount of time spent reading and debugging code because you can easily find where the variable or constant is declared. A common syntax is to prefix each variable or constant with *m_* if it's module-level or *g_* if it's public (the "g" stands for "global"). If the variable or constant is procedure-level, an additional prefix isn't used.

Do I Need to Declare My Variables and Constants?

Declaring variables is one of the most common programming practices, and by most programming standards it's a necessity. It allows for more readable code and lets Visual Basic know what type of data you're working with. If you don't declare a variable or constant as a specific type, Visual Basic, by default, declares the variable as a Variant data type.

The Variant data type allows you to set any type of data to a variable. For example, if MyVariable is declared as a Variant data type, you can set it to equal a String, an Integer, a Boolean, or any other data type. The ability to assign any data type to a variable is useful in cases where you're not sure what type of data has been entered in a database or what type of data the user will enter.

When Visual Basic runs a line of code that uses a variable or constant declared as a Variant data type, however, it must determine what the variable type is, possibly slowing your program's execution. Also, a variable or constant declared as a Variant data type uses more memory.

Making Decisions with Condition Blocks

In any production process, whether you're producing a report, a car, or software, you need to decide what materials you need and how to control the flow of those materials through your personnel, your departments, and your technologies. At each point in the process, you may gather input from sources like quality control or computer sensors and select alternative flows for the material. In Visual Basic, you decide what data you need to work with, create a program flow to work with the data, gather input from users or data sources on your system or network, and produce a result.

In many situations, you select a path depending on conditions, just like on a drive from city to city. When travelling, you choose which roads to take depending on weather, traffic, scenery, and time. Your Visual Basic program is no different. Once you decide what conditions determine the flow, your program will follow a logical path to the final output. Visual Basic provides a number of syntax choices to allow you to evaluate information and run appropriate code, depending on which criteria and conditions you specify.

Pick an Option with If...Then...Else Statements

In Visual Basic the most common and simplest condition statements are *If...Then* and *If...Then...Else*. These statements allow you to evaluate a condition (or set of conditions) in order to run a particular block of statements. (You already used this structure in the procedure you wrote to determine a data type.)

1. In the Code window, create a new procedure by typing **Sub IfThenCondition** and pressing ENTER.

2. Between the lines Sub IfThenCondition and End Sub, add the following line of code:

```
sInput = InputBox("Enter a number greater than 10.")
```

As discussed earlier, the built-in Visual Basic *InputBox* function prompts the user to enter a value in a text box and returns a string representing the value that the user enters. In this case, you prompt the user to enter a number greater than 10.

3. After the line containing the *InputBox* function, enter the following If...Then condition block:

```
If sInput > 10 Then
    MsgBox "You entered a number greater than 10."
End If
```

Within this If...Then condition block, if the value entered by the user is greater than 10, the program displays the message box. Otherwise, nothing else happens.

4. Place the cursor anywhere in the *IfThenCondition* procedure and press F5. You'll see the InputBox prompting you to enter a number greater than 10. If the condition is evaluated to True (that is, the input value is a number greater than 10), the program displays the confirmation message. If the number is less than or equal to 10, no message is displayed.

5. Enter a number greater than 10 and click OK.

6. Click OK to close the message box.

7. Add the following two lines between the line containing the *MsgBox* function and End If of the If...Then condition block you just created:

```
Else
    MsgBox "You entered a number less than 10."
```

The If...Then...Else condition block goes one step further. It provides an alternative if the condition isn't met. Now, if you enter a number less than 10, you see a different message box.

8. Press F5.

9. Enter a number less than 10 and then click OK.

10. Click OK to close the message box.

11. Within the If...Then...Else condition block you created above, add the following two lines just above the line Else:

```
ElseIf sInput = 10 Then
    MsgBox "You entered the number 10."
```

Finally, the If...Then...ElseIf condition block goes yet another step and adds more flexibility than the If...Then...Else condition block. With the If...Then...ElseIf condition block, you can evaluate more than one condition within the same block. Now, a different message box is displayed for all three cases for the input value. This value can either be greater than, equal to, or less than 10.

The completed If...Then...ElseIf condition block should look like this:

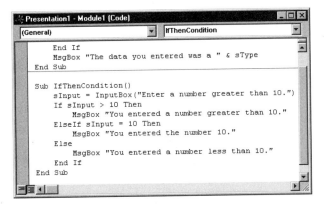

12. Press F5.

13. Enter the number 10 and click OK.

14. Click OK to close the message box.

Select Among Options with Select Case

The Select Case condition block is very similar to the If...Then...ElseIf condition block. Select Case evaluates the test expression in the first line and afterward compares it to the value in each case.

1. In the procedure you created above, delete the If...Then...ElseIf condition block and replace it with a Select Case statement. The revised procedure looks like this:

```
Sub IfThenCondition()
    sInput = InputBox("Enter a number greater than 10.")
    Select Case sInput
    Case Is > 10
        MsgBox "You entered a number greater than 10."
    Case Is = 10
        MsgBox "You entered the number 10."
    Case Is < 10
        MsgBox "You entered a number less than 10."
    End Select
End Sub
```

Pay particular attention to the similarities between the overall structure of the Select Case condition with the If...Then...ElseIf condition block. In the Select Case condition block, the variable *sInput* is the test expression and you enter it at the beginning of the condition block. Then a number of Case statements follow to handle the possible conditions of the test expression.

2. Run the procedure and enter numbers as you did before. The procedure responds the same way.

Repeating Actions with Loops

You'll often find occasions where you'll want to continually change a value and run some code repeatedly with the incremented value. At other times you'll want to delay running code until the value of a variable meets certain conditions. In Visual Basic, looping structures come in a variety of options to suit either case.

Count with For...Next

The For...Next loop both runs a block of code repeatedly and incrementally increases or decreases a variable you specify. The incremental changes in value to the variable can be in steps with positive or negative integers. By default, the incremental step value is +1.

1. Create a new procedure called *ForNext*.

2. Within the procedure, declare the two integers i and iTotal by adding the following two lines of code:

```
Dim iTotal As Integer
Dim i As Integer
```

3. Add the following For...Next loop:

```
For i = 1 To 5
    iTotal = iTotal + i ^ 2
Next i
```

The For...Next loop increments the integer variable *i* by a value of 1. The loop has a range from 1 to 5. Thus, *i* is initially assigned a value of 1 the first time the loop runs, and then in the following loop *i* has a value of 2, and so on. The variable *iTotal* is used to sum the square of each of the values from 1 to 5 (the range of the For...Next loop).

4. Add a message box after the For...Next loop to display the final value of the variable *iTotal* by adding the following line of code:

```
MsgBox iTotal
```

The complete procedure should look like this:

```
Sub ForNext()
    Dim iTotal As Integer
    Dim i As Integer
    For i = 1 To 5
        iTotal = iTotal + i ^ 2
    Next i
    MsgBox iTotal
End Sub
```

5. Press F5.

The final value of *iTotal* is 55. The line within the loop, iTotal = iTotal + i ^ 2, adds the square of the numbers between 1 and 5 (that is, $1 + 4 + 9 + 16 + 25$).

Note   You could also step backward by setting the range from 5 to 1 and adding the keyword Step and –1 just after the range. The resulting code would look like this:

```
For i = 5 To 1 Step -1
```

The variable *i* is initially assigned a value of 5, then 4, then 3, and so on. In this case, stepping through backward would produce the same result as the procedure you wrote.

Step Out Early

If you want to exit the loop when the value of *iTotal* is greater than 5, you can add an If...Then condition within the loop. If the condition is met, Visual Basic will exit the For...Next loop.

1. In the procedure you just created, add the following If...Then condition block within the For...Next loop, just after the line `iTotal = iTotal + i ^ 2`:

```
If iTotal > 5 Then
    MsgBox i
    Exit For
End If
```

The code `Exit For` tells Visual Basic to exit the For...Next loop that's currently running. The message box just before the Exit For statement shows the value of iCount just before exiting the loop.

2. Press F5.

Now you'll see two message boxes. The first shows the value of the counter *i* used in the For...Next loop, which is 3. The second displays the value of *iTotal*, which is 14. Once you jump from a loop, you usually continue with an action right after the loop and use the values altered in the loop in the following actions.

Using the Do...Loop

The Do...Loop structure continues to run code within the loop structure until a certain condition is met. Unless you specify a condition for exiting or stopping a Do...Loop structure, it loops without stopping. You can specify such a condition in three ways: repeat until something changes, continue while things are the same, and leave a loop early.

Repeat Until Something Changes

The first way to exit a loop structure is to add the keyword Until after the word Loop and then specify the condition.

1. Create a procedure called *DoLoopUntil*.

2. Declare the variable *iCount* as an integer and create a Do...Loop structure by adding the following lines of code:

```
Dim iCount As Integer
Do
     iCount = iCount + 2
Loop Until iCount > 100
```

In the Do...Loop structure, the program increments the variable *iCount* by a value of 2 each time through the loop. When the value of *iCount* is greater than 100, the loop exits.

3. Just after the line `iCount = iCount + 2` in the Do...Loop structure, add the following:

```
Debug.Print iCount
```

During each successive loop, `Debug.Print` prints the value of *iCount* in the Immediate window so you can see *iCount* being incremented.

4. If the Immediate window isn't displayed, in the Visual Basic Editor, on the View menu, click Immediate Window (or press CTRL+G as a shortcut).

5. Add a message box after the Do...Loop structure indicating that the loop has finished:

```
MsgBox "The loop has finished."
```

The complete procedure should look like this:

```
Sub DoLoopUntil()
     Dim iCount As Integer
     Do
          iCount = iCount + 2
          Debug.Print iCount
     Loop Until iCount > 100
     MsgBox "The loop has finished."
End Sub
```

6. Press F5 to run the procedure.

Continue While Things Are the Same

The second way to exit a Do...Loop structure is to add the keyword While after the word Loop and then specify the condition.

1. In the Do...Loop structure you just created, delete the line `Loop Until iCount > 100` and replace it with:

```
Loop While iCount <= 100
```

2. Press F5. The procedure performs like the one in the previous example.

If you closely compare the logic of the Until condition and the While condition, you'll see that they specify the same condition and produce the same result.

Important   In both previous cases, you could place the keywords *Until* and *While* (plus the condition following them) after the word *Do* instead of *Loop*. You can type **Until** or **While** after the word *Do* or after the word *Loop*, but not after both words in one procedure. The difference this makes to your code is that if you place *Until* and *While* after the word *Loop*, the program evaluates the statements at least once before reaching the Until or While condition. If you place them after the word *Do*, the program evaluates the condition following the keyword *Until* or *While* immediately, before any lines within the Do...Loop structure run. If the condition is false, the program won't execute the loop at all. For more information, in the Visual Basic Editor, ask the Assistant for help using the words "Using Do...Loop Statements."

Exit a Loop Early

The third way to exit a Do...Loop structure is to use only a condition statement in the lines of code within the Do...Loop structure.

1. In the Do...Loop structure, delete the line `Loop While Count <= 100` and replace it with the following If...Then condition and Loop statements:

```
If iCount > 100 Then Exit Do
Loop
```

The complete procedure looks like this:

```
Sub DoLoopUntil()
    Dim iCount As Integer
    Do
        iCount = iCount + 2
        Debug.Print iCount
        If iCount > 100 Then Exit Do
    Loop
    MsgBox "The loop has finished."
End Sub
```

2. Press F5. The procedure performs the same as the ones in the two preceding examples.

3. Exit PowerPoint.

Parsing Filenames with For...Next

You may find that your program handles files and filenames in many scenarios. For example, your program may prompt the user to specify a filename under which information will be saved. To verify that the specified pathname of the filename is valid, you need to parse the filename string for the pathname. To *parse* means to separate into more easily processed components (groups of characters, in this case) and to analyze them. The section File Management in Chapter 4 describes more ways to parse all parts of a filename. The following example examines one way to parse any text string (in this case, a file name).

Parse Filenames

Once you develop a function to extract the pathname from a filename string, you use the debugging tools of the Visual Basic Editor to step through each line of code and see the different values assigned to variables.

1. Open the Visual Basic Editor in any Microsoft Office application. (The following code and steps work identically in each application.)

2. Insert a new code module. In the Code window, type **Sub ParseFileName** and press ENTER to create a new procedure.

3. Add the following line of code to the procedure:

```
MsgBox GetPath("C:\Temp\Test.txt")
```

The string value you specified as the first argument of the MsgBox statement is the value returned from the function *GetPath*. (*GetPath* is a *Function* procedure that you'll create in the steps below. Recall that a *Function* procedure is like a *Sub* procedure except that it returns a value.) *GetPath* takes one string argument, representing the filename. In this case, the value you pass to the *GetPath* function is "C:\Temp\Test.txt", which does not necessarily exist on your system but is used as a test to verify that the *GetPath* function works.

4. Below the End Sub statement of the *ParseFileName* procedure, add a blank line by pressing ENTER. Create a new function by typing **Function GetPath(sFileName As String) As String** and pressing ENTER.

The function *GetPath* accepts an argument, *sFileName*, which is declared as a String data type. The *GetPath* function is itself declared as a String data type, which indicates that you assign a string to *GetPath*. By default, the value of *GetPath* is initially an empty string, or "".

5. Within the *GetPath* function, add the following declaration statements:

```
Dim sChar As String, i As Integer
```

6. After the declarations in the *GetPath* function, add the following For...Next loop:

```
For i = Len(sFileName) To 1 Step -1
Next i
```

Because you specify the Step keyword and a step value at the end of the For statement, the loop iterates from the value representing the length of the string sFileName down to 1. The Visual Basic function *Len* is built into the Visual Basic language. The *Len* function returns the number of characters in the string you specify. In this case, the variable *sFileName*, or "C:\Temp\Test.txt", is the string value, and its length is 16.

7. Within the For...Next loop, add the following line:

```
sChar = Mid$(sFileName, i, 1)
```

The program assigns the variable *sChar* to the value returned by the Visual Basic built-in *Mid$* function. The *Mid$* function accepts three arguments: *string*, *start*, and *length*. The arguments are used to return a specified number of characters from the string. The *string* argument represents the string from which you want to extract a subset of characters. The *start* argument specifies the character position in the string at which to start extracting characters. The *length* argument indicates the number of characters to extract.

In the preceding *Mid$* function, Visual Basic extracts one character from the string value represented by sFileName, or "C:\Temp\Test.txt", starting from the position i. The value of i is set by the For...Next loop.

8. After the *Mid$* function, add the following If...Then condition block:

```
If sChar = "\" Then
End If
```

The If...Then condition block indicates that if the string sChar equals a backslash, the statements within the block run.

9. Within the If...Then condition block, add the following two lines:

```
GetPath = Left$(sFileName, i - 1)
Exit For
```

Although the Visual Basic function *Left$* is similar to the *Mid$* function, it accepts only two arguments: *string* and *length*. The *Left$* function extracts the number of characters specified by the *length* argument, starting at the left end of the string.

When you enter the If...Then condition block, you assign to the *GetPath* function the pathname (the pathname is a subset of the filename previously passed to the *GetPath* function) and the For...Next loop exits.

10. Place the cursor in the *ParseFileName* procedure and press F5.

You'll see a message box with the string value "C:\Temp". The *GetPath* function iterates through the specified filename string, evaluating each character in the filename string, starting from the right-most character and working backward. When it finds a character equal to a backslash, it extracts the characters to the left of the backslash in the filename string, which indicates the pathname. The pathname is assigned to *GetPath*, and a message box displays the result of *GetPath*.

Tip If you want to extract only the portion of the filename without the path in the string "C:\Temp\Test.txt", you can change the line with the *Left$* function to the following: GetPath = Right$(sFileName, Len(sFileName) - i). The *Right$* function is similar to the *Left$* function, but it extracts the number of characters specified by the *length* argument, starting at the right end of the string. Notice also that you can nest functions inside other functions. In this case, the result of *Len* is an argument to the *Right$* function.

Debugging Your Code

All developers need to learn debugging. And when you're debugging, you can use several tools to track down problems within the logic of the written code. The Visual Basic Editor has a number of debugging tools usually found only in advanced development environments, such as Microsoft Visual C++.

Breakpoints

When Visual Basic runs your code, you can break execution at a specific line of code and evaluate the current state of variables. When you press F5 to run your code or select a menu item or toolbar button that calls a specific macro, Visual Basic is in *run mode* because it's running code. If you add a breakpoint at a specific line of code, Visual Basic changes to *break mode*. While in break mode, you can do one of three things: stop execution, continue execution, or step through your code line by line. Stepping through code allows you to evaluate variables used in your code and see the exact path of code execution that Visual Basic is following.

Set Breakpoints in Code

1. In the *ParseFileName* procedure, place the cursor in the line `MsgBox GetPath("C:\Temp\Test.txt")` and press F9.

    The F9 key is a keyboard shortcut to clicking Toggle Breakpoint on the Debug menu in the Visual Basic Editor. The line is now highlighted in dark red, indicating that when Visual Basic runs this line of code, it will enter break mode. You remove this breakpoint by placing the cursor within the line of code and pressing F9 again or by clicking the dot in the left margin next to the line of code.

Click the dot to toggle the breakpoint.

Press F9 to set a breakpoint.

2. With a breakpoint set for the MsgBox statement, and with the cursor placed in the *ParseFileName* procedure, press F5.

    Visual Basic will start code execution by entering the *ParseFileName* procedure and will break at the first line within the procedure. In break mode, Visual Basic highlights the next line it'll run.

The text in the title bar of the Visual Basic Editor indicates that the Visual Basic code execution for the specified project is in break mode.

This line will run next.

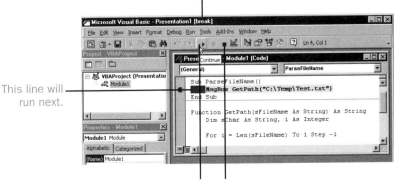

If you want Visual Basic to continue code execution until the next breakpoint (if another exists), you can click the Continue button or press F5.

Click the Reset button to stop and reset your code.

3. Press F8 several times to step through the code.

The F8 key is a shortcut to clicking Step Into on the Debug menu. As you'll see below, stepping through code by pressing F8 allows you to examine the values of variables and see the exact path Visual Basic code execution will take. You can press F5 anytime to continue code execution until the next breakpoint (if there is one). If you want to stop code execution while in break mode, click the Reset button (two buttons to the right of Continue) or click Reset on the Run menu in the Visual Basic Editor.

Tip   If you don't add a breakpoint anywhere in your code, you can start code execution in break mode by placing the cursor in the procedure you want to run and pressing F8. Visual Basic automatically enters break mode and highlights the first line of the procedure containing the cursor.

---

4. Press F5 to finish running the macro. Click OK to close the message box.

The Data Tips Window

As you step through your code, there are several ways you can track a variable's value. The easiest way is to place the cursor over the variable in question when Visual Basic is in break mode. The Visual Basic Editor will display a tip window with the current value of the variable, object property, or function. The Data Tips window is similar to the ToolTip displayed when the cursor is over a toolbar button.

Display Data Tips

1. With the same breakpoint set, place the cursor in the *ParseFileName* procedure and press F5 to start running the code.

2. Step through the code by pressing F8 until code execution reaches the If...Then condition block.

3. Place the cursor over the variable *sChar* in the line `If sChar = "\" Then`. You'll see the Data Tips window showing the current value of *sChar*, which is the letter "t". The letter "t" is the last character in the string "C:\Temp\Test.txt" and is the first character to which *sChar* is assigned.

If you don't see the Data Tips window, click Options on the Tools menu in the Visual Basic Editor. On the Editor tab on the Options dialog box, select the Auto Data Tips check box and click OK.

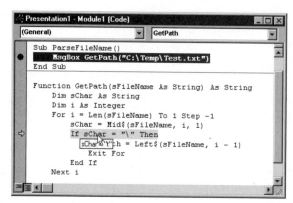

4. Continue pressing F8 to step through the code, and each time the For...Next loop reaches the If...Then condition block, display the Data Tips window by placing the cursor over the variable *sChar*.

5. Press F5 to finish running the macro. Click OK to close the message box.

The Visual Basic Editor provides three other windows in which you can display the current value of variables. They are the Watch, Locals, and Immediate windows.

The Watch Window

You can select a variable in a code module and drag it to the Watch window, where its contents are automatically updated each time the value changes during code execution.

Add Watch Variables

1. If you don't see the Watch window, click Watch Window on the View menu in the Visual Basic Editor.

2. Double-click the variable *sChar* in the code module. (You can select any of the three occurrences of *sChar*.)

3. Drag the selected variable name to the Watch window. You can also add variables to the Watch window by selecting the var-iable in code, clicking Add Watch on the Debug menu, and clicking OK.

4. Select the variable *i* in the code module and drag it to the Watch window.

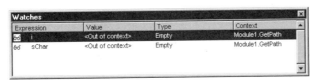

The "out of context" message in the Value column in the Watch window indicates that the corresponding variable hasn't been used yet within the currently running module. Once a variable has been referenced within the currently running module, the Value column displays the current value assigned to that variable. With a variable that hasn't been declared yet (either by assigning a value to it or by explicitly creating it with the Dim statement), the third column, Type, displays the notation "Empty." When Visual Basic encounters a statement that declares the variable, it displays the appropriate data type (such as Integer, String, Single, or Long).

The fourth column in the Watch window indicates context, which defines the scope of the variables. The variables *sChar* and *i* are declared at the procedure level, within the *GetPath* function. The context of each variable in the Watch window is listed as Module1.GetPath. Module1 represents the name of the code module containing the function *GetPath*.

5. Step through your code by placing the cursor within the *ParseFileName* procedure and pressing F8 several times.

As you step through your code, the values of the variables *sChar* and *i* are updated in the Watch window. The Watch window allows you to monitor the values of as many variables as you choose. The program sets the value of *i* in the first line of the For...Next loop and the value of *sChar* in the next line.

6. Press F5 to finish running the macro. Click OK to close the message box.

The Locals Window

Although the Locals window is very similar to the Watch window, you don't need to add the variables to be watched. By default, the Locals window automatically displays the values of all declared variables in the current procedure.

Observe the Values of Local Variables

1. If you don't see the Locals window, on the View menu in the Visual Basic Editor click Locals Window.

2. Place the cursor in the *ParseFileName* procedure.

3. Press F8 several times to step through your code again, until you reach the end of the first iteration through the For...Next loop in the *GetPath* function.

If the Locals window or any of the Editor windows isn't big enough to display the needed information, move or resize it as you would any other window.

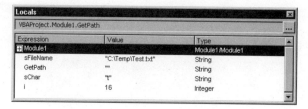

The program displays the values of all variables used in the *GetPath* function in the Locals window, including *sFileName*, which was passed to the *GetPath* function, and the value of *GetPath* itself. If there were any module-level variables, you could click the plus sign (+) beside the Module1 item in the Expression list to display their values.

4. Press F5 to finish running the macro. Click OK to close the message box.

The Immediate Window

The third window that the Visual Basic Editor provides as a debugging tool is the Immediate window. It's more versatile than the Data Tips, Watch, or Locals window. You can either explicitly "print" a value of a variable to the Immediate window, or you can type or paste a line of code into the window, press ENTER to run the code, and observe the results.

Print to the Immediate Window

1. If you don't see the Immediate window, on the View menu in the Visual Basic Editor click Immediate Window or press CTRL+G.

2. In the Code window, in the *GetPath* function, add the following line below the line that sets the value of the variable *sChar* (sChar = Mid$(sFileName, i, 1)):

```
Debug.Print sChar
```

The Debug.Print method accepts one argument, which is the variable or value you want to print to the Immediate window. In this case, you'll print the value of *sChar* to the Immediate window.

3. Place the cursor in the *ParseFileName* procedure and press F8 several times until the procedure ends. The program prints the value of the variable *sChar* to the Immediate window during each iteration through the For...Next loop.

Execute a Line of Code in the Immediate Window

1. Step through your code, starting within the *ParseFileName* procedure, until you reach the line setting the value of *sChar* in the *GetPath* function.

2. Click in the bottom of the Immediate window, type **Print i**, and press ENTER. The value of i will be printed below the line you typed. You can also determine the value of any property of any object defined within the current scope of code execution.

3. Exit your application.

Tip   In the Print statement in the preceding example, you can replace the word "Print" with a question mark (?) so the line appears as ?i. The question mark is a shortcut to the word "Print" in the Immediate window.

Chapter Summary

This chapter described how to create a procedure in which you:

- write Visual Basic code
- declare variables and constants
- process string and numerical data from user input
- control program flow using Visual Basic decision-making statements and
- repeat a series of steps with looping structures

Chapter 3

Creating Custom Dialog Boxes

Estimated time: 120 minutes

- Create custom dialog boxes.

- Use ActiveX controls in your dialog boxes to create dialog box elements, such as a list box or a tabbed dialog box.

- Create a Microsoft Office wizard similar to the Fax Wizard in Microsoft Word and the AutoContent Wizard in Microsoft PowerPoint.

- Integrate the Office Assistant into your wizards.

A dialog box in any Microsoft Windows application serves a number of purposes. It can, for example, provide information by displaying a message, request information by providing a text box for input, and list a set of choices using a list box. In the Microsoft Visual Basic Editor in any of the Office applications, a custom dialog box is called a *UserForm*. UserForms are the "drawing pad" on which you design custom dialog boxes. In most cases throughout Office, you use UserForms to reproduce built-in dialog boxes. The elements within a UserForm, such as a button, list box, or a text box, are ActiveX controls. Retrieving user input and displaying information are just two of the things you can do with these controls.

After explaining how to build and use UserForms, this chapter goes on to describe how to build a wizard similar in look and style to the wizards used in Word and PowerPoint. Learning to build the wizard dialog box will also help you become familiar with writing the Visual Basic for Applications code that controls elements on the dialog box.

Note Building dialog boxes in the Visual Basic Editor isn't the same as building dialog boxes in the Microsoft Visual Basic 5.0 or 6.0 development products. UserForms in the Visual Basic Editor in Office and forms in Visual Basic 5.0/6.0 use different technologies. In Part 6, Chapters 13 and 14 describe how to create COM add-ins in Visual Basic 6.0. The examples in this chapter use UserForms in the Visual Basic Editor. However, a similar wizard dialog box is built using Visual Basic 6.0 and is provided in the Chapter 14 practice folder. Some differences exist in how these boxes are built, but the coding styles and practice are similar.

Quick Guide

The following table lists a common set of tasks when creating UserForms.

Task	Description
Create a UserForm	In the Visual Basic Editor, on the Insert menu, click UserForm.
Add a control from the Toolbox to a UserForm	In the Toolbox, click the control, and then on the UserForm drag the control to the size you want.
Set the value of a property for a control on a UserForm	In the Properties window, select the control from the Object drop-down list, click the property name in the left column, and type or select a value in the right column.
Create code for the event procedure of a control on a UserForm	Double-click the control, and then in the Code window, select a procedure from the Procedure drop-down list, and type the code between the Sub and End Sub statements.
Add controls to the Toolbox	In the Editor, on the Tools menu, click Additional Controls, select the controls you want to add from the Available Controls list, and click OK.
Add tabs to a UserForm	In the Toolbox, click the MultiPage control and drag it to the UserForm.

Creating a Basic Dialog Box

This chapter tells you how to create common elements of the dialog boxes you see throughout Office and Windows. For example, some dialog boxes contain two list boxes, and you can selectively move items from one list to the other. If you click Templates and Add-Ins on the Tools menu in Word and then click Organizer on the Templates and Add-Ins dialog box, you'll see an example of this. The Organizer dialog box is also a tabbed dialog box, and this chapter describes how to build custom tabbed dialog boxes.

Create a UserForm

1. Start Microsoft Excel. On the Tools menu, point to Macro, and then click Visual Basic Editor on the submenu.

2. In the Editor, on the Insert menu, click UserForm.

A UserForm is a "drawing pad" upon which you design a custom dialog box.

The components of your custom dialog box come from the Visual Basic for Applications Toolbox.

The Toolbox contains a graphical list of ActiveX controls that you can add to a UserForm. To learn the name of each control, move the cursor over it. When you create a UserForm, Visual Basic lists a default set of ActiveX controls. You can easily add more ActiveX controls to the list, which you'll learn to do later in this chapter.

3. In the Toolbox, click the CommandButton control.

4. On the UserForm, drag the control to the size you want, and then drag it to the position you want. Use the following illustration as a guide:

CommandButton control

UserForm1

CommandButton1

5. In the Toolbox, click the TextBox control.

6. On the UserForm, drag the control to the size you want, and then drag it to the position you want. Use the illustration on the following page as a guide.

TextBox control

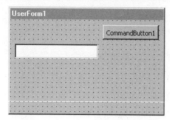

Label control

7. Add one more CommandButton control and a Label control to the UserForm. Again, you can use the following illustration as a guide.

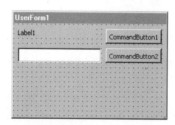

If you have to add several controls to a UserForm, you might speed things up by using one of the shortcut methods. The shortcut methods create controls in a default size, but you can use the size handles to resize them later. In Excel, you can use any of the following methods to add controls from the Toolbox to a UserForm:

- Click a control in the Toolbox, and then click in the UserForm. The control appears where you click.

- Drag a control from the Toolbox to the UserForm. The control appears where the mouse pointer is when you release the mouse button.

- Double-click a control in the Toolbox, and then click in the UserForm once for each control you want to create. Each control appears where you click. Click the Select Objects button (the arrow icon) when you want to "turn off" the mode of inserting controls where you click.

Set the Properties of Controls

Before you can display your controls in a dialog box and put them to use, you need to set their properties. Properties determine the captions of controls, the values they can accept or display, when they are available, and so on.

When the Properties window is open, you can also display the properties of a control by clicking the control.

1. On the View menu, click Properties Window; or press F4 as a shortcut.
     The Properties window lists the properties of the selected control in the left column and the corresponding property values in the right column.

2. Near the top of the Properties window, select CommandButton1 from the Object drop-down list.

3. Click the Alphabetic tab.

4. In the left column of the Properties window, select the Name property (shown in parentheses).

5. Type **cmdOK** and press ENTER.

6. Repeat steps 2 through 5 for CommandButton2. This time, however, select CommandButton2 from the Object drop-down list and type **cmdCancel** as the value of the Name property.

7. Continue setting the other properties for all the controls using the values shown in the following table.

> The Object drop-down list in the Properties window will show the new names for CommandButton1 and CommandButton2 (cmdOK and cmdCancel, respectively).

Control	Property	Value
CommandButton1	Name	cmdOK
CommandButton2	Name	cmdCancel
CommandButton1	Caption	OK
CommandButton2	Caption	Cancel
CommandButton2	Cancel	True
Label1	Name	lblMyLabel
Label1	Caption	(Enter text and click OK.)
TextBox1	Name	txtInput

Note   When you add controls to a UserForm, Visual Basic automatically assigns a unique name to the control. The default name for a given control is the type of control it is—such as a label or command button—followed by a number; the number is incremented each time you add another control of the same type. For example, after you add the first command button, the default name of the next command button is CommandButton2. If you delete or add more controls than the examples in this chapter tell you to do, the names of your controls will be different. Make sure that you set the properties of the correct control.

8. Click any blank area on the UserForm so that the Properties window lists the UserForm's properties. In the Properties window, type the value **Text Input** for the Caption property.

9. Resize and move the controls on the UserForm just as you would a drawing shape on a document, worksheet, or slide. The following illustration shows how Excel will display the completed dialog box. Use it as a guide in moving and resizing the controls on your UserForm.

You just added four controls to your UserForm: two CommandButton controls, a TextBox control, and a Label control. You'll use these controls to gather user input and place text in a cell on an Excel worksheet.

*If your UserForm
is behind the
Code window,
display it by
clicking
UserForm1
(UserForm) on
the Window
menu.*

Gather User Input

1. Double-click the cmdOK command button. When the Code window opens, type the following program statements between the `Private Sub cmdOK_Click` and `End Sub` statements:

```
If txtInput.TextLength > 0 Then
    ActiveSheet.Cells(1, 1).Value = txtInput.Text
    Unload UserForm1
Else
    MsgBox "Please enter some text.", vbCritical
End If
```

The TextLength property of the TextBox control returns the number of characters of the text string in the TextBox control. If you entered text (indicated by a TextLength greater than 0), that text in the TextBox control is inserted into cell A1 in the active worksheet. Thereafter, the program closes, or *unloads*, the UserForm by calling the *Unload* function and passing to it the name of the UserForm (UserForm1 in this case) as the argument. If the value of TextLength is 0, no text was entered and the program displays a message box asking the user to enter some text.

2. Double-click the cmdCancel command button and type the following program statement in the Code window between the `Private Sub cmdCancel_Click` and `End Sub` statements:

```
Unload Me
```

When the user activates this button by clicking it, the UserForm is unloaded. To unload the UserForm, the program calls the Unload statement and passes the name of the UserForm—in this case the keyword *Me* (which represents the UserForm where the code and control exist)—as the argument. It's a common Windows design not to run any actions other than closing the dialog box when you press a Cancel command button.

3. In the Editor, if the Project Explorer window isn't open, click Project Explorer on the View menu.

4. In the Project Explorer window, double-click UserForm1 to activate the window containing the UserForm.

5. On the Standard toolbar in the Visual Basic Editor, click the Run Sub/ UserForm button. The Text Input program runs in Excel.

*Run Sub/
UserForm*

6. Without entering text in the text box, click OK. You'll see a message box asking you to enter some text.

7. Click OK to close the message box.

8. To end the program, click Cancel, or enter text in the text box and click OK.

   The code behind the Cancel button in the *cmdCancel_Click* event procedure contains the code Unload Me, which was added in step 2. Thus, clicking the cmdCancel control unloads the UserForm and ends your program. You can also end the program by pressing ESC. Because you set the Cancel property of the cmdCancel control to True, pressing ESC when the UserForm is active has the same effect as clicking the cmdCancel control. This is the usual Windows behavior.

   This was a simple example of how to use ActiveX controls on your UserForm. In the next few procedures, we'll create several UserForms that use many of the Toolbox's ActiveX controls.

Using the Controls in the Toolbox

Although Office provides a set of ActiveX controls in the Visual Basic Editor Toolbox, chances are you'll have other ActiveX controls registered on your system that you also may want to use in a Visual Basic UserForm.

Add a Control to the Toolbox

1. In the Editor, click Insert, and then click UserForm to insert a new UserForm.

2. On the Tools menu, click Additional Controls. The Additional Controls dialog box, as shown on the next page, displays a list of the registered ActiveX controls available on your system. (Your list may be different.)

3. Just to observe the process, select any item on the list and click OK. You'll see an icon representing the ActiveX control in the Toolbox.

4. Click the newly added ActiveX control in the Toolbox and drag the control to the UserForm.

These steps work in exactly the same way in the Visual Basic Editor in any Office application.

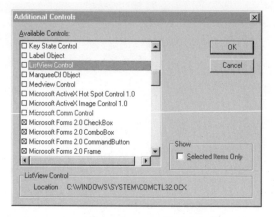

5. While the control is selected, press F1 to get more information about the control. (Help isn't available for all controls.) You can also right-click the control and then click Properties on the shortcut menu. Scroll through the properties to learn about the control.

6. You may want to remove the control from the Toolbox. To do that, right-click the control and then click Delete <control name> on the shortcut menu.

Hundreds of ActiveX controls are available through third-party vendors and on the Internet. If you require functionality in your program that you can't get from the list of controls on your machine, you can get ActiveX controls from other developers.

Note The Toolbox in the Visual Basic Editor adjusts to accommodate the number of controls in it. When you add controls to the Toolbox, you can resize the dialog box to display them all.

Creating List Dialog Boxes

When you start creating Visual Basic projects and features for Office, you'll often come across scenarios in which you'll want to position your ActiveX controls on your UserForm to resemble the dialog boxes in Microsoft Access, Word, Excel, PowerPoint, or Outlook. You'll also find many dialog boxes in Word, Excel, and PowerPoint that share a set of controls and a layout, although the tasks of the dialog boxes may be very different.

Move Items Between Two List Boxes

A common dialog box layout is to have two ListBox controls with Add, Remove, and Remove All command button controls in between. You see this layout when you're asked to select items from one full list in order to create a subset of items. The Define Custom Show dialog box in PowerPoint is an example of this layout, which you'll create below in Excel.

1. Without exiting Excel, start PowerPoint. In the opening PowerPoint dialog box, select Blank Presentation and click OK. In the New Slide dialog box, select any AutoLayout and click OK.

2. On the Slide Show menu, click Custom Shows, and click the New button. You're going to create a dialog box in Excel that's similar to the Define Custom Show dialog box.

3. Click Cancel, click Close, and exit PowerPoint without saving changes.

4. In the Visual Basic Editor of Excel, click UserForm on the Insert menu.

5. In the Toolbox, click the ListBox control and drag the control to the left side of the UserForm.

6. Click the ListBox control again and drag the control to the right side of the UserForm.

7. Move and size the controls using the following illustration as a guide:

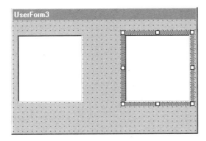

8. Add two CommandButton controls, placing the first control between the two list boxes and the second one just below the first.

9. Add two more CommandButton controls, placing them below the second list box, ListBox2. (The fourth command button is to the right of the third.) Use the following illustration as a guide:

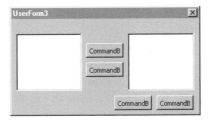

10. In the Properties window, set the following values. You may need to resize the window to see the complete control names.

Control	Property	Value
CommandButton1	Name	cmdAdd
CommandButton1	Caption	Add >
CommandButton2	Name	cmdRemove
CommandButton2	Caption	< Remove
CommandButton3	Name	cmdOK
CommandButton3	Caption	OK
CommandButton4	Name	cmdCancel
CommandButton4	Cancel	True
CommandButton4	Caption	Cancel
ListBox1	Name	lstEmployees
ListBox2	Name	lstAttendees

Tip   When working with controls in Visual Basic code, you commonly add a three-letter prefix to the names of the ActiveX controls. The prefix indicates what type of control is being referenced in code. For the controls listed in the Toolbox of the Visual Basic Editor, use the following prefixes: *chk* for check box, *cbo* for combo box, *cmd* for command button, *img* for image, *lbl* for label, *lst* for list box, *mpg* for multipage, *opt* for option button, *scb* for scroll bar, *spn* for spin button, *txt* for textbox, and *tgl* for toggle button.

To enter property values more efficiently, click the control on the UserForm before typing its values in the Properties window.

If your UserForm is behind the Code window, display it by clicking UserForm3 (UserForm) on the Window menu.

11. Double-click the cmdAdd command button and type the following statements in the Code window between the `Private Sub cmdAdd_Click` and `End Sub` statements:

```
Dim i As Integer
For i = 0 To lstEmployees.ListCount - 1
    If lstEmployees.Selected(i) = True Then
        lstAttendees.AddItem _
            lstEmployees.List(i)
        lstEmployees.RemoveItem i
        lstEmployees.Selected(i) = False
    End If
Next i
```

The For...Next loop, discussed in the previous chapter, iterates through each item in the lstEmployees list box and checks to see whether the item is selected. If it is, it's added to the lstAttendees list box and removed from the lstEmployees list box. The Selected property of the lstEmployees list box control returns a Boolean value indicating whether the item is selected.

12. Double-click the cmdRemove command button and type the following program statements in the Code window between the `Private Sub` `cmdRemove_Click` and `End Sub` statements:

```
Dim i As Integer
For i = 0 To lstAttendees.ListCount - 1
    If lstAttendees.Selected(i) = True Then
        lstEmployees.AddItem lstAttendees.List(i)
        lstAttendees.RemoveItem i
    End If
Next i
```

The structure and sequence of this code segment is exactly the same as the code assigned to the cmdAdd command button, but it moves items in the opposite direction (that is, from the lstAttendees list box to the lstEmployees list box).

13. Double-click any blank area on the UserForm, select Initialize from the Procedure drop-down list in the Code window (the list on the right), and type the following program statements in the Code window between the `Private Sub UserForm_Initialize` and `End Sub` statements:

```
With lstEmployees
    .AddItem "Dave"
    .AddItem "Rob"
    .AddItem "Greg"
    .AddItem "Christina"
    .AddItem "Mark"
End With
```

When you add the Employees list box to the UserForm, it doesn't contain any of the items in the list. The With...End block adds five items to fill the list box when the UserForm is first initialized, just before it's displayed on the screen. In an actual program, the program would probably load the data from a file stored on disk.

14. Double-click the cmdOK and cmdCancel command buttons and type **Unload Me** between the `Sub` and `End Sub` statements.

Now you're ready to go.

15. Run the dialog box by pressing F5, and click each button to reveal its functionality.

When you click the Add button, the program removes selected items in the left list box and adds them to the right list box. The opposite happens when you click the Remove button.

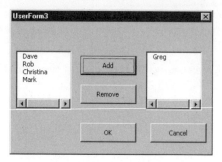

Save button

16. Click the Save button to save your work.

Creating Tabbed Dialog Boxes

Tabbed dialog boxes are now very common in Windows, and their use has spread throughout Office. The Toolbox in the Visual Basic Editor contains a tool you can use to create tabbed dialog boxes with ease: the MultiPage control.

Add Tabs to a UserForm

1. In the Visual Basic Editor, insert a new UserForm.

2. In the Toolbox, click the MultiPage control and drag the control to the UserForm.

3. Add two CommandButton controls to the UserForm so that the UserForm looks like the following illustration:

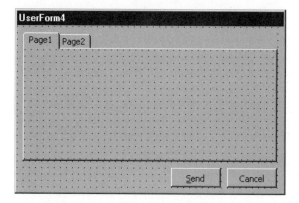

4. Set the properties of the command buttons so that they have names and captions matching the illustration.

On the first page of the MultiPage control, you'll copy the controls from the UserForm you created in the example "Move Items Between Two List Boxes" earlier in this chapter. (If you followed the steps sequentially, that form was named UserForm2.)

5. In the Project window, double-click UserForm2.

6. Select all of the controls except the cmdOK and cmdCancel command button controls by holding down the CTRL key and clicking the two list boxes and the Add and Remove buttons.

7. In the Editor, on the Edit menu, click Copy to copy the selected controls to the Clipboard.

8. In the Project Explorer window, double-click the name of the UserForm to which you added the MultiPage control. If you followed all steps in this chapter sequentially, the name of the UserForm is UserForm3.

9. Select the MultiPage control and click the center of the first page (Page1). This selects the first page.

10. In the Editor, on the Edit menu, click Paste to paste the controls to the first page. Move and size the controls as shown in the illustration.

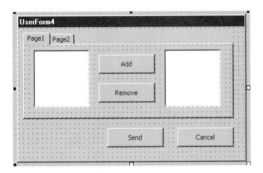

11. In the Project Explorer window, double-click UserForm2 and then double-click a blank area on the form.

12. On the Edit menu, click Select All to select all of the code.

13. On the Edit menu, click Copy.

14. In the Project Explorer window, double-click UserForm3, and then double-click a blank area on the form outside of the MultiPage control. If there is any code in the Code window, select it, and press DELETE.

15. On the Edit menu, click Paste.

16. Press F5 to run the dialog box.

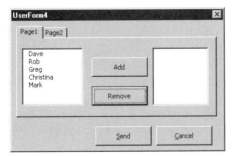

17. Click Cancel to close the box, and then save your changes and close the workbook.

You may also want to experiment by clicking the second tab (Page2) of the MultiPage control and adding any controls you want from the Toolbox.

Examine the Fully Functional Dialog Box

In the UserForm.xls file in the Chapter 3 practice folder, you can examine a fully functional dialog box. For example, the second tab of the MultiPage control contains a number of common controls such as spinners and option buttons. The file also provides fully functional code for each control. In particular, you can look through the code behind UserForm3 in the Chapter 3 practice file. This should give you a good start in creating your own UserForms.

Open

1. In Excel, click the Open button and then change to the Chapter 3 practice folder.

2. Select the UserForm.xls workbook, and then click the Open button.

3. Switch to the Visual Basic Editor.

4. Run the dialog box and examine the code that makes it work.

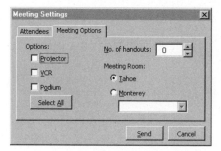

The controls and code for this dialog box are in the UserForm3 UserForm.

5. Exit Excel without saving changes.

Developing Office Wizards

Wizards are common features of many software applications. Not only do they guide you through a series of tasks and often help you save time creating documents, they also step you through many prebuilt content templates and provide you with ideas, starter text, formatting, and organization. The new style of Office wizards now lets you navigate more easily, both backward and forward, through the steps and allows you to track your progress visually through the task steps so you have a sense of where you are and where you're going.

It's even easier if you integrate the Office Assistant with wizards. The Assistant gives you tips for going through the steps as well as visual examples and step-by-step instructions for specific tasks.

Wizard Look and Style

The wizard dialog box has three main features: navigation buttons, a subway map, and tab pages. The subway map is optional but is provided in many Office wizards. Your wizard works equally well without it.

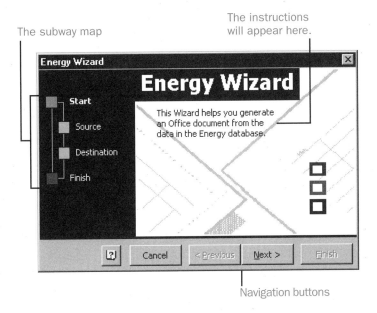

The Energy Wizard has the same look and style as the Fax Wizard in Word. To access the Fax Wizard, click New on the File menu in Word, and in the Letter And Faxes tab, select the Fax Wizard icon and click OK. (The details of the AutoContent Wizard in PowerPoint differ slightly from those of the wizards in Word, but the look and style of the two wizard types are the same.) In this chapter, you'll use the details of the Fax Wizard in Word as the model. The code for the wizard UserForm will be very generic so that you can easily plug the same code into a wizard in any Office application.

Set Up a Multiple-Step Wizard Dialog Box

You can easily build dialog boxes with multiple steps by using the MultiPage control. The MultiPage control is a container of controls within a collection of pages. As you'll see, the MultiPage control makes it simple to design each page because you can add controls to one page and display the controls of another page.

1. Start Word. Display the Visual Basic Editor and insert a new UserForm.

2. In the Properties window, change the default name in the Name property of the new UserForm from UserForm1 to frmWizard.

MultiPage control

3. In the Toolbox, click the MultiPage control and then click the frmWizard UserForm.

4. In the Properties window, change the default name in the Name property from MultiPage1 to mpgSteps. (The prefix *mpg* represents "multipage.")

5. Right-click the first tab of the mpgSteps control and click New Page on the shortcut menu.

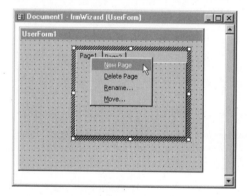

This adds a new page to the mpgSteps control. The tab caption of the new page is Page3.

6. Click the tab with the caption Page1 and change the Name property in the Properties window to pgStart. (The prefix *pg* represents "page.") Change the Caption property from Page1 to Start.

7. Click the tab with the caption Page2 and change the Name property to pgStep1. Change the Caption property to Step1.

8. Click the tab with the caption Page3 and change the Name property to pgFinish. Change the Caption property to Finish.

Your MultiPage control has three pages. The first page is the Start screen, or the screen that the wizard displays first. The last page is the Finish screen, which the wizard displays once the user completes all the steps in the wizard. The page between the first and last pages will become the step in the wizard where the user sets options and enters information that the wizard needs to complete its overall task. Each subsequent step in the wizard requires its own page. In the section later in this chapter titled "Add a New Step in the Wizard," you'll learn how to add another new page and, hence, another new step in your wizard.

By default, the program sets the style of the MultiPage control to the enumeration value fmTabStyleTabs, which represents a value of 0. Later in this chapter, when you start adding controls to each page in the control, you'll set the Style property of the MultiPage control to fmTabStyleNone so that the tabs aren't displayed in the wizard dialog box. Some wizards display tabs, but the style you're creating in this chapter doesn't.

Add Navigation Buttons

Most well-designed wizards provide a set of common navigation buttons along the lower edge of the wizard dialog box. These navigation buttons are Cancel, Previous, Next, and Finish. With the introduction of the Office Assistant, you can add another button that allows you to display tips or instructions from the Assistant.

1. Move the MultiPage control mpgSteps to the upper-right area of the frmWizard UserForm.

2. Resize the UserForm to slightly increase its width. Double-click the CommandButton control in the Toolbox, and then click four times in the lower area of the UserForm, working from left to right, to create four command buttons. Use the following illustration as a guide:

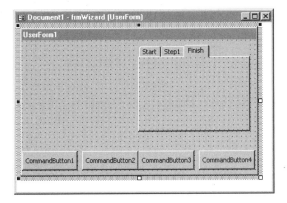

Note By double-clicking a control in the Toolbox, you can add more than one of a particular control to a UserForm without having to continuously click the control in the Toolbox. You can't resize or select any other control in the UserForm until you click the Select Objects arrow in the Toolbox.

*Select Objects
arrow*

3. Click the Select Objects arrow in the Toolbox so that you can select the controls in the UserForm, and then change the properties of the CommandButton controls to the following:

Control	Property	Value
CommandButton1	Name	cmdCancel
CommandButton1	Caption	Cancel
CommandButton1	Cancel	True
CommandButton2	Name	cmdPrevious
CommandButton2	Caption	< Previous
CommandButton2	Accelerator	P
CommandButton3	Name	cmdNext
CommandButton3	Caption	Next >
CommandButton3	Accelerator	N
CommandButton4	Name	cmdFinish
CommandButton4	Caption	Finish
CommandButton4	Accelerator	F

You should set the Cancel property of the Cancel button to True so that the user can press ESC to cancel the wizard dialog box. Allowing the user to cancel a dialog box by pressing ESC is a standard Windows programming practice.

4. Double-click the Previous button and add the following line to the *cmdPrevious_Click* event procedure:

```
mpgSteps.Value = mpgSteps.Value - 1
```

The Value property of the MultiPage control mpgSteps is an integer that indicates the currently active page. A value of 0 represents the first page in the control. The maximum value of this property is the number of pages minus 1. Each time you click the Previous button, the program decreases the value of the mpgSteps control by 1 and displays the previous step.

Remember, because the code belongs exclusively to an object (the frmWizard UserForm), the code is contained in a class module. If a module doesn't belong to an object, it's referred to as a code module (or as a standard module in more recent versions of Visual Basic).

5. In the Object drop-down list of the frmWizard Code window, select cmdNext and add the following line to the *cmdNext_Click* event procedure:

```
mpgSteps.Value = mpgSteps.Value + 1
```

Each time you click the Next button, you increase the value of the mpgSteps control by one and display the next step.

6. In the Object drop-down list of the frmWizard Code window, select cmdCancel and add the following line to the *cmdCancel_Click* event procedure:

```
Unload Me
```

The Visual Basic keyword *Me* is an implicit reference to the UserForm in which the code is currently running. Thus, *Me* represents the frmWizard UserForm. When you click the Cancel button or press ESC, you close the dialog box and unload it from memory.

7. In the Object drop-down list of the frmWizard Code window, select cmd-Finish and add the following line to the *cmdFinish_Click* event procedure:

```
Unload Me
```

For now, the Finish button closes the UserForm. Later in this chapter, however, to the *cmdFinish_Click* event procedure you'll add code that checks the values entered in the steps in the wizard and then calls a number of procedures to perform the wizard's overall task before unloading the dialog box from memory.

8. In the Object drop-down list, select mpgSteps and add the following lines to the *mpgSteps_Change* event procedure:

```
Select Case mpgSteps.Value
    Case 0
        cmdNext.Enabled = True
        cmdPrevious.Enabled = False
        cmdFinish.Enabled = False
    Case m_iTotalSteps - 1
        cmdNext.Enabled = False
        cmdPrevious.Enabled = True
        cmdFinish.Enabled = True
    Case Else
        cmdNext.Enabled = True
        cmdPrevious.Enabled = True
        cmdFinish.Enabled = False
End Select
```

When the value of the MultiPage control mpgSteps is changed by the *cmdNext_Click* or *cmdPrevious_Click* event procedure, the Change event of the mpgSteps control is triggered. The Select Case statement you added evaluates the current value of the mpgSteps control and determines the appropriate course of action. If the value is 0, the program displays the Start page and disables the Previous button because there are no more pages before the Start.

If the value is equal to the module-level variable *m_iTotalSteps* minus one, the program displays the Finish page and disables the Next button because there are no more pages after the Finish. In this case, however, it enables the Finish button. The variable *m_iTotalSteps* is declared in step 10 and represents the total number of pages in the mpgSteps control. If the value of the mpgSteps control is neither the first nor last page, both the Previous and Next buttons are enabled.

9. In the Object drop-down list of the frmWizard Code window, select UserForm. In the Procedure drop-down list of the module, select

Initialize and add the following lines to the *UserForm_Initialize* event procedure:

```
m_iTotalSteps = mpgSteps.Pages.Count
mpgSteps.Value = 0
Call mpgSteps_Change
```

Before the dialog box is displayed, you need to initialize the state of some controls and then set the value of the variable *m_iTotalSteps*. This is done in the *UserForm_Initialize* event procedure, which runs just before the dialog box is displayed on the screen. In the *Initialize* event procedure of the frmWizard UserForm, *m_iTotalSteps* is set to the number of pages in the mpgSteps control.

The second line of code above sets the value of the mpgSteps control to 0 so that the Start page is shown when the UserForm is displayed. Despite the fact that the value of the mpgSteps control is set, the *mpgSteps_Change* event procedure may not run if the value of the mpgSteps is 0 while you're designing the UserForm. Thus, you explicitly call the *mpgSteps_Change* event procedure so that the navigation button is also initialized.

10. In the Declarations section of the frmWizard Code window (at the top of the code window before the first procedure), add the following module-level declaration:

```
Dim m_iTotalSteps As Integer
```

Tip   If the Option Explicit statement isn't included at the beginning of the frmWizard Code window, you should add it by typing "Option Explicit" before the module-level declaration you added in the previous step. If you want the Option Explicit statement to be added to any code module by default, on the Tools menu in the Visual Basic Editor, click Options, and then click Require Variable Declaration in the Editor tab of the Options dialog box. See "Do I Need to Declare My Variables and Constants?" in Chapter 2 for more information.

---

11. In the frmWizard UserForm, resize and move the navigation Command-Button controls, using the following illustration as a guide. Then press F5 to display the dialog box.

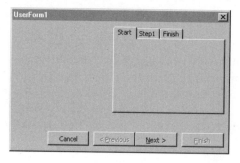

The program disables the Finish and Previous buttons and shows the first page (the Start page) in the MultiPage control when the wizard is displayed. Click the Next and Previous buttons to see the pages of the MultiPage control being activated and the navigation buttons being enabled and disabled.

12. Click Cancel, and then in the Project Explorer, right-click the frmWizard project item located in the Forms folder. Click Export File on the shortcut menu.

13. In the Export File dialog box, change to the Chapter 3 subfolder in the Office VBA practice folder, type the name **frmWizardTemplateBasic** in the File Name text box, and click Save.

This example gave you the basics of setting up a wizard dialog box. In steps 12 and 13, you exported the UserForm so that you can use it as a starting point when you create a new wizard. In the next example, you'll continue building onto your wizard by adding the subway map panel on the left side of the UserForm.

Create a Subway Map

The "subway map" is a new style of Office wizard that permits easy navigation through the wizard's steps by giving a visual representation of where you are within the wizard. Each "station" on the subway map represents a step in the wizard, and the current station, or step, is green. If you want to skip a step or jump to a specific step, you can do so by using the subway map panel.

1. In the Editor, in the Project Explorer, double-click the frmWizard project item. In the Toolbox, click the Image control, and then click in the upper-left area of the UserForm. In the Properties window, change the name of the Image control from Image1 to imgLeftPane.

Image control

2. Click the Image control in the Toolbox again and click the UserForm just below the imgLeftPane control. Change the name of the Image control from Image1 to imgBottomStripe.

3. To change the color of the Image controls you just inserted, select both Image controls by first selecting either one and then holding down the CTRL key to select the other. In the Properties window, click the value of the BackColor, and then click the arrow. Click the Palette tab and select the color black.

4. Move and resize the imgLeftPane and imgBottomStripe controls so that the UserForm looks like the following illustration:

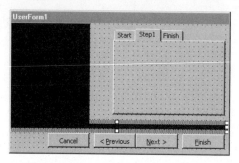

5. Click the Image control in the Toolbox and then click the imgLeftPane control. Change the name of the newly inserted Image control to imgSubway. You're placing imgSubway on top of imgLeftPane.

6. In the Properties window, change the BackStyle property of the imgSubway control to 0 – fmBackStyleTransparent. Change the BorderColor property by clicking the arrow, clicking the Palette tab, and selecting light gray. The value &H00C0C0C0& appears, which represents light gray.

7. Add another Image control and place it in the upper-left corner of the imgSubway control. Change the name to imgStart and set the BorderStyle property to 0 – fmBorderStyleNone. Resize the control so that it looks like the following illustration:

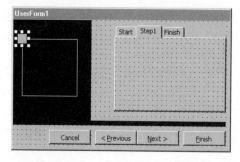

8. Click the imgStart control. On the Edit menu, click Copy. On the Edit menu, click Paste twice to create two copies of the control. In the Properties window, select Image1 from the drop-down list and change its name to imgStep1. Similarly, change the name of Image2 to imgFinish.

9. Move the imgStep1 and imgFinish controls so that they are on the border of the imgSubway control.

If the imgStep1 and imgFinish controls are underneath the mpgSteps control, select the selection border around the mpgSteps control and move the control temporarily out of the way. Also, if one image is underneath the other, select one by clicking its name in the drop-down list in the Properties window to select the control on the UserForm. Then drag the control to a new location on the UserForm.

10. In the Toolbox, click the Label control, and then click the UserForm just beside the imgStart control. Set the following properties for the Label control:

Property	Value
Name	lblStart
BackStyle	0 – fmBackStyleTransparent
Caption	Start
ForeColor	&H00FFFFFF& (or white in the Palette tab)

11. Select the lblStart control by clicking any other control and then clicking the lblStart control. (If you initially click only the lblStart control, you'll select the caption of the control, not the control itself.) On the Edit menu, click Copy, and then paste the control twice.

12. Move one of the pasted Label controls beside the imgStep1 control, name it lblStep1, and set the Caption property to Step1. Move the second pasted Label control beside the imgFinish control, name it lblFinish, and set the Caption property to Finish.

13. Move and resize the controls so that the UserForm looks like the following illustration:

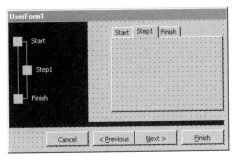

Make sure the label controls are slightly wider than the text they contain.

14. Select the controls imgStart, lblStart, imgStep1, lblStep1, imgFinish, and lblFinish, and then in the ControlTipText property in the Properties window, type **To skip to this step, click here.** Each subway map image and label has the same ToolTip text, which is the same as that in Word's Fax Wizard.

You've completed the layout of the subway map. What remains is to add the code that allows you to use the map to navigate through the steps.

Indicate Active and Visited Steps in the Subway Map

The subway map has to indicate which step is currently active and which steps you have visited. You indicate the currently active step by setting two properties of the controls in the subway map. First, set the BackColor property of the Image control, or station, to light green. Second, set the font of the station label to bold. Once you move on to another step in the wizard, the program sets the BackColor property of the Image control of the previous station to dark gray to indicate that you have previously visited it.

View Code

1. In the Project Explorer, select the frmWizard project item and click the View Code button, which is the leftmost button on the Project Explorer toolbar.

2. At the top of the module, just after the module-level declaration *m_iTotalSteps*, add the following module-level declaration:

```
Dim m_sCurStep As String
```

The variable *m_sCurStep* is the name of the current step, and it's used to keep track of the current step. Once you move to another step, you can use the value in the variable *m_sCurStep* to determine what the previous step was and to reset its properties so that the previous step appears visited.

3. In the Object drop-down list of the frmWizard Code window, select mpgSteps so that the *mpgSteps_Change* event procedure appears. Add the following procedure call just before the Select Case statement so that the call is the first line of the *mpgSteps_Change* event procedure:

```
SetSubwayMap
```

Every time the *mpgSteps_Change* event procedure runs, the *SetSubwayMap* procedure is called so that the images and labels of the map can be initialized.

4. At the bottom of the module, create the *SetSubwayMap* procedure by adding the following code:

```
Sub SetSubwayMap()
    Controls("img" & m_sCurStep).BackColor = &H808080
    Controls("lbl" & m_sCurStep).Font.Bold = False
    Select Case mpgSteps.Value
        Case 0
            m_sCurStep = "Start"
        Case m_iTotalSteps - 1
            m_sCurStep = "Finish"
        Case Else
            m_sCurStep = "Step" & mpgSteps.Value
    End Select
```

```
        Controls("img" & m_sCurStep).BackColor = vbGreen
        Controls("lbl" & m_sCurStep).Font.Bold = True
End Sub
```

The *SetSubwayMap* procedure performs three tasks. The first task is to use the m_sCurStep value to determine what the previous step is. The program calls the *SetSubwayMap* procedure when the value of the mpgSteps control has been changed. Before you update the value of m_sCurStep to reflect the current step, you reset the control properties of the previous step so that it appears visited. You do this by setting the BackColor property of the Image control to dark gray (&H808080) and the font of the Label control to roman (not bold).

For the second task of the procedure, the Select Case statement evaluates the current value of the mpgSteps control and sets the variable *m_sCurStep* to the name of the current step. You then use the value of *m_sCurStep* to set the BackColor property of the current Image control to light green (vbGreen). The Visual Basic color enumeration vbGreen represents the value &HFF00.The third task of the procedure is to set the associated Label control's font to bold.

5. In the Object drop-down list of the frmWizard Code window, select UserForm. In the Procedure drop-down list in the upper-right area of the Code window, select Initialize and add the line:

```
m_sCurStep = "Start"
```

The *UserForm_Initialize* event procedure should now look like this:

```
Private Sub UserForm_Initialize()
    m_iTotalSteps = mpgSteps.Pages.Count
    m_sCurStep = "Start"
    mpgSteps.Value = 0
    mpgSteps_Change
End Sub
```

6. In the Project Explorer, select the frmWizard project item and click the View Object button, which is just to the right of the View Code button on the Project Explorer toolbar.

View Object

7. Select the imgFinish control on the frmWizard UserForm. In the Properties window, change the BackColor property to red in the Palette tab (a value of &H000000FF&).

The color red is used as an initial indicator that this step is the last one in the wizard (or the last station on the subway map).

8. Click anywhere on the frmWizard UserForm and press F5 to run the UserForm.

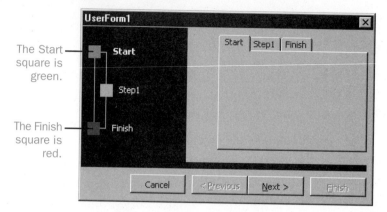

The Start square is green.

The Finish square is red.

Click the Next and Previous buttons to see the program activate the pages of the MultiPage control, enable and disable the navigation buttons, and update the properties of the subway map's Image and Label controls. The last remaining task is to add the code that allows you to click the controls on the subway map to navigate between the steps.

Add Code to the Subway Map

1. Close and unload the frmWizard UserForm by clicking the Cancel or Finish button.

2. Double-click the imgStart control of the subway map and add the following line to the *imgStart_Click* event procedure:

```
mpgSteps.Value = 0
```

3. In the Object drop-down list, select lblStart and add the following line to the *lblStart_Click* event procedure:

```
mpgSteps.Value = 0
```

4. In the Object drop-down list, select imgStep1 and add the following line to the *imgStep1_Click* event procedure:

```
mpgSteps.Value = 1
```

5. In the Object drop-down list, select lblStep1 and add the following line to the *lblStep1_Click* event procedure:

```
mpgSteps.Value = 1
```

6. In the Object drop-down list, select imgFinish and add the following line to the *imgFinish_Click* event procedure:

```
mpgSteps.Value = m_iTotalSteps - 1
```

7. In the Object drop-down list, select lblFinish and add the following line to the *lblFinish_Click* event procedure:

```
mpgSteps.Value = m_iTotalSteps - 1
```

8. Press F5 to run the UserForm.

Click the Image and Label controls on the subway map to see the program enable and disable the Previous and Next buttons and activate the pages of the MultiPage control.

Add a New Step in the Wizard

You need to use the naming convention for the controls of the subway map so that a new step can be added easily. The following example shows how to set up your code to add more steps as needed.

1. Close and unload the frmWizard UserForm by clicking the Cancel or Finish button.

2. In the frmWizard UserForm, select the imgStep1 control. With the CTRL key pressed, select the lblStep1 control adjacent to it.

3. On the Edit menu, click Copy and then click Paste. The program pastes copies of the controls imgStep1 and lblStep1 into the center of the UserForm and selects both copies.

4. Click the selection border of either one of the controls and drag the two controls so that the imgStep1 control sits on the border of the imgSubway control.

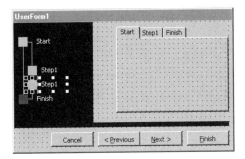

5. Rename the pasted Image control to imgStep2 and the Label control to lblStep2. Change the Caption of lblStep2 to Step2.

6. Move imgStep1, lblStep1, imgStep2, and lblStep2 so that these controls are evenly spaced on the border of the imgSubway control.

7. Click the mpgSteps MultiPage control and then right-click any of the tabs. On the shortcut menu, click New Page. The program adds a new page to the control with the default tab caption Page1.

8. In the Properties window, change the Caption property of Page1 to Step2 and then change the Name property to pgStep2.

9. Right-click any tab in the MultiPage control. On the shortcut menu, click Move. The Page Order dialog box, which lists the pages within the MultiPage control, is displayed.

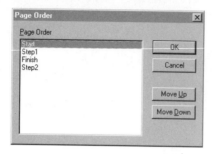

10. In the Page Order dialog box, select Step2 in the Page Order list and click the Move Up button to move the Step2 page after the Step1 page and before the Finish page. Click OK.

11. Double-click the imgStep2 control. In the *imgStep2_Click* event procedure, add the following line:

```
mpgSteps.Value = 2
```

12. In the Object drop-down list, select lblStep2 and add the following line to the *lblStep2_Click* event procedure:

```
mpgSteps.Value = 2
```

13. Press F5 to run the UserForm. Click the Next button, or click the label Step2 to navigate and activate the second step in the wizard.

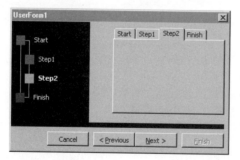

14. Close and unload the frmWizard UserForm by clicking the Cancel or Finish button.

15. Right-click the frmWizard project item in the Project Explorer and then click Export File on the shortcut menu. In the Export File dialog box, change to the Chapter 3 practice folder and in the File Name text box, type the name **frmWizardTemplateSubway** and click Save.

You've completed the wizard UserForm with its subway map. In step 15, you exported the UserForm so that you can use it as a starting point when you create a new wizard with a subway map. The final process in setting up the wizard UserForm is to add the new element that all wizards in Office can include: the Office Assistant.

Note   Because none of the code in the UserForm you've created so far is specific to any Office application, you can import the wizard UserForm into a Visual Basic for Applications project in any application.

Integrating the Office Assistant into Wizards

Most of the wizards in Office now have a toggle button alongside the Cancel, Previous, Next, and Finish navigation buttons in the wizard dialog box. When you press the toggle button you display the Office Assistant, which displays in its balloon a tip for the current step in the wizard. Tips are often helpful the first few times you use a wizard; but once you're familiar with it, you may no longer need them. The Assistant provides an easy method for creating helpful steps by displaying tips that you don't have to add directly on the wizard UserForm. In that way, using the Assistant helps prevent your wizard from appearing cluttered.

Add the Assistant Button

1. Click the frmWizard project item and then click the View Object button in the Project Explorer.

View Object

2. Click the ToggleButton control in the Toolbox and then click the frmWizard UserForm to the left of the Cancel button.

ToggleButton control

3. In the Properties window, remove the text from the Caption property so that no caption is displayed, and change the Name property to tglAssistant. (The prefix *tgl* represents "toggle.")

4. Click the Picture property, and then click the ellipsis button in the right column to display the Load Picture dialog box. Change to the Chapter 3 practice folder and select the bitmap file Assistnt.bmp. Click Open.

Ellipsis

5. Resize the tglAssistant ToggleButton control so its height is the same as that of the other navigation buttons and its width equals its height, as shown in the illustration on the following page.

6. Run the UserForm and click the tglAssistant ToggleButton control. When you first click it, the control stays pressed. To return the toggle button to its initial state, click it again.

Now that you've added the Assistant toggle button to your wizard, you need to write the code that will determine the current step in the wizard and display the appropriate tip when the user clicks the Assistant button.

Make the Assistant Display a Tip

1. Close and unload the frmWizard UserForm by clicking the Cancel or Finish button.

2. In the Project Explorer, right-click the Energy Wizard project, and then click Import File on the shortcut menu. In the Import File dialog box, change to the Chapter 3 practice folder and select the file modAsst.bas. Click Open.

   The file modAsst.bas contains all the code that will display tips in the Assistant balloon and close it when necessary. In the following steps, you'll add calls to procedures in the standard code module you just imported. The module name is modAssistant.

3. Select the frmWizard project item and then click the View Code button in the leftmost corner of the Project Explorer toolbar.

View Code

4. In the Object drop-down list of the frmWizard Code window, select UserForm. In the *UserForm_Initialize* event procedure, add the call to the *VisibleCheck* procedure so that the procedure appears as follows:

```
Private Sub UserForm_Initialize()
    m_iTotalSteps = mpgSteps.Pages.Count
    m_sCurStep = "Start"
    mpgSteps.Value = 0
    mpgSteps_Change
    modAssistant.VisibleCheck
End Sub
```

Before the wizard is displayed, the Assistant's visible state is determined in the *VisibleCheck* procedure in the modAssistant module. This procedure also contains code that handles cases where the Assistant isn't installed; if this is the case, the Assistant button is disabled.

5. On the frmWizard UserForm, double-click the tglAssistant ToggleButton control. In the *tglAssistant_Click* event procedure, add the following code:

```
modAssistant.ToggleAssistant
```

The *ToggleAssistant* procedure determines the value of the tglAssistant ToggleButton control and then decides whether to display or hide the Assistant.

6. In the Object drop-down list of the frmWizard Code window, select mpgSteps. In the *mpgSteps_Change* event procedure, add the following If...Then condition block after the call to the *SetSubway* procedure:

```
If tglAssistant.Value = True Then
    modAssistant.SetBalloonText
End If
```

Each time the page changes in the wizard, the program evaluates the value of the Assistant button. If the button is clicked, the program calls the *SetBalloonText* procedure and the tip for the current step is displayed in the Assistant balloon.

7. Finally, in the Object drop-down list of the frmWizard Code window, select cmdCancel and add the following code to the *cmdCancel_Click* event procedure, so that the procedure appears as follows:

```
Private Sub cmdCancel_Click()
    If tglAssistant.Value = True Then
        modAssistant.CloseBalloon
    End If
    Unload Me
End Sub
```

Repeat this step but select cmdFinish from the Object drop-down list. Copy the identical code from within the *cmdCancel_Click* event procedure to the *cmdFinish_Click* event procedure. Later, when you extend the wizard to perform some operation in your program, add a line of code that calls a new procedure to conduct that action. Add the new line after the line Unload Me in the *cmdFinish_Click* event procedure.

The If...Then condition block determines whether the Assistant balloon is displaying a wizard tip by evaluating the value of the tglAssistant ToggleButton control. If the toggle button is clicked (in the up position), the Assistant balloon is closed.

8. Press F5 to run the wizard and then click the Assistant button to display the tip for the current step.

The Assistant balloon should appear and the tip "Start" should appear, which represents the tip for the currently active step. Click the Next button to see the next tip and continue through the steps to see the Assistant balloon being updated to reflect the current step.

The current step...   ...is reflected in the Assistant balloon.

9. Close and unload the frmWizard UserForm by clicking the Cancel or Finish button.

10. Right-click the frmWizard project item in the Project Explorer and then click Export File on the shortcut menu. In the Export File dialog box, change to the Chapter 3 practice folder, and in the File Name text box, type the name **frmWizardTemplateAssistant** and click Save.

The wizard UserForm with navigation buttons, subway map, and Assistant integration is complete. In step 10, you exported the UserForm so that you can use it as a starting point when you create a new wizard with a subway map and the Office Assistant.

Tip The contents of all three UserForms that you saved in this chapter— frmWizardTemplateBasic, frmWizardTemplateSubway, and frmWizardTemplate-Assistant—are also provided in the Chapter 3 practice folder of the practice files CD-ROM. The files are named frmBasic, frmSubwy, and frmAsst.

Customizing Wizard Steps

By adding controls to the steps in your wizard, and with the help of two common Windows dialog boxes, you can finish creating common elements of the look and style of wizards in Word and PowerPoint. In the following steps, you add an image to the start and finish steps of the wizard dialog box.

A text box that allows you to enter a path to a file or folder is a common element of a wizard dialog box and many other dialog boxes in Office. Usually adjacent to the text box is a button with the caption "Browse," which allows the user to browse for a file or folder rather than having to enter the path in the text box. The following steps describe the addition of the text box and the Browse button. In the last section of this chapter, you'll hook up the Browse button to common Windows dialog boxes that allow the user to browse for a file or folder.

Prepare the Wizard Start Screen

1. On the frmWizard UserForm, click the first tab in the mpgSteps MultiPage control to activate the first page.

   Make sure that the text "pgStart Page" appears in the drop-down list at the top of the Properties window.

2. In the Properties window, click the Picture property and then click the ellipsis button in the right column. In the Load Picture dialog box, change to the Chapter 3 practice folder and select the file Start.bmp. Click Open.

Ellipsis

   The background of the first page of the MultiPage control now displays a bitmap similar in look and style to that of the Fax Wizard in Word and the AutoContent Wizard in PowerPoint.

3. Set the PictureSizeMode property value to 1 – fmPictureSizeModeStretch.

4. Click the selection border of the MultiPage control. The text "mpgSteps MultiPage" appears in the drop-down list at the top of the Properties window.

5. Scroll down the Properties window and change the Style property from 0 – fmTabStyleTabs to 2 – fmTabStyleNone.

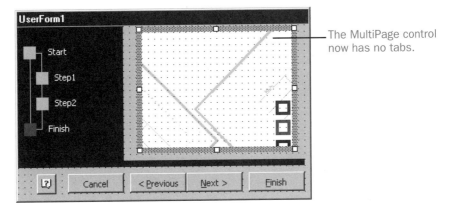

The MultiPage control now has no tabs.

   The pages haven't disappeared, just the tabs. Switching between the pages of the MultiPage control isn't as simple as clicking the tab of the specific page. To navigate the pages of the MultiPage control, click anywhere within the MultiPage control to activate the current page and use the drop-down list at the top of the Properties window to activate the specific page. You should work without the tabs in the MultiPage control so that you can precisely place controls within the pages.

6. Resize the mpgSteps MultiPage control so that it fills the space between the imgLeftPane and imgBottomStripe controls and the right side of the UserForm.

Image control

7. Click the Image control in the Toolbox and then click in the upper-left area of the first page of the mpgSteps control. Add a Label control just below the Image control and set the properties as follows:

Control	Property	Value
Image1	Name	imgTitleBack
Image1	BackColor	&H00000000& (or black from the Palette tab)
Label1	Name	lblTitle
Label1	Caption	Energy Wizard
Label1	BackStyle	0 – fmBackStyleTransparent
Label1	Font	Set the Font Style to Bold and the Font Size to 20.
Label1	ForeColor	&H00FFFFFF& (or white in the Palette tab)

8. Move the lblTitle control onto the imgTitleBack control.

9. Add a Label control under and slightly to the right of the lblTitle control, set its Name to lblStartDescription, set its BackStyle to 0 – fmBackStyleTransparent, and enter its caption as **This Wizard helps you generate an Office document from the data in the Energy database.** Move and size the controls using the following illustration as a guide:

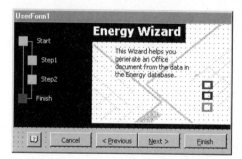

The page that first appears when you first load the wizard is now complete.

Add Controls for Each Step in the Wizard

1. Click within the MultiPage control and select pgStep1 Page from the drop-down list in the Properties window. This activates the second page in the mpgSteps MultiPage control.

2. Click the Label control in the Toolbox and click in the upper area of the second page of the mpgSteps control. Add a TextBox control below the Label control and a CommandButton control below the TextBox control.

3. Set the properties of the controls added to the second page. If you followed the steps throughout the chapter, the default names for the controls added will be the same as those listed below:

Control	Property	Value
Label1	Name	lblSource
Label1	Caption	Energy Database:
Label1	Accelerator	E
TextBox1	Name	txtDataSource
CommandButton1	Name	cmdBrowse
CommandButton1	Caption	Browse...
CommandButton1	Accelerator	B

The accelerator keys for controls on the pages in the MultiPage control should never be P, N, or F because these values are reserved for the navigation buttons Previous, Next, and Finish, respectively, at the bottom of the wizard UserForm.

4. Add a Label control below the Browse button. Add a TextBox control below the Label control and a CommandButton control below the TextBox control. Set the properties of the controls added as follows:

Control	Property	Value
Label1	Name	lblTemplate
Label1	Caption	Energy Template:
Label1	Accelerator	n
TextBox1	Name	txtTemplate
CommandButton1	Name	cmdBrowseTemplate
CommandButton1	Caption	Browse...
CommandButton1	Accelerator	r

5. Resize and move the controls on the second page so that the UserForm appears similar to the following illustration:

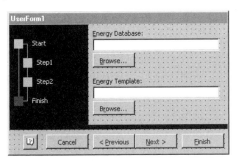

6. Click within the MultiPage control and select pgStep2 Page from the drop-down list in the Properties window. This activates the third page in the mpgSteps MultiPage control.

7. Click the Label control in the Toolbox and click at the top of the second page of the mpgSteps control. Add a TextBox control below the Label control and a CommandButton control below the TextBox control. Set the properties of the controls as listed below:

Control	Property	Value
Label1	Name	lblDestination
Label1	Caption	Destination folder:
Label1	Accelerator	D
TextBox1	Name	txtDestination
CommandButton1	Name	cmdBrowseFolder
CommandButton1	Caption	Browse...
CommandButton1	Accelerator	B

8. Change the Caption property of lblStep1 and lblStep2 on the subway map to Source and Destination, respectively. Adjust the width of both label controls so that the caption text fits, leaving some extra space so that it'll still fit when the text is made bold. Move and size the controls using the following illustration as a guide:

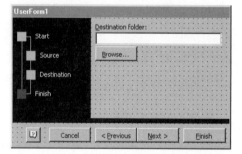

Prepare the Wizard Finish Screen

1. Click within the MultiPage control and select pgFinish Page from the drop-down list in the Properties window. The last page in the mpgSteps MultiPage control is activated.

2. In the Properties window, click the Picture property and then click the ellipsis button in the right column. In the Load Picture dialog box, change to the Chapter 3 practice folder and select the file Finish.bmp. Click Open.

3. Set the PictureSizeMode property value to 1 – fmPictureSizeModeStretch.

4. Click the Image control in the Toolbox and click in the upper-left of the first page of the mpgSteps control. Add a Label control just below the Image control and set the properties as shown on the next page.

Ellipsis

Control	Property	Value
Image1	Name	imgFinishTitleBack
Image1	BackColor	&H00000000& (or black from the Palette tab)
Label1	Name	lblFinishTitle
Label1	Caption	Energy Wizard
Label1	BackStyle	0 – fmBackStyleTransparent
Label1	Font	Set the Font Style to Bold and the Font Size to 16.
Label1	ForeColor	&H00FFFFFF& (or white in the Palette tab)

5. Add a Label control under the lblFinishTitle control and slightly to the right, set its Name to lblFinishDescription, its BackStyle to 0 – fmBackStyleTransparent, and its caption to **You are now ready to generate the Office document. Click Finish.**

6. Move the lblFinishTitle control onto the imgFinishTitleBack control and resize the controls so that the wizard UserForm appears as follows:

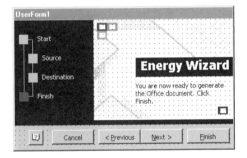

7. Click the Save button to save the work you've done so far.

You've now completed the last page that appears, as well as each step in the wizard. In the next section, you'll add code that will allow you to interact with the controls you've added to your wizard.

Save

Using Dialog Boxes from Windows

In order to save developers who are writing applications for Windows from having to create certain dialog boxes from scratch, Windows provides a set of common dialog boxes. Among them are the File dialog box, which you use to open, save, or browse for files on your computer or computer network; the Browse For Folder dialog box, which you use to specify a folder name; and the Color dialog box, which allows you to choose a specific color.

In the wizard you're creating, you'll take advantage of the File and Browse For Folder dialog boxes. The code provided in the practice files allows you to use these dialog boxes without knowing too much about the code itself, which uses more advanced Windows-based programming techniques. You can learn more about the specifics of this code and Windows programming using the Visual Basic programming language by referring to books on the Visual Basic and Windows application programming interfaces (APIs).

Add a Common Windows Dialog Box to Your Wizard

1. In the Project Explorer, right-click the Energy Wizard project and click Import File on the shortcut menu. In the Import File dialog box, change to the Chapter 3 practice folder and select the file modFlDlg.bas. Click Open.

   The file modFlDlg.bas contains code that allows you to display the Windows system File dialog box, which is the same dialog box as the Import File dialog box you just used. The name of the imported standard module is modFileDialog, and it also contains a user-defined type that you can use to set properties such as the caption in the title bar of the File dialog box.

2. Click within the MultiPage control and select pgStep1 Page from the drop-down list in the Properties window. Double-click the first Browse button and add the following code to the *cmdBrowse_Click* event procedure, so that the procedure appears as follows:

```
Private Sub cmdBrowse_Click()
    Dim sFileName As String
    Dim udtFileDialog As FileDialog

    With udtFileDialog
        .CustomFilter = "Access Database (*.mdb)" & _
            Chr$(0) & "*.mdb" & Chr$(0) & Chr$(0)
        .DefaultExt = "*.mdb"
        .Title = "Browse"
        sFileName = modFileDialog _
            .WinFileDialog(udtFileDialog, 1)
    End With
    If Len(sFileName) > 0 Then
        txtDataSource.Text = sFileName
    End If
End Sub
```

The variable *udtFileDialog* is declared as the user-defined type FileDialog, which is declared as public in the modFileDialog module. You use the user-defined type to set the filters that are displayed in the Files Of Type drop-down list in the File dialog box.

The default extension is then set to the filter extension that the Files Of Type drop-down list will display first. When you click the cmdBrowse control, you use the Access Database type filter. The title bar caption of the File dialog box is set to the text "Browse."

When you display the dialog box, the folder you'll see by default is the most recently used folder. The section File Management in Chapter 4 describes how to set which folder is initially displayed in this dialog.

The value of sFileName is then set to the value returned by the function *WinFileDialog*, which displays the File dialog box. The If…Then condition block determines whether you clicked Cancel in the File dialog box or selected a valid file and clicked Open. If you selected a valid file, the program enters its full path in the txtDataSource text box. If you clicked Cancel, the value of sFileName is an empty string.

3. In the Object drop-down list of the module, select cmdBrowseTemplate and copy the same code to the *cmdBrowseTemplate_Click* event procedure that you added in the previous step to the *cmdBrowse_Click* event procedure. Change the two lines setting the value of CustomFilter and DefaultExt to the following:

```
.CustomFilter = "Document Template (*.dot)" & _
    Chr$(0) & "*.dot" & Chr$(0) & Chr$(0)
.DefaultExt = "*.dot"
```

When you click the cmdBrowseTemplate control, the filters used are of the Document Template type.

4. Change the line `txtDataSource.Text = sFileName` in the *cmdBrowseTemplate_Click* event procedure to:

```
txtTemplate.Text = sFileName
```

If a valid file was selected, its full path is entered in the txtDataSource text box.

5. Select pgStep2 Page from the drop-down list in the Properties window and then select cmdBrowseFolder from the drop-down list in the Properties window. Add the following code to the *cmdBrowseFolder_Click* event procedure:

```
Private Sub cmdBrowseFolder_Click()
    Dim sPath As String
    sPath = modBrowseFolder.BrowseForFolder
    If Len(sPath) > 0 Then
        txtDestination.Text = sPath
    End If
End Sub
```

The function *BrowseForFolder* in the modBrowseFolder module displays the Windows system Browse For Folder dialog box shown on the following page. (Your Browse For Folder dialog box will look different.)

6. In the Project Explorer, right-click the Energy Wizard project and click Import File on the shortcut menu. In the Import File dialog box, change to the Chapter 3 practice folder and select the file modBrwse.bas. Click Open.

The file modBrwse.bas contains code that allows you to display the Windows system Browse For Folder dialog box. The name of the imported standard module is modBrowseFolder.

View Object

7. Click the frmWizard project item and then click the View Object button in the Project Explorer to display the wizard UserForm.

8. Press F5 to run the wizard. Step through the wizard and click each of the Browse buttons in the steps. The wizard now allows you to find the files.

9. Close and unload the frmWizard UserForm by clicking the Cancel or Finish button.

10. Right-click the frmWizard project item in the Project Explorer and then click Export File on the shortcut menu. In the Export File dialog box, change to the Chapter 3 practice folder, and in the File Name text box, type the name **frmWizardComplete** and click Save.

Chapter Summary

Creating custom dialog boxes is the same in the Visual Basic Editor of any Office application. You can insert ActiveX controls from the Control Toolbox in the Visual Basic Editor, and set properties for ActiveX controls using the Properties window. Using ActiveX controls, you can create some of the common elements or style of dialog boxes that are displayed in Office. For example, in this chapter you created a wizard similar in look and style to the Fax Wizard in Word and the AutoContent Wizard in PowerPoint. Integrating the common Windows dialog boxes, such as the Browse For Folder and Open dialog boxes, helps you build custom dialog boxes similar to those you see throughout Office applications.

Preview of the Next Chapter

This next part describes how you can use code to create new documents; to open, save, print, and close them; and how to find them on a file system. It also tells you how to write code to trap events when a document is created, opened, saved, printed, or closed. Finally, it discusses how you can insert and manipulate content in a document once it's loaded into an Office application.

Chapter 4

Creating and Managing Files and Documents

- Work with various coding techniques used to find files to open and to find folders to save files to. Use the same techniques to parse fully qualified filenames to retrieve the path or filename.

- Display system-defined dialog boxes in which users select a file to open or a folder to save a file to. Customize the Microsoft Office File dialog box to make searching for files and folders easier.

- Work with the programmatic equivalents of the following commands: New, Open, Close, Save, Save As, Save as Web Page, Print, and Properties.

- Create and open Microsoft Word, Microsoft Excel, and Microsoft PowerPoint files. Create Microsoft Outlook folder items such as e-mail and appointments.

- Save Word, Excel, and PowerPoint documents in HTML format for viewing in a Web browser.

- Set and retrieve properties of a document, such as its Author and Title.

Before you can insert or manipulate content in applications like Word, Excel, PowerPoint, or Microsoft Access, you need to create a new document or open an existing one. When you've finished inserting and manipulating content, you need to determine where the document is going to reside. Before saving a document, you might want to add properties that distinguish it from others or help categorize it in a set of documents. A server, for example, may have a document library that organizes information about documents, manages them, and provides functionality such as version control and backup facilities.

The functionality provided by the commands on the File menus in Word, Excel, PowerPoint, and Access help you create and manage documents. The File menu is used to create new documents and open existing ones; to save, close, and print documents; and to set document properties. This chapter describes the programmatic equivalents of the following commands: New, Open, Close, Save, Save As, Save as Web Page, Print, and Properties.

This chapter also discusses the programmatic equivalents of locating where a document is situated or finding a folder to store a document—similar to the functionality provided by the New, Open, and Save As dialog boxes. The next chapter, "Managing Documents With Events," describes how to set up event procedures that are triggered when the actions new, open, save, close, and print occur either through Microsoft Visual Basic code or from the user clicking a File menu command.

Quick Guide

This chapter has three main parts. Because you have to specify where a document is or where it is to be located in order to open or save it, the first part describes how to write Visual Basic code that allows you to retrieve specific file folders, determine if a file or folder exists, and parse filenames to retrieve.

The second part describes the methods and properties associated with the new, open, save, close, and print actions in Word, Excel, and PowerPoint. It also explains the use of the new, save, close, and print actions with an Outlook mail item. The chapter doesn't discuss the use of these actions in Access (with the exception of Open) because they depend on the data access object library you work with (Microsoft DAO Object Library or Microsoft ActiveX Data Objects Library).

The final part discusses how to set and retrieve built-in document properties such as Author. It also explains custom document properties, which allow you to define your own document properties that you can use, for example, in document management systems. The following table provides a quick reference to the methods and properties discussed in the chapter.

(continued)

Quick Guide *(continued)*

Task	Description
Creating a new document	Use the *Add* method on the following document collections in Word, Excel, and PowerPoint: *Documents, Workbooks,* and *Presentations.*
Opening an existing document	Use the *Open* method on the following collection objects: *Documents, Workbooks,* and *Presentations.* The filename of the file to be opened is passed as the first argument in the *Open* method in each application.
Save a document to a new location	To save a new document that has no file path or change the saved location of an existing (opened) document, use the *SaveAs* method. You specify the filename as the first argument and the file format type as the second argument in each application.
Close a document loaded in an application	Use the *Close* method on the document object *(Document, Workbook,* and *Presentation)* in each application. Word and Excel also provide the *Close* method on the *Documents* and *Workbooks* collection object in order to close all opened documents. The *Close* method on the collection object is equivalent to clicking the Close All command on the File menu. The Close All command is displayed only when you hold down the SHIFT key and click the File menu.
Print a document	Use the *PrintOut* method on the document object *(Document, Workbook,* and *Presentation)* in each application. PowerPoint provides a *PrintOptions* object in addition to the *PrintOut* method that provides functionality equivalent to the *PrintOut* method in Word and Excel. You can access the *PrintOptions* object from the *Presentation* object.

Retrieve built-in document properties in Word, Excel, or PowerPoint	Use the BuiltInDocumentProperties property of the *Document* object in Word, the *Workbook* object in Excel, or the *Presentation* object in PowerPoint to specify the property value you want. For example:
	`sProperty = ActivePresentation. _`
	`    BuiltInDocumentProperties("Author")`

Set document properties using Visual Basic code	Assign the property values to the appropriate property index in the *BuiltInDocumentProperties* collection. For example:
	`ActiveDocument _`
	`    .BuiltInDocumentProperties("Company") _`
	`    = "My Company"`

(continued)

Quick Guide *(continued)*

Task	Description
Locate, create, remove, and copy files and folders	You can use the combination of Visual Basic for Applications built-in functions, Windows application programming interfaces (APIs), and functionality in the Microsoft Scripting Runtime object library to find files and folders and to parse filenames.
Parse filenames	Use Visual Basic for Applications built-in functions that manipulate text strings. Built-in text manipulation functions include *Left$, Right$, Mid$, Trim$, Len*, and *InStr*.

The code you use to locate, create, remove, and copy file folders, as well as to parse filenames, involves a number of different functions. The following section describes them.

File Management

Before opening a file in Word, Excel, PowerPoint, or Access, you need to determine the filename of the document to be opened. When you save a document, you need to specify a filename. When you work with the Office applications, you use the Open and Save As dialog boxes to navigate through the file system on your machine, your network, or your Web server to open or save a document. In your Visual Basic programs, to find files and folders you can use a combination of Visual Basic for Applications built-in functions, Windows application programming interfaces (APIs), and the Microsoft Scripting Runtime object library.

In addition to using code to find files and folders programmatically, you can use Windows APIs to display Windows system dialog boxes that allow the user to specify a file or folder. This section describes how to display the system file dialog box and the folder dialog box that allows your users to browse for a specific folder. The following table briefly describes the code you need in order to do common file management tasks, including parsing a string representing a filename:

Task	Code Description
Check if a file exists	Len(Dir$(sFileName))
Check if a folder exists	Len(Dir$(sFileName, vbDirectory))
Get the application data folder	Use the Windows API SHGetSpecialFolderLocation.
Get the Temp folder on the user's system	Use the Windows API GetTempPath.

(continued)

(continued)

Task	Code Description
Remove a file	Use the built-in VBA function *Kill(Pathname)*.
Parse through a filename and retrieve the filename without the path	In a custom function, use the built-in *InStrRev* function to return the position of the first occurrence of the backslash ("\") within the filename from the end of the filename string. The position returned by *InStrRev* is used in the built-in *Mid$* function to return the characters of the filename string to the right of the backslash ("\").
Parse through a filename and retrieve the path	In a custom function similar to the one described immediately above, you use the built-in *Mid$* function to return the characters of the filename string to the left of the backslash ("\").
Browse for a file	Import the code module modFlDlg.bas from the practice folders.
Browse for a folder	Import the code module modBrwse.bas from the practice folders.
(All tasks listed in this table.)	Use the *FileSystemObject* object in the Microsoft Scripting Runtime object library.

Check If a File Exists

Sometimes you need to determine if a file exists before you attempt to open it or overwrite it. Using a combination of the *Len* and *Dir* functions built into the Visual Basic for Applications language, you can easily check if a file exists and take the appropriate action if it does or doesn't. In this scenario, you use the *Dir* function to return a string representing the name of a file that matches a specified file. You can also use the *Dir* function to return a string representing a directory, as the next example describes.

Start the Visual Basic Editor in any Office application and click Module on the Insert menu. Copy the following code and after placing the cursor in the procedure, press F5. If the folder "C:\Temp" or the file Test.txt does not exist, a message box indicating the file does not exist will be displayed. Change the filename or folder assigned to the variable *sFileName* to a file that exists on your system and a message indicating the file exists will be displayed.

```
Sub CheckIfFileExists()
    Dim sFileName As String
    sFileName = "C:\Temp\Test.txt"
    If Len(Dir$(sFileName)) Then
        MsgBox "File exists."
    Else
        MsgBox "File does not exist."
    End If
End Sub
```

In this procedure, the first argument of the *Dir* function takes a string expression representing the name of the file being checked to see if it exists. If it isn't found, the *Dir* function returns a zero-length string (""). Instead of checking if the *Dir* function equals a zero-length string in the If...Then statement in the procedure, you use the *Len* function to determine the length of the string. The *Len* function returns a value of type Long representing the number of characters in a specified string. If *Len* returns a value greater than zero, the file exists.

Tip   You can also use the *Dir* function to iterate through all files in a folder. See the online Visual Basic for Applications Help files for more information.

Check If a Folder Exists

The second argument, *attributes*, of the *Dir* function, is an optional constant or numeric expression whose combined value specifies file attributes. You can set the *Attributes* argument to one or a sum of the VbFileAttribute constants. In the following procedure, you set the *attributes* argument to the value vbDirectory, specifying that the *Dir* function should determine if the filename specified by the first argument of the *Dir* function can be found.

Start any Office application and in a standard code module in the Visual Basic Editor, copy the following code, place the cursor in the procedure, and press F5. If the folder "C:\TempFoo" does not exist, a message box indicating that the folder does not exist will be displayed. Change the folder assigned to the variable *sPath* to a folder that exists on your system and a message indicating the folder exists will be displayed.

```
Sub CheckIfFolderExists()
    Dim sPath As String
    sPath = "C:\TempFoo\"
    If Len(Dir$(sPath, vbDirectory)) Then
        MsgBox "Folder exists."
    Else
        MsgBox "Folder does not exist."
        MkDir sPath
    End If
End Sub
```

Note the differences between this procedure and the preceding one. You set the variable *sPath* in this procedure to a folder name instead of a filename. And unlike in the preceding example, you specify the second argument of the *Dir* function. The last line in the If...Then...Else statement in the procedure above uses the Visual Basic for Applications language's built-in *MkDir* function. The *MkDir* function creates a new folder. If the folder didn't exist, you'd use the *MkDir* function to create it.

Get the Temp Folder

If you use the Windows Explorer on your machine to scroll through the Temp folder, you'll find that Windows applications have created a lot of files and folders to temporarily store data. You may find in your Visual Basic for Applications programs that you also need to create a temporary text file, for example, to store data while your program executes. At a later point in your program, you can clean up any temporary data files using the *Kill* function that's built into the Visual Basic for Applications language. In order to store data temporarily, you need to determine where the Temp folder is located on the user's machine. Although the Visual Basic for Applications language and Office offer no simple ways to retrieve the Temp folder path, both Windows and the Microsoft Scripting Runtime object library do. Later in this chapter, you'll learn how to use the Microsoft Scripting Runtime object library. This section tells you how to use the function *GetTempPath* that's built into Windows.

Windows provides a very extensive set of application programming interfaces, or APIs, that allows developers to create applications for the Windows platform. Although the Visual Basic for Applications language, along with objects, methods, and properties found in Office, provide ways to set and retrieve information, in some cases functionality isn't provided. Using Windows APIs, you can access a lot of the same functionality but often can go well beyond that offered by the Visual Basic for Applications language.

> **Tip** For a more in-depth discussion of the use of Windows APIs in your Visual Basic for Applications programs, see the book *Microsoft Office 2000 Visual Basic Programmer's Guide* from Microsoft Press. You can also search the Microsoft KnowledgeBase on the World Wide Web at *http://support.microsoft.com/support/*.

```
Public Declare Function GetTempPath Lib "kernel32" _
    Alias "GetTempPathA" ( _
        ByVal nBufferLength As Long, _
        ByVal lpBuffer As String _
    ) As Long

Function GetTempDir()
    Dim sPath As String * 255, lTempPathLength As Long
    lTempPathLength = GetTempPath(255, sPath)
    GetTempDir = Mid$(sPath, 1, lTempPathLength)
    Debug.Print GetTempDir
End Function
```

In a new standard code module in the Visual Basic Editor in any Office application, copy the public declaration of the function *GetTempPath* at the top of the code module. The code in the custom *GetTempDir* function calls the Windows API GetTempPath. Place the cursor directly in the *GetTempDir* function and press F5. The Temp folder path is printed to the Immediate window in the Visual Basic Editor. Whenever you want to retrieve the Temp folder path, call the *GetTempDir* function from anywhere in your code.

Get a Special Folder

In Office 2000, files that are created or modified by the user, or created by default, are saved in the user's profile in the Application Data folder. The subfolders under the Application Data folder contain configuration preferences and options for each user. If the administrator for the user's machine set the user up with a roaming profile, information under the Application Data folder will roam as the user logs onto one Windows 2000 machine after another. Information under this folder is part of the user's profile. For example, on a typical installation of Office 2000, user-customized templates will be saved to a folder called Templates:

%windir%\Profiles\<username>\Application Data\Microsoft\Templates

The folder path above is typical of Windows NT4 or Windows 2000 users. If the user is using a Windows 95 or Windows 98 operating system, the folder will appear as:

%windir%\Application Data\Microsoft\Templates

The file Normal.dot that's used by Word is stored under this folder. If you click Save As on the File menu in PowerPoint and chose the Design Template (*.pot) file type in the Save as Type drop-down list, the 'Save in' folder changes to the folder specified above. If you also want to give your users the choice of saving files and data to a subfolder under the Application Data folder, you can use the Windows API SHGetSpecialFolderLocation.

Start the Visual Basic Editor of any Office application, right-click the Project Explorer, select the Import File command on the shortcut menu, and in the Import File dialog box, navigate to this book's practice folders. In the Chapter 4 practice folder, select the code module file SHGetFdr.bas. This module contains the declarations and custom function *GetSpecialFolder* that retrieves any special folder defined by Windows. Place the cursor in the *Main* procedure and press F5. All special folders defined by the user's operating system are printed to the Immediate window. In another code module, you can retrieve a specific folder by copying the following procedure to a new code module.

```
Sub GetUserTemplateFolder()
    Dim sAppDataPath As String, sUserTemplatePath As String
    sAppDataPath = GetSpecialFolder(CSIDL_APPDATA)
    sUserTemplatePath = sAppDataPath & "Microsoft\Templates\"
    Debug.Print sUserTemplatePath
End Sub
```

This procedure retrieves the Templates folder that Office applications use to store user-created or user-modified Office templates. Before running this procedure, make sure you've imported the file SHGetFdr.bas from the Chapter 4 practice folder. The path to the Templates folder, similar to the paths specified above, will be printed to the Immediate window. In the file SHGetFdr.bas, you'll find a number of constants defined for each special folder. The constant names begin with the prefix "CSIDL_". Type each of the following lines in the Immediate window in Visual Basic Editor and press ENTER to retrieve the user's desktop folder and the user's My Documents folder.

```
?GetSpecialFolder(CSIDL_DESKTOP)
?GetSpecialFolder(CSIDL_PERSONAL)
```

Parse Filenames

You'll often find that your code will retrieve a filename that contains both the name of the file and the path to the file. In many cases, you may need to do one of the following with the filename:

- Strip off the path to the file to retrieve only the file's name

- Strip off the file's name to retrieve only the path

- Determine the file extension

Using Visual Basic code, you can write custom functions that take a filename and return only the necessary portion of the filename string. Using the new *InStrRev* function built into the Visual Basic for Applications language (it's not available in Office 97), you can retrieve the position of the backslash ("\") character, starting from the end of the string. Once you know this position, you can use the *Mid$* function built into the Visual Basic for Applications language to retrieve the portion of the string you require.

The first argument of the *InStrRev* function specifies the string to be searched, while the second argument specifies the string to be searched for in the first argument. The procedure below, *TestGetPathAndFileName*, calls the three custom functions, *GetFileName, GetFileExtension*, and *GetPath* and prints the return values of the custom functions to the Immediate window.

Note that the only difference between the custom functions *GetFileName* and *GetPath* is the second and third argument of the *Mid$* function. In the *GetFileName* function, you set the *Start* argument to the character position of the backslash plus one. You set the *Start* argument specified in the *Mid$* function in the *GetPath* function to 1, but you set the *Length* argument to include all characters up to the position of the backslash.

```
Sub TestGetPathAndFileName()
    Debug.Print GetFileName("C:\Temp\12345Foo.txt")
    Debug.Print GetFileExtension("C:\Temp\12345Foo.txt")
    Debug.Print GetPath("C:\Temp\12345Foo.txt")
End Sub

Function GetFileName(sFileName As String) As String
    Dim iPosn As Integer
    iPosn = InStrRev(sFileName, "\")
    GetFileName = Mid$(sFileName, iPosn + 1)
End Function
```

```
Function GetFileExtension(sFileName As String) As String
    Dim iPosn As Integer
    iPosn = InStrRev(sFileName, ".")
    GetFileExtension = Mid$(sFileName, iPosn + 1)
End Function

Function GetPath(sFileName As String) As String
    Dim iPosn As Integer
    iPosn = InStrRev(sFileName, "\")
    GetPath = Mid$(sFileName, 1, iPosn - 1)
End Function
```

The results printed to the Immediate window will be "12345Foo.txt", "txt", and "C:\Temp", respectively. If you want *GetPath* to return the path and include the backslash at the end of the path string, change the line setting *GetPath* to the following, which excludes the subtraction of one in the *Mid$* function.

```
GetPath = Mid$(sFileName, 1, iPosn)
```

Note In the Visual Basic for Applications language used in Office 2000, the following string manipulation functions are new and didn't exist in Office 97: *InStrRev, Join, Split, Replace,* and *StrReverse.* These functions complement the existing string manipulation functions in Office 97: *Left, Right, Mid, LTrim, RTrim, Trim, Len, StrComp,* and *InStr.* See the online Help file in the Visual Basic Editor for more information on these new functions built into the language.

Differences from Visual Basic for Applications in Office 97

In Office 97, the built-in *InStrRev* function doesn't exist in the Visual Basic for Applications language. Therefore, in the custom function *GetFileName*, defined in the previous example, your code needs to iterate through each character of the filename starting from the right end of the filename string.

```
Function GetFileName97(sFileName As String) As String
    Dim sChar As String, i As Integer
    For i = Len(sFileName) To 1 Step -1
        sChar = Mid$(sFileName, i, 1)
        If sChar = "\" Then
            GetFileName97 = Mid$(sFileName, i + 1)
            Exit For
        End If
    Next i
End Function
```

When you find the first backslash ("\"), use the built-in *Mid$* function to return the characters of the filename string to the right of the backslash ("\"). The *GetFileName97* function will appear as listed above when typed into a code module in the Visual Basic Editor in Office 97. Type **?GetFileName97 ("C:\Temp\12345Foo.txt")** in the Immediate window and the same result is printed. This custom function works the same in the Visual Basic Editor in Office 2000. You can easily modify this function to return the path and file extension.

Using Dialog Boxes from Windows

In addition to using code to find files and folders programmatically, you can use Windows APIs to display Windows system dialog boxes that allow the user to specify a file or folder. Two common system dialog boxes are the File dialog box, which is used to open, save, or browse for files on your computer or computer network, and the Browse For Folder dialog box, which is used to specify a folder name. This section describes how to display to your users the Windows system File dialog box and Browse For Folder dialog box so they can locate a document or find a folder to store a document.

Note   Word and Excel provide a method to display the Office File dialog box (the dialog box displayed when you click Open or Save As on the File menu). Chapter 5 describes how to display in Word and Excel the Office "Save As" File dialog box in the document Save event so that you can determine the filename specified by the user.

   The Visual Basic code you need to write to display the dialog boxes, however, is different in each application. In addition, you can't programmatically display the dialog box in PowerPoint, Access, or Outlook. The Windows File dialog box isn't as feature-rich as the Office File dialog box. However, the Windows File dialog box allows you to write code once and have it work in any application. There's one way to customize the Office File dialog box and that's described in the section of this chapter entitled "Customizing the Office File Dialog Box."

Display the Windows File Dialog Box

Starting with Windows 95 and Windows NT version 4.0, the Windows File dialog box provided user-interface features that are similar to the Windows Explorer. Windows 98 expands the functionality of the Windows File dialog box by providing a shortcut to the Desktop folder and letting the user increase the size of the dialog box by clicking at its bottom-right and dragging it to an appropriate size.

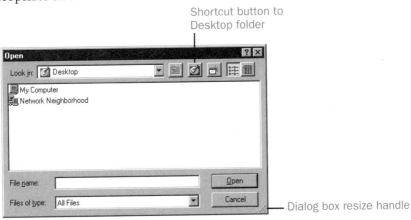

Shortcut button to
Desktop folder

Dialog box resize handle

In Windows 2000, the Windows File dialog box looks very similar to the Office File dialog box, providing a bar (similar to the look and style of the Outlook bar in Outlook) of folder shortcuts at the left.

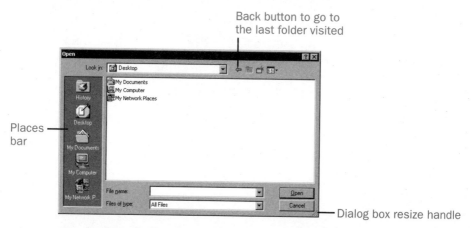

Back button to go to the last folder visited

Places bar

Dialog box resize handle

The main functionality of the Windows File dialog box is to enable the user to select a file to open or insert or to specify a filename and folder to save a file. You can display the Windows File dialog box by using one of the following two Windows application programming interfaces (API): *GetOpenFileName* and *GetSaveFileName*. These APIs return a valid file to the programmer that is fully qualified with the pathname. If no file is selected or specified, they return an empty string, indicating that the user clicked Cancel in the dialog box.

Insert Code to Display the Windows File Dialog Box

In the Project Explorer in the Visual Basic Editor for any Office application, right-click any VBA project and click Import File on the shortcut menu. In the Import File dialog box, change to the Chapter 4 practice folder, select the file modFlDlg.bas, and click Open.

The file modFlDlg.bas contains code that allows you to display the Windows system File dialog box, which is the same dialog box as the Import File dialog box you just used to import the module. In the Properties window of the Visual Basic Editor, the name of the imported standard module is modFileDialog, and it contains a user-defined type that you can use to set properties such as the caption in the title bar of the File dialog box. To use the code in the modFileDialog module, insert a new code module by clicking Module on the Insert menu and add the following procedure. After adding the procedure, place the cursor in the procedure and press F5 to run. The system File dialog box will be displayed.

```
Sub GetFileWithSystemFileDialog()
    Dim sFileName As String
    Dim udtFileDialog As FileDialog
```

```
With udtFileDialog
    .CustomFilter = "Text Files (*.txt)" _
        & Chr$(0) & "*.txt" & Chr$(0) _
        & Chr$(0)
    .DefaultExt = "*.txt"
    .Title = "Browse"
    .InitialDir = "C:\"
    sFileName = modFileDialog _
        .WinFileDialog(udtFileDialog, 1)
End With
If Len(sFileName) > 0 Then
    Debug.Print sFileName
End If
End Sub
```

Initial directory

Dialog box title

File type filter and default file extension

You declare the variable *udtFileDialog* as the user-defined type FileDialog, which you declare as public in the modFileDialog module. For more information on user-defined types, see the online Visual Basic for Applications Help file in the Visual Basic Editor. You use the user-defined type to set the custom filters that are displayed in the Files of Type drop-down list in the File dialog box.

You then set the default extension to the filter extension that's to be initially displayed in the Files of Type drop-down list. The filter that's used when the procedure is executed is the Text Files type. You set the title bar caption of the File dialog box to the text "Browse." The InitDir specifies what folder is displayed when the dialog box is displayed. You can use any of the techniques described in this chapter to retrieve a folder path and set it to InitDir.

You then set the value of the string variable *sFileName* to the value returned by the function *WinFileDialog*, which displays the File dialog box. The function *WinFileDialog* is defined in the imported code module modFileDialog. The If...Then condition block determines whether Cancel is clicked in the File dialog box or a valid file is selected and Open is clicked. If a valid file is selected, its full path is printed to the Immediate window in the Visual Basic Editor. If Cancel is clicked in the File dialog box, the value of *sFileName* is an empty string.

File filter and extension   The value of CustomFilter is a string containing pairs of a display string and extension(s), separated by a Null character, represented in code as Chr$(0). The entire string set to CustomFilter is terminated by two Null characters. For example:

```
"Text File" & Chr$(0) & "*.txt" & Chr$(0) & Chr$(0)
```

or

```
"Word Files" & Chr$(0) & "*.doc;*.dot" & Chr$(0) _
    & "Text Files" & Chr$(0) & "*.txt" & Chr$(0) & Chr$(0)
```

The value set to DefaultExt is the default extension that will be added to the filename if the user doesn't specify one. The preceding procedure, *GetFileWithSystemFileDialog*, would add the file extension "txt" to the filename.

Displaying more than one file type in the same filter in the Files of Type drop-down list   To display more than one file type in the Files of Type drop-down list, change the two lines setting the value of CustomFilter and DefaultExt to the following:

```
.CustomFilter = "Web Pages (*.htm; *.html)" & _
    Chr$(0) & "*.htm;*.html" & Chr$(0) _
    & Chr$(0)
.DefaultExt = "*.htm; *.html"
```

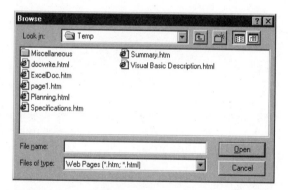

Displaying more than one filter in the Files of Type drop-down list   In order to display more than one filter in the Files of Type drop-down list, change the two lines setting the value of CustomFilter and DefaultExt to the following:

```
.CustomFilter = "Access Database (*.mdb)" & _
    Chr$(0) & "*.mdb" & Chr$(0) & _
    "PowerPoint Presentation (*.ppt)" & _
    Chr$(0) & "*.ppt" & Chr$(0) & _
    Chr$(0)
.DefaultExt = "*.mdb"
```

The default extension value, DefaultExt, is set to the first file type *.mdb, though it could have been *.ppt.

Display the Windows Browse Dialog Box

In the Project Explorer in the Visual Basic Editor of any Office application, right-click any VBA project and click Import File on the shortcut menu. In the Import File dialog box, change to the Chapter 4 practice folder, select the file modBrwse.bas, and click Open.

The file modBrwse.bas contains code that allows you to display the Windows system Browse For Folder dialog box. In the Visual Basic Editor's Properties window, the imported standard module's name is modBrowseFolder. To use the code in the modBrowseFolder module, insert a new code module by clicking Module on the Insert menu and add the following procedure:

```
Sub GetFolderSpecifiedByUser()
    Dim sPath As String
    sPath = modBrowseFolder.BrowseForFolder
    If Len(sPath) > 0 Then
        Debug.Print sPath
    End If
End Sub
```

The function *BrowseForFolder* in the modBrowseFolder module displays the Windows system Browse For Folder dialog box. The If...Then condition block determines whether Cancel is clicked in the Browse For Folder dialog box or a folder is selected and OK is clicked. If a folder is selected, its path is printed to the Immediate window in the Visual Basic Editor. If Cancel is clicked in the Browse For Folder dialog box, the value of *sPath* is an empty string.

Customizing the Office File Dialog Box

When you click Open or Save As on the File menu in most Office applications, you see the Office File dialog box. Like the Windows File dialog box, it most commonly enables the user to select a file to open, to specify a filename and folder to save a file to, and to browse for a file to insert into a document.

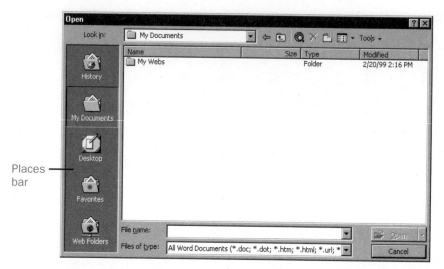

Places
bar

Tip You can also display the Office File dialog box programmatically through Visual Basic code—but only in Word and Excel. The Microsoft KnowledgeBase article, ID Q161930, "XL97: How to Use the *GetOpenFilename* Method," at *http://support.microsoft.com* or on your Microsoft Developer Network (MSDN) CD (if you have a membership), describes how to display the Office File dialog box in Excel.

As previously noted, Chapter 5 discusses how you can display the Office "Save As" File dialog box. This dialog box allows you to handle scenarios such as determining what filename a user specified in the Save As dialog box. If the document does not have certain properties set and the filename indicates the file will be saved to a specific folder location on a network, for example, you can cancel the document Save event. Chapter 5 provides the samples for this scenario in Word and Excel.

Remember that you can't display the File dialog box in PowerPoint, Access, or Outlook through code. However, you can still customize the Office File dialog box so that no matter when and in what application it's displayed, the user's experience will be the same. The one part of the Office File dialog box you can customize is the places bar at the left of the dialog box. The places bar is similar in look and style to the Outlook bar in Outlook.

The Places Bar

The places bar commonly contains up to five positions that you use to display an icon and a caption that provide a shortcut to a folder on the user's machine, network share, or Web server share. By default, the places bar displays icons in order from top to bottom for the folders History, My Documents, Desktop, Favorites, and Web Folders.

Note This section assumes that you're familiar with using the basics of the Windows Registry, such as navigating to a key and adding string values. The following description discusses which settings stored in the Windows Registry you use to customize the places bar in the Office File dialog box. You can use Windows Registry application programming interfaces (APIs) in your Visual Basic programs to manipulate these Registry settings. See the article with ID Q145679—"HOWTO: Use the Registry API to Save and Retrieve Settings" in the Microsoft KnowledgeBase on the Web at *http://support.microsoft.com* or your Microsoft Developer Network (MSDN) CD if you have a membership. See *http://msdn.microsoft.com* for more information about MSDN memberships.

Office uses the Windows Registry to determine if these shortcut icons appear on the places bar. Under the Windows Registry key, HKEY_CURRENT_USER \Software\Microsoft\Office\9.0\Common\Open Find\Places, there are two subkeys: StandardPlaces and UserDefinedPlaces.

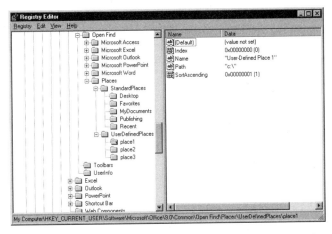

Each of the subkeys under StandardPlaces corresponds to the shortcut icons displayed by default in the Office File dialog box. The Publishing subkey corresponds to the Web Folders shortcut icon in the dialog box, and the Recent subkey corresponds to the History shortcut icon. If you want to display a user-defined place in the places bar, you need to complete the following steps. In short, user-defined places are displayed only if a position is available in the places bar and one or more StandardPlaces aren't visible.

1. To turn off the display of any of the default shortcut icons on the places bar, under the appropriate subkey under the StandardPlaces key, add a DWORD value to the subkey, name it Show, and then set its value to 0.

    If the Show value already exists, change its value from 1 to 0. To insert a DWORD value, click New on the Edit menu in the Windows Registry and then click DWORD value on the submenu. You can edit the name of the value when the DWORD value is added, or you can right-click the value and click Rename on the shortcut menu. To change the value of the DWORD value, double-click it and type the appropriate value in the Value Data text box in the Edit DWORD Value dialog box.

2. Under the UserDefinedPlaces key, add a subkey with any name.

3. Add two string values, Name and Path, under the new subkey.

4. For the Name value, add a string that will be used as the caption for the user-defined place in the places bar. For the Path value, add a string that the user-defined place will navigate the user to in the Office File dialog box.

The following graphic shows the History, Favorites, and Web Folders turned off and three user-defined places displayed.

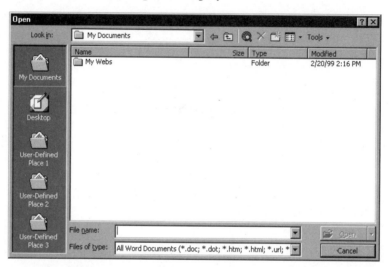

You can also specify two other DWORD values, Index and SortAscending, under the user-defined place subkey. Index indicates the position of the user-defined place in the places bar with respect to other user-defined places. For example, you can sort the places sequentially, regardless of the order of keys in the registry. If Index isn't specified, the user-defined places are sorted in the order of the keys in the registry. The registry key order is defined by the order in which the key is added under the UserDefinedPlaces key.

The SortAscending value determines whether the display of files in the Office File dialog box should be in alphabetical order or reverse alphabetical order. A value of 1 indicates alphabetical order and a value of 0 indicates reverse alphabetical order.

The following list explains the behaviors of the places bar in the Office File dialog box:

- If Name or Path doesn't exist, the place doesn't show up in the dialog box.

- If Path is defined but contains an empty string, it does show up in the dialog box, but clicking on the place doesn't change the folder view in the dialog box.

- If Name is defined but contains an empty string, the generic icon for a user-defined place is displayed but no caption is displayed. Clicking on the place still changes the folder view in the dialog box, as long as Path has a valid string.

Load Any File Using ShellExecute

The ShellExecute Windows application programming interface (API) allows your program to open any file. ShellExecute parses the filename passed to it and determines what the file string represents. The following list describes the common types of files that the file string represents, and which the ShellExecute API opens:

- Executable files such as Notepad.exe or any Office application

- Any document file on your computer or network share

- Any Web page or file over the Intranet or Internet

- URL (*.url) shortcuts

- Desktop (*.lnk) shortcuts

- E-mail name

Tip   For more information, search the Microsoft Developer's Network at *http:// msdn.microsoft.com* or *http://support.microsoft.com* by using "ShellExecute" in a search, or if you have a subscription to MSDN, type ShellExecute in the Search tab of the MSDN Library window.

The following *LoadMiscFiles* procedure calls the custom procedure *LoadFile* to load each of the different files specified. Because the first is an HTTP file, ShellExecute will launch whatever browser is registered to open Web pages. As you'll see in the description of the *SaveAs* method later in this chapter, you use ShellExecute to display saved Web pages from Word, Excel, or PowerPoint in the Web browser.

The procedure's second line passes the *mailto* syntax that's commonly used in Web pages to load your machine's default e-mail application and to open a new message. The third line launches Notepad, and the last line displays the Windows Explorer showing the contents of the Temp folder on the C drive.

```
Declare Function ShellExecute Lib "shell32.dll" _
    Alias "ShellExecuteA" ( _
        ByVal Hwnd As Long, _
        ByVal lpOperation As String, _
        ByVal lpFile As String, _
        ByVal lpParameters As String, _
        ByVal lpDirectory As String, _
        ByVal nShowCmd As Long _
    ) As Long

Sub LoadFile(FileName As String)
    ShellExecute 0, "Open", FileName, "", "", 1
End Sub
```

```
Sub LoadMiscFiles()
    LoadFile "http://www.microsoft.com"
    LoadFile "mailto:mspress@microsoft.com"
    LoadFile "notepad.exe"
    LoadFile "C:\Temp"
End Sub
```

As you'll see in the description of the *Print* method later in this chapter, you can use ShellExecute to print files. The only difference from the code above is in the line ShellExecute in the *LoadFile* procedure, where the string "Open" is replaced with "Print."

Using the Object *FileSystemObject*

What you've learned so far about finding files and folders through code has involved the use of Windows application programming interfaces (APIs) and built-in functions in the Visual Basic for Applications language, or both. Microsoft, however, also provides an object library that you can reference in your Visual Basic programs, and it provides objects, methods, and properties you can use to access the file system where your program is executed.

In the Visual Basic Editor, click References on the Tools menu to display the References dialog box. Scroll down the list of Available References and select the item Microsoft Scripting Runtime. Click OK to set a reference to the Microsoft Scripting Runtime object library.

The filename of the Microsoft Scripting Runtime object library is scrrun.dll, and it should be installed in the Windows system folder in a typical installation of Office 2000.

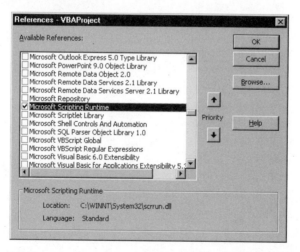

Important   Before you can execute any of the following procedures, make sure that you set a reference to the Microsoft Scripting Runtime object library in your Visual Basic project. In the follow procedures, the variable *fileSystemObj* is set to the *FileSystemObject* defined in the Microsoft Scripting Runtime object library. The New keyword in the declaration indicates that the *fileSystemObj* object variable is set when it's first used in code.

When To Use the Microsoft Scripting Runtime Object Library

As you'll see in the following procedures, by using the *FileSystemObject* and other objects defined in the Microsoft Scripting Runtime object library, you can replace most of the file management tasks discussed earlier in this chapter. So when should you use one or the other? If you don't want to depend on the Microsoft Scripting Runtime object library, you can do most file management tasks using Windows APIs and built-in functions in the Visual Basic for Applications language.

If you only need to determine if a file or folder exists a few times in your code, it's not worth depending on the Microsoft Scripting Runtime object library. If your program does a lot of file management and if depending on the Microsoft Scripting Runtime object library isn't an issue for your solution, you'll find it's much easier to write and understand the code to handle file management tasks by using the *FileSystemObject* in the Microsoft Scripting Runtime object library.

Note   It's possible that the Microsoft Scripting Runtime object library, contained in the file scrrun.dll, may not be installed on every user's machine. If you've purchased and installed Microsoft Visual Basic 6.0, the Microsoft Scripting Runtime object library can be distributed royalty-free. If you're developing a COM add-in, as described in Chapters 13 and 14, and you use this object library, you need to consider packaging this file for the deployment of your COM add-in solution. The last section of Chapter 13 tells you how to use the Package and Deployment Wizard. However, the Microsoft Scripting Runtime object library ships with Microsoft Visual Studio 6, Microsoft Internet Explorer 5, Microsoft Windows 98, Windows NT 4, and Windows 2000. So if your users have any of these products, you don't need to redistribute it.

Check If a File Exists

This procedure is similar to using the combination of the built-in functions *Len* and *Dir* in the Visual Basic for Applications language. The main difference is in the expression evaluated in the If...Then statement. In the following procedure, the *FileExists* method of the *FileSystemObject* returns True if the specified file exists and False if it doesn't.

```
Sub CheckIfFileExists()
  Dim fileSystemObj As New Scripting.FileSystemObject
  Dim sFileName As String
    sFileName = "C:\Temp\Test.txt"
    If fileSystemObj.FileExists(sFileName) Then
      MsgBox "File exists."
    Else
      MsgBox "File does not exist."
    End If
End Sub
```

Check If a Folder Exists

This procedure is also similar to using the combination of the built-in functions *Len* and *Dir* in the Visual Basic for Applications language. As above, the main difference is in the expression evaluated in the If...Then statement. In the following procedure, the *FolderExists* method of the *FileSystemObject* returns True if the specified folder exists and False if it doesn't. In addition, you use the *CreateFolder* method in place of the *MkDir* function built into the Visual Basic for Applications language.

```
Sub CheckIfFolderExists()
    Dim fileSystemObj As New Scripting.FileSystemObject
    Dim sPath As String
    sPath = "C:\TempFoo\"
    If fileSystemObj.FolderExists(sPath) Then
        MsgBox "Folder exists."
    Else
        MsgBox "Folder does not exist."
        fileSystemObj.CreateFolder sPath
    End If
End Sub
```

Get the Temp Folder

You can easily retrieve the Temp folder by using the *GetSpecialFolder* method on the *FileSystemObject* object and specifying the SpecialFolderConst constant value TemporaryFolder. Instead of having to use a module-level declaration and at least two procedure-level variable declarations when you use the GetTempFolder Windows API, you only need two lines when using the *FileSystemObject*. (The sTempPath doesn't need to be declared and set to the return value of the *GetSpecialFolder* method.) The Temp folder path in this procedure is printed to the Immediate window in the Visual Basic Editor.

```
Sub GetTempDirUsingFileSystemObject()
    Dim fileSystemObj As New Scripting.FileSystemObject
    Dim sTempPath As String
    sTempPath = fileSystemObj.GetSpecialFolder(TemporaryFolder)
    Debug.Print sTempPath
End Sub
```

Get a Special Folder

Unlike the Windows API SHGetSpecialFolderLocation described earlier in this chapter, the *FileSystemObject* object only lets you retrieve three special folders. They're defined as SpecialFolderConst constants: SystemFolder, TemporaryFolder, and WindowsFolder. In the previous procedure, change the value specified in the *GetSpecialFolder* method to either SystemFolder or WindowsFolder. In this case, using the Windows API SHGetSpecialFolderLocation is more robust because it allows you to return folders like the user's Desktop and Favorites folders.

Unlike using the built-in *InStrRev* function in the Visual Basic for Applications language, you can use the *GetFileName, GetExtensionName,* and *GetParentFolderName* methods on the *FileSystemObject* to return the filename without the path, the file extension, or the path without the filename, respectively. Instead of creating separate custom functions, you need only two lines of code in each case. The result of running each procedure below is printed to the Immediate window and the values will be "12345Foo.txt", "txt", and "C:\Temp," respectively.

```
Sub GetFileNameUsingFileSystemObject()
    Dim fileSystemObj As New Scripting.FileSystemObject
    Debug.Print fileSystemObj _
        .GetFileName("C:\Temp\12345Foo.txt")
End Sub

Sub GetFileExtensionUsingFileSystemObject()
    Dim fileSystemObj As New Scripting.FileSystemObject
    Debug.Print fileSystemObj _
        .GetExtensionName("C:\Temp\12345Foo.txt")
End Sub

Sub GetPathUsingFileSystemObject()
    Dim fileSystemObj As New Scripting.FileSystemObject
    Debug.Print fileSystemObj _
        .GetParentFolderName("C:\Temp\12345Foo.txt")
End Sub
```

New and Open

As you'll see in Chapter 6, the most common thing you do in Office applications like Word, Excel, and PowerPoint is to specify an area in a document and then manipulate the content. If you want to create content in a new document or in an existing document that isn't currently loaded into the application, you first need to create a new file or open an existing one. This necessity isn't limited to Word, Excel, and PowerPoint documents. You may also need to create new e-mail messages in Outlook, for example, or open an existing database in Access to retrieve data for a report in Word.

The *Open* Method

If you click Open on the File menu in Word, Excel, PowerPoint, or Access, you see the Open dialog box. You use the Open dialog box to navigate to a file, and then you click Open to open the file in the application. When you need to open an existing document—such as a Word document, Excel workbook, PowerPoint presentation, or Access database—using Visual Basic code, the functional equivalent is the *Open* method. The *Open* method lets your programs open documents that exist in the file system on the user's machine, on a network share, and on an HTTP or FTP server. You can use the *Open* method to open any file type listed in the Files of Type drop-down list in the Open dialog box.

What the *Open* Method Does

The *Open* method adds a document item to the existing collection of documents in an Office application. Hence, you can access the *Open* method in Word, Excel, and PowerPoint from the *Documents, Workbooks*, and *Presentations* collection objects, respectively. In the definition of the *Open* method in Word, Excel, and PowerPoint, you need the first argument, named *FileName*, and it's consistent in all three applications. In the *FileName* argument, you specify a valid file that's fully qualified with the pathname. Using the techniques described in the first section of this chapter, "File Management," you build a string to be passed into the *FileName* argument of the *Open* method. The table on the following page lists the definition of the *Open* method in Word, Excel, and PowerPoint. These definitions are copied from the Details pane of the Object Browser in the Visual Basic Editor.

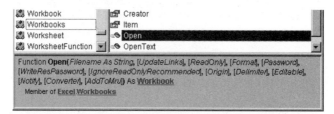

Creating New Documents and Opening Existing Ones Invisibly

The ability to load a document invisibly is one of the major similarities between the *Open* method and the method to create a new document, the *Add* method on the *Documents* and *Presentations* collection objects in Word and PowerPoint, respectively. This ability lets you load documents and manipulate them in the background. When your program has finished adding and formatting content in the document, you can make the document visible to the user or just save it to a new file location and close it.

The sample procedures describing the *Add* method for creating new documents show you how to create documents invisibly and to choose when to make them visible. You can apply the same technique to the *Open* method in Word and PowerPoint. The integrated Office solutions in Chapters 7 and 8 use this technique to create documents invisibly, add content, save the documents, and make them visible to the user.

Note   The following table, like the other tables in the chapter, lists the definition of a document management method (*Add, Open, SaveAs, Close, PrintOut*). These definitions are copied from the Details pane of the Object Browser in the Visual Basic Editor. The purpose of this type of table is to show the similarities and differences between the methods in the Office applications. You can see similarities and differences by the name of the arguments defined for each method.

Document Collection Object	Definition of the *Open* Method
Word - Documents	Function Open(**FileName**, [ConfirmConversions], [ReadOnly], [AddToRecentFiles], [PasswordDocument], [PasswordTemplate], [Revert], [WritePasswordDocument], [WritePasswordTemplate], [Format], [Encoding], [Visible]) As Document
Excel - Workbooks	Function Open(**FileName** As String, [UpdateLinks], [ReadOnly], [Format], [Password], [WriteResPassword], [IgnoreReadOnlyRecommended], [Origin], [Delimiter], [Editable], [Notify], [Converter], [AddToMru]) As Workbook
PowerPoint - Presentations	Function Open(**FileName** As String, [ReadOnly As MsoTriState], [Untitled As MsoTriState], [WithWindow As MsoTriState = msoTrue]) As Presentation

Excel also provides an *OpenText* method on the *Workbooks* collection object. In Word and PowerPoint, you can use the *Open* method to open Text files (*.txt) or any other file type listed in the Files of Type drop-down list in the Open dialog box. In Access, you can use the Microsoft ActiveX Data Objects 2.1 Library to open an existing database with the *Open* method, as described in the integrated Office solution in Chapter 8.

Using the *Open* Method To Open Web Pages and Documents on a Web Server

You can use the *Open* method to open the common Office document types, such as Word documents and templates (*.doc, *.dot), Excel workbooks and templates (*.xls, *.xlt), and PowerPoint presentations and templates (*.ppt, *.pot). You can also use the *Open* method to open Web pages (*.htm, *.html). You don't need to specify anything different in the *Open* method, as long as you specify a filename that is fully qualified with the pathname.

(continued)

If the Web page or Office document exists on an HTTP or FTP server, the filename specified in the *FileName* argument is similar to the address typed in the Address bar of your Web browser. For example, if you specify *http://www.microsoft.com/* as the *FileName* argument in the *Open* method in Word's *Documents* collection object, Office will download the default Web page from this Web site address and load it into Word. If you type the following line of the code in the Immediate window in the Visual Basic Editor in Word, a read-only HTML document is opened.

```
Documents.Open FileName:="http://www.microsoft.com/"
```

If your computer is not connected to the Internet, this line of code will generate the run-time error '424: Object required'. If your computer is connected to the Internet, an error may occur if it cannot connect to the address. If this is the case, start the Web browser on your machine and type in the Web address specified above to ensure that navigation to this site is possible from your computer. If your computer is connected to an Intranet, change the address of this line of code to an address on your Intranet.

Using the *SaveAs* method described later in this chapter, you can save this Web page to a different file folder or server location.

Using the *Add* Method to Create New Documents

You use the *Add* method to create a new document in Word, Excel, and PowerPoint. You'll find the *Add* method in many places throughout the Office objects, and you use it consistently when adding an item to a collection. When you want to add an item to the collection of documents, use the *Add* method to create a new document on the *Documents, Workbooks*, and *Presentations* collection objects, respectively.

The following table lists the definition of the *Add* method in Word, Excel, and PowerPoint for the *Documents, Workbooks*, and *Presentations* collection objects, respectively. These definitions are copied from the Details pane of the Object Browser in the Visual Basic Editor.

Document Collection Object	Definition of the *Add* Method
Word - Documents	Function Add([Template], [NewTemplate], [DocumentType], [Visible]) As Document
Excel - Workbooks	Function Add([Template]) As Workbook
PowerPoint - Presentations	Function Add([WithWindow As MsoTriState = msoTrue]) As Presentation

Word

When the *Add* method on the *Documents* collection is executed, you can specify the *Visible* argument to False so that you create the new document in the background. You can then add content to the document, and when you're done you can make the document visible. The following procedure copies the contents of the main text of the active document in Word and creates a new document with the copied content.

The procedure adds the document invisibly so the user doesn't see the content being pasted. It also applies the styles of the template attached to the active document to the new document. You can do a lot more document and content manipulation when the document is invisible. Word provides the *Visible* argument in both the *Add* and *Open* methods of the *Documents* collection object. The *Visible* argument is new to Word in Office 2000 and isn't available in Word 97.

```
Sub AddDocument()
    Dim docNewCopy As Document, sTmplName As String
    Dim iViewType As WdViewType

    With ActiveDocument
        .Range.Copy
        sTmplName = .AttachedTemplate.FullName
    End With
    iViewType = ActiveWindow.View.Type

    Set docNewCopy = Application.Documents.Add( _
        Template:=sTmplName, Visible:=False)
    With docNewCopy
        .AttachedTemplate = ActiveDocument.AttachedTemplate
        .Range.Paste
        If Application.Visible = True Then
            .ActiveWindow.Visible = True
        End If
        .ActiveWindow.View.Type = iViewType
    End With
End Sub
```

As the Set statement in this procedure shows, the *Visible* argument of the *Add* method of the *Documents* collection object is set to False. The new document is added to the *Documents* collection without a window (it's invisible). The *Document* object returned by the *Add* method is assigned to the *docNewCopy* variable. This variable is used in the With...End block to paste text in its main range as well as to attach the template used in the original document.

The line `.ActiveWindow.Visible = True` in the With...End block creates a new document window for the invisible document. The ActiveWindow property on the *Document* object returns a *Window* object in Word. The Visible property on the *Window* object is then set to True. This line should always be used to make an invisible Word document visible. The last line in the With...End block changes the view of the document window to the same type as the original document window.

Note The If...Then statement determines if the Word application window is visible. If it is, the Visible property on the *Window* object returned by the ActiveWindow property is set to True. If it isn't, you don't need to set the Visible property. That's because if (and when) the Word application window is made visible, by setting the Visible property on the *Application* object to True, you make all invisible documents visible. This behavior is similar to PowerPoint's.

Excel

Unlike Word and PowerPoint, Excel doesn't provide an argument to create a document invisibly. However, you can set the Visible property of a workbook window to False, manipulate its contents, and then make the workbook window visible again. In the following procedure, the *Add* method on the *Workbooks* collection object returns a *Workbook* object that's assigned to the *wbNew* variable. The visible state of the workbook's window is immediately set to False. The procedure adds a new workbook, changes its name to "My Data," and sets the workbook's window to True.

```
Sub AddWorkbook()
    Dim wbNew As Workbook, shNew As Worksheet
    Set wbNew = Application.Workbooks.Add
    With wbNew
        wbNew.Windows(1).Visible = False
        Set shNew = .Worksheets.Add
        shNew.Name = "My Data"
        wbNew.Windows(1).Visible = True
    End With
End Sub
```

Within the With...End block, you could add or manipulate a lot more content, and you may want to do that when your program needs to create a new workbook, to insert data from a database into worksheets, to create new charts, and then to make the workbook visible to the user. In Chapter 8, this technique of creating an Excel workbook invisibly is used when a workbook containing a worksheet and chart is created from data in an Access database.

PowerPoint

The one and only argument that PowerPoint provides in the *Add* method on the *Presentations* collection object is the *WithWindow* argument. The functionality provided by the *WithWindow* argument is equivalent to Word's *Visible* argument in the *Add* method of the *Documents* collection object. PowerPoint provides the *WithWindow* argument in both the *Add* and *Open* methods of the *Presentations* collection object. (PowerPoint 97 also provides this argument.) The following procedure adds a new presentation and assigns the *Presentation* object returned by the *Add* method to the *presNew* variable. Within the With...End block, you use a For...Next loop to add five slides. You set the text of each slide's title to "Slide" plus the number of the slide.

```
Sub AddPresentation()
    Dim sld As Slide, i As Integer
    Dim presNew As Presentation
    Set presNew = Presentations.Add(WithWindow:=msoFalse)
    With presNew
        For i = 1 To 5
            Set sld = .Slides.Add(i, ppLayoutText)
            sld.Shapes.Title.TextFrame _
                .TextRange = "Slide " & i
        Next i
        If Application.Visible = msoTrue Then
            .NewWindow
        End If
    End With
End Sub
```

As in the previous examples in Word and Excel, you can do more content insertion and manipulation within the With...End block before making the invisible presentation visible. In Chapter 8, this technique of creating a PowerPoint presentation invisibly is used when a presentation is created from data in an Access database.

Note The If...Then statement determines if the PowerPoint application window is visible. If it is, the *NewWindow* method on the *Presentation* object is executed. If it isn't, you don't need to use the *NewWindow* method. That's because if (and when) the PowerPoint application window is made visible, by setting the Visible property on the *Application* object to True, you make all invisible presentations visible. This behavior is similar to Word's. If you did use the *NewWindow* method while the PowerPoint application window is invisible and the application window is set to visible, two document windows will exist for the new presentation: one originally created with the *Add* method on the *Presentations* object and the other created with the *NewWindow* method.

Document Windows in the Windows Taskbar

Word, Excel, and PowerPoint all display a document item on the Windows Taskbar each time you create or open a document. If you create and open a number of documents in your solution, you may want to use the technique of creating and opening a document invisibly, as previously described in the Word, Excel, and PowerPoint examples. You can also set a property in Excel, PowerPoint, and Access so that the document windows aren't displayed in the Windows Taskbar. The check box "Windows in Taskbar" is provided in Excel, PowerPoint, and Access's Options dialog boxes under the Show group of the View tab.

(continued)

Document Windows in the Windows Taskbar *(continued)*

These applications also provide a programmatic way to set this option through Visual Basic code. In Excel and PowerPoint, you can use the ShowWindowsInTaskbar Boolean property on the *Application* object. This returns the state of the check box and gives the developer the opportunity to change it.

```
Sub ShowInTaskbarCheck()
    Dim bShowInTaskbar As Boolean
    bShowInTaskbar = Application.ShowWindowsInTaskbar
    Application.ShowWindowsInTaskbar = False
    ' do something that creates/manipulates documents
    Application.ShowWindowsInTaskbar = bShowInTaskbar
End Sub
```

In this code you set the declared *bShowInTaskbar* Boolean variable to the current state of the ShowWindowsInTaskbar property. The property is then set to False and documents and content can be manipulated. Then the ShowWindowsInTaskbar property is returned to the original value stored in the *bShowInTaskbar* Boolean variable. The recommended way to insert and manipulate multiple documents and not distract the user on-screen is to use the techniques of creating or opening a document invisibly. However, the description of ShowWindowsInTaskbar here is provided as an alternative (mainly for Visual Basic programs created in Office 97).

Save and Close

If you click Save As on the File menu in Word, Excel, or PowerPoint, you'll see the Save As dialog box. You'll also see it if you click Close on the File menu and the document hasn't been saved before. You use the Save As dialog box to navigate to a folder, specify a filename and then click Save to save the file in the specified file folder. When you need to save a document loaded in Word, Excel, or PowerPoint using Visual Basic code, the functional equivalent is the *SaveAs* method.

The *SaveAs* method allows your programs to save documents loaded in an Office application in the file system on the user's machine, on a network share, and on an HTTP or FTP server. You can use the *SaveAs* method to save any file type listed in the Files of Type drop-down list in the Save As dialog box. The *Close* method allows your programs to close documents, and this method often follows the *SaveAs* method.

What the *SaveAs* Method Does

The *SaveAs* method saves a document in an existing collection of documents in an Office application, and, hence, the *SaveAs* method in Word, Excel, and PowerPoint is accessible from the *Document, Workbook,* and *Presentation* objects, respectively. In the definition of the *SaveAs* method in Word, Excel, and

PowerPoint, the first argument, named *FileName*, allows you to specify a valid filename that is fully qualified with a valid pathname. Using the techniques described in the first section of this chapter, "File Management," you build a string to be passed into the *FileName* argument of the *SaveAs* method.

You use the second argument of the *SaveAs* method, named *FileFormat*, to specify what file format you want to use to save the document. You'll get more details about this in the "Saving Files in the Most Common File Formats" section later in this chapter. The following table lists the definition of the *SaveAs* method in Word, Excel, and PowerPoint. These definitions are copied from the Details pane of the Object Browser in the Visual Basic Editor and are listed to show a side-by-side comparison of the method in each application. The *FileName* and *FileFormat* are the only two arguments that are found in all three versions of the *SaveAs* method.

Document Object	Definition of the *Save As* Method
Word—Document	Sub SaveAs([FileName], [FileFormat], [LockComments], [Password], [AddToRecentFiles], [WritePassword], [ReadOnlyRecommended], [EmbedTrueTypeFonts], [SaveNativePictureFormat], [SaveFormsData], [SaveAsAOCELetter])
Excel—Workbook	Sub SaveAs([Filename], [FileFormat], [Password], [WriteResPassword], [ReadOnlyRecommended], [CreateBackup], [AccessMode As XlSaveAsAccessMode = xlNoChange], [ConflictResolution], [AddToMru], [TextCodepage], [TextVisualLayout])
PowerPoint—Presentation	Sub SaveAs(FileName As String, [FileFormat As PpSaveAsFileType = ppSaveAsPresentation], [EmbedTrueTypeFonts As MsoTriState = msoTriStateMixed])

Methods and Properties Related to the *SaveAs* Method

A number of methods and properties related to the *SaveAs* method aren't discussed in detail here. These members include *Save, Saved, SaveCopyAs, Name, Path, FullName*, and *DisplayAlerts*. With the exception of *SaveCopyAs* and *DisplayAlerts*, all these members exist in Word, Excel, and PowerPoint.

You should also note that Excel provides a *SaveAs* method on the *Worksheet* object and *Chart* object. This allows you save an individual worksheet or a chart in a workbook to a file on disk. Only Excel provides this ability to save granular parts of a document. In Word and PowerPoint you can copy a portion of a document, create a new document, paste the contents, and then save the new document.

The *Save* method   In all three applications, you use the *Save* method when you don't need to specify a filename. If you've previously used the *SaveAs* method to save a file, you can call the *Save* method on the *Document, Workbook*, or *Presentation* object to save changes in a document. If the document in Word and Excel hasn't been saved before, the Save As dialog box prompts the user for a filename when the *Save* method is executed. In Word and Excel, the Save As dialog box isn't displayed if the DisplayAlerts property on the *Application* object is set to wdAlertsNone in Word and False in Excel. The following sidebar discusses the DisplayAlerts property.

In PowerPoint, if the presentation hasn't been saved before, PowerPoint will save the file without prompting the user for a filename when the *Save* method is executed. PowerPoint assigns a default name to the file. The default name is the name given to a presentation when it's first created. The Name property on the Presentation, as described in the section below entitled '"Determining the filename, path, and fully qualified name," is the name used as the filename.

The *Saved* property   Word, Excel, and PowerPoint all provide the Saved property on the *Document, Workbook*, and *Presentation* objects, respectively. This property returns True if a document hasn't changed since it was last saved. If the Saved property returns False, Word and Excel display a prompt telling the user to save changes when closing the document. You can explicitly set the Saved property to True, but if you do, the user won't be prompted to save changes when closing the document and all changes made to the document since it was last saved will be lost. Commonly, you set the Saved property explicitly to True if a modified document should be closed without either saving it or prompting the user to save it.

The *SaveCopyAs* method   In Excel and PowerPoint, the *SaveCopyAs* method saves a copy of the workbook or presentation to a file but doesn't modify the open workbook or presentation. You can access the *SaveCopyAs* method from the *Workbook* and *Presentation* objects. The *SaveCopyAs* method is useful when you want to make a copy of a workbook or presentation in another file format or filename but don't want to modify the current file format or change the location of a workbook or presentation.

Using DisplayAlerts to Prevent Built-In Dialog Boxes and Alerts From Being Displayed

When you call methods like the *Save* method, the Office application will, depending on certain conditions, display a built-in dialog box. In the case of the *Save* method, as previously noted, if the document hasn't been saved before, the Save As dialog box prompts the user for a filename when the *Save* method is called. In some cases, you may not want the Office application to display built-in dialog boxes like the Save As dialog box. In addition, you may not want the Office application to display messages such as "Do you want to save the changes you made to documentX?" when, by clicking Close on the File menu, you close a document that was modified but not saved before.

(continued)

**Using DisplayAlerts to Prevent Built-In
Dialog Boxes and Alerts From Being Displayed** *(continued)*

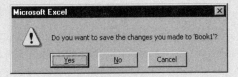

In Word and Excel, to prevent the application from displaying dialog boxes and message boxes, you can use the DisplayAlerts property on the *Application* object. If the property is set to wdAlertsAll in Word or True in Excel, Word and Excel display certain built-in dialog boxes or message boxes when your Visual Basic code is running. The default value is wdAlertsAll in Word and True in Excel. If the property is set to wdAlertsNone in Word or False in Excel, no built-in dialog boxes or message boxes are displayed when your code is running. If a dialog box or message box normally requires user input, Word and Excel choose the default response.

```
Application.DisplayAlerts = wdAlertsAll      'Word
Application.DisplayAlerts = True             'Excel
```

The DisplayAlerts property doesn't exist in PowerPoint, and PowerPoint never displays any built-in dialog or message boxes when your code is running. The behavior in PowerPoint when code is running is similar to what happens when you set DisplayAlerts to wdAlertsNone in Word or to False in Excel. In most cases, if user input is required, PowerPoint uses the default response.

Instead of DisplayAlerts, Access has something similar called UserControl, which you can access from the *Application* object. If UserControl is set to True, built-in dialog boxes or message boxes are displayed. If it's set to False, they're not. In Outlook, dialog boxes or message boxes are displayed when code is running, but in most cases you can write code so that no built-in dialog boxes or message boxes have to be displayed when your code is running.

Determining the filename, path, and fully qualified name   When you open or save a document in Word, Excel, or PowerPoint, you can use the Name, Path, and FullName properties on the *Document, Workbook*, or *Presentation* objects, respectively, to determine the file's name without the path, the file's path only, or the full name that includes both the filename and the path. The value returned by the FullName property is often referred to as the fully qualified filename and it's a concatenation of the Path and Name property values. The following procedure works in a code module in the Visual Basic Editor in Word—though it can work in Excel and PowerPoint if you change the expression in the With line to `ActiveWorkbook` and `ActivePresentation` respectively. You'll also need to change the *FileFormat* argument to a value listed in the Binary column of the table below.

```
Sub SaveAsDOC()
    Dim sTempPath As String
    sTempPath = "C:\Temp\"
    With ActiveDocument
        .SaveAs FileName:=sTempPath & "WordDoc", _
            FileFormat:=wdFormatDocument
        Debug.Print .Name
        Debug.Print .Path
        Debug.Print .FullName
    End With
End Sub
```

In the Immediate window in the Visual Basic Editor in Word, the following three values are printed: WordDoc.doc, C:\Temp, and C:\Temp\WordDoc.doc.

Determining if a document is new and has yet to be saved   The most common way to determine if a document in Word, Excel, and PowerPoint is a new document and has yet to be saved is to use the Path property on the *Document, Workbook*, and *Presentation* objects, respectively. If the Path property returns an empty string, the document has yet to be saved to disk. If the Path property returns a valid path string, the document has been saved to disk.

Saving Files in the Most Common File Formats

The file types listed in the Save as Type drop-down list in the Save As dialog box are all represented as WdSaveFormat, XlFileFormat, or PpSaveAsFileType constants in Word, Excel, and PowerPoint, respectively. The two file formats listed in the table below are the binary and HTML file formats, although Word, Excel, and PowerPoint all provide at least eight more possible file types.

The binary file format refers to a file with the extension doc in Word, xls in Excel, and ppt in PowerPoint. The HTML file format refers to a file with the extension htm or html. The following table lists the two common file formats you use to save a Word, Excel, or PowerPoint document. You'd use one of the values in the last two columns when you specify the *FileFormat* argument in the *SaveAs* method.

Application	Constant Name	Binary	HTML
Word	WdSaveFormat	wdFormatDocument (extension: .doc)	wdFormatHTML
Excel	XlFileFormat	xlWorkbookNormal (extension: .xls)	xlHTML
PowerPoint	PpSaveAsFileType	ppSaveAsPresentation (extension: .ppt)	ppSaveAsHTML

Office 2000 introduced the HTML file format as a native format supported by Word, Excel, and PowerPoint. This means that you can take any document, workbook, or presentation, save it as a Web page in HTML file format, and then reopen the file in the application that created the HTML document.

```
Sub SaveAsHTML()
    Dim sTempPath As String
    sTempPath = "C:\Temp\"
    ActiveDocument.SaveAs FileName:=sTempPath & "WordDoc", _
        FileFormat:=wdFormatHTML
    ActiveWorkbook.SaveAs FileName:=sTempPath & "ExcelDoc", _
        FileFormat:=xlHtml
    ActivePresentation.SaveAs FileName:=sTempPath & "PPTPres", _
        FileFormat:=ppSaveAsHTML
End Sub
```

This procedure lists the code that uses the *SaveAs* method in Word, Excel, and PowerPoint to save a document as an HTML file. You can easily change the line of code to save the active document in binary file format by changing the value of the *FileFormat* argument to a value listed in the Binary column of the preceding table.

You can copy this code into a code module in the Visual Basic Editor in Word, Excel, or PowerPoint, but you need to remove the lines that don't apply to the application. For example, if you want to copy the procedure in the Visual Basic Editor in Word, remove the lines starting with `ActiveWorkbook` and `ActivePresentation`, which are used in Excel and PowerPoint, respectively. The code for all three applications is shown above in one procedure to show the similarity in the use of the *SaveAs* method when specifying the *Filename* and *FileFormat* arguments.

Tip   To determine the file format of a document that's saved in Excel, you can use the FileFormat property on the *Workbook* object. In Word, you can use the combination of the Type and Kind properties on the *Document* object in order to determine if the document is a template, a document, or an e-mail message. PowerPoint has no property that indicates the file type of the presentation. However, in all three applications you can use the techniques described earlier in this chapter to parse the filename of the document and retrieve its extension. The extension will then indicate what file format the document has been saved in.

Preview Saved HTML Pages in the Web Browser

If you click Web Page Preview on the File menu in Word, Excel, or PowerPoint, a copy of the active document is saved as a Web page (an HTML file) and displayed in the Web browser on your machine. You can mimic this behavior by saving the active document using *SaveAs* or *SaveCopyAs* in Excel and PowerPoint and then using the *ShellExecute* Windows application programming interface (API) to load the Web page document in the Web browser.

Insert a new standard code module in the Visual Basic Editor in Excel, type the following code, place the cursor in the *SaveAsHTMLPreview* procedure, and press F5. The procedure saves the active workbook in Excel in HTML file format and displays the resulting saved document in the file system in the user's Web browser.

```
Declare Function ShellExecute Lib "shell32.dll" _
    Alias "ShellExecuteA" ( _
        ByVal Hwnd As Long, _
        ByVal lpOperation As String, _
        ByVal lpFile As String, _
        ByVal lpParameters As String, _
        ByVal lpDirectory As String, _
        ByVal nShowCmd As Long _
    ) As Long


Sub LoadFile(FileName As String)
    ShellExecute 0, "Open", FileName, "", "", 1
End Sub


Sub SaveAsHTMLPreview()
    Dim sFileName As String
    Application.DisplayAlerts = False
    sFileName = "C:\Temp\ExcelDoc.HTM"
    ActiveWorkbook.SaveAs FileName:=sFileName, _
        FileFormat:=xlHtml
    LoadFile FileName:=sFileName
    Application.DisplayAlerts = True
End Sub
```

The *Close* Method

The *Close* method in Word, Excel, and PowerPoint closes a document in an existing collection of documents. You can access it from the *Document, Workbook*, and *Presentation* objects, respectively. In the definition of the *Close* method in Word and Excel, the first argument, named *SaveChanges*, allows you to specify whether changes to the document are saved when the document is closed.

The following table lists the definition of the *Close* method in Word, Excel, and PowerPoint. These definitions are copied from the Details pane of the Object Browser in the Visual Basic Editor and are listed to show a side-by-side comparison of the method in each application.

Document Object	Definition of the *Close* Method
Word—Document	Sub Close([SaveChanges], [OriginalFormat], [RouteDocument])
Excel—Workbook	Sub Close([SaveChanges], [Filename], [RouteWorkbook])
PowerPoint—Presentation	Sub Close()

All arguments in the *Close* method in Word and Excel are optional. In most cases, you won't need to specify the *SaveChanges* argument because you can use the *Save* or *SaveAs* method before the *Close* method. For example, the following procedure saves the active workbook in Excel and then closes the workbook.

```
Sub SaveAndClose()
    ActiveWorkbook.SaveAs "C:\Temp\Test.xls"
    ActiveWorkbook.Close
End Sub
```

In PowerPoint, if the presentation has been modified when the *Close* method is called, PowerPoint doesn't display an alert prompting the user to save changes and doesn't save changes to the presentation before closing it. Changes made to the presentation since the previous save are lost. If you want to ensure that all changes are saved, you must explicitly call the *Save* method or the *SaveAs* method on the *Presentation* object before using *Close*.

Print

If you click Print on the File menu in Word, Excel, or PowerPoint, you see the Print dialog box. You use it to set print criteria such as the print range or number of copies, and then you click OK to print the file through the specified printer. When you need to print a document loaded in Word, Excel, or PowerPoint using Visual Basic code, the functional equivalent is the *PrintOut* method. The *PrintOut* method allows your programs to print documents loaded in an Office application using a specified printer. You can use the *PrintOut* method (or *PrintOptions* object in PowerPoint) to print any file with the settings provided in the Print dialog box.

What the *PrintOut* Method Does

The *PrintOut* method prints a document, and you can access it from the *Document*, *Workbook*, and *Presentation* objects in Word, Excel, and PowerPoint, respectively. The *PrintOut* methods in Word, Excel, and PowerPoint have four arguments in common: *From, To, Copies,* and *Collate.* The table on the next page lists the definition of the *PrintOut* method in Word, Excel, and PowerPoint. These definitions are copied from the Details pane of the Object Browser in the Visual Basic Editor and are listed to show a side-by-side comparison of the method in each application.

Application	Definition of the *PrintOut* Method
Word—Document	Sub PrintOut([Background], [Append], [Range], [OutputFileName], [From], [To], [Item], [Copies], [Pages], [PageType], [PrintToFile], [Collate], [ActivePrinterMacGX], [ManualDuplexPrint], [PrintZoomColumn], [PrintZoomRow], [PrintZoomPaperWidth], [PrintZoomPaperHeight])
Excel—Workbook	Sub PrintOut([From], [To], [Copies], [Preview], [ActivePrinter], [PrintToFile], [Collate], [PrToFileName])
PowerPoint—Presentation	Sub PrintOut([From As Long = -1], [To As Long = -1], [PrintToFile As String], [Copies As Long], [Collate As MsoTriState])

The following procedure lists the code that uses the *PrintOut* method in Word, Excel, and PowerPoint. You can copy it into a code module in the Visual Basic Editor in Word, Excel, or PowerPoint, but you need to remove the lines that don't apply to the application. For example, if you copy the procedure in the Visual Basic Editor in Word, remove the lines starting with ActiveWorkbook and ActivePresentation, which are used in Excel and PowerPoint, respectively.

```
Sub PrintDocument()
    ActiveDocument.PrintOut From:="1", To:="2", _
        Copies:=2, Collate:=True
    ActiveWorkbook.PrintOut From:=1, To:=2, _
        Copies:=2, Collate:=True
    ActivePresentation.PrintOut From:=1, To:=2, _
        Copies:=2, Collate:=True
End Sub
```

The code for all three applications is shown above in one procedure to show the similarity in the use of the *PrintOut* method when four of the most common arguments of the *PrintOut* method are used. The *From* and *To* arguments, however, mean different things in each application. In Word, Excel, and PowerPoint, the *From* and *To* arguments refer to pages, worksheets, and slides, respectively. Note that the type of value required for the *From* and *To* arguments in Word is a value of type String. Therefore, quotes are used around the value of the argument. In Excel and PowerPoint, the values of the *From* and *To* arguments are of type Integer.

Differences in PowerPoint

In addition to the *PrintOut* method on the *Presentation* object, which is similar to the *PrintOut* method in Word and Excel, PowerPoint provides a *PrintOptions* object, which contains print options for a presentation. The properties on the *PrintOptions* object in PowerPoint are functionally equivalent to passing arguments to the *PrintOut* method in Word and Excel. The unique functionality provided by the *PrintOptions* object is that its settings are stored with the presentation so that when you next open and print the presentation, you can use the same options without resetting them. The following procedure is functionally equivalent to the *PrintOut* method listed in the previous procedure. Two collated copies of the first and second slides in the active presentation are printed.

```
Sub UsingPrintOptionsInPowerPoint()
    With ActivePresentation
        With .PrintOptions
            .RangeType = ppPrintSlideRange
            .Ranges.Add 1, 2
            .NumberOfCopies = 2
            .Collate = True
            .PrintColorType = ppPrintColor
            .PrintHiddenSlides = True
            .FitToPage = True
            .FrameSlides = True
            .OutputType = ppPrintOutputSlides
        End With
        .PrintOut
    End With
End Sub
```

You use the RangeType property to indicate that only part of the presentation is to be printed. You then use the Ranges property to specify which slides to print.

Using ShellExecute to Print a File

As discussed earlier in this chapter in the "File Management" section, you can use the Windows API ShellExecute to print files without explicitly starting an application like Word, Excel, or PowerPoint, opening the appropriate file, and calling the *PrintOut* method. Insert a new standard code module in the Visual Basic Editor in any Office application, type the following code, place the cursor in the *PrintMiscFile* procedure, and then press F5. The file specified by the string "C:\Temp\docwrite.html" is printed. Change this file string to a valid file on your computer.

```
Declare Function ShellExecute Lib "shell32.dll" _
    Alias "ShellExecuteA" ( _
        ByVal Hwnd As Long, _
        ByVal lpOperation As String, _
        ByVal lpFile As String, _
        ByVal lpParameters As String, _
        ByVal lpDirectory As String, _
        ByVal nShowCmd As Long _
    ) As Long
```

```
Sub PrintFile(FileName As String)
    ShellExecute 0, "Print", FileName, "", "", 1
End Sub

Sub PrintMiscFile()
    PrintFile "C:\Temp\docwrite.html"
End Sub
```

Using Document Properties

Each file you create in an Office application contains a set of document properties. The set is a combination of built-in document properties that Office defines—including Title, Author, Subject, and Comments—and custom document properties that you can define for the document. You conduct the setting and retrieval of built-in and custom document properties in the user interface through the Properties dialog box. Clicking Properties on the File menu in Word, Excel, or PowerPoint accesses the Properties dialog box. In Access, click Database Properties on the File menu.

> **Note**   The object model associated with the document properties of a file is provided through the Microsoft Office 9.0 Object Library. You access the document properties through the BuiltInDocumentProperties property in Word, Excel, and PowerPoint, as the example below demonstrates. In Access, setting and returning document properties of a database is slightly more involved. You can set the built-in and custom properties by using the *SummaryInfo* and *UserDefined Document* object in the *Documents* collection. For more information, in Access ask the Assistant for help using the words "database properties."

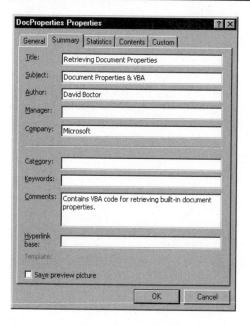

Retrieve Built-In Document Properties

Suppose you want to build an index of all the documents kept on a local file server, cataloged by such document properties as Author, Title, Subject, and Comments. You retrieve these and other built-in document properties through the *DocumentProperties* object using the BuiltInDocumentProperties property of Word's *Document* object, Excel's *Workbook* object, and PowerPoint's *Presentation* object.

1. Start Word. Open the Visual Basic Editor, insert a new module, and create a new procedure by typing **Sub GetDocumentProperties**.

2. Add the following With...End block:

```
With ActiveDocument.BuiltInDocumentProperties
End With
```

Note   If you're running this procedure in PowerPoint, you should change `ActiveDocument` to `ActivePresentation`. If you're running it in Excel, change it to `ActiveWorkbook`.

---

3. In the With...End block created in step 2, type the following lines:

```
Debug.Print "Author: " & .Item("Author").Value
Debug.Print "Subject: " & .Item("Subject").Value
Debug.Print "Title: " & .Item("Title").Value
Debug.Print "Comments: " & .Item("Comments").Value
```

These properties are common to Word, Excel, and PowerPoint, and they always return a value. If any one isn't set, the value returns an empty string. The `Debug.Print` statement prints the specified string in the Immediate window, which you can display by clicking Immediate Window on the View menu in the Editor. The *MsgBox* function can serve the same purpose, but it displays the value in a message box that you have to close in order to continue working with the application or the Editor. The Debug.Print statement allows you to continue working without disruption.

4. Just after the built-in properties specified above and before the `End With` statement, add the following lines:

```
Debug.Print "Number of Words: " & _
    .Item("Number of Words").Value
Debug.Print "Number of Pages: " & _
    .Item("Number of Pages").Value
```

Unlike in step 3, where the properties you added are common to Word, Excel, and PowerPoint, here few built-in document properties are specific to either Word or PowerPoint. These properties are listed in the Statistics tab in the Properties dialog box.

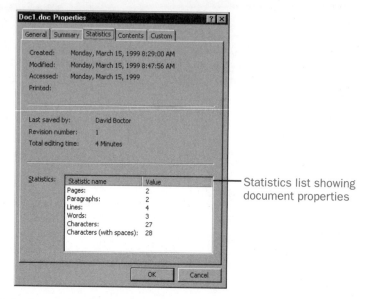

Statistics list showing document properties

5. If the Immediate Window isn't open, click Immediate Window on the View menu.

6. Place the cursor in the *GetDocumentProperties* procedure and press F5 to run it. The specified built-in document properties for Word appear in the Immediate window.

How Retrieving Some Document Properties Results in an Error

Some properties, such as Author and Title, can only be returned and can't be set by the user. These properties are invalid until the first time they are set by the Office application. For example, the built-in document property Last Save Time isn't valid until the first time you save the document, workbook, or presentation. The Last Print Date built-in document property is also invalid until the first time you print the document, workbook, or presentation.

```
Debug.Print "Last Save Time: " & _
    .Item("Last Save Time").Value
Debug.Print "Last Print Date: " & _
    .Item("Last Print Date").Value
```

If you add the two lines above to the With…End block added in step 2 of the preceding example, an error would occur, and the valid values wouldn't be displayed in the Immediate window.

Set Document Properties

Because you don't usually set document properties first in a document, you can easily overlook them. Some companies require that every document that's sent electronically to customers has its document properties set. For example, you may want to explicitly set the built-in Company document property to be the same company-wide and set some comments in the built-in Comments document property. In the following example, document properties are set for the active document. However, in Chapter 5, document events such as Save and Close are used to prompt the user to set specific document properties before these actions are completed.

1. Start the Visual Basic Editor in Word and click Module on the Insert menu.

2. In the code module, add the following lines:

```
Sub SetProperties
    With ActiveDocument.BuiltInDocumentProperties
        .Item("Company").Value = "My Company"
        .Item("Comments").Value = _
            "Please send mail to Dave@MyCompany.com"
    End With
End Sub
```

3. Place the cursor in the procedure and press F5.
    The values for the built-in document properties Company and Comments are set.

Note   Because you're altering the document properties, this results in a state in which the document has been changed. Therefore, when you close the document and the document properties are changed, an alert is displayed asking whether you want to save the document. If you do not want this alert to be displayed, use code to explicitly save the document, using the Save method on the *Document* object after the With...End block.

---

4. On the File menu, click Properties. The property information is added to the Company and Comments text boxes on the Summary tab.

Get Current User's Name

When you want to build an index of all the documents kept on a file server, cataloged by such document properties as Author, Title, Subject, and Comments, you may want to retrieve information such as the user's network logon name (if the user is using a machine on a computer network). This can allow you, for example, to build a change history table stored in a document or on a server. This information may be useful when you handle a document's Open, Save, or

Close event, allowing you to automatically enter information into a document when the document is saved or closed. The next chapter discusses the use of document events, such as New, Open, Save, Close, and Print.

Using the GetUserName Windows API   To retrieve the user's network logon name, you can use the Windows application programming interface (API) function *GetUserName*. The GetUserName Windows API returns the name of the user currently logged on to the system. If the user isn't logged onto the system, GetUserName returns an empty string. On a Windows NT 4 or Windows 2000 system, the user is required to log on before accessing the computer's file system; on a Windows 95 or Windows 98 system, however, the user is not required to log on. In the Visual Basic Editor of any Office application, insert a new standard code module and copy the following two functions along with the declaration, which must be typed at the top of the code module.

```
Declare Function GetUserName Lib "advapi32.dll" _
    Alias "GetUserNameA" ( _
        ByVal lpBuffer As String, _
        nSize As Long _
    ) As Long

Function CurrentUserName() As String
    Dim sBuffer As String * 25, lReturn As Long
    lReturn = GetUserName(sBuffer, 25)
    CurrentUserName = Left$(sBuffer, InStr(sBuffer, Chr(0)) - 1)
End Function

Sub GetCurrentUserName()
    Dim sUserName As String
    sUserName = CurrentUserName
    If Len(sUserName) Then
        Debug.Print sUserName
    Else
        Debug.Print "User not logged on."
    End If
End Sub
```

Place the cursor in the *GetCurrentUserName* procedure and press F5. The procedure assigns the string variable *sUserName* to the return value of the custom *CurrentUserName* function, defined above as the *GetCurrentUserName* procedure. In the custom *CurrentUserName* function, the procedure calls the Windows API GetUserName and removes any trailing spaces on the return string value. In the *GetCurrentUserName* procedure, if the length of the return value of the custom *CurrentUserName* function is more than zero, the user's name is printed to the Immediate window in the Visual Basic Editor. If the length of the string is zero, the Windows API GetUserName returns an empty string, indicating that the user isn't logged onto the computer system.

Managing Items in Outlook

This chapter has described and compared the methods and properties related to creating or opening documents in Word, Excel, and PowerPoint. Chapters 7 and 8 describe integrated Office solutions involving the creation of documents and content based on data in an Access database. They also describe the creation of an Outlook mail message. Below is a procedure similar to the one used in Chapters 7 and 8. It's provided here in the context of creating types of documents in other Office applications.

In the Visual Basic Editor in Outlook, insert a new standard code module and copy the following procedure. You can see the similarities of the methods for saving, closing, and printing. Outlook uses the *CreateItem* method to create all item types supported in Outlook, such as appointment, mail, contact, and notes. In other Office applications, you use the *Add* method to create new documents in which content will reside.

```
Sub NewMailItem()
    Dim itemNewMail As Outlook.MailItem
    Set itemNewMail = Application.CreateItem(olMailItem)
    With itemNewMail
        .To = "Energy Committee"
        .CC = "Executive Board"
        .Subject = "New energy usage documents"
        .Body = "The following documents reflect" & _
            " the energy usage for the circuit." & _
            vbCrLf
        '.Attachments.Add sFile
        .Display
        .Save
        .SaveAs Path:="C:\Temp\" & .Subject & ".msg", _
            Type:=olMSG
        MsgBox "Item has been saved to the Drafts folder."
        .PrintOut
        .Close SaveMode:=olPromptForSave
    End With
End Sub
```

The *Save* method in Outlook saves the mail item in this procedure to the Drafts folder. The *SaveAs* method saves a copy of the mail item to the file system. The *Path* argument in the *SaveAs* method in Outlook is equivalent to the *FileName* argument in the *SaveAs* method in Word, Excel, and PowerPoint. In the procedure above, you use the subject as the filename of the saved message. This is similar to Outlook's functionality in which you open a mail message in Outlook, click Save As on the File menu, and then click Save in the SaveAs dialog box.

The file's default name is the subject of the mail message. The second argument of the *SaveAs* method is named *Type* and is equivalent to the

FileFormat argument in the *SaveAs* method in Word, Excel, and PowerPoint. The *Type* argument can be one of the OlSaveAsType constants, including olDoc, olHTML, olMSG, olRTF, or olTXT. The constant olDoc saves the message as a Word document.

The *PrintOut* method here doesn't take any arguments, unlike the *PrintOut* method in Word, Excel, and PowerPoint. It simply prints out the Outlook item. The above procedure prints the mail message.

Finally, the *Close* method is similar to Word's and Excel's in that it provides an argument that tells the application whether the user should be prompted to save. In the procedure above, you set the *SaveMode* argument to olPrompt-ForSave, to prompt the user if changes should be saved. However, setting this argument is redundant in this example because the mail item is already saved using the *Save* method. However, the *SaveMode* argument is useful when you create a skeleton mail message, allow the user to make changes to the item, and then close the message programmatically using the *Close* method.

Chapter Summary

Finding and loading a document is a common task when using any Office application. This chapter described how to programmatically find a document on disk as well as find a folder location to save a document to. Using Visual Basic, you can also display a File dialog box to allow your users to find a file or folder. Once you've determined where a file is located or if a folder exists, you can use the *Open* and *SaveAs* methods provided in Word, Excel, and PowerPoint to open existing documents or to save loaded documents. Use the *Add* method to create new documents, and use the *Print* method to print a document from Word, Excel, or PowerPoint. The *Close* method closes a document when you no longer require it to be loaded in memory.

Chapter 5

Managing Documents with Events

Chapter Objectives   Estimated time: 60 minutes

- Use an event procedure to trap when the following File menu commands are clicked: New, Open, Close, Save, Save As, Save as Web Page, and Print—or when the same actions occur programmatically.

- Understand when the new, open, save, close, and print events are triggered in Microsoft Word, Microsoft Excel, and Microsoft PowerPoint and know the differences among these events in each application.

- Add or remove content such as header or footer information to òr from documents when they are opened or before they are saved, printed, or closed.

- Set and retrieve document properties such as Author and Title, as well as determine if a specific document property is set before you save, print, or close a document.

The main functionality for creating and managing Microsoft Office documents is reflected in the commands on the File menu in Word, Excel, PowerPoint, Microsoft Access, and Microsoft Outlook. You use the File menu, among other things, to create new documents and to open, save, close, and print existing ones. When you use the mouse or a keyboard shortcut to invoke one of these File menu commands, Office determines what command has been invoked and what action should be carried out.

When one of these actions, or events, occurs, your Microsoft Visual Basic for Applications program can respond, allowing you to determine when a document is created, opened, saved, closed, or printed. This chapter describes the event procedures that are called in your programs when any one of the following commands or their programmatic equivalents (as described in Chapter 4) are invoked through the File menu or through Visual Basic code: New, Open, Close, Save, Save As, Save as Web Page, and Print. After you set up event procedures to handle the occurrence of the actions New, Open, Save, Close, and Print, you can develop solutions like the following:

- When you create or open a document in Word, Excel, or PowerPoint, you can insert or manipulate specific content.

- Before you save a document, you're required to set document properties such as the Author and Title. If they aren't there, the save operation will be cancelled.

Quick Guide

This quick guide lists and describes the events you can respond to when you create, open, save, print, or close any document in Word, Excel, or PowerPoint. The steps following this quick guide also show how to set up the event procedures in your Visual Basic code. The event procedures are called whenever the user generates the action of creating, opening, saving, printing, or closing any Word, Excel, or PowerPoint document through the File menu or programmatically through code, using any of the methods described in the previous chapter.

The following table lists the events you'll call. Their names, such as NewDocument, WorkbookOpen, and PresentationSave, appear in the name of the event procedure you set up in your program.

Event	Word	Excel	PowerPoint
New	NewDocument	NewWorkbook	NewPresentation
Open	DocumentOpen	WorkbookOpen	PresentationOpen
Save	DocumentBeforeSave	WorkbookBeforeSave	PresentationSave
Close	DocumentBeforeClose	WorkbookBeforeClose	PresentationClose
Print	DocumentBeforePrint	WorkbookBeforePrint	PresentationPrint

Excel and PowerPoint also provide the WorkbookNewSheet and PresentationNewSlide events, which are called when a worksheet or slide is added to a workbook or presentation, respectively.

Outlook doesn't have direct equivalents to these events except for Open, Write, and Close. It has a NewInspector event that can be related to the NewDocument event, but NewInspector is triggered not just for new items, but any time an item in a folder is displayed. You can determine if the message is new by using the CurrentItem and the Sent or Saved property. Access doesn't have direct equivalents to these events.

Important In some cases you'll find that you can't perform certain operations when the code is executed within an event procedure. For example, if you add the line `Pres.Close` in the *NewPresentation* event procedure in PowerPoint, an error will occur indicating that this operation can't be performed in the event procedure. Also, an application may not allow your program to quit the application (that is, execute `Application.Quit`) in an event procedure.

Setting Up a Document Event

All the event procedures used to handle document events in Word, Excel or PowerPoint have one thing in common: the document being created, opened, saved, printed, or closed is passed in as the first argument in the event procedure. The naming of the first argument passed into each event procedure is consistent. In Word, the argument is declared as a *Document* object and is named Doc. In Excel, the argument is declared as a *Workbook* object and is named *Wb*. In PowerPoint, the argument is declared as a *Presentation* object and is named Pres. The following example lists the event procedures you use to respond to the action of opening a document in Word, Excel, and PowerPoint, respectively:

```
Sub App_DocumentOpen(ByVal Doc As Document)

Sub App_WorkbookOpen(ByVal Wb As Workbook)

Sub App_PresentationOpen(ByVal Pres As Presentation)
```

Event Naming Convention

In each application the event name follows the name of the document object. The document object in Word, Excel, and PowerPoint is *Document, Workbook*, and *Presentation*, respectively, and each appears in the name of document events for each application.

If the word *Before* is prefixed to the event name, it indicates that the event procedure is called before the action is actually carried out by Word, Excel, or PowerPoint, giving you the opportunity to prevent the application from carrying out the action's default behavior. For example, in Word and Excel, if a document that is being saved doesn't contain a particular property, you can alert the user and cancel the save event. As the previous table shows, PowerPoint doesn't provide any document events that can be cancelled.

Set Up an Event Procedure

The following steps show a simple tip for debugging and testing your solution and for determining exactly when an event procedure is called. Always remember to create a new class module and declare an object of type *Application* with events before the application's events can be used.

Note You will use the first, second, and fourth steps of the list that follows to set up each of the document event procedures in this chapter. If you complete them once, you don't need to repeat these steps.

---

1. Start Word, Excel, or PowerPoint and press ALT+F11 to start the Visual Basic Editor. This example uses Word.

2. Click Class Module on the Insert menu, add the following code in the class module, and press ENTER.

```
Public WithEvents App As Application
```

Once you press ENTER, the new *App* object, declared with events, appears in the Object drop-down list in the class module. When you select the new object in the Object drop-down list, the Procedures drop-down list displays the events for the *Application* object.

3. Select the object *App* in the Object drop-down list in the class module and, in the Procedures drop-down list, select any event listed in the table at the beginning of the Quick Guide section. Add the following lines within the event procedure.

```
Static i As Integer
i = i + 1
Debug.Print "EventProcedureName: " & i
```

These three lines are handy for debugging your solution and determining exactly when the event procedure is called. After everything is set up in step 5, every time you create a new document or open, save, print, or close a document, the event should fire. You use the static integer variable *i* so that when the text from the code line `Debug.Print` is printed to the Immediate window in the Visual Basic Editor, you can see a change from line to line in the printed text.

You should change the text `EventProcedureName` to the procedure name of the event you selected from the Procedures drop-down list.

4. Click Module on the Insert menu. In the module, named Module1 by default, add the following code:

```
Dim AppEvents As New Class1

Sub InitEvents()
    Set AppEvents.App = Application
End Sub
```

Before an event procedure will run, you must connect the declared object *App* in the class module to the *Application* object. Note that the class name *Class1* stated just after the *New* keyword in the declaration statement should be the name of the class module you declared as the *App* variable in step 2. The class module inserted in step 2 is, by default, Class1, but you can change the name of the class module to anything. If you do, you must also change the class name after the *New* keyword in the above declaration.

5. Place the cursor in the *InitEvents* procedure and press F5 to run the project. After you run the *InitEvents* procedure, the *App* object in the class module points to the *Word Application* object, and the event procedures in the class module will run when the events occur.

6. Position the Office application window so you can see the Immediate window in the Visual Basic Editor. Perform the action of the event you selected in step 3 above. For example, if you selected the WindowSelectionChange event in Word, start clicking around in the Word document, inserting new content and selecting the text and shapes.

In the Immediate window, you should see the text `Window-SelectionChange` or the name of the event you used in step 3 to replace the text `EventProcedureName`. The name of the event is followed by a number. When you perform another action, the number is changed incrementally.

No matter what event you write code for, use this technique to help you debug and test your solutions. It also helps you determine exactly when an event is triggered. The rest of the chapter goes into more depth on each event that is triggered by a user's interaction with and manipulation of content in the active document. You can either use the lists from each of the descriptions for each event or use the technique described in this example to determine when an event triggers.

The Document New Event

The procedure for the document New event is called *after* you create a new document. Word, Excel, or PowerPoint create a new document, display it, and then, if it's set up in your program, call the document New event. This event can't be cancelled. You can create new documents with the New command on the File menu or on the Standard toolbar. The *Add* method on the *Documents, Workbooks*, and *Presentations* collection objects, described in the previous chapter, also triggers the *New* event procedure.

```
Sub App_NewDocument(ByVal Doc As Document)
Sub App_NewWorkbook(ByVal Wb As Workbook)
Sub App_NewPresentation(ByVal Pres As Presentation)
```

There are no differences in how the New event is defined in each application or when it's called. In all three applications, the application creates the document first and then calls the event procedure. PowerPoint calls the *NewPresentation* event procedure after it creates the presentation but before it displays the New Slide. As previously noted, however, PowerPoint doesn't allow your code to perform operations like closing the newly created presentation in the *NewPresentation* event procedure. If the *NewPresentation* event procedure executes the code `Pres.Close`, an error will occur.

Example Scenario

The following examples for Word, Excel, and PowerPoint each perform the same operation: when you create a new document, the application adds the text *Created on*, followed by the current date and time, to the footer at the bottom left of each page. The text format for the footer is italicized. The date and time values are static once they're inserted so their values do not change as the date and time changes. Although the code to indicate the date format m/d/yy and the hours:minutes and am/pm formats is different in each application, the same date and time format is inserted.

Set Up the NewDocument Event in Word

Before following the steps below, make sure you complete steps 1, 2, and 4 in the section "Set Up an Event Procedure" after the Quick Guide.

1. In Word, start the Visual Basic Editor and then double-click the Class1 project item in the Project Explorer to make it the active window.

2. Click *App* from the Object drop-down list and then select NewDocument from the Procedures drop-down list in the class module. In the *NewDocument* event procedure, add the following code:

```
Private Sub App_NewDocument(ByVal Doc As Document)
    With Doc.Sections(1).Footers(wdHeaderFooterPrimary).Range
        .InsertDateTime DateTimeFormat:="M/d/yy h:mm am/pm", _
            InsertAsField:=False, DateLanguage:=wdEnglishUS
        .InsertBefore Text:="Created on "
        .Font.Italic = True
    End With
End Sub
```

To insert a footer in Word, use the Footers property to access the footer text range of the document. You insert the date and time with the *InsertDateTime* method on the *Range* object and you insert the text 'Created on' before the date and time with the *InsertBefore* method.

3. In the Project Explorer, double-click the Module1 project item to make it the active window, place the cursor in the *InitEvents* procedure, and press F5.

4. Switch to Word and click the New button on the Standard toolbar. The text, date, and time are inserted at the bottom left of each page. To view the footer, click Print Layout on the View menu and scroll down to the bottom of the page.

To insert a header or footer in Excel, you use the PageSetup property on the *Worksheet* object to access the *PageSetup* object. On the *PageSetup* object, you use the LeftFooter property to set the footer. Other similar properties are CenterFooter, RightFooter, LeftHeader, CenterHeader, and RightHeader. To insert text or the date and time in any header or footer position in Excel, you need to apply header and footer information to all the worksheets in a workbook.

Before following the steps below, make sure you complete steps 1, 2, and 4 in the section "Set Up an Event Procedure" after the Quick Guide.

1. In Excel, start the Visual Basic Editor and then double-click the Class1 project item in the Project Explorer to make it the active window.

2. Click *App* from the Object drop-down list and then select NewWorkbook from the Procedures drop-down list in the class module. In the *NewWorkbook* event procedure, add the following code:

```
Private Sub App_NewWorkbook(ByVal Wb As Workbook)
    Dim sh As Worksheet
    For Each sh In Wb.Worksheets
        sh.PageSetup _
            .LeftFooter = "&""""Italic,Italic""""Created on " _
            & FormatDateTime(Date$) & _
            " " & FormatDateTime(Time$)
    Next sh
End Sub
```

Excel doesn't provide the ability to insert the current date and/or time that are static and don't change. However, you can use the *Date$* and *Time$* functions built into the Visual Basic for Applications language. If you use &D and &T in the string assigned to the LeftFooter property, the current date and time will be displayed in the footer whenever you view the footer or print the worksheet. The string assigned to the LeftFooter property would then appear as follows: "&""Italic""""Created on &D &T".

3. In the Project Explorer, double-click the Module1 project item to make it the active window, place the cursor in the *InitEvents* procedure, and press F5.

4. Switch to Excel and click the New button on the Standard toolbar.

When you view a worksheet normally, you won't see the header and footer. Header and footer information is only displayed in a worksheet's Print Preview mode and on printed pages. To see or set headers and footers in Excel, click Page Setup on the File menu and click the Header/Footer tab. In this example, a custom footer is set. Therefore, to see the custom footer, click the Custom Footer button between the Header and Footer previews.

Note   Excel also provides an event that is called when you add a new worksheet to a workbook. The *WorkbookNewSheet* event procedure is called when you add a worksheet by clicking Worksheet on the Insert menu. The event procedure is defined as:

```
Sub App_WorkbookNewSheet(ByVal Wb As Workbook, _
    ByVal Sh As Object)
```

Set Up the NewPresentation Event in PowerPoint

Before following the steps below, make sure you complete steps 1, 2, and 4 in the section "Set Up an Event Procedure" after the Quick Guide.

In PowerPoint, you add text to the DateTime placeholder, which is located at the bottom left of the presentation's slide master by default. The index position of the DateTime placeholder in the *Placeholders* collection of the presentation's slide master is 3 by default. If a different default presentation template is used when you create new presentations, the DateTime placeholder may not exist. The PowerPoint example in the Print section near the end of this chapter describes how to write a function to determine if a specific placeholder type exists in a presentation.

1. In PowerPoint, start the Visual Basic Editor and then double-click the Class1 project item in the Project Explorer to make it the active window.

2. Click *App* from the Object drop-down list and then select NewPresentation from the Procedures drop-down list in the class module. In the *NewPresentation* event procedure, add the following code:

```
Private Sub App_NewPresentation(ByVal Pres As Presentation)
    With Pres
        With .SlideMaster.Shapes.Placeholders(3).TextFrame
            .WordWrap = msoFalse
            .AutoSize = ppAutoSizeShapeToFitText
            With .TextRange
                .Text = ""
                .InsertDateTime _
                    DateTimeFormat:=ppDateTimeMMddyyHmm, _
                    InsertAsField:=msoFalse
                .InsertBefore "Created on "
                .Font.Italic = msoTrue
            End With
        End With
    End With
End Sub
```

You use the *SlideMaster* object, which you access using the SlideMaster property on the *Presentation* object, to set footer information on all the slides in a presentation. All slides, with the exception of title slides, share the same slide master. If you set the text in a placeholder on the slide master, it applies to all slides. In the *NewPresentation* event procedure, you access the DateTime placeholder on the *Shapes* collection of the SlideMaster for the new presentation.

3. In the Project Explorer, double-click the Module1 project item to make it the active window, place the cursor in the *InitEvents* procedure, and press F5.

4. Switch to PowerPoint and click the New button on the Standard toolbar.
To change the text in the Footer or Slide Number placeholder, select Header and Footer on the View menu and display the Slide tab.

Note PowerPoint also provides an event that's called when you add a new slide to a presentation. The *PresentationNewSlide* event procedure is called when you add a slide by clicking New Slide on the Insert menu or by pasting it from another presentation. The event procedure is defined as:

```
Sub App_PresentationNewSlide(ByVal sld As Slide)
```

The Document Open Event

The procedure for the document Open event is called *after* you open a document. Word, Excel, or PowerPoint will load an existing document, display it, and then, if it's set up in your program, call the document Open event. This event can't be cancelled. You can open documents with the Open command on the File menu or on the Standard toolbar. The *Open* method on the *Documents, Workbooks*, and *Presentations* collection objects, described in the previous chapter, also triggers the *Open* event procedure.

```
Sub App_DocumentOpen(ByVal Doc As Document)

Sub App_WorkbookOpen(ByVal Wb As Workbook)

Sub App_ PresentationOpen(ByVal Pres As Presentation)
```

There are no differences in how the Open event in each application is defined or when it's called. In all three applications, the application opens the document first and then calls the event procedure.

Example Scenario

In the following examples for Word, Excel, and PowerPoint, the application retrieves the opened document's file extension in order to evaluate the opened document's file format type. You may need to know the opened document's file format in order to set specific custom menu or toolbar commands or to set document properties.

For each event procedure example to function properly, you need to add the following custom function to the class module where the document *Open* event procedure is defined for each application. The custom function *GetFileExtension* is described in Chapter 4 in the section entitled "Parse Filenames." The function takes a filename as an argument into the function and returns just the extension of the filename.

```
Private Function GetFileExtension(sFileName As String) As String
    Dim iPosn As Integer
    iPosn = InStrRev(sFileName, ".")
    GetFileExtension = Mid$(sFileName, iPosn + 1)
End Function
```

In all three following examples, the Name property of the *Document, Workbook*, and *Presentation* object in Word, Excel, and PowerPoint, respectively, returns the document's filename. If the document isn't newly created and is a file on disk, the Name property will contain an extension. In the case here, the opened document will contain a file extension. The expression in the Select Case statement evaluates the upper case of the extension returned by the custom *GetFileExtension* function.

Each application prints the file format type to the Immediate window in the Visual Basic Editor. Note that the Select Case statement in each event procedure doesn't cover all possible file format types in each application. The examples only parse for the most common format types.

Set Up the DocumentOpen Event in Word

Before following the steps below, make sure you complete steps 1, 2, and 4 in the section "Set Up an Event Procedure" after the Quick Guide.

1. In Word, start the Visual Basic Editor and then double-click the Class1 project item in the Project Explorer to make it the active window.

2. Click *App* from the Object drop-down list and then select DocumentOpen from the Procedures drop-down list in the class module. In the *DocumentOpen* event procedure, add the following code:

```
Private Sub App_DocumentOpen(ByVal Doc As Document)
    Select Case UCase$(GetFileExtension(Doc.Name))
        Case "HTM", "HTML"
            Debug.Print "HTML file"
        Case "DOC"
            Debug.Print "Document file"
        Case "DOT"
            Debug.Print "Document template file"
        Case "TXT"
            Debug.Print "Text file"
    End Select
End Sub
```

3. In the Project Explorer, double-click the Module1 project item to make it the active window, place the cursor in the *InitEvents* procedure, and press F5.

4. Switch to Word and click the Open button on the Standard toolbar.

5. Open a file and then switch back to the Visual Basic Editor. If the file you open is a Word document, template, HTML, or text file, the extension of the file is printed in the Immediate window.

Set Up the WorkbookOpen Event In Excel

1. In Excel, start the Visual Basic Editor and then double-click the Class1 project item in the Project Explorer to make it the active window.

2. Click *App* from the Object drop-down list and then select WorkbookOpen from the Procedures drop-down list in the class module. In the *WorkbookOpen* event procedure, add the following code:

```
Private Sub App_WorkbookOpen(ByVal Wb As Workbook)
    Select Case UCase$(GetFileExtension(Wb.Name))
        Case "HTM", "HTML"
            Debug.Print "HTML file"
        Case "XLS"
            Debug.Print "Workbook file"
        Case "XLT"
            Debug.Print "Workbook template file"
        Case "TXT"
            Debug.Print "Text file"
    End Select
End Sub
```

3. In the Project Explorer, double-click the Module1 project item to make it the active window, place the cursor in the *InitEvents* procedure, and press F5.

4. Switch to Excel and click the Open button on the Standard toolbar.

5. Open a file and then switch back to the Visual Basic Editor. If the file you open is an Excel workbook, template, HTML, or text file, the extension of the file is printed in the Immediate window.

Before following the steps below, make sure you complete steps 1, 2, and 4 in the section "Set Up an Event Procedure" after the Quick Guide.

Set Up the PresentationOpen Event in PowerPoint

1. In PowerPoint, start the Visual Basic Editor and then double-click the Class1 project item in the Project Explorer to make it the active window.

2. Click *App* from the Object drop-down list and then select PresentationOpen from the Procedures drop-down list in the class module. In the *PresentationOpen* event procedure, add the following code:

```
Private Sub App_PresentationOpen(ByVal Pres As Presentation)
    Select Case UCase$(GetFileExtension(Pres.Name))
        Case "HTM", "HTML"
            Debug.Print "HTML file"
        Case "PPT"
            Debug.Print "Presentation file"
        Case "POT"
            Debug.Print "Presentation template file"
    End Select
End Sub
```

Before following the steps below, make sure you complete steps 1, 2, and 4 in the section "Set Up an Event Procedure" after the Quick Guide.

3. In the Project Explorer, double-click the Module1 project item to make it the active window, place the cursor in the *InitEvents* procedure, and press F5.

4. Switch to PowerPoint and click the Open button on the Standard toolbar.

5. Open a file and then switch back to the Visual Basic Editor.

   If the file you open is a PowerPoint presentation, template, or HTML, the extension of the file is printed in the Immediate window.

The Document Save Event

The procedure for the document Save event is called *before* you save a document. Word, Excel, or PowerPoint will call the document *Save* event procedure, if it's set up in your program, before saving the document and before displaying the Save As dialog box (if you haven't previously saved the document on disk). In Word and Excel, you *can* cancel this event. Therefore, the name of the event is prefixed with the word *Before*. In PowerPoint, you can't keep this event from occurring and, thus, its name isn't prefixed with *Before*.

Note If either Word, Excel, or PowerPoint is in its sequence of closing a document and the changes to it will be saved, the application calls the document *Save* event procedure *after* the document *Close* event procedure.

You can save documents with the Save, Save As, or Save as Web Page commands on the File menu or with the Save command on the Standard toolbar. The *Save* or *SaveAs* method on the *Document, Workbook,* and *Presentation* objects, described in the previous chapter, also triggers the document *Save* event procedure.

```
Sub App_DocumentBeforeSave(ByVal Doc As Document, _
    SaveAsUI As Boolean, Cancel As Boolean)

Sub App_WorkbookBeforeSave(ByVal Wb As Workbook, _
    ByVal SaveAsUI As Boolean, Cancel As Boolean)

Sub App_PresentationSave(ByVal Pres As Presentation)
```

The main difference between the document Save event in Word, Excel, and PowerPoint is that both Word and Excel allow the developer to cancel the save action but PowerPoint does not. When the user clicks on the Save command or on a related save command, or when the *Save* or *SaveAs* method on the document object is executed, the event procedure listed above is called in the appropriate application. In Word and Excel, your code can prevent Word and Excel from actually saving the changes in the document if you set to True the *Cancel* Boolean argument passed into the event procedure. In Word and Excel, the second argument in the event procedure definition is the *SaveAsUI* Boolean argument and it allows you to set whether the Save As dialog box will be displayed.

Evaluating the Filename
Entered in the Save As Dialog Box

Many common scenarios exist where you need to retrieve the filename and path that the user enters in the Save As dialog box, parse the filename, and, based on the value, perform a specific operation. For example, if the user wants to save a document to a specific folder location on the network or an HTTP server, you can make sure the user enters certain document properties before the document is saved. If the user doesn't, your code can cancel the Save event. Word and Excel provide a way to display the Office Save As dialog box and parse the entered filename to handle this scenario.

In Word, start the Visual Basic Editor and in a standard code module, insert the following procedure. Press F5 to run the procedure. The Save As dialog box is displayed when the *Display* method on the *Dialog* object is executed. After you select a file and click Save, the string value of the filename returned by the dialog box is evaluated and printed to the Immediate window. If the filename doesn't consist of a path to a Web Folder, the *Save* function of the Save As dialog box is executed using the *Execute* method of the *Dialog* object.

```
Sub UsingSaveAsDialogInWord()
    Dim dlgSaveAs As Dialog, sFileName As String
    Set dlgSaveAs = Dialogs(wdDialogFileSaveAs)
    dlgSaveAs.Display
    sFileName = dlgSaveAs.Name
    If Left$(sFileName, 4) = "http" Then
        Debug.Print "Web Folder: " & sFileName
    Else
        Debug.Print CurDir & "\" & dlg.SaveAs.Name
        dlgSaveAs.Execute
    End If
End Sub
```

You can use similar code in the DocumentBeforeSave event in Word to cancel the Save event if the user wants to save to a specific folder but certain conditions are not met. See the steps "Evaluate and Cancel the Document Save Event Based on the Filename " in this section for an example.

In Excel, start the Visual Basic Editor and in a standard code module, insert the following procedure. Press F5 to run the procedure. The Save As dialog box is displayed when the *GetSaveAsFilename* method on the *Application* object is executed. After you select a file and click Save, the string value of the filename returned by the dialog box is

(continued)

**Evaluating the Filename
Entered in the Save As Dialog Box** *(continued)*

evaluated and printed to the Immediate window. If the filename doesn't consist of a path to a Web Folder, the *SaveAs* method of the *Workbook* object is used to save the active workbook with the filename specified in the Save As dialog box.

```
Sub UsingSaveAsDialogInExcel()
    Dim sFileName As String
    sFileName = Application.GetSaveAsFilename
    If Left$(sFileName, 4) = "http" Then
        Debug.Print "Web Folder: " & sFileName
    Else
        Debug.Print sFileName
        ActiveWorkbook.SaveAs sFileName
    End If
End Sub
```

You can use similar code in the WorkbookBeforeSave event in Excel to cancel the Save event if the user wants to save to a specific folder but certain conditions are not met. See the *WorkbookBeforeSave* event procedure in the sample file XlEvents.bas in the Chapter 5 practice folder for an example of evaluating and cancelling the workbook Save event based on the filename.

You can also display the Microsoft Windows system File dialog box, which enables your code to determine the filename, path, and file type specified by the user. For a description of how to use and display the Windows system File dialog box in this and similar scenarios, see the "File Management" section of Chapter 4.

Example Scenario

In the following examples for Word, Excel, and PowerPoint, the code in the document *Save* event procedure evaluates whether the user who is saving the document is logged onto the network. If the user is logged on, the procedure retrieves the user's name and adds text to the built-in document property (Comments), indicating that the user is logged on.

For each event procedure example to function properly, you need to add the following Windows application programming interface (API) declaration and custom function to the top of the class module where the document *Save* event procedure is defined for each application. Note the keyword *Private* added to the beginning of the GetUserName declaration. When you add a Windows API declaration in a class module, the keyword *Private* must appear in the declaration. If you add the API declaration in a standard code module, the *Private* keyword isn't required and you can use the API from any code module.

```
Private Declare Function GetUserName Lib "advapi32.dll" _
    Alias "GetUserNameA" (ByVal lpBuffer As String, _
        nSize As Long _
    ) As Long

Function CurrentUserName() As String
    Dim sBuffer As String * 25, lReturn As Long
    lReturn = GetUserName(sBuffer, 25)
    CurrentUserName = Left$(sBuffer, InStr(sBuffer, Chr(0)) - 1)
End Function
```

In all three examples below, the custom *CurrentUserName* function is called and its return value is assigned to the string variable *sUserName*. If the length of the string returned by the custom *CurrentUserName* function is greater than zero, the procedure uses the user's name in a text string assigned to the built-in Comments document property. If the length of the string is zero, the Windows API GetUserName returned an empty string, indicating that the user isn't logged onto the computer system. You use the BuiltInDocumentProperties property of the *Document, Workbook*, and *Presentation* objects in Word, Excel, and PowerPoint, respectively, to access the Comments document property.

In Word and Excel, rather than assigning the string "Last saved by user not logged on" to the Comments document property, you can display a message indicating to the user that the document or workbook can't be saved unless the user is logged on. After the message box is displayed, the *Cancel* Boolean argument passed as the third argument in the event procedure is set to True, therefore preventing the save action from being processed by Word or Excel. If you want to prevent the save action, replace the Else statement in the following event procedures for Word and Excel with the following Else statement:

```
Else
    MsgBox "This document cannot be saved unless " & _
        "you are logged on."
    Cancel = True
```

The example scenario described in the document *Close* event procedures sets the *Cancel* argument to True when the Subject document property isn't set.

Set Up the DocumentBeforeSave Event in Word

1. In Word, start the Visual Basic Editor and then double-click the Class1 project item in the Project Explorer to make it the active window.

2. Click *App* from the Object drop-down list and then select Document-BeforeSave from the Procedures drop-down list in the class module. In the *DocumentBeforeSave* event procedure, add the following code:

```
Sub App_DocumentBeforeSave(ByVal Doc As Document, _
    SaveAsUI As Boolean, Cancel As Boolean)

    Dim sUserName As String
    sUserName = CurrentUserName
```

Before following the steps below, make sure you complete steps 1, 2, and 4 in the section "Set Up an Event Procedure" after the Quick Guide.

```
    If Len(sUserName) Then
        Doc.BuiltinDocumentProperties("Comments").Value = _
            "Last saved by user logged on as " & sUserName
    Else
        Doc.BuiltinDocumentProperties("Comments").Value = _
            "Last saved by user not logged on."
    End If
End Sub
```

3. In the Project Explorer, double-click the Module1 project item to make it the active window, place the cursor in the *InitEvents* procedure, and press F5.

4. Switch to Word and click New on the Standard toolbar to create a new document.

5. Add some text to the document and click the Save button on the Standard toolbar.

6. To view the comments added to the document properties collection, display the Properties window of the saved file by clicking Properties on the File menu and selecting the Summary tab.

Evaluate and Cancel the Document Save Event Based on the Filename

1. Replace the code in the *DocumentBeforeSave* event procedure added in step 2 above with the following code:

```
Sub App_DocumentBeforeSave(ByVal Doc As Document, _
    SaveAsUI As Boolean, Cancel As Boolean)

    Dim dlgSaveAs As Dialog, sFileName As String
    SaveAsUI = False
    Cancel = True

    Set dlgSaveAs = Dialogs(wdDialogFileSaveAs)
    dlgSaveAs.Display
    sFileName = dlgSaveAs.Name

    If Left$(sFileName, 4) = "http" Then
        If Len(Doc.BuiltInDocumentProperties("Subject") _
                .Value) = 0 Then
            MsgBox "Please enter a document subject " & _
                "before saving to a Web Folder.", _
                vbCritical
            Exit Sub
        End If
    End If
```

```
        dlgSaveAs.Execute
End Sub
```

2. In the Project Explorer, double-click the Module1 project item to make it the active window, place the cursor in the *InitEvents* procedure, and then press F5.

3. Switch to Word and click Save As on the File menu.

In the DocumentBeforeSave event, the *SaveAsUI* Boolean argument passed into the *DocumentBeforeSave* event procedure is set to False so that your code can explicitly display the Save As dialog box. Because the *SaveAsUI* Boolean argument is set to False, Word will not display the Save As dialog box after the *Save* event procedure is executed. The *Cancel* Boolean argument passed into the event procedure is set to True in order to cancel Word's default behavior of saving the document. Your code will use the Execute method of the Save As dialog box to explicitly save the document. The Save As dialog box is displayed using the Display method of the Dialog object.

After you select a file and click Save, the string value of the filename returned by the dialog box is evaluated. If the filename consists of a path to a Web Folder, the code evaluates if the user added text to the built-in document property Subject in the Properties dialog. If the Subject document property is not set, a message box is displayed and the Save event procedure is exited without saving the document. Otherwise, the save function of the Save As dialog box is executed using the *Execute* method of the Dialog object.

Set Up the WorkbookBeforeSave Event in Excel

1. In Excel, start the Visual Basic Editor and then double-click the Class1 project item in the Project Explorer to make it the active window.

2. Click *App* from the Object drop-down list and then select Workbook-BeforeSave from the Procedures drop-down list in the class module. In the *WorkbookBeforeSave* event procedure, add the following code:

Before following the steps below, make sure you complete steps 1, 2, and 4 in the section "Set Up an Event Procedure" after the Quick Guide.

```
Private Sub App_WorkbookBeforeSave(ByVal Wb As Workbook, _
    ByVal SaveAsUI As Boolean, Cancel As Boolean)

    Dim sUserName As String
    sUserName = CurrentUserName
    If Len(sUserName) Then
        Wb.BuiltinDocumentProperties("Comments").Value = _
            "Last saved by user logged on as " & sUserName
    Else
        Wb.BuiltinDocumentProperties("Comments").Value = _
            "Last saved by user not logged on."
    End If
End Sub
```

3. In the Project Explorer, double-click the Module1 project item to make it the active window, place the cursor in the *InitEvents* procedure, and then press F5.

4. Switch to Excel and click New on the Standard toolbar to create a new workbook.

5. Add some text to the cells in the workbooks and click the Save button on the Standard toolbar.

6. To view the comments added to the document properties collection, display the Properties window of the saved file by clicking Properties on the File menu and selecting the Summary tab.

Set Up the PresentationSave Event in PowerPoint

Before following the steps below, make sure you complete steps 1, 2, and 4 in the section "Set Up an Event Procedure" after the Quick Guide.

1. In PowerPoint, start the Visual Basic Editor and then double-click the Class1 project item in the Project Explorer to make it the active window.

2. Click *App* from the Object drop-down list and then select PresentationSave from the Procedures drop-down list in the class module. In the *PresentationSave* event procedure, add the following code:

```
Private Sub App_PresentationSave(ByVal Pres As Presentation)
    Dim sUserName As String
    sUserName = CurrentUserName
    If Len(sUserName) Then
        Pres.BuiltinDocumentProperties("Comments").Value = _
            "Last saved by user logged on as " & sUserName
    Else
        Pres.BuiltinDocumentProperties("Comments").Value = _
            "Last saved by user not logged on."
    End If
End Sub
```

3. In the Project Explorer, double-click the Module1 project item to make it the active window, place the cursor in the *InitEvents* procedure, and then press F5.

4. Switch to PowerPoint and click New on the Standard toolbar to create a new presentation.

5. Add some text to the presentation and click the Save button on the Standard toolbar.

6. To view the comments added to the document properties collection, display the Properties window of the saved file by clicking Properties on the File menu and selecting the Summary tab.

Note If PowerPoint is in its sequence of closing a presentation and if changes to the presentation will be saved, the *PresentationSave* event procedure is called after you close the presentation's document window. The presentation, however, is still in memory and can be manipulated. Attempting to change any aspect of the presentation's document window will result in an error.

The Document Close Event

The procedure for the document Close event is called *before* you close a document. Word, Excel, and PowerPoint will call the document *Close* event procedure, if it's set up in your program, before you close the document.

Note If the document has been changed since it was last saved to disk, the document Close event is called before the user is asked to save the changes. After the document *Close* event procedure is executed, the message box that's displayed contains a Yes, a No, and a Cancel button. If the user clicks Cancel, Word, Excel, or PowerPoint cancels the close operation and the document is *not* closed.

In Word and Excel, you *can* cancel this event. Therefore, the event's name is prefixed with the word *Before*. In PowerPoint, you can't cancel this event and, thus, its name isn't prefixed with *Before*. You have at least eight common ways to close a document in Word, Excel, and PowerPoint. These are listed and described in the table on the following page.

```
Sub App_DocumentBeforeClose( _
ByVal Doc As Document, Cancel As Boolean)

Sub App_WorkbookBeforeClose( _
    ByVal Wb As Workbook, Cancel As Boolean)

Sub App_PresentationClose(ByVal Pres As Presentation)
```

The main difference between the document Close event in Word, Excel, and PowerPoint is that both Word and Excel allow the developer to cancel the close action while PowerPoint does not. When the user clicks on Close or a related close command, or when the *Close* or related close method on the document object is executed, the event procedure listed above is called in the appropriate application. In Word and Excel, if you set to True the *Cancel* Boolean argument passed into the event procedure, your code can prevent Word and Excel from actually closing the document.

Closing a Document

The following table lists the ways you can close a document in Word, Excel, and PowerPoint:

Way to close	Description
Use the keyboard shortcut ALT+F4	ALT+F4 executes the Close command on the Control-menu, displayed when you click the application's (or document's) icon on the title bar at the top left of a window. The Control-menu, and hence the ALT+F4 keyboard shortcut, is available to all Windows applications, by default.
Use the keyboard shortcut CTRL+F4	CTRL+F4, not to be confused with ALT+F4, is available in Word, Excel, and PowerPoint. It doesn't work for Outlook windows or many other applications. This keyboard shortcut closes the active document window.
Click the Close window button	In Word, the Close window button is the 'x' located at the top right of a document window, next to the Minimize and Maximize button on all document windows. In Excel and PowerPoint, the Close window button exists for a document window *and* the application window. It's located at the right end of the menu bar and at the right end of the title bar, respectively.
Click Close All on the File menu	The Close All command is only available in Word and Excel. To display the Close All command, you must hold down the SHIFT key and then click the File menu. When the File menu is displayed, Close All is displayed in place of the Close command.
Click Close on the File menu	This command is available in Word, Excel, and PowerPoint.
Click Exit on the File menu	This command is available in Word, Excel, and PowerPoint.
Application.Quit method	This method is available in Word, Excel, and PowerPoint.
Document.Close method	This method is available in Word, Excel, and PowerPoint.
Documents.Close method	This method is only available in Word and Excel. It's equivalent to the Close All command available on the File menu when you hold down the SHIFT key and then click the File menu.

(continued)

(continued)

Way to close	Description
Window.Close method	This method is available in Word, Excel, and PowerPoint. If only one document window is open for the document, the document is actually closed. More than one document window in Word, Excel, and PowerPoint for any given document can exist if you click on the New Window command on the Window menu. If more than one window for a document is open, the Close method closes only the specified window, while the document and its other windows remain open. This is similar to clicking on the 'x' at the top right of a document window.

Example Scenario

In the following examples for Word, Excel, and PowerPoint, the code in the document *Close* event procedure evaluates if the built-in document property, Subject, is set before you close the document. If the Subject isn't set, in Word and Excel the *Cancel* argument in the event procedure is set to True and the close action is cancelled. The user sees a message saying that the Subject document property hasn't been set before the event is cancelled. In PowerPoint, the event can't be cancelled and therefore, the message that the user sees is slightly different. It suggests that the user reopen the document and set the Subject document property.

Note the use of the text characters represented by the built-in Visual Basic for Applications language function *Chr$*. Chr$(10) and Chr$(13) together represent a linefeed and carriage return in between the two sentences of the message. You use the BuiltInDocumentProperties property of the *Document, Workbook,* and *Presentation* object in Word, Excel, and PowerPoint, respectively, to access the Subject document property. If the Subject document property value doesn't contain text, the string returned by the Value property is equal to the Visual Basic for Applications constant vbNullString, which represents an empty string ("").

Set Up the DocumentBeforeClose Event in Word

1. In Word, start the Visual Basic Editor and then double-click the Class1 project item in the Project Explorer to make it the active window.

2. Click *App* from the Object drop-down list and then select DocumentBeforeClose from the Procedures drop-down list in the class module. In the *DocumentBeforeClose* event procedure, add the following code:

```
Private Sub App_DocumentBeforeClose( _
    ByVal Doc As Document, Cancel As Boolean)
```

Before following the steps below, make sure you complete steps 1, 2, and 4 in the section "Set Up an Event Procedure" after the Quick Guide.

```
    If Doc.BuiltinDocumentProperties("Subject") _
        .Value = vbNullString Then
        MsgBox "Before this document can be closed, the " & _
            "subject of this document must be entered." & _
            Chr$(10) & Chr$(13) & Chr$(10) & Chr$(13) & _
            "Click Properties on the " & _
            "File menu to set the Subject.", vbCritical
        Cancel = True
    End If
End Sub
```

3. In the Project Explorer, double-click the Module1 project item to make it the active window, place the cursor in the *InitEvents* procedure, and then press F5.

4. Switch to Word and click New on the Standard toolbar to create a new document.

5. Add some text to the document and click the Close button on the File menu.

Set Up the WorkbookBeforeClose Event in Excel

Before following the steps below, make sure you complete steps 1, 2, and 4 in the section "Set Up an Event Procedure" after the Quick Guide.

1. In Excel, start the Visual Basic Editor and then double-click the Class1 project item in the Project Explorer to make it the active window.

2. Click *App* from the Object drop-down list and then select WorkbookBeforeClose from the Procedures drop-down list in the class module. In the *WorkbookBeforeClose* event procedure, add the following code:

```
Private Sub App_WorkbookBeforeClose( _
    ByVal Wb As Workbook, Cancel As Boolean)

    If Wb.BuiltinDocumentProperties("Subject") _
        .Value = vbNullString Then
        MsgBox "Before this workbook can be closed, the " & _
            "subject of this workbook must be entered." & _
            Chr$(10) & Chr$(13) & Chr$(10) & Chr$(13) & _
            "Click Properties on the " & _
            "File menu to set the Subject.", vbCritical
        Cancel = True
    End If
End Sub
```

3. In the Project Explorer, double-click the Module1 project item to make it the active window, place the cursor in the *InitEvents* procedure, and press F5.

4. Switch to Excel and click New on the Standard toolbar to create a new workbook.

5. Add some text to the workbook and click the Close button on the File menu.

Set Up the PresentationClose Event in PowerPoint

1. In PowerPoint, start the Visual Basic Editor and then double-click the Class1 project item in the Project Explorer to make it the active window.

2. Click *App* from the Object drop-down list and then select PresentationClose from the Procedures drop-down list in the class module. In the *PresentationClose* event procedure, add the following code:

```
Private Sub App_PresentationClose(ByVal Pres As Presentation)
    If Pres.BuiltinDocumentProperties("Subject") _
        .Value = vbNullString Then
        MsgBox "A subject was not entered for this " & _
            "presentation." & _
            Chr$(10) & Chr$(13) & Chr$(10) & Chr$(13) & _
            "Please reopen this presentation and " & _
            "click Properties on the " & _
            "File menu to set the Subject.", vbCritical
    End If
End Sub
```

Before following the steps below, make sure you complete steps 1, 2, and 4 in the section "Set Up an Event Procedure" after the Quick Guide.

3. In the Project Explorer, double-click the Module1 project item to make it the active window, place the cursor in the *InitEvents* procedure, and then press F5.

4. Switch to PowerPoint and click New on the Standard toolbar to create a new presentation.

5. Add some text to the presentation and click the Close button on the File menu.

The Document Print Event

The procedure for the document Print event is called *before* a document is printed. Word, Excel, or PowerPoint will call the document *Print* event procedure if it's set up in your program before the document is printed. In Word and Excel, this event *can* be cancelled. Therefore, the name of the event is prefixed with the word *Before*. In PowerPoint, this event can't be cancelled and thus, the event name isn't prefixed with *Before*.

You can print documents using the Print command on the File menu or on the Standard toolbar. The *PrintOut* method on the *Document, Workbook,* and *Presentation* objects, described in the previous chapter, also triggers the document *Print* event procedure. In PowerPoint, the print event also triggers when the *PrintOut* method on the *PrintOptions* object, accessed from the *Presentation* object, is executed.

```
Sub App_DocumentBeforePrint( _
    ByVal Doc As Document, Cancel As Boolean)

Sub App_WorkbookBeforePrint( _
    ByVal Wb As Workbook, Cancel As Boolean)

Sub App_PresentationPrint(ByVal Pres As Presentation)
```

Example Scenario

The following examples for Word, Excel, and PowerPoint are similar to the examples described after the Quick Guide section in the document *New* event procedures. When you print a document, the application adds the text "MyCompany Confidential" to the header at the top left of each page. Because PowerPoint doesn't support headers on a slide, it adds text to the footer of each slide. The added text is formatted to be bolded and its font name set to Arial. You can replace the text string "MyCompany" with the name of your company.

Set Up the DocumentBeforePrint Event in Word

To insert a header in Word, use the Headers property to access the document's header text range. The text "MyCompany Confidential" is inserted at the top left of each page. To view the header, click Print Layout on the View menu and scroll to the top of the page.

Before following the steps below, make sure you complete steps 1, 2, and 4 in the section "Set Up an Event Procedure" after the Quick Guide.

1. In Word, start the Visual Basic Editor and then double-click the Class1 project item in the Project Explorer to make it the active window.

2. Click *App* from the Object drop-down list and then select Document-BeforePrint from the Procedures drop-down list in the class module. In the *DocumentBeforePrint* event procedure, add the following code:

```
Sub App_DocumentBeforePrint( _
    ByVal Doc As Document, Cancel As Boolean)

    With Doc.Sections(1).Headers(wdHeaderFooterPrimary).Range
        .Text = "MyCompany Confidential"
        With .Font
            .Bold = True
            .Name = "Arial"
        End With
    End With
End Sub
```

3. In the Project Explorer, double-click the Module1 project item to make it the active window, place the cursor in the *InitEvents* procedure, and press F5.

4. Switch to Word and click New on the Standard toolbar to create a new document.

5. Add some text to the document and click the Print option on the File menu.

Set Up the WorkbookBeforePrint Event in Excel

In Excel, to insert a header or footer you use the PageSetup property on the *Worksheet* object to access the *PageSetup* object. On the *PageSetup* object, you use the LeftHeader property to set the header. To insert text in any header or footer position, you need to apply header and footer information to all the worksheets in a workbook.

Before following the steps below, make sure you complete steps 1, 2, and 4 in the section "Set Up an Event Procedure" after the Quick Guide.

1. In Excel, start the Visual Basic Editor and then double-click the Class1 project item in the Project Explorer to make it the active window.

2. Click *App* from the Object drop-down list and then select Workbook-BeforePrint from the Procedures drop-down list in the class module. In the *WorkbookBeforePrint* event procedure, add the following code:

```
Private Sub App_WorkbookBeforePrint( _
    ByVal Wb As Workbook, Cancel As Boolean)

    Dim sh As Worksheet
    For Each sh In Wb.Worksheets
        sh.PageSetup.LeftHeader = _
            "&""Arial,Bold""MyCompany Confidential"
    Next sh
End Sub
```

3. In the Project Explorer, double-click the Module1 project item to make it the active window, place the cursor in the *InitEvents* procedure, and then press F5.

4. Switch to Excel and click New on the Standard toolbar to create a new workbook.

5. Add some text to the workbook and click the Print button on the File menu.

As described in the *New* event procedure for Excel earlier in this chapter, when you view a worksheet normally, you don't see the header and footer. You only see header and footer information when the worksheet is in Print Preview mode or when it's printed. To see or set headers and footers in Excel, click Page Setup on the File menu and click the Header/Footer tab. In this example, a custom header is set. Therefore, to see the custom header, click the Custom Header button between the Header and Footer previews.

Set Up the PresentationPrint Event in PowerPoint

Before following the steps below, make sure you complete the steps 1, 2, and 4 in the section "Set Up an Event Procedure" after the Quick Guide.

In this procedure, PowerPoint adds the text "MyCompany Confidential" to the Footer placeholder, which is located at the bottom center of the presentation's slide master by default. The index position of the Footer placeholder in the *Placeholders* collection of the presentation's slide master is 4 by default. You use the *SlideMaster* object, accessed through the SlideMaster property on the *Presentation* object, to set footer information on all the slides in a presentation. All slides, with the exception of title slides, share the same slide master. If you set the text in a placeholder on the slide master, it applies to all slides.

1. In PowerPoint, start the Visual Basic Editor and then double-click the Class1 project item in the Project Explorer to make it the active window.

2. Click *App* from the Object drop-down list and then select PresentationPrint from the Procedures drop-down list in the class module. In the *PresentationPrint* event procedure, add the following code:

```
Private Sub App_PresentationPrint(ByVal Pres As Presentation)
    With Pres
        With .SlideMaster.HeadersFooters.Footer
            .Text = "MyCompany Confidential"
            .Visible = msoTrue
        End With
        With .SlideMaster.Shapes.Placeholders(4) _
                .TextFrame.TextRange.Font
            .Bold = msoTrue
            .Name = "Arial"
        End With
    End With
End Sub
```

3. In the Project Explorer, double-click the Module1 project item to make it the active window, place the cursor in the *InitEvents* procedure, and then press F5.

4. Switch to PowerPoint and click New on the Standard toolbar to create a new presentation.

5. Add some text to the presentation and click the Print button on the File menu.

In the preceding *PresentationPrint* event procedure, the Footer placeholder is accessed on the *Shapes* collection of the SlideMaster for the presentation. To change the text of this placeholder or any other placeholder on a slide master, select Header and Footer on the View menu and display the Slide tab.

When the Placeholder Doesn't Exist

The index position of the Footer placeholder in the *Placeholders* collection of the presentation's slide master is 4 by default. For example, the *Print* event procedure you added in the code example above uses the value of 4. However, if the presentation template applied to the presentation doesn't contain the Footer placeholder on the slide master, or if the user deleted the Footer placeholder on the slide master, you use the custom function *PlaceholderShape* to determine if a specific placeholder type exists in a presentation and, if it doesn't, to put the placeholder back in the presentation.

To make the document *Print* event procedure in PowerPoint more robust, you revise the *Print* event procedure with four lines added below the With Pres statement. The first line declares the variable *shpPlaceholder*, which is set to the return value of the custom *PlaceholderShape* function. This function returns the *Shape* object representing the Footer placeholder. You clear the Footer placeholder's text by setting the TextRange property to an empty string (""). Note also the change in the With statement in the last With…End block in the event procedure. This With…End block sets the font attributes in the placeholder. You use the *shpPlaceholder* variable in place of `.SlideMaster.Shapes _ .Placeholders(4)`.

Retrieve or Add a Placeholder Shape

1. Replace the code in the *PresentationPrint* event procedure added in the previous code example with the following *PresentationPrint* event procedure. Also add the custom function *PlaceholderShape* after the event procedure.

```
Private Sub App_PresentationPrint(ByVal Pres As Presentation)
    With Pres
        Dim shpPlaceholder As Shape
        Set shpPlaceholder = PlaceholderShape( _
            .SlideMaster.Shapes, ppPlaceholderFooter, True)
        shpPlaceholder.TextFrame.TextRange = ""

        With .SlideMaster.HeadersFooters.Footer
            .Text = "MyCompany Confidential"
            .Visible = msoTrue
        End With
```

```
        With shpPlaceholder.TextFrame.TextRange.Font
            .Bold = msoTrue
            .Name = "Arial"
        End With
    End With
End Sub


Function PlaceholderShape(shpColl As Shapes, _
    iType As PpPlaceholderType, _
    bAddPlaceholderIfMissing As Boolean) As Shape

    Dim shpPlaceHolder As Shape
    For Each shpPlaceHolder In shpColl.Placeholders
        If shpPlaceHolder.PlaceholderFormat.Type = iType Then
            Set PlaceholderShape = shpPlaceHolder
            Exit Function
        End If
    Next shpPlaceHolder
    If bAddPlaceholderIfMissing Then
        Set PlaceholderShape = _
            shpColl.AddPlaceholder(Type:=iType)
    End If
End Function
```

2. In the Project Explorer, double-click the Module1 project item to make it the active window, place the cursor in the *InitEvents* procedure, and then press F5.

3. Switch to PowerPoint and display the slide master by clicking Master on the View menu and then Slide Master from the submenu. In the slide master, delete the Footer placeholder.

4. Click the Print button on the File menu.

Because the *PlaceholderShape* function is generic, you can use it to determine if a specific type of placeholder exists on a slide and, if it doesn't, to add the placeholder to the slide or slide master. You need to pass three arguments to the function. The first is the *Shapes* collection of the slide or slide master on which you want to search for a specific type of placeholder. The second argument is the placeholder type you want to search for. And the third argument is a Boolean indicating whether the placeholder shape should be added if it doesn't exist in the *Shapes* collection.

In this example, the Footer placeholder will be replaced once the *PresentationPrint* event procedure is executed. The next chapter provides a full description of placeholders in PowerPoint.

Chapter Summary

Setting up event procedures to trap the document New, Open, Save, Close, and Print events in Word, Excel, and PowerPoint allows you to build programs that can supplement the functionality built into these applications. In Word and Excel, you can cancel the built-in behavior of the Save, Close, and Print document events. This ability to cancel the document Save event as well as manually display the Office Save As dialog box provides a way for you to evaluate a specified filename and perform specific actions if conditions are not satisfied. For example, you can determine if certain document properties or header and footer information is set before you save, print, or close a document.

Chapter 6

Inserting and Manipulating Content

Chapter Objectives

- Use code to locate content in a document and use methods and properties to modify the content, regardless of what's on the user's screen.

- Understand how to insert and manipulate the main content types in Microsoft Word, Microsoft Excel, and Microsoft PowerPoint.

- Insert and iterate through specific content types, such as text, tables, cells, and shapes.

- Apply formatting to content, such as font, border, and fill color attributes.

- Understand the different ways of manipulating text in Word, Excel, and PowerPoint.

When you use Microsoft Office applications like Word, Excel, and PowerPoint, your most common task is to specify an area in a document and then manipulate the content. The content you insert and manipulate can be of any type, such as text, tables, charts, and shapes. The formatting you apply generally consists of font, border, and fill attributes. Using the mouse pointer or keyboard, you scroll in the document to search visually for an area that you then manipulate with menu and toolbar commands.

Using Microsoft Visual Basic for Applications, you write code to do what you did visually: locate an area in the document and manipulate the content with methods and properties in the object model. The difference with using Visual Basic code is that you can locate and manipulate content without changing what's displayed on the user's screen. You can choose to write your code so that content manipulation occurs:

- In the background, with the changes then being displayed to the user on screen.

- Only in the background, without any visual changes on the user's display.

- Directly to the content in visual display to the user.

This chapter tells you how to use Visual Basic code to locate a specific area in a document and create and manipulate content such as text, tables, charts, and shapes in that area. It also describes common differences between object model members that manipulate similar content types, such as text.

In Chapters 7 and 8, you'll learn how to create instances of an Office application behind the scenes and create content without having to show the applications. In Chapter 10, you'll learn how to write code that identifies for you, based on events from the keyboard and mouse, what content the user interacts with. Based on this information, you can perform actions such as updating custom toolbars and displaying custom menus and shortcut menus.

Tip   This chapter describes the most common elements of handling content in Word, Excel, and PowerPoint. It also compares the ways in which common content elements (such as text) are different in Word, Excel, and PowerPoint. If you want to quickly see the methods and properties that Word, Excel, and PowerPoint use to insert and manipulate content, use the Macro Recorder.

Chapter 1 outlines the use of the Macro Recorder. It's highly recommended as the fastest way to learn the methods and properties required to insert and manipulate content. In several cases, the examples in this chapter were generated from the Macro Recorder and then modified for style.

Also, when the Word, Excel, or PowerPoint Visual Basic Editor is active, use the online help by pressing F1 to get more information about specific methods and properties used in this chapter. If the Office Assistant is displayed, type 'Working with Range objects' in the text box in its balloon. If the Help window is displayed, type the same thing in the Answer Wizard tab's text box.

Quick Guide: Content Objects

Each Office application deals with a different type of content. Word handles text, Excel handles grids of cells containing data, PowerPoint handles shapes and text in shapes on a slide, Microsoft Access handles structured data stored in a database, and Outlook handles items stored in your mailbox. What the main object in each application is tells you how good it is at handling and manipulating a certain type of content. For example, Word's text-handling objects, methods, and properties are far more robust than Excel's, while Excel's elements are more robust for manipulating data in cells. The following table tells you which object is used to retrieve and manipulate the most common type of data in each Office application (with the exception of Access). The table also lists the simplest code that can access each object.

(continued)

Quick Guide: Content Objects *(continued)*

Application	Content object	Content type	Code to access object
Word	Range	Text	`ActiveDocument.Range`
Excel	Range	Cells	`ActiveSheet.Range`

PowerPoint	Shapes, TextRange	Shapes, text	`ActiveWindow.View.Slide.Shapes`
			`ActiveWindow.View.Slide _`
			`.Shapes(i).TextFrame.TextRange`
			where *i* represents the index position of the shape in the *Shapes* collection.

Outlook	Items	Mail, notes, tasks, etc. in a folder	`ActiveExplorer.Session _`
			`.GetDefaultFolder( _`
			`olFolderInbox).Items`

Although Word and Excel call their main objects *Range,* the word means something different in each application, although both represent the application's main content type. In Word the *Range* object represents the text in a document, but in Excel the *Range* object represents the cells in the workbook.

PowerPoint has two main objects, the *Shapes* collection object and the *TextRange* object, although text can only be retrieved through the *Shapes* collection. PowerPoint's text object, methods, and properties are almost as robust as Word's (while Excel's text-handling methods are very simple).

Outlook represents every item as an item in an Outlook folder. Each specific item has a type, and a specific item object exists for the item type. For example, the *MailItem* object represents a specific mail item in your Inbox.

In Access, your data is represented in a table in a database. The *RecordSet* object is commonly used to retrieve data. In Chapter 8, you'll retrieve data from a database for use in creating a Word, Excel, and PowerPoint document. The code in the Quick Guide in Chapter 8 lists how to retrieve data in an Access database. You'll execute the first procedure in the Quick Guide from within an Access database, and you'll execute the second procedure from the Visual Basic Editor within another Office application.

(continued)

Quick Guide: Content Objects *(continued)*

Accessing Content In Multiple Ways

You may find as you gain experience with Visual Basic that sometimes there is more than one way to retrieve or set content, or information about content, in Word, Excel, PowerPoint, or Outlook. For example, if you start with a new workbook in Excel, the following lines set the same cell to the same value.

```
ActiveSheet.Cells(1, 1).Value = "Region"
ActiveSheet.Range("A1").Value = "Region"
ActiveSheet.Cells.Range("A1").Value = "Region"
```

In fact, because the Value property on the *Range* object in Excel is the default property, you really don't need to specify Value in the lines above. If you remove the `.Value` from each line above, the lines will still be functionally equivalent. In Word, PowerPoint, and Outlook, you'll find different lines of code that produce the same result. However, each way is slightly different—better suited for specific scenarios and for developing more compact, efficient code. Each section in this chapter describes cases in which there is more than one way to locate and manipulate content.

Accessing Content Through Word's *Range* Object

Word's programming model centers around the *Range* object, which represents a contiguous area of text. The *Range* object allows you to retrieve or set text, and apply text formatting in any position in a document. On this object, you'll find the methods and properties that allow you to manipulate or create text. As you'll learn in the following examples, when you insert content other than text, you need to specify where the content, such as a shape or embedded object, is anchored.

A range of text has a starting and ending character position and exists in distinct parts of the document, such as the main body, headers, footers, endnotes, and comments. Thus, there are many ways to access the *Range* object, including access from a cell in a table, a header, or a paragraph object. The following line of code provides the most common access to the *Range* object:

```
ActiveDocument.Range.Text
```

If you type this line after a question mark ('?') in the Immediate window in the Visual Basic Editor in Word, the program will print the main text of the document in the Immediate window.

Tip The code listed here that describes how to insert and manipulate document content in Word is also found in the WdContnt.bas code module in the Chapter 6 practice folder on the CD that comes with this book.

Handling Text

The *Range* object allows you access to all text, no matter where it is in a document. You can set the *Range* object so that it represents all or only a portion of a range of text. If you set a variable to the line ActiveDocument.Range, the variable represents the range of text in the main body in a document. This could be anywhere from a single paragraph to many pages of text. Within every *Range* object, you can return more granular units of text. The *Range* object allows you to iterate through units of text from as large as a section to as small as a paragraph, sentence, word, and even a single character.

Determining Where Text Belongs

Whenever you return a *Range* object, you can use the Paragraphs, Sentences, Words, or Character properties to return the collection of paragraphs, sentences, words, or characters from a range of text. One of the nice things about the *Range* object in Word is that from any *Range* object you can navigate up and down the text "hierarchy" tree. What this means is that if you assign a variable representing a word to a *Range* object, you can determine what sentence, paragraph, or section the word is in. The same holds for any unit of text.

```
Sub NavigateUpTextHierarchy()
    Dim rng As Range
    If ActiveWindow.Selection.Type = wdSelectionIP Then
        Set rng = ActiveWindow.Selection.Range
        Debug.Print rng.Words(1)
        Debug.Print rng.Sentences(1)
        Debug.Print rng.Paragraphs(1).Range
    End If
End Sub
```

Even if a *Range* object represents an insertion point (as is commonly the case), when you return the active selection in a window, you can determine what word the insertion point is in. (An insertion point occurs when the blinking cursor is between two characters of text.) See Chapter 9 for more information. In the procedure above, the If...Then statement determines if the selection is an insertion point. If it is, you set the *rng* variable to the range that represents the insertion. Although there's no text in the *rng,* the last three lines in the If...Then block print to the Immediate window in the Visual Basic Editor in Word the text of the word, sentence, and paragraph where the insertion point resides.

Iterate Through Words

The following are two different procedures that each search for the word *the* and keep track of how many instances are found. The first procedure can be very slow, depending on how many words the document has. The For Each...Next loop iterates through the *Words* collection in the main body text of the document. The If...Then statement uses the built-in Visual Basic for Applications functions *Trim$* and *LCase$* to remove the spaces after the text of the word and sets the text of the word to lowercase. The number of occurrences found is printed to the Immediate window.

Note In Word, a unit of text representing a word consists of the text of the word followed by the space between the text and the next word. If you double-click on a word in a Word document, the text and the space after the text is highlighted. The same principle holds for sentences. A sentence in Word consists of the text in the sentence followed by the space after the period. A paragraph includes the text, the space after the end of the text (if any), and the paragraph marker.

```
Sub IterateThroughWords()
    Dim wrd As Range, iCount As Integer
    For Each wrd In ActiveDocument.Range.Words
        If Trim$(LCase$(wrd.Text)) = "the" Then
            iCount = iCount + 1
        End If
    Next wrd
    Debug.Print "The word 'the' used " & iCount & " times."
End Sub
```

You can also use Word's *Find* object as a method of finding the number of instances a word is found in a document. As you'll see later in this section, the functionality in the *Find* object represents the functionality in the Find dialog box in Word. Your code uses the *Find* object to take advantage of Word's built-in search compatibilities rather than relying on the previous procedure's word iteration.

```
Sub IterateThroughWordsUsingFindMethod()
    Dim iCount As Integer
    With ActiveDocument.Range.Find
        .ClearFormatting
        .MatchWholeWord = True

        Do While .Execute(FindText:= "the", _
                Forward:=True, Format:=True) = True
            With .Parent ' returns Range object
                iCount = iCount + 1
                .Move Unit:=wdWord, Count:=1
            End With
        Loop
    End With
```

```
    Debug.Print "The word 'the' used " & _
        iCount & " times."
End Sub
```

The use of the *Find* object is described starting on page 195 under the heading "Find and Replace."

Insert Paragraphs

When you build document content programmatically, you commonly have to insert paragraphs. Word provides two convenient methods for creating a new paragraph before or after an existing one: *InsertParagraphBefore* and *InsertParagraphAfter*. When you access a range representing an existing paragraph or the beginning or end of a paragraph, you can use either method to insert a new paragraph.

You can also use the *InsertBefore* and *InsertAfter* methods to insert text. The following procedure assumes that the active document contains at least three paragraphs. The code inserts two new paragraphs before the third one, inserts text into the second new paragraph added, and then adds another paragraph after the second. This gives the appearance of adding a blank line, a new paragraph, and another blank line between the initial second and third paragraphs.

```
Sub InsertNewParagraphWithLineSpaces()
    Dim rng As Range
    Set rng = ActiveDocument.Paragraphs(3).Range
    With rng
        .InsertParagraphBefore
        .InsertParagraphBefore
        .InsertBefore "New paragraph."
        .InsertParagraphBefore
    End With
End Sub
```

Of course, you can reduce the code above to just insert a new paragraph between the second and third paragraphs without the two blank lines by removing the two extra lines containing the *InsertParagraphBefore* method.

```
Sub InsertNewParagraph()
    Dim rng As Range
    Set rng = ActiveDocument.Paragraphs(3).Range
    With rng
        .InsertParagraphBefore
        .InsertBefore "New paragraph."
    End With
End Sub
```

Another very common task in solutions is to insert content at the end of text in a document's main body. The following procedure inserts text at the end of a range using the combination of the *InsertParagraphAfter* and *InsertAfter* methods:

```
Sub InsertNewParagraphWithInsertAfter()
    Dim rngEndOfDoc As Range
    With ActiveDocument.Paragraphs.Last.Range
        .InsertParagraphAfter
        .InsertAfter "New paragraph."
    End With
End Sub
```

The section "Inserting Content at the End of a Document" below describes in more depth how to add content in this location.

Iterate Through Paragraphs in a Bulleted or Numbered List

Word provides a way of determining if a paragraph exists within a list. Two main list types exist: numbered and bulleted. To detect if a paragraph, sentence, word, or character exists in a list, you can use the ListType property on the *ListFormat* object. You can access the *ListFormat* object from a *Range* object.

```
Sub IterateThroughParagraphsInBulletedLists()
    Dim para As Paragraph
    For Each para In ActiveDocument.Paragraphs
        If para.Range.ListFormat _
            .ListType = wdListBullet Then
            Debug.Print para.Range.Text
        End If
    Next para
End Sub
```

This procedure iterates through the paragraphs in the main body of the active document. If the list type is bulleted, the text of the bulleted paragraph is printed to the Immediate window in the Visual Basic Editor.

Inserting Content at the End of a Document

You'll often find Office Visual Basic for Applications solutions that use Word to create a report based on, for example, data in a database. You write the code so that it inserts text and data progressively into the document. The main heading is inserted, followed by text, then data, and so on. At each point, the code finds the end of the document and inserts new content. Other scenarios that involve inserting content at the end of the document include adding a new section or an appendix to an existing document. Use the following With...End block to return a *Range* object that represents the end of a document. The *Range* object returned consists only of the last character in the main text.

```
Dim rngEndOfDoc As Range
Set rngEndOfDoc = ActiveDocument.Range
```

```
With rngEndOfDoc
    .Collapse Direction:=wdCollapseEnd
    ' use methods here to insert text into document
End With
```

Once you've returned the last character in the main body of text in a document, you can use a few methods to insert content at the end of the document.

Insert a Paragraph at the End of the Main Body

The *Collapse* method collapses a range to the starting or ending position, depending on what direction you specify in the *Direction* argument of the *Collapse* method. The starting and ending points become equal when a range is collapsed.

```
Sub InsertNewParagraphUsingCollapse()
    Dim rng As Range
    Set rng = ActiveDocument.Range
    With rng
        .Collapse Direction:=wdCollapseEnd
        .InsertParagraphAfter
        .InsertAfter "End of document."
    End With
End Sub
```

As mentioned in the Quick Guide section at the beginning of this chapter, in code there is more than one way to accomplish the same task. The main difference between this procedure and the following one is how the range at the end of the document is returned. In the following procedure, the *Collapse* procedure isn't required when the range of the last paragraph is accessed:

```
Sub InsertNewParagraphUsingInsertAfter()
    With ActiveDocument.Paragraphs.Last.Range
        .InsertParagraphAfter
        .InsertAfter "End of document."
    End With
End Sub
```

Insert a Table at the End of a Document

When you add a table to a document, you need to specify the range where the table is to appear. If the range is more than an insertion point, the table replaces the range when inserted. In the following procedure, you insert the table at the end of the document. In the With...End block, a paragraph of text that represents a heading for the table is added before the table.

The *InsertParagraphAfter* method inserts the new paragraph at the end of the document. The range is then collapsed to a single character position at the end of the document. The text "Data: " is added and formatted as bold. A second paragraph is inserted, the range collapsed again and the new table with five rows and three columns is inserted.

```
Sub InsertTableAtEndOfDocument()
    Dim rngEndOfDoc As Range
    Set rngEndOfDoc = ActiveDocument.Range
    With rngEndOfDoc
        .InsertParagraphAfter
        .Collapse Direction:=wdCollapseEnd
        .Text = "Data: "
        .Font.Bold = True

        .InsertParagraphAfter
        .Collapse Direction:=wdCollapseEnd
        .Tables.Add rngEndOfDoc, 5, 3
    End With
End Sub
```

Alternately, you can set *rngEndOfDoc* to the range of the last paragraph. To do this, change the object expression of the Set statement in the procedure above to `ActiveDocument.Paragraphs.Last.Range`. For another example of this, see the code in the section on the previous page.

Insert a Table Between Paragraphs

You use similar code to insert a table between paragraphs as you do to add it to the end of the document's main body. The main difference is that instead of specifying the range of the document and then collapsing the range to a single character position, you return the range of the paragraph where you want to insert the table.

```
Sub InsertTableBetweenParagraphs()
    Dim rng As Range
    Set rng = ActiveDocument.Paragraphs(1).Range
    With rng
        .Collapse Direction:=wdCollapseEnd
        .Tables.Add rng, 5, 3
    End With
End Sub
```

Text Formatting

You can access the methods and properties that allow your code to format text through the *Range* object to such objects as *Font* and *ParagraphFormat*. The *Font* object, which is found in Word, Excel, and PowerPoint, is used to set text attributes such as bold, italic, and color. The *ParagraphFormat* object allows your code to set properties such as indent level, borders, and shading. The *ParagraphFormat* object contains access to objects, methods, and properties that represent functionality in the Paragraph and the Borders And Shading dialog boxes. You can access both of these dialog boxes from the Format menu in Word.

```
Sub FormatText()
    With ActiveDocument.Paragraphs(1).Range

        With .Font
            .Bold = True
            .Italic = True
            .Color = wdColorBlueGray
        End With

        With .ParagraphFormat
            .FirstLineIndent = InchesToPoints(1)
            .Alignment = wdAlignParagraphCenter
            With .Borders(wdBorderTop)
                .LineStyle = wdLineStyleSingle
                .LineWidth = wdLineWidth050pt
            End With
            With .Borders(wdBorderBottom)
                .LineStyle = wdLineStyleSingle
                .LineWidth = wdLineWidth225pt
            End With
        End With

    End With
End Sub
```

This procedure applies formatting to the first paragraph of the active document and sets font attributes of the first paragraph, along with setting the indent of the first line of the paragraph to 1 inch. It centers the paragraph alignment and applies top and bottom borders of different widths.

Stories

A Word document can contain text in parts that are distinct from one another. For example, you insert headers and footers that are independent of the text in the main body. Word calls each distinct area of text a *story* and represents the distinction in the *StoryRanges* collection. This collection allows you to access the 11 different types of stories that can be part of a document. A document's main body, which has most of your text, is referred to as the *main text* story. If a document contains not only main body text, but also headers, footers, and comments, there are four stories: main text, header, footer, and comment. The enumeration WdStoryType contains the 11 different story constants. Some examples of constants are the values wdMainTextStory, wdFootnotesStory, wdEndnotesStory, and wdCommentsStory.

Since you most commonly access the main text story, Word provides two ways to access it. The Range property and the Content property on the *Document* object each returns a *Range* object representing the document's main text. In Word the lines on the next page all return a *Range* object representing the same text in the document.

```
ActiveDocument.Content
ActiveDocument.Range
ActiveDocument.StoryRanges(wdMainTextStory)
```

If you typed a question mark ('?') followed by any of the lines above in the Immediate window in Word's Visual Basic Editor, the same text content would be printed. Since the Text property is the default property of the *Range* object, Visual Basic returns the text of the range specified in the line of code.

Text Styles

The Style drop-down list on Word's Formatting toolbar lists a document's built-in and user-defined paragraph and character styles. The most common styles are the predefined set in the Normal.dot template: Normal, Heading 1, Heading 2, and Heading 3. Depending on how you use and define the template and styles, the list can vary considerably. Word has a number of built-in styles that are listed as constants in the WdBuiltInStyle enumeration. The name of each built-in style depends on the language version of Word you installed on a machine. For example, the name for the built-in style "Normal" changes to its Japanese equivalent on a Japanese installation of Word. The constants let you determine if a paragraph has a specific built-in style without having to worry about what the local name of the style is. Word automatically determines the local name of a style.

```
Sub IterateThroughParagraphsByStyle()
    Dim para As Paragraph
    For Each para In ActiveDocument.Paragraphs
        If para.Style = _
            ActiveDocument.Styles(wdStyleNormal) Then
            Debug.Print para.Range.Text
        End If
    Next para
End Sub
```

This procedure uses the constant wdStyleNormal to determine if the name of the style applied to a paragraph, represented by the object variable *para*, is the same as the built-in Normal style. If so, the text is printed to the Immediate window in the Visual Basic Editor.

Create an Outline Document Based on Another Document's Paragraph Styles

You can use the technique just described to do things like copy paragraphs that have particular styles. In the following procedure, you create a new document based on the text of the active document. You use a For Each...Next loop to iterate through the paragraphs of the active document, and the Select Case statement determines if the paragraph style is Heading 1, Heading 2, or Heading 3. If the paragraph style is any of these styles, the procedure copies the formatted text to the end of the text range of the new document created. The new document represents the outline of the active document.

```
Sub CreateOutlineDocument()
    Dim para As Paragraph
    Dim docActive As Document, docOutline As Document

    Set docActive = ActiveDocument
    Set docOutline = Application.Documents.Add

    For Each para In docActive.Paragraphs
        Select Case para.Style

        Case docActive.Styles(wdStyleHeading1), _
            docActive.Styles(wdStyleHeading2), _
            docActive.Styles(wdStyleHeading3)

            With docOutline.Range
                .Collapse wdCollapseEnd
                .FormattedText = _
                    para.Range.FormattedText
                .InsertParagraphAfter
            End With
        End Select
    Next para
End Sub
```

One of the interesting things in this procedure is the line:

```
.FormattedText = para.Range.FormattedText
```

The FormattedText property returns a range containing not just the text but the character formatting from the specified range as well. The line of code above retrieves the formatted text in the active document and applies the formatted text in the new outline document. If you don't want to apply the same text formatting to the outline document, replace the line above with the following one, which sets just the text in the new outline document.

```
.Text = para.Range.Text
```

PowerPoint and Excel don't have an equivalent to the FormattedText property. Excel does, however, provide a *PasteSpecial* method to specify inserting rich text formatting for the cell data and text. This allows you to copy and paste cell data and text, along with cell and text formatting, from one cell to another in any workbook. PowerPoint doesn't have an equivalent to the *PasteSpecial* method.

Find and Replace

Word has the best text-finding capabilities in Office. You'll find this quality reflected in the Find dialog box in Word, which you access by clicking Find on the Edit menu. In Excel and PowerPoint, the Find dialog box doesn't provide as many choices for narrowing down a text search. The following procedures were written so that the procedure that actually finds and replaces the text is separate from the code that specifies what text needs to be found and what text should replace it. This allows you to call the *FindAndReplace* procedure from many places in your project.

```
Sub TestFindAndReplace()
    FindAndReplace sFindText:="dog", _
        sReplaceWithText:="CAT"
End Sub

Sub FindAndReplace(sFindText As String, _
    sReplaceWithText As String)

    With ActiveDocument.Range.Find
        .ClearFormatting
        .MatchWholeWord = True

        Do While .Execute(FindText:=sFindText, _
            Forward:=True, Format:=True) = True

            With .Parent ' returns Range object
                .Text = sReplaceWithText
                .Bold = True
                .Move Unit:=wdWord, Count:=1
            End With
        Loop
    End With
End Sub
```

For example purposes, note that the text that's found and replaced is bolded. Although it's added here to provide a visual indicator in the active document where the text has been replaced, you should remove this line. This example also assumes that you have the word "dog" in your document. You can replace the find and replace text in *TestFindAndReplace* with any text.

Find and Replace Hyperlinks

Word 2000, like Excel and PowerPoint, makes it easy for you to create HTML documents that you can display in your Web browser with the same fidelity as in Word. You just save your documents with the HTML file format in the Save As dialog box or with the *SaveAs* method (as discussed in Chapter 4). HTML documents in your Web browser commonly contain hyperlinks. Office's new Insert Hyperlink dialog box, which you display by clicking Hyperlink on the Insert menu, provides a simple way to add hyperlinks to document content.

```
Sub TestFindAndReplaceHyperlinks()
    FindAndReplaceHyperlinks sFindText:="Microsoft", _
        sHyperlink:="http://www.microsoft.com"
End Sub
```

```
Sub FindAndReplaceHyperlinks( _
    sFindText As String, sHyperlink As String)
    Dim rng As Range

    With ActiveDocument.Content.Find
        .ClearFormatting

        Do While .Execute(FindText:=sFindText, _
            Forward:=True, Format:=True) = True

            Set rng = .Parent
            With rng
                .Hyperlinks.Add rng, sHyperlink
                .Font.Color = wdColorSeaGreen
                .Move Unit:=wdWord, Count:=1
            End With
        Loop
    End With
End Sub
```

In the active document add some text with the word "Microsoft" scattered throughout. Run the *TestFindAndReplaceHyperlinks* subroutine from a code module in the Visual Basic Editor in Word. This procedure passes the text to be searched for in the active document. It also passes the hyperlink URL that should be added to the text when it's found. When the Do...Loop in the second procedure finds an instance of the search text "Microsoft," the program inserts the hyperlink *http://www.microsoft.com* and sets the color of the text "Microsoft" to sea green. To preview the HTML document in the Web browser, click Web Page Preview from the File menu in Word. Click on the word "Microsoft" and the Web browser should navigate to Microsoft's home page (if your computer is connected to the Internet).

Tables

Tables are common content elements found in many Office documents. The following two procedures create a simple five-row by three-column table at the end of the active document's main body. The new table is set to the variable *tbl*, and the second With...End block in the procedure sets properties of the table. Within the With...End block, you format the table to the Classic 1 format (listed in the Table AutoFormat dialog box, Table menu). The program then calls the procedure *InsertTableData,* which fills the second and third columns with random values.

```
Sub InsertTable()
    Dim tbl As Table, rngEndOfDoc As Range
    Set rngEndOfDoc = ActiveDocument.Range
```

```
    With rngEndOfDoc
        .Collapse Direction:=wdCollapseEnd
        Set tbl = .Tables.Add(rngEndOfDoc, 5, 3)
    End With

    With tbl
        .AutoFormat Format:=wdTableFormatClassic1
        InsertTableData tbl
        .Columns.AutoFit
    End With
End Sub

Sub InsertTableData(tbl As Table)
    Dim x As Integer, y As Integer
    With tbl
        For x = 2 To .Rows.Count
            For y = 2 To .Columns.Count
                .Cell(x, y).Range.Text = _
                    Format$(Rnd(x + y), "####0.00")
            Next y
        Next x
    End With
End Sub
```

Because the data's source can vary, you write the code to insert data into the table so that it exists in a separate procedure. This code separation keeps table insertion and formatting separate from the data that's inserted.

Shapes: Inline and Floating

You can insert shapes into a Word document as either *floating* shapes or *inline* shapes. Word is the only application that has two distinct shape collections. Excel and PowerPoint have only the *Shapes* collection, but Word has both the *InlineShapes* and the *Shapes* collections. The difference, as the name *InlineShapes* implies, is that some shapes will exist between two text characters (that is, in line with the text). The inline shape resides within a character position in a range's text stream. Objects in the *Shapes* collection, on the other hand, float on a content layer above or below the text in the Word document.

Although text can be wrapped around an object so that the object appears to be inline with the text, technically the object lives above the text. AutoShapes can only be free-floating, but pictures, for example, can be inserted as either inline or free-floating. You can change the layout of a picture shape by using the *ConvertToInlineShape* method and the *ConvertToShape* method to convert shapes from one type to the other. Also, you can choose from any of the wrapping styles to convert the shape from one type to the other by selecting a picture, clicking Format Picture on the Format menu, and displaying the Layout tab.

Using Excel's *Range* and *Chart* Objects

Excel's programming model centers around the *Range* object, which represents any single cell or adjacent or nonadjacent blocks of cells on a worksheet. The *Range* object allows you to retrieve or set data in cells as well as apply formatting to cells in a worksheet. When you work with a worksheet on screen, you can select a range of cells and then hold down the CTRL key while selecting another range of cells. Each range of cells selected is a contiguous block. In this case, if you set a variable to the selection in the active window in Excel, the *Range* object would contain a combination of cells from both cell blocks. You can iterate through the cells in the range to return data such as a cell's address to apply settings to all cells simultaneously.

You can access the *Range* object in several ways, such as from the selection in the active window, a hyperlink object, and a worksheet object. The following line of code provides the most common access to the *Range* object. The code assumes that the active sheet is a worksheet rather than a chart. The Cells property returns a *Range* object representing all cells in the active worksheet.

```
ActiveSheet.Cells
```

Tip The code listed here that describes how to insert and manipulate workbook content in Excel is also found in the XlContnt.bas code module in the Chapter 6 practice folder on the CD that comes with this book.

Handling Cell Data

As you learned in the Quick Guide at the beginning of this chapter, there are multiple ways to access and manipulate content. If you start with a new workbook in Excel, the following lines set the same cell to the same value:

```
ActiveSheet.Cells(1, 1).Value = "Region"
ActiveSheet.Range("A1").Value = "Region"
ActiveSheet.Cells.Range("A1").Value = "Region"
```

In fact, because the Value property on the *Range* object in Excel is the default property, you really don't need to specify *Value* in the lines above. If you remove the .Value from each line, they'll still be functionally equivalent. Each way is inherently different and suited for specific scenarios and for developing more compact, efficient code. The following procedure provides a very simple way of retrieving data in a cell. The value and formula of the first ten cells in the first column of the active worksheet are printed to the Immediate window in the Visual Basic Editor in Excel.

```
Sub ReadingValueInCells()
    Dim i As Integer
    For i = 1 To 10
        Debug.Print ActiveSheet.Cells(i, 1).Value
        Debug.Print ActiveSheet.Cells(i, 1).Formula
    Next i
End Sub
```

Display the Address of a Range

By default, a range's Address property is provided in the A1-style reference. This means that the address of a cell is returned as a string such as "A1" or "B4" as opposed to "R1C1" or "R4C2" (or row 4, column 2). In Excel the A1-style reference is displayed in the Name box to the left of the Formula bar. Reference styles can be one of the following XlReferenceStyle constants: xlA1 or xlR1C1. If you returned the address of a single cell, for example, A1, the value returned from the Address property on the *Range* object is "A1." In a custom dialog box, you may want to display the address without the dollar signs so that the user sees a simpler address value.

```
Sub GetAddressOfSelection()
    Dim rng As Range
    If TypeName(ActiveWindow.Selection) = "Range" Then
        Set rng = ActiveWindow.Selection
        Debug.Print rng.Address
        Debug.Print StrippedAddress(rng.Address)
    End If
End Sub

Function StrippedAddress(str As String) As String
    Dim i As Integer, temp As String
    For i = 1 To Len(str)
        If Mid$(str, i, 1) <> "$" Then
            temp = temp & Mid$(str, i, 1)
        End If
    Next i
    StrippedAddress = temp
End Function
```

This procedure returns the address of the currently selected cells. If the selection isn't a range (that is, a shape is selected), the procedure is exited. Otherwise, the procedure passes the address of the range to the *StrippedAddress* function to remove dollar signs. If you select one or more cells in the active worksheet and run the *GetAddressOfSelection* procedure in a module in the Visual Basic Editor in Excel, the result is printed to the Immediate window.

Insert a New Row and Column of Cells

In order to insert cell content, you may have to insert new cells first. The following procedure uses the *Insert* method on the *Range* object to insert a new row at the top of the active worksheet and a new column at the left. If the active sheet isn't a worksheet (that is, it's a chart sheet), the procedure is exited. Otherwise, the use of the Rows property returns a *Range* object representing the first row of the active worksheet and the use of the Columns property returns a *Range* object representing the first column.

```
Sub InsertRowAndColumnByShiftingCells()
    Dim sh As Worksheet
    Set sh = ActiveSheet
    If TypeName(sh) <> "Worksheet" Then Exit Sub
    sh.Rows("1:1").Insert Shift:=xlDown
    sh.Columns("A:A").Insert Shift:=xlRight
End Sub
```

Cell Formatting

To format cells, you use objects, methods, and properties similar to those in Word and PowerPoint. When you access a *Range* object, you can use objects such as *Borders* and *Font* to manipulate the border and font attributes of the cells in the range. You access both attributes through the *Range* object by using the Borders and Font properties, respectively. In the following procedure, you set the *rng* variable to the selection in the active window if the selection is one or more cells. Other selections could include charts or shapes. Chapter 9 provides further information on working with selections in Excel.

```
Sub FormatCell()
    Dim rng As Range
    If TypeName(ActiveWindow.Selection) <> _
        "Range" Then Exit Sub
    Set rng = ActiveWindow.Selection
    If TypeName(rng) <> "Range" Then Exit Sub
    With rng
        With .Borders(xlEdgeBottom)
            .LineStyle = xlContinuous
            .Weight = xlThick
            .ColorIndex = 1
        End With
        With .Font
            .Name = "Arial"
            .Color = RGB(112, 220, 21)
            .Bold = True
            .Italic = True
        End With
    End With
End Sub
```

Once you set the range to the *rng* variable, the line style of the bottom edge border of each cell is set so there's a continuous, thick black line. If the cell displays any value, the text font will be Arial and boldface and the color will be green. You can change this example so that the *rng* variable is set to any cell range in a workbook.

Handling Text

The methods and properties you use to insert and manipulate text in a cell in Excel are not as rich as those in Word and PowerPoint. In Word and PowerPoint you can access and manipulate text by any unit of text. For example, you can access text by characters, words, sentences, or paragraphs. In Excel, however, you have two options—you can access all the text in a cell at once, or you can access a set of text characters in a cell.

In Word and PowerPoint, you can use the Text property to return and set text. In Excel, on the other hand, the Text property on the *Range* object is read-only. For example, you can use the Text property to read the text in a cell, but you have to use the Value property to write text into a cell. Because you can also use the Value property to read text in a cell, you don't need to use the Text property on the *Range* object. When you access the *Range* object that represents a cell, you can use the Value property to return all text in the cell.

Format Text in Cells

If you want to apply formatting or change text in any part of a text string in a cell, use the *Characters* collection object, which is the only unit of text you can retrieve from a cell. Using the Characters property on the *Range* object, you can access the *Characters* collection object and format characters in the text string. To return a specific sequence of characters, you specify the *Start* and *Length* arguments in the Characters property of the *Range* object. In the following procedure, set the variable *rng* to the selection in the active window. If the selection isn't a cell, the procedure exits. If the selection is more than one cell, the procedure applies the value and formatting of text to each cell in the selection.

```
Sub FormatCellText()
    Dim rng As Range
    If TypeName(ActiveWindow.Selection) <> _
        "Range" Then Exit Sub

    Set rng = ActiveWindow.Selection
    rng.Value = "This is some text"

    With rng.Characters(Start:=1, Length:=7).Font
        .Name = "Arial"
        .FontStyle = "Regular"
        .Size = 10
        .Shadow = True
        .Underline = xlUnderlineStyleSingle
        .ColorIndex = 21
    End With
```

```
    With rng.Characters(Start:=9, Length:=4).Font
        .Name = "Arial"
        .Bold = True
        .Size = 11
        .Underline = xlUnderlineStyleNone
        .ColorIndex = xlAutomatic
    End With
End Sub
```

The value of the cells in the *rng* variable is set to "This is some text." Two arguments are specified in the Characters property of the *Range* object. The first is the *Start* argument, which represents the character position in the cell text string at which the part to be returned begins. The second argument, *Length*, indicates the number of characters to return. Both arguments are optional. If you don't specify either one, `rng.Characters` returns a *Characters* collection object that represents all the characters in a cell's text string. Excel's Characters property is similar to the *Mid* function, which is built in to the Visual Basic for Applications language. See Chapter 4 for information on the *Mid* function (as used to parse a filename string) or use the online help in the Visual Basic Editor to learn more.

You use the Font property on the *Characters* collection object to return the *Font* object in Excel. You can use the Name and Size properties to change the name and size of the font, and you use other properties to apply more settings to characters such as color, bold, and italics.

Worksheets

The breakdown of content in Excel is similar to that of PowerPoint. In a PowerPoint presentation, the content resides on a slide. In an Excel workbook, the content resides in a worksheet. The *Worksheets* collection allows your code to iterate through and work with specific worksheets in a workbook. You can also use the *Worksheets* collection object to add a new worksheet and hence, new content.

Iterate Through the Worksheet Collection

The following procedure iterates through worksheets in the *Worksheets* collection object. Each worksheet is assigned to the variable *sh* and the name and index of each worksheet is printed to the Immediate window in the Visual Basic Editor in Excel.

```
Sub IterateThroughWorksheets()
    Dim sh As Worksheet
    For Each sh In ActiveWorkbook.Worksheets
        Debug.Print "Sheet name: " & sh.Name
        Debug.Print "Sheet Index: " & sh.Index
    Next sh
End Sub
```

The Index property returns a number representing the position of the worksheet in the *Worksheets* collection. The Index number is directly related to the position of the worksheet's tab on screen. The Name property returns the name visible on the tab. You can also use the value returned by the Name property as the *Index* argument in the Worksheets(*index*) property on the *Workbook* object so your code can return a specific *Worksheet* object.

Insert Worksheets

You use the *Add* method of the *Worksheets* collection to insert a new worksheet in the workbook. The *Add* method takes four arguments: *Before, After, Count,* and *Type*. If you don't specify the *Before* or *After* argument, a new worksheet is inserted before the active worksheet in the active workbook. This is the same behavior as inserting a new worksheet by clicking the Worksheet command on the Insert menu.

```
Sub InsertWorkSheet()
    Dim sh As Worksheet, shNew As Worksheet
    Dim wb As Workbook
    For Each sh In ActiveWorkbook.Worksheets
        If sh.Name = "Sheet3" Then
            Set wb = sh.Parent
            Set shNew = wb.Worksheets.Add(Before:=sh)
            shNew.Name = "New Sheet"
            Exit For
        End If
    Next sh
End Sub
```

In this procedure, you use the For Each...Next loop to iterate through the *Worksheets* collection. You use the If...Then block to determine the name of the worksheet implicitly assigned to the variable *sh* by the For Each...Next loop. If the worksheet name is "Sheet3," the program adds a new worksheet before Sheet3, sets its name to "New Sheet," and exits the loop.

Tip   In the preceding procedure, *sh.Parent* returns the *Workbook* object. The parent of a worksheet isn't the *Worksheets* collection, but the workbook. In all cases in Word, Excel, and PowerPoint, the parent of an item in a collection isn't the collection, but the parent of the collection. In many cases the Parent property of an object returns an object defined as the generic Object type. If you replace the If...Then block in the preceding procedure with the following, when you type the dot ('.') after *sh.Parent*, the Auto List Members drop-down list doesn't appear.

```
If sh.Name = "Sheet3" Then
    Set shNew = sh.Parent.Worksheets.Add(Before:=sh)
    shNew.Name = "New Sheet"
    Exit For
End If
```

Note   To take advantage of the Auto List Members drop-down list again, the preceding procedure declared a new variable *wb* as type Workbook and assigned *wb* to *sh.Parent*. When you use the variable *wb* in your code, the Auto List Members drop-down list will appear. See the sidebar "When Auto List Members Doesn't Appear" under the section "Auto List Members" in Chapter 1.

Using Find and Replace

To insert a hyperlink into an Excel workbook, you select a range of cells and then click Hyperlink on the Insert menu. In Visual Basic for Applications, you can use Excel's *Find* method, which quickly iterates through all the content in a workbook, searches for specified text, and adds a hyperlink. When the method finds text matching the criteria, it adds a hyperlink to a cell's text and sets the hyperlink to the URL specified in the procedure *TestFindAndReplace*. Adding hyperlinks to documents will become even more common now that Office 2000 adds the capability to easily save Word, Excel, and PowerPoint documents in HTML format for display in your Web browser. If you type the word "Microsoft" in several workbook cells and then run the *TestFindAndReplace* procedure, all cells containing the text "Microsoft" would have a hyperlink to *http://www.microsoft.com* inserted.

In the following procedure, the For Each...Next loop iterates through the *Worksheets* collection of the active workbook and implicitly assigns the object variable *sh* to the next *Worksheet* object in the collection. Within the loop, the *Find* method searches through all the cells in the worksheet for the value specified in the *What* argument of the *Find* method. The Set statement assigns the object variable *rng* to the cell range returned by the *Find* method.

```
Sub TestFindAndReplace()
    FindAndReplaceHyperlink sFindText:="Microsoft", _
        sHyperlink:="http://www.microsoft.com"
End Sub


Sub FindAndReplaceHyperlink(sFindText As String, _
        sHyperlink As String)
    Dim rng As Range, sh As Worksheet
    Dim sFirstAddress As String

    For Each sh In ActiveWorkbook.Worksheets
        Set rng = sh.Cells.Find(What:=sFindText, _
            LookIn:=xlValues, MatchCase:=True)

        If Not rng Is Nothing Then
            sFirstAddress = rng.Address
```

```
            Do
                If Trim$(rng.Text) = sFindText Then
                    rng.Hyperlinks.Add _
                        Anchor:=rng, Address:=sHyperlink
                End If
                Set rng = sh.Cells.FindNext(rng)
            Loop While rng.Address <> sFirstAddress
        End If
    Next sh
End Sub
```

You use the variable *rng* to store the cell range in the worksheet that has text matching the value of sFindText. If the trimmed value of the cell found by the *Find* or *FindNext* method is equal to the sFindText value, the program adds a hyperlink to the cell. The *Add* method of the *Hyperlinks* object accepts three arguments. The first argument, *Anchor*, represents the cell range where the hyperlink is to be anchored. The second argument, *Address*, represents the hyperlink address, which can be a filename or URL, and is the same value that's entered in the "Type the file or Web page name" text box in the Insert Hyperlink dialog box. The optional third argument, *SubAddress,* isn't specified here.

Tables

Because most of Excel's content is inherently organized in cells, tables are second nature. Hence, unlike Word, the capability of explicitly inserting and returning access to a *Table* object doesn't exist in Excel. Excel creates tables by organizing cell data to appear as a table.

Organizing and setting data in cells commonly occurs relative to a specific cell. For example, as the following example shows, if you select cell B5, then `ActiveWindow.Selection.Range("B1")` returns cell C5 because B1 is relative to the *Range* object, B5, that is returned by the Selection property. On the other hand, the code `ActiveSheet.Range("B5")` always returns cell B5. To see this in operation, select cell B5 in the active worksheet, switch to the Visual Basic Editor in Excel, and add the following line in the Immediate window:

```
?ActiveWindow.Selection.Range("B1").Address
```

When you press ENTER after the line, the program prints the value "C5". In the following example, the data for the table, including row and column headings, are entered relative to the starting cell B5. Later, you use the text in the cells that represent the row and column headings, as well as the cells containing data, to create a chart in Excel.

Insert Tables

The following two procedures create a simple five-row by three-column table. You create the table starting at cell B5 in the active worksheet, setting the variable *rngStart* to cell B5. You enter all values for the table, including the labels for the x axis and legend, in the worksheet relative to cell B5. Within the

With…End block, you set the heading for each row and column to the appropriate cell value. You call the procedure *InsertTableData,* which fills the second and third columns with random values. The cell B5, represented by the variable *rngStart,* is passed as the one and only argument to the *InsertTableData* procedure.

```
Sub InsertTable()
    Dim sh As Worksheet, rngStart As Range

    If TypeName(ActiveSheet) <> "Worksheet" Then Exit Sub
    Set sh = ActiveSheet

    Set rngStart = sh.Range("B5") ' starting cell
    With rngStart
        .Cells(1, 1) = "Region"
        .Cells(1, 2) = "Projected"
        .Cells(1, 3) = "Actual"
        .Cells(2, 1) = "Northwest"
        .Cells(3, 1) = "Northeast"
        .Cells(4, 1) = "Southwest"
        .Cells(5, 1) = "Southeast"
    End With

    InsertTableData rngStart
    rngStart.Range("A1:C5").Columns.AutoFit

    ' InsertChartObject sh:=sh, rngSource:=rngStart.Range("A1:C5")
End Sub
```

Note that the last line in the procedure contains a comment at the beginning of the line. You'll use this line in the next example when the example is extended to insert a chart with the data in the table.

You write the code to insert data into the table so that it exists in a separate procedure. That's because the source of the data can vary. By keeping the code separate, you keep table insertion and formatting separate from the data that's inserted.

```
Sub InsertTableData(rngStart As Range)
    Dim x As Integer, y As Integer
    Dim iNumOfRows As Integer, iNumOfCols As Integer
    iNumOfRows = 5: iNumOfCols = 3
    With rngStart
        For x = 2 To iNumOfRows
            For y = 2 To iNumOfCols
                .Cells(x, y).Value = Format$(Rnd(x + y), "###0.00")
            Next y
        Next x
    End With
End Sub
```

Just before the end of the *InsertTable* procedure, you set the width of columns B through D on the active worksheet to AutoFit, which lets you achieve the best fit based only on the contents of cells. Note the code used just above the last line of the *InsertTable* procedure. You use the Range property on the range represented by the variable *rngStart*. The argument in the Range property specifies the cells A1 through C5, relative to B5. That is, starting from cell B5, take three columns to the left and five rows down and AutoFit the columns based on the data in this range of cells

Charts

You commonly use charts to help analyze data. In Excel a chart can exist in two locations. The first is as a chart sheet and the second is as an embedded chart object on a worksheet. A chart sheet displays a tab on screen. In Chapter 8, you'll see how to insert a new chart sheet into an Excel workbook. You create the chart sheet from data in a worksheet and then copy and paste the chart to a PowerPoint presentation. In the following example, you extend the *InsertTable* example to create an embedded chart on the same sheet where the table data is inserted.

The example uses the *ChartObjects* collection object to create a new chart placed in the worksheet passed into the *InsertChartObject* procedure. You can also use the *Add* method on the *Charts* collection object to insert a new chart. The difference, however, is that when you use the *Add* method on the *Charts* collection object, you create and locate a chart on a new chart sheet rather than placing the chart in an existing worksheet. You access charts located as a sheet in the workbook by using the Charts property on the *Workbook* object. On the other hand, you access charts embedded on a worksheet by using the ChartObjects property on the *Worksheet* object.

Insert Charts

In the *InsertTable* procedure in the previous example, remove the comment from the beginning of the following line. This line is the last line in the *InsertTable* procedure and it calls the *InsertChartObject* procedure, passing two arguments. The first is the worksheet where the table data is inserted, and the second is the range representing the table data.

```
InsertChartObject sh:=sh, rngSource:=rngStart.Range("A1:C5")
```

The *chrtObject* variable is declared as a ChartObject in the *InsertChartObject* procedure and is set to the embedded chart object created by the *Add* method of the *ChartsObjects* collection object. The first With...End block determines the left and top position of the chart object on the worksheet specified by the *sh* argument. You determine the left value by adding 10 points (units) to the right edge of the cell range. In the second With...End block, you set the chart type along with the chart's source data and other properties, such as the chart and axes title. You set the data source for the chart to the range `rngStart.Range("A1:C5")`, which is passed into the *InsertChartObject* procedure. You set the name of the embedded chart object to "Q2 Sales."

```
Sub InsertChartObject(sh As Worksheet, rngSource As Range)
    Dim chrtObject As ChartObject
    Dim lLeft As Long, lTop As Long

    With rngSource
        lLeft = .Columns.Left + .Columns.Width + 10
        lTop = .Rows.Top
    End With

    Set chrtObject = sh.ChartObjects.Add(Left:=lLeft, _
        Top:=lTop, Width:=328.5, Height:=192.75)
    chrtObject.Name = "Q2 Sales"

    With chrtObject.Chart
        .ChartType = xlColumnClustered
        .SetSourceData Source:=rngSource, PlotBy:=xlColumns
        .HasTitle = True
        .ChartTitle.Characters.Text = "Q2 Sales"
        With .Axes(xlCategory, xlPrimary)
            .HasTitle = True
            .AxisTitle.Characters.Text = "Region"
        End With
        With .Axes(xlValue, xlPrimary)
            .HasTitle = True
            .AxisTitle.Characters.Text = "Increase"
        End With
    End With
End Sub
```

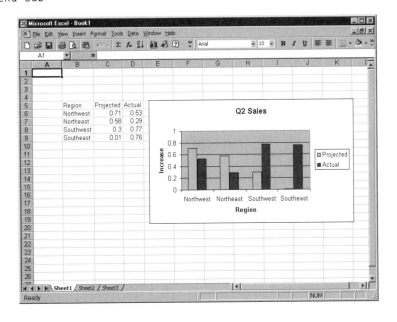

Change the Location of a Chart

In the previous example, you used the *ChartObjects* collection object to create a new chart. The new chart is created as an embedded chart on the worksheet passed into the *InsertChartObject* procedure. You can switch the location of an embedded chart to a new sheet (and vice versa) by using the *Location* method on the *Chart* object. For example, if an embedded chart exists on a worksheet, such as this example created, you can specify the *Where* argument in the *Location* method as xlLocationAsNewSheet to move the chart to a new sheet.

```
Sub ChangeLocationOfEmbeddedChart()
    Dim chrtSheet As Chart
    Set chrtSheet = ActiveSheet.ChartObjects("Q2 Sales") _
        .Chart.Location(Where:=xlLocationAsNewSheet)
    chrtSheet.Name = "Q2 Sales"
End Sub
```

This procedure changes the location of the embedded chart object, named "Q2 Sales" in the *InsertChartObject* procedure, to a new sheet. The procedure sets the name of the sheet to "Q2 Sales" as well.

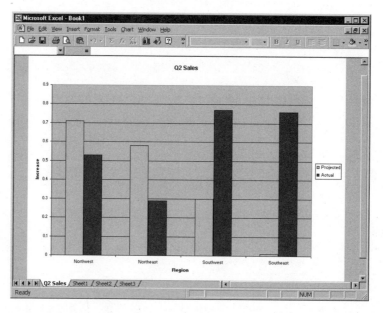

Manipulating Shapes In PowerPoint

PowerPoint's programming model centers around two objects: *Shape* and *TextRange*. Although Word and Excel each provide a *Shapes* collection object that is consistent with PowerPoint's *Shapes* collection object, shapes aren't the main content type in these two applications: text and cells are, respectively. In PowerPoint, the *Shape* object is vital because all content in a presentation, including text, exists in a shape. Even if a slide has nothing but text, the text is contained in a shape of a specific type.

To access text, first you have to access the shape in the *Shapes* collection object on a slide, and then access the text in a shape using the *TextRange* object. The *TextRange* object represents a continuous area of text within a shape. The *TextRange* object, which is very similar to and nearly as robust as Word's *Range* object, allows you to retrieve or set text, as well as apply formatting to text, in any shape in a presentation. You can only access the *TextRange* object by first accessing a shape.

Tip   The code listed here that describes how to insert and manipulate presentation content in PowerPoint is also found in the PpContnt.bas code module in the Chapter 6 practice folder on the CD that comes with this book.

The Shapes Collection

Each slide in a PowerPoint presentation contains a *Shapes* collection. To access a *Shapes* collection, you first need to access a specific slide in a presentation's *Slides* collection. A shape represents any object on a slide, including a text box, an AutoShape, an OLE object, a picture, a table, or a chart. You can access a *Shape* object using the *Shapes* collection or the *ShapeRange* collection. The *Shapes* collection represents all shapes on a slide, and a *ShapeRange* collection can represent all or a subset of shapes on a slide. As you'll see in this section, the *ShapeRange* collection is useful in cases where formatting is applied to multiple shapes.

Set Properties to Multiple Shapes in a Selection

The *ShapeRange* collection object usually consists of a subset of shapes that exist in the *Shapes* collection for a particular slide. When you work with selected shapes in the active window, you'll commonly work with the *ShapeRange* collection. Users generally select multiple shapes and apply settings to the shapes in the selection. Before running the following procedure, insert a number of different shapes on the slide in the active window, such as a rectangle, *ActiveX* control, line, WordArt, and text box. Then select all shapes and run the following procedure from a module in the Visual Basic Editor in PowerPoint:

```
Sub SetShapeProperties()
    If ActiveWindow.Selection.Type <> _
        ppSelectionShapes Then Exit Sub

    With ActiveWindow.Selection.ShapeRange
        With .Fill
            .ForeColor.RGB = RGB(255, 0, 102)
            .OneColorGradient Style:=msoGradientHorizontal, _
                Variant:=2, Degree:=0.23
        End With
        .Line.ForeColor.RGB = RGB(200, 100, 150)
```

```
        With .TextFrame.TextRange
            With .Font
                .Name = "Arial"
                .Size = 24
                .Bold = msoTrue
                .Color.RGB = RGB(255, 255, 0)
            End With
        End With
    End With
End Sub
```

The preceding procedure sets properties such as fill color, fill gradient, line border color, and font attributes to the selected shapes. Although some properties may not apply to specific shapes in the selection, using the *ShapeRange* collection object saves you from having to filter which shapes certain properties don't apply. Therefore, you can write your code generically and PowerPoint will determine if the property can or can't be applied to a specific shape in the *ShapeRange* collection. This is the same as the course of action in PowerPoint when you select a number of different types of shapes on a slide and click on the Fill Color button on the Drawing toolbar or the Bold button on the Formatting toolbar.

Shape Ranges

In some cases, you may want to iterate through the selected shapes, and apply property settings only to a specific shape. The following procedure determines if the slide title shape is in the selection of shapes in the active window. If the slide title shape *is* in the selection, the procedure positions the title shape back to specific left and top coordinates. You can change the code within the nested If…Then block to set or retrieve any property of the title shape.

```
Sub CheckIfShapeExistsInShapeRange()
    Dim shp As Shape
    If ActiveWindow.Selection.Type <> _
        ppSelectionShapes Then Exit Sub

    For Each shp In ActiveWindow.Selection.ShapeRange
        If shp.Type = msoPlaceholder Then
            If shp.PlaceholderFormat _
                .Type = ppPlaceholderTitle Then
                shp.Left = 53.5
                shp.Top = 36
            End If
        End If
    Next shp
End Sub
```

This example uses the objects and properties associated with placeholders to determine if a specific shape is found on a slide or in a selection. Placeholders are described after the following example.

Work with the Slide Master and Default Properties

You can extend the previous example and make it more robust. To do so, set the left and top coordinates of the slide title shape to the default position of the title shape on the slide master of the presentation. This procedure is useful in scenarios where you may want to reset the position of a placeholder, such as the slide title, back to its default coordinates (based on the slide master).

```
Sub WorkingWithSlideMaster()
    Dim shp As Shape, sldMaster As Master

    If ActiveWindow.Selection.Type <> _
        ppSelectionShapes Then Exit Sub

    For Each shp In ActiveWindow.Selection.ShapeRange
        If shp.Type = msoPlaceholder Then
            If shp.PlaceholderFormat _
                .Type = ppPlaceholderTitle Then
                Set sldMaster = ActiveWindow.View.Slide.Master
                With sldMaster.Shapes _
                    .Placeholders(ppPlaceholderTitle)
                    shp.Left = .Left
                    shp.Top = .Top
                End With
            End If
        End If
    Next shp
End Sub
```

You can view the master for the slides in the presentation by clicking Master on the View menu and then selecting Slide Master from the submenu in PowerPoint. In the preceding procedure, you declare the variable *sldMaster* as a *Master* object. It's set to the master of the slide in the active window. The slide title shape's coordinates are set to the coordinates of the title shape on the slide master.

Because the nested If...Then only looks for the placeholder of type ppPlaceholderTitle, the *sldMaster* will always be set to the master that's in view when you click Slide Master on PowerPoint's Master submenu. If the slide layout is a title slide (see the discussion on slide layout later in the chapter), the slide title shape would be of the placeholder type ppPlaceholderCenterTitle.

Placeholders

Placeholders are special kinds of shapes specific to PowerPoint and aren't found in Word's or Excel's *Shapes* collection. Placeholders are tied to the layout of a slide. For example, you commonly insert slides with either the title layout or, more commonly, the body layout. The body layout has both a title placeholder and a body placeholder. When you work with text and insert new slides in Outline view, slides are created with the body layout by default.

Using placeholders, you can access shapes like the slide title or body placeholder shape no matter where the placeholder shape is in the collection. When you change the z-order of a shape on the slide, the index position of a placeholder or any other shape in the *Shapes* collection changes. As a result, it's easier to use in your code the *Placeholders* collection, accessed from the *Shapes* collection, to access the most common shape elements on a slide.

```
Sub InsertSlideAndAccessPlaceholders()
    Dim sldNew As Slide
    Set sldNew = ActivePresentation.Slides _
        .Add(Index:=1, Layout:=ppLayoutText)
    With sldNew.Shapes
        .Placeholders(1) _
            .TextFrame.TextRange.Text = "Ideas..."
        .Placeholders(2) _
            .TextFrame.TextRange.Text = "Use VBA."
        With .AddShape(msoShapeCloudCallout, _
            50, 50, 120, 100)
            .TextFrame.TextRange.Text = "Thoughts?"
        End With
    End With
End Sub
```

This procedure inserts a new slide with the layout ppLayoutText. This layout represents a slide with the title and body placeholders. You then use the *Placeholders* collection to insert text in the title and body placeholders. The procedure adds a new AutoShape and positions it near the top left of the body placeholder.

Iterate Through Title and Body Placeholders and Print to a Text File

To retrieve the main text in a presentation, you usually need to access the title and body placeholder on a slide. Some slides, however, may not have the title or body placeholder. And because there are up to 16 different placeholder PpPlaceholderType constants that represent the possible placeholder types, you may also be searching for other placeholders on a slide. The three procedures listed in this section work together to iterate through the slides in the active presentation and retrieve the slide title and body placeholder text, if either exists. They print the retrieved text to a text file under the Temp folder on the C: drive. You can change the file path "C:\Temp" to an appropriate path on your machine.

In this example, the procedure sends the content of a PowerPoint presentation to a text file, but you can use the content of a PowerPoint presentation to be the basis of a new Word document. This functionality is similar to pointing to Send To on the File menu and then clicking Microsoft Word on the submenu in PowerPoint. Chapter 7 describes the reverse operation; that is, you use a Word document as a basis for creating a new PowerPoint presentation.

The first of the following three procedures is the main one. You set the variable *sOutputFile* to the output text file and use the Open statement to open the text file in Output mode. The Output mode indicates that if the file exists on disk, its content will be overwritten. The For Each...Next loop iterates through each slide in the presentation. The first line within the For Each...Next loop prints the slide title in the text file. The procedure retrieves the slide title by using the function *SlideTitle*. The section "Iterate Through Titles in a Presentation" later in this chapter describes the *SlideTitle* function.

```
Sub PrintContentsOfPresentationToTextFile()
    Dim sld As Slide, shpBodyPlaceHolder As Shape
    Dim iFreeFile As Integer, sOutputFile As String
    sOutputFile = "C:\Temp\ActivePresentationText.txt"
    iFreeFile = FreeFile
    Open sOutputFile For Output As iFreeFile

    For Each sld In ActivePresentation.Slides
        Print #iFreeFile, SlideTitle(sld)
        If PlaceholderExists(sld.Shapes, _
            ppPlaceholderBody, shpBodyPlaceHolder) Then
            Print #iFreeFile, shpBodyPlaceHolder _
                .TextFrame.TextRange.Text
        End If
        Print #iFreeFile,
    Next sld

    Close #iFreeFile

    ' ShellExecute 0, "Open", sOutputFile, "", "", 1
End Sub

Function PlaceholderExists(shpColl As Shapes, _
    iType As PpPlaceholderType, _
    shpPlaceHolder As Shape) As Boolean

    For Each shpPlaceHolder In shpColl.Placeholders
        If shpPlaceHolder.PlaceholderFormat.Type = iType Then
            PlaceholderExists = True
            Exit Function
        End If
    Next shpPlaceHolder
End Function
```

```
Function SlideTitle(sld As Slide) As String
    Dim sPrefix As String, sSlideTitle As String

    If sld.Shapes.HasTitle Then
        sSlideTitle = sld.Shapes.Title.TextFrame.TextRange.Text
    End If

    sPrefix = sld.SlideNumber & ". "
    If Len(sSlideTitle) Then
        SlideTitle = sPrefix & sSlideTitle
    Else
        SlideTitle = sPrefix & "Slide " & sld.SlideNumber
    End If
End Function
```

After the slide title is retrieved, the If…Then block in the first procedure then uses the *PlaceholderExists* function to determine if the body placeholder exists. Because this function is generic, you can use it to determine if any placeholder exists. You need to pass three arguments to the function. The first is the *Shapes* collection of the slide you want to search on for a specific type of placeholder; the second is the placeholder type you want to search for; and the third is an object declared as type *Shape*. If the *PlaceholderExists* function finds the specified placeholder type, the procedure sets the object variable *shpPlaceholder* to the placeholder. If the placeholder exists, the procedure prints the text contents in the body placeholder to the output text file, followed by a blank line.

Copy the three preceding procedures in a code module in the Visual Basic Editor in PowerPoint, switch back to PowerPoint, and click New on the File menu. In the Presentations tab, select a presentation that's installed on your machine. Click OK. Switch back to the Visual Basic Editor and run the *PrintContentsOfPresentationToTextFile* procedure. Navigate to the output text file in the Microsoft Windows Explorer to see the results.

Opening and Displaying the Output Text File from Code

You can extend the preceding example to automatically open the text file after it's been closed for output. This is the same operation you saw in Chapter 4, where the program automatically opens the HTML document saved to disk in the Web browser installed on your machine. The last line in the first procedure in the preceding example contains the following line, which is commented out:

```
ShellExecute 0, "Open", sOutputFile, "", "", 1
```

Remove the comment from the beginning of the line, and then add the following Windows API to the top of the code module:

```
Declare Function ShellExecute Lib "shell32.dll" _
    Alias "ShellExecuteA" ( _
        ByVal Hwnd As Long, _
        ByVal lpOperation As String, _
```

```
      ByVal lpFile As String, _
      ByVal lpParameters As String, _
      ByVal lpDirectory As String, _
      ByVal nShowCmd As Long _
   ) As Long
```

Run the *PrintContentsOfPresentationToTextFile* procedure again. This time, the output text file should be opened and displayed in Microsoft Notepad. You can use this functionality in any scenario, no matter where you write Visual Basic code.

Slides

As discussed earlier in this chapter, PowerPoint's content breakdown is similar to Excel's. Excel organizes content in worksheets, and PowerPoint uses slides. In PowerPoint, the *Slides* collection allows your code to iterate through and work with specific slides in a presentation. You can also use the *Slides* collection object to add a new slide and, hence, new content.

Iterate Through the Slides Collection

The following procedure iterates through slides in the *Slides* collection object. The procedure assigns each slide to the variable *sld* and prints the slide name, number, and index to the Immediate window in the Visual Basic Editor in PowerPoint.

```
Sub IterateThroughSlides()
    Dim sld As Slide
    For Each sld In ActivePresentation.Slides
        Debug.Print "Slide name: " & sld.Name
        Debug.Print "Slide number: " & sld.SlideNumber
        Debug.Print "Slide Index: " & sld.SlideIndex
    Next sld
End Sub
```

By default, PowerPoint gives a new name to each slide created, although there's no way to change a slide's name through the menus, toolbars, or dialog boxes. You can only do that by setting the Name property through Visual Basic code. You can also use the value returned by the Name property as the *index* argument in the Slides(*index*) property on the *Presentation* object so that your code can return a specific *Slide* object.

The SlideIndex property returns a number representing the position of the slide in the *Slides* collection. The SlideIndex number is directly related to the position of the slide on screen. The Name property returns the name of the slide. The SlideNumber property on the *Slide* object returns the slide number visible on the slide. You can set the slide number in PowerPoint by selecting the Slide number check box in the Slide tab of the Header and Footer dialog box. You can access this dialog box by clicking Header and Footer on the View menu.

Insert Slides

You use the *Add* method of the *Slides* collection to insert a new slide in the presentation. The *Add* method takes two arguments, *Index* and *Layout,* and you need both. The *Index* argument represents the position of the new slide in the *Slides* collection. If you want to add the slide to the end of the *Slides* collection, you need to set the *Index* argument to the number of the slides in the collection plus one. The code would appear as:

```
With ActivePresentation.Slides
    Set sldNew = .Add(Index:=.Count + 1, _
        Layout:=ppLayoutText)
End With
```

If you want to insert a new slide at the end of the *Slides* collection, replace the Set sldNew statement in the following procedure with the With...End block above.

```
Sub InsertSlide()
    Dim sldNew As Slide
    Set sldNew = ActivePresentation.Slides _
        .Add(Index:=1, Layout:=ppLayoutText)
    With sldNew
        .Shapes(1).TextFrame.TextRange.Text = "Ideas..."
        .Shapes(2).TextFrame.TextRange.Text = "Use VBA."
        With .Shapes.AddShape(msoShapeCloudCallout, _
            50, 50, 120, 100)
            .TextFrame.TextRange.Text = "Thoughts?"
        End With
    End With
End Sub
```

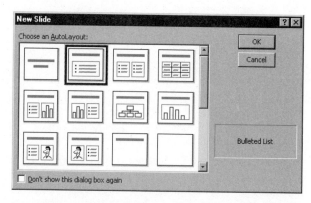

The *Layout* argument allows your code to specify the slide layout for the new slide. Every slide in PowerPoint has a slide layout. You need to set a *Layout*

argument to a PpSlideLayout constant. When you insert a new slide in PowerPoint by clicking New Slide on the Insert menu in PowerPoint's application window, the New Slide dialog box displays all the possible slide layouts. The name of the layout appears at the right in the dialog box. Most layout names in the dialog box are similar to their associated PpSlideLayout constant. In the preceding procedure, the PpSlideLayout constant ppLayoutText represents the Bulleted List layout in the New Slide dialog box.

Iterate Through Titles in a Presentation

A slide's title and body placeholder are two elements you'll commonly find on slides. The slide title is commonly used to display a list of *Slides* in a presentation. The following procedure allows you to return a list of slide titles exactly like the list you'll find in the Slide Navigator in Slide Show. In Slide Show view, right-click on the slide, click Go, and click Slide Navigator on the submenu.

You can also see a list of slide titles in the Insert Hyperlink dialog box by clicking Hyperlink on the Insert menu and then selecting Place in This Document on the Link To bar at the left of the dialog box. In the Visual Basic Editor in PowerPoint, run the following procedure. The list of slide titles is printed in the Immediate window.

```
Sub RetrieveSlideTitleList()
    Dim sld As Slide
    Dim sPrefix As String, sSlideTitle As String

    For Each sld In ActivePresentation.Slides
        If sld.Shapes.HasTitle Then
            sSlideTitle = sld.Shapes.Title _
                .TextFrame.TextRange.Text
        End If
```

```
            sPrefix = sld.SlideNumber & ". "
            If Len(sSlideTitle) Then
                Debug.Print sPrefix & sSlideTitle
            Else
                Debug.Print sPrefix & "Slide " & _
                    sld.SlideNumber
            End If
        Next sld
End Sub
```

PowerPoint provides a shortcut that allows you to easily determine if a slide title exists and if so, to access the title shape. Instead of using the Shapes*(Index)* property on the *Slide* object or the Placeholders(Index) property on the *Shapes* collection object to return the slide title, you can use the Title property on the *Shapes* object. This property provides a shortcut to the Title shape.

Even though the majority of slides have a slide title, some may not. Either the slide layout is blank (ppSlideLayoutBlank) or the user deleted the slide title shape. Therefore, before you access the slide title shape using the Title property on the *Shapes* object, your code should first use the HasTitle property. If the slide does have a title, the string variable *sSlideTitle* is set to the text of the slide title shape. The If...Then...Else block determines if the length of text assigned to the variable *sSlideTitle* is greater than zero. If so, the procedure prints the slide title to the Immediate window. If not, it prints the slide number to the Immediate window.

Handling Text

In a PowerPoint presentation, all text has to exist in a shape. The *TextRange* object allows you to insert or manipulate text content in a shape. You can set the *TextRange* object so that it represents all or only a portion of a range of text. A *TextRange* object can consist of text that represents a single paragraph (a bulleted list item, for example) or all text in a shape (such as all bulleted items).

Within every *TextRange* object, you can return more granular units of text—just as you can in Word with the *Range* object. The *TextRange* object allows you to iterate through units of text as large as all the text in a shape and as small as a paragraph (usually a bulleted item), a sentence, a word, and, finally, a character. The *TextRange* object in PowerPoint is equivalent in purpose to the *Range* object in Word. Many methods and properties on both of these objects are similar as well.

> ### Determine If a Shape Can Contain Text and Set Bullets of Unindented Items

You can't apply a number of properties on the *Shape* or *ShapeRange* object to all shapes. You can use the Paragraphs, Sentences, Words, or Character properties on the *TextRange* object to return the collection of paragraphs, sentences, words, or characters from a range of text. However, you can't access the text range on shapes like a line, WordArt, bitmap placeholder, or *ActiveX* control. Before you try to access text in a range of shapes—in a selection, for example —you need to determine if a shape can contain text.

To access text, you need to first access the *TextFrame* object. In hierarchical object terms, a *Shape* object contains a *TextFrame*. The *TextFrame* contains a *TextRange* object that actually represents text. Some shapes don't contain a *TextFrame* object. To determine if a shape does contain one, and therefore can contain text, you can use the HasTextFrame property on the *Shape* object. Thereafter, if a shape does contain text, you can access the text in the shape and set its properties.

```
Sub IterateParagraphsAndSetBullets()
    Dim para As TextRange
    Dim shp As Shape, iCount As Integer

    If ActiveWindow.Selection.Type <> _
        ppSelectionShapes Then Exit Sub
    For Each shp In ActiveWindow.Selection.ShapeRange
        If shp.HasTextFrame Then
            iCount = 0

            For Each para In shp.TextFrame _
                .TextRange.Paragraphs
                If para.IndentLevel = 1 Then
                    With para.ParagraphFormat.Bullet
                        If .Type <> ppBulletNone Then
                            .Font.Name = "Arial"
                            .RelativeSize = 0.75
                            iCount = iCount + 1
                            .Character = 48 + iCount
                        End If
                    End With
                End If
            Next para

        End If
    Next shp
End Sub
```

Before running this procedure, insert different shapes on the active slide, such as a line, an *ActiveX* control, some WordArt, and a rectangle. Add text to the rectangle, the title, and the body placeholder, if they exist. Select all shapes on the slide and then run the procedure. Make sure that the body text is bulleted. The procedure determines if the selection in the active window is a range of shapes. If so, the first For Each...Next loop iterates through the shapes in the selected shape range. If the shape contains a text frame, the nested For Each...Next loop iterates through the paragraphs in the text range of the selected shape.

The If...Then statement evaluating the bullet Type property is used to determine if there is a bullet visible for the paragraph. If there is, then the For...Each loop proceeds to add a number as the bullet. If a bullet does not exist, the bullet of the paragraph is unaffected. Every bulleted item in a shape, including those that are indented below a main bulleted item, is considered a paragraph. You access the list of bulleted items by using the Paragraphs property on the *TextRange* object. The Paragraphs property returns the collection of paragraphs in the text range of a shape. You can use the IndentLevel property to return specific paragraphs in a shape. The preceding procedure sets the bullet character to a number if the bullet exists for the paragraph. This procedure mimics the functionality of automatically numbering bulleted items in a shape.

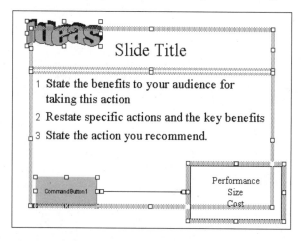

Navigate Through the Units of Text

Unlike in Word, in PowerPoint your code can only navigate down the text "hierarchy" tree. For example, if you select a bulleted item on a slide in the active window, you can access the sentence, word, and character collections in the bulleted item. However, if you had selected a word, you cannot return the sentence or paragraph the word belonged to. The *Range* object in Word, on the other hand, allows you to return the paragraph where a range of text, such as a word, is contained.

The following procedure prints to the Immediate window in the Visual Basic Editor in PowerPoint the first paragraph, sentence, and word of a text selection. For example, in a body placeholder on a slide, type in two bulleted items where the first item has two or more sentences. Select all of the text in the shape and then run the following procedure in a module in the Visual Basic Editor.

```
Sub NavigateDownTextHierarchy()
    Dim rng As TextRange
    If ActiveWindow.Selection.Type = ppSelectionText Then
        Set rng = ActiveWindow.Selection.TextRange
        Debug.Print rng.Paragraphs(1)
```

```
        Debug.Print rng.Sentences(1)
        Debug.Print rng.Words(1)
    End If
End Sub
```

Iterate Through Words

PowerPoint is similar to Word in that a unit of text representing a word consists of the text of the word followed by the space between the text and the next word. If you double-click on a word in a Word document or in a shape in PowerPoint, the text and the space after the text is highlighted. The same principle holds for sentences. A sentence in Word and PowerPoint consists of the sentence's text followed by the space between the period and the next sentence. A paragraph includes the text, space after the end of the text (if any), and the paragraph marker.

```
Sub SpaceAfterTextUnits()
    Dim rng As TextRange
    If ActiveWindow.Selection.Type = ppSelectionText Then
        Set rng = ActiveWindow.Selection.TextRange
        Debug.Print rng.Words(1) & Chr(34)
        Debug.Print rng.Words(1).TrimText & Chr(34)
        Debug.Print rng.Sentences(1) & Chr(34)
        Debug.Print rng.Paragraphs(1) & Chr(34)
    End If
End Sub
```

Before running this procedure, add text to a body placeholder and add two sentences to the first bulleted item. Select all text in the bulleted item and run the procedure. The procedure prints the text of the first word, sentence, and paragraph (which represents the bulleted item) to the Immediate window, followed by a quote. Chr(34) represents the quote character ("), which allows you to see the spaces after each unit of text.

Unlike in Word, in PowerPoint you can use the TrimText property to remove all spaces and paragraph markers before and after a unit text. The built-in *Trim$* function in the Visual Basic for Applications language works only for removing spaces before and after a text string. The TrimText property in PowerPoint also removes paragraph markers after, for example, a sentence or paragraph. The TrimText property is useful when you retrieve the last paragraph in a shape and don't want the paragraph marker along with the text.

Insert Paragraphs

When you build presentation content programmatically, you commonly have to insert paragraphs. PowerPoint, like Word, provides two convenient methods for creating a new paragraph before or after an existing one: *InsertBefore* and *InsertAfter*. When you access a range representing an existing paragraph or the beginning or end of one, you can use either of these two methods to insert a new paragraph.

The following procedure assumes that the active presentation contains at least two slides and two shapes on the second slide. The procedure also assumes that the second shape on the second slide has at least two bulleted items. The code inserts a new paragraph at the end of the text range in the shape using the *InsertAfter* method on the *TextRange* object. The *InsertAfter* method takes one argument representing the new text to be added in the new paragraph. This procedure adds a new paragraph after the first paragraph in the shape. Note that in the text string assigned to the variable *sNewPara*, a carriage return, represented by Chr(13), is added to the end of the text. When the text string is set to the new paragraph, the carriage return ensures that the new paragraph is separate from the paragraph after the new paragraph.

```
Sub InsertNewParagraphBetweenParagraphs()
    Dim shp As Shape, rngText As TextRange
    Dim sNewPara As String

    sNewPara = "New paragraph between items." & Chr(13)
    Set shp = ActivePresentation.Slides(2).Shapes(2)
    With shp.TextFrame.TextRange.Paragraphs(1)
        Set rngText = .InsertAfter(NewText:=sNewPara)
        rngText.Font.Italic = msoTrue
        rngText.IndentLevel = 2
    End With
End Sub
```

Another very common task in programming solutions is to insert content at the end of text in the body placeholder or any shape. The following procedure inserts text at the end of a text range using the *InsertAfter* method. However, in this case it adds the carriage return character at the beginning of the text string assigned to the string variable *sNewPara*.

```
Sub InsertNewParagraphAtEndOfTextRange()
    Dim shp As Shape, rngText As TextRange
    Dim sNewPara As String

    sNewPara = Chr(13) & "New paragraph."
    Set shp = ActivePresentation.Slides(2).Shapes(2)
    With shp.TextFrame.TextRange
        Set rngText = .InsertAfter(NewText:=sNewPara)
        rngText.Font.Italic = msoTrue
    End With
End Sub
```

Tables

PowerPoint 2000 is the first version of PowerPoint that offers a way of creating tables that's similar to the functionality provided by the Draw Table command on Word's Tables And Borders toolbar. The following two procedures create a simple five-row by three-column table. They create the table on a new slide inserted at the end of the *Slides* collection in the active presentation. You should note that your code can insert a table that has up to 25 rows and 25 columns. This is also the row and column limit that's set when you create the table using the Tables And Borders toolbar.

Insert Tables

First you set the new table to the *Table* variable *tbl*. PowerPoint doesn't provide the ability to apply predefined formats to your table as Word does using the Table AutoFormat on the Table menu. Since you can't format a table with a preset table format, you need to explicitly format the table through code. You do this by using the *SetTableFormatting* procedure. You call the procedure *InsertTableData* to fill the second and third columns with random values after you apply formatting.

As described in this chapter's Word and Excel table examples, you could, for example, replace the code in *InsertTableData* with code that accesses data in an Access database.

Note   The result of the table appears in the following graphic. Note the formatting applied to specific sets of cells. For example, the text in the first row is bold and italicized. The text in the first column is left aligned, while the text in the second and third columns is center aligned.

Q2 Sales: Increase (%)

Region	Projected	Actual
Northwest	0.47	0.30
Northeast	0.62	0.65
Southwest	0.26	0.28
Southeast	0.83	0.82

Note The code to create this table is listed below and is also found in the PpContnt.bas code module under the Chapter 6 practice folder on the CD that comes with this book. Also note that the first two lines in the code belong at the top of the standard code module. If Option Explicit is already listed at the top of your code module, you do not need to type it again. However, the module-level variable, *m_sldSales,* is used in the other procedures listed below.

```vb
Option Explicit
Dim m_sldSales As Slide

Sub InsertTable()
    Dim tbl As Table
    Dim iNumOfRows As Integer, iNumOfColumns As Integer

    ' create new slide and add title text
    With ActivePresentation
        Set m_sldSales = .Slides.Add( _
            Index:=.Slides.Count + 1, _
            Layout:=ppLayoutTitleOnly)
    End With
    m_sldSales.Shapes.Title.TextFrame _
        .TextRange = "Q2 Sales: Increase (%)"

    ' insert table
    iNumOfRows = 5: iNumOfColumns = 3
    Set tbl = m_sldSales.Shapes.AddTable(iNumOfRows, _
        iNumOfColumns, 54, 156, 612, 324).Table

    SetHeadingRowText tbl
    SetFirstColumnText tbl
    InsertTableData tbl
End Sub

Sub InsertTableData(tbl As Table)
    ' fill cells with random data
    Dim x As Integer, y As Integer
    For x = 2 To tbl.Rows.Count
        For y = 2 To tbl.Columns.Count
            tbl.Cell(x, y).Shape.TextFrame.TextRange _
                .Text = Format$(Rnd(), "###0.00")
        Next y
    Next x
End Sub
```

Important   When you select a set of cells in a table on a slide and click on the Bold button on the Formatting toolbar, for example, PowerPoint applies formatting to all cells in the selection. However, PowerPoint doesn't allow you to mimic the same behavior through code. You have to explicitly create a shape range of cells and apply formatting to the set of cells. The code provides a good structure to apply formatting to a specific set of cells in a table. The remaining procedures are called from the preceding *SetTableFormatting* procedure.

The *GetRowArray*, *GetColumnArray* and *GetTableCellArray* procedures return an array used to create a collection of shapes within a *ShapeRange* object. Using the *ShapeRange* object, you can apply formatting to all cells at once. The *GetRowArray* and *GetColumnArray* procedures are designed to allow your code to specify what row or column of table cells should be returned as a shape range. The procedures also allow your code to specify if the shape range of a row or column of cells should skip the first cell. For example, if the first cell in a column is part of a heading row, you may want to skip formatting the cell like the others in a column.

```
Sub SetHeadingRowText(tbl As Table)
    tbl.Cell(1, 1).Shape.TextFrame _
        .TextRange.Text = "Region"
    tbl.Cell(1, 2).Shape.TextFrame _
        .TextRange.Text = "Projected"
    tbl.Cell(1, 3).Shape.TextFrame _
        .TextRange.Text = "Actual"
End Sub

Sub SetFirstColumnText(tbl As Table)
    tbl.Cell(2, 1).Shape.TextFrame _
        .TextRange.Text = "Northwest"
    tbl.Cell(3, 1).Shape.TextFrame _
        .TextRange.Text = "Northeast"
    tbl.Cell(4, 1).Shape.TextFrame _
        .TextRange.Text = "Southwest"
    tbl.Cell(5, 1).Shape.TextFrame _
        .TextRange.Text = "Southeast"
End Sub
```

Table Cell Borders in PowerPoint

Because tables are a group of shapes, you can use the *Shape* object to manipulate cell formatting such as the line format of the shape representing a cell. You should not, however, use the *LineFormat* of the *Shape* object to manipulate the borders of a cell in a table. Doing so results in unpredictable behavior for the borders of a cell. Instead, use the Borders property of the *Cell* object, which can be accessed from the *Table* object.

(continued)

Table Cell Borders in PowerPoint *(continued)*

The following procedure uses the Borders property to remove the left and right border for each cell in the table created by the previous set of procedures. For the following procedure to work, you need to make sure you select the entire table, switch back to the Visual Basic Editor in PowerPoint, insert the cursor in the procedure, and then press F5 to run it.

```
Sub TableCellBorders()
    Dim tbl As Table
    Dim iRow As Integer, iCol As Integer

    Set tbl = ActiveWindow.Selection.ShapeRange.Table
    For iRow = 1 To tbl.Rows.Count
        For iCol = 1 To tbl.Columns.Count
            With tbl.Cell(iRow, iCol)
                .Borders(ppBorderLeft).Visible = msoFalse
                .Borders(ppBorderRight).Visible = msoFalse
            End With
        Next iCol
    Next iRow
End Sub
```

Chapter Summary

When a document is created or an existing document opened, you can insert or manipulate content such as text, tables, shapes, and other objects, such as charts. How to manipulate content varies between Word, Excel, and PowerPoint, and this chapter discussed the similarities and differences between the three applications. To manipulate content in Word, the main object you'll use is the *Range* object, which allows you to manipulate text. In Excel, you'll use the main object, also named *Range,* to manipulate content in a range of cells. In PowerPoint, you'll use two main objects: the *Shape* object and the *TextRange* object. You'll employ these objects the most when using Visual Basic code to insert and edit content in documents. Chapter 8 describes how to use the main object in Access, the *RecordSet* object, to retrieve data content in an Access database.

Preview of the Next Chapter

In the previous three chapters, Chapters 4 through 6, you first learned how to create or open Office documents through code, and then insert and manipulate content in those documents. In the next chapter, Chapter 7, as well as in Chapter 8, you'll go one step further. Instead of creating or opening a document from within an Office application, using instructions in Chapter 7, you'll create or open documents in one application from code running in another Office application. To do so, you'll first learn how to start another Office application and load documents. In Chapter 8, you'll use data in an Access database to start Word, Excel, PowerPoint, and Outlook, create new documents, insert content, and save the documents to disk.

Part 3

Working Across Applications

Chapter 7

Communicating Across Microsoft Office

Chapter Objectives   Estimated time: 45 minutes

- Use Microsoft Visual Basic code to start an application or access an application that's running.

- Use the Visual Basic functions *CreateObject* and *GetObject* and the New keyword to create and return a reference to an application.

- Access a file loaded in a running instance of an application.

- Use a Microsoft Office application invisibly to create documents and content.

- Exchange information between Office applications.

These days many computing situations require the interaction of two or more Office applications. Such interactions often combine different forms of the same material (such as text, charts, tables, and slides). A company's sales figures, for example, may be stored in a Microsoft Access database, presented in a report written in Microsoft Word, analyzed with a Microsoft Excel worksheet, and summarized in a Microsoft PowerPoint presentation. To be able to use the same content in different Office applications, you need to establish communication among them.

In Visual Basic for Applications, you make a connection between two applications either by using the Visual Basic functions *CreateObject* or *GetObject* or by using the keyword New in a declaration statement. Either of the two functions or the keyword New establishes a link to another Office application, giving you the power to use content from one application inside another.

Quick Guide: *CreateObject, GetObject*, and the *New* Keyword

This chapter describes the use of the *CreateObject* and *GetObject* functions and the *New* keyword. They are built into the Visual Basic for Applications language to start an instance of an Office application. Once you start an application, you use content from one application to create a document in another. This chapter shows how to access a running instance of Excel in order to retrieve data from a worksheet. This chapter also uses PowerPoint to create a presentation from a Word document. Chapter 8 uses data from an Access database to create documents and content in Word, Excel, and PowerPoint, as well as an e-mail message in Outlook. The following table lists the tasks you'll commonly use to communicate among applications.

Task	Description

Create a new instance of an object	Return a reference to the object with the *CreateObject* function, and then assign the reference to a variable with the Set statement. For example:
	`Set appXl = CreateObject _`
	`    ("Excel.Application")`
	The underscore indicates that the line of code continues on the next line.

Declare a variable as a generic object type	Type the variable name between Dim and As Object. For example: `Dim MyObject As Object`
Reference application object libraries	In the Visual Basic Editor, click References on the Tools menu, select the object libraries for the applications your program will work with, and click OK.
Declare a variable as a specific object type	With the appropriate object library selected in the References dialog box, type **Dim**, followed by the variable name, **As**, and the object type. For example: `Dim appPPT As PowerPoint.Application` In this example, the Microsoft PowerPoint 9.0 Object Library must be referenced.
Declare an object variable and assign an instance of an object to it in one step	Type **Dim**, followed by the variable name, **As New**, and the application object name. For example: `Dim appPPT As New PowerPoint.Application`
Assign an instance of an object that is already loaded to an object variable	Return a reference to the object with the *GetObject* function and *Class* argument, and then assign the reference to the variable with the Set statement. For example: `Set appWd = GetObject(, "Word.Application")`

(continued)

Quick Guide: *CreateObject, GetObject,* and the *New* Keyword *(continued)*

Task	Description
Start an application, open an existing file, and assign it to an object variable in one step	Return a reference to the object with the *GetObject* function and *pathname* argument, and then assign the reference to the variable with the Set statement. For example: `Set wbBook1 = GetObject("Book1.xls")`
Disconnect a variable from an object	Assign the value Nothing to the variable. For example: `Set appPPT = Nothing`

Starting Office Applications Using *CreateObject*

All applications in Office provide at least one type of object you can create with the *CreateObject* function: the *Application* object. However, both Word and Excel provide other types of objects you can create with the *CreateObject* function. The following table lists all the Office object types you can create:

Application	Object type	Class
Access	Application	Access.Application
Excel	Application	Excel.Application
Excel	Worksheet	Excel.Sheet
Excel	Chart	Excel.Chart
Outlook	Application	Outlook.Application
PowerPoint	Application	PowerPoint.Application
Word	Application	Word.Application
Word	Document	Word.Document

When you create an Excel worksheet or chart, you also implicitly create a new instance of the Excel application. The same holds true when you create a Word document, in which case you create a new instance of the Word application.

CreateObject(*ApplicationName.ObjectType*) is the syntax for the *CreateObject* function. *ApplicationName* is the name of the application that provides the object you want to create, and *ObjectType* is the type or class of object you'll create. The Class column in the previous table shows the concatenation of the *ApplicationName* and the *ObjectType* (with a period in between). The following procedure, added to and executed in a code module in a Visual Basic Editor other than Excel, shows the *CreateObject* function in the context of Visual Basic for Applications code. The example that follows it describes a similar procedure.

```
Public appXl As Object

Sub UsingCreateObject()
    Set appXl = CreateObject("Excel.Application")
    Debug.Print appXl.Name
    appXl.Visible = True
End Sub
```

Create a New Instance of an Object

To create an object for use with Visual Basic for Applications, you have to assign the object that *CreateObject* returns to an object variable. You do this by completing the following steps:

1. Start Excel. On the Tools menu, point to Macro, and then click Visual Basic Editor on the submenu.

2. In the Editor, click Module on the Insert menu.

3. In the inserted code module, create a new procedure by typing **Sub UsingCreateObject** and pressing ENTER.

4. In the first line of the procedure, add the following line of code:

```
Dim appPPT As Object
```

Tip   As discussed in Chapter 2, it's a common programming practice to give variable and constant names a prefix indicating the object type. The prefix *o* can be used generically to denote any type of object variable, but in many cases you'll see a prefix that's more specific, such as *app*, to denote the *Application* object.

With this step, you're declaring the variable *appPPT* as the generic Object type. This lets you use that variable to represent any type of application object that you create (or any instance of an even wider range of objects). As you'll see in the next example, you should declare each object variable by using the specific object type whenever possible.

5. Add the following line after the variable declaration statement:

```
Set appPPT = CreateObject("PowerPoint.Application")
```

This assigns to the object variable *appPPT* the results of the *CreateObject* function and tells the function what type of object to create (in this case, an instance of the *PowerPoint* application object). At this point, you can add code to create and manipulate the content of a PowerPoint presentation.

Checking Syntax in Visual Basic

When you press F5 to run your code, Visual Basic first conducts a process called *compiling*, in which your program is translated into machine language. During this process, Visual Basic checks to see whether a specific object provides the properties and methods you specified in code. Visual Basic also determines whether you've assigned valid values to variables that are declared as a particular type.

If your code has no syntax errors and compiles, Visual Basic knows what your variables are. If you declare a variable as a specific object type that belongs to an application other than the one in which you're writing your code, you must first make a reference to the other application's object library (demonstrated in the following example). When Visual Basic compiles your code, referencing an object library allows it to find all the information about an object, its methods, and its properties.

6. Add one last line in the procedure:

```
appPPT.Visible = True
```

As discussed at the beginning of this chapter, each *Application* object in Office has a Visible property allowing you to choose whether or not to display the application window. This allows you to create invisible documents and content that won't distract your program's user and then to display the application when it's needed.

7. Place the cursor in the procedure and press F5. When the code in this procedure runs in Excel, the PowerPoint application starts and displays the application window on the screen. Once you create an object, you can reference it in code by using the object variable you declared, and you can use any of the properties and methods within the application's object library.

8. Exit PowerPoint without saving your changes.

Creating an Instance of an Application

To work with an application other than the one where you execute your Visual Basic code, you must first set an object variable so that it represents the application you want to use. To do this, you can either create a new instance of the application or access an existing instance of an application (one that's currently running). When you start an instance of a Word, Excel, PowerPoint, Access, or Outlook application by using the *CreateObject* or *GetObject* function or the *New* keyword, the application window isn't displayed on the screen or the Windows taskbar.

The Visible Property on the *Application* Object

Each *Application* object in Office, with the exception of Outlook, provides a Visible property that allows you to display the application window after you create the application. In many Visual Basic for Applications programming scenarios, you create an *Application* object first, and then, before displaying the application window, you manipulate documents that you open or create. Once you finish, you display the application window with the document or documents. This technique allows you to make changes without distracting your program's user.

Starting More than One Instance of an Application

As the accompanying table shows, when you use *CreateObject* or the *New* keyword to create an instance of an Office application, Visual Basic creates a new instance of the application on the system for all applications except PowerPoint and Outlook. This means that if Word or Excel is already running and visible, *CreateObject* or the *New* keyword actually loads another instance of Word or Excel. For example, two Windows processes will have the Word executable loaded: the one visible and the other started using *CreateObject* or the *New* keyword. If you exit the visible instance, the other instance of Word remains. You must explicitly close the instance created by your code.

Application	New instance created when using *CreateObject* or *New* keyword
Access	Yes
Excel	Yes
Outlook	No
PowerPoint	No
Word	Yes

In the case of PowerPoint and Outlook, a new instance isn't created and *CreateObject* and the *New* keyword attaches to an existing instance of these applications (if either one is running).

Note When you use the *CreateObject* function to create a new instance of an *Application* object, you assign the *Application* object returned by the function to an object variable. In this case, and in the case where the *New* keyword is used in a variable declaration to create a new instance of an *Application* object, you need to declare the object variable at either a procedure, module, or public level. For example, as described in Chapter 2, if the object variable is declared at a module or public level, the application associated with the *Application* object remains loaded even after the procedure that creates the application is executed.

Replacing *CreateObject* with Strongly Typed Variables and the Keyword *New*

When you declare variables as type Object, as you did in step 4 of the preceding example, Visual Basic doesn't know what the exact type of object is until it tries to create it the first time. Declaring objects as the generic Object type has benefits, but more often you'll want to declare an object variable as the specific type of object that it represents.

Using Strongly Typed Variables

When you declare an object variable as a specific type, your code runs faster and the Visual Basic Editor can help reduce the number of errors in your code. One way the Editor can do this is with the Auto List Members feature, which displays all of the properties and methods supported by the object. This feature lets you see easily whether the option you're trying to use actually exists. However, you must take an additional step before using the Auto List Members feature with objects that aren't part of the application containing your Visual Basic code: you must make sure that the object library containing the object that you want to reference is loaded into the Editor.

Load the PowerPoint Object Library

1. Switch to the Visual Basic Editor of Excel.

2. On the Tools menu, click References.

These three object libraries are always referenced by default.

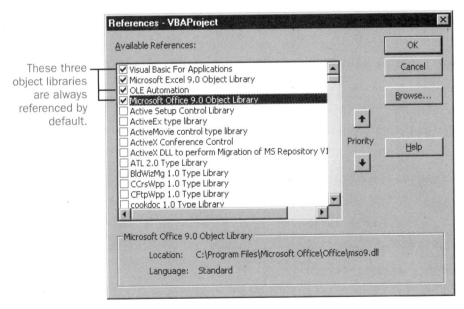

The References dialog box displays a list of every object library currently registered on your system. In addition to the object library for the application containing your Visual Basic code (in this example, Excel), three object libraries are always referenced by default:

- Visual Basic for Applications

- Microsoft Office 9.0 Object Library

- OLE Automation

Visual Basic individually saves the items selected in the list of Available References for each Visual Basic for Applications project. This means that setting a reference to a particular object library won't create the same *reference* in every Visual Basic for Applications project you have open.

It's not enough to select the library name in the list. Make sure you select the checkbox before you click OK.

3. Scroll down the list, select the check box next to the Microsoft PowerPoint 9.0 Object Library, and click OK.

You have set a reference to the Microsoft PowerPoint 9.0 Object Library for your current Visual Basic project. Second, you now have access to all the PowerPoint objects, methods, and properties, and when you work with an object variable that is declared as a PowerPoint object type, the Auto List Members drop-down list appears when you enter your Visual Basic code. Third, when you add a reference to an object library, it appears in the Libraries drop-down list in the Editor's Object Browser so you can browse through the object model and conduct member searches if necessary. For more information about the Object Browser, see "Learning the Members of the Object Model" in Chapter 1.

4. Create a new procedure by typing **Sub SetReferences** and pressing ENTER.

5. Add the following line:

```
Dim appPPT As PowerPoint.Application
```

Right after you type the word **As** and a space, the Auto List Members drop-down list appears and PowerPoint is listed (scroll through the list or type **pow** to see it). The Auto List Members drop-down list appears again right after you type the period (.) after the word "PowerPoint". Continue to type the word **Application**; "Application" will appear selected in the Auto List Members drop-down list. Once you enter it, this line declares the variable *appPPT* as an *Application* object of PowerPoint.

Tip When the Auto List Members drop-down list appears and you type the first few letters of the member name you need, Visual Basic automatically selects an item in the list that matches what you type. You can then press TAB to complete your statement with the selected item and then close the drop-down list.

---

6. Add the following two lines:

```
Set appPPT = CreateObject ("PowerPoint.Application")
appPPT.Visible = True
```

   Right after you type the period (.) after the variable name *appPPT*, the Auto List Members drop-down list appears and displays a list of the properties and methods belonging to PowerPoint. Thus, when you declare a variable as a specific type, Visual Basic provides you with a list of the object's property and method members. You don't have to remember which properties and methods the object supports because the Auto List Members drop-down list displays them.

Note   The Auto List Members drop-down list also appears when you type the equal sign (=) to set the value of a property. In this case, the Auto List Members drop-down list displays the possible values you can assign to the Visible property, including two additional True values, msoCTrue and msoTrue, which are the numeric values 1 and –1, respectively. You don't need to worry about the uses of the values now, and any of the True values (including True itself) makes the window visible. More specifically, you can use "True" in the place of "msoTrue" or "False" in the place of "msoFalse." They are both equivalent.

---

7. Place the cursor in the procedure and press F5. When you run this procedure, Visual Basic compiles your project and checks your code's syntax, ensuring that you have valid values assigned to variables. Once Visual Basic compiles your code, it runs slightly faster than if you didn't declare your object variables as a specific type.

8. Exit PowerPoint without saving changes.

Multiple Application Instances

As noted in the section "Starting More than One Instance of an Application" earlier in this chapter, with Word, Excel and Access, you can create more than one instance of an application. With PowerPoint and Outlook, if the application isn't already running, the *Application* object created using the *CreateObject* function starts PowerPoint or Outlook. If PowerPoint is running, for example, *CreateObject* returns the same *Application* object that's currently loaded in memory. For the Word, Excel and Access applications, each time you use the *CreateObject* function a new instance is created.

Using the Keyword *New*

Dim, Sub, End, and so on are *keywords*, words recognized as part of the Visual Basic programming language. These keywords are essential to your programming efforts because they're the ones that control the way Visual Basic interprets your instructions. The keyword *New* provides a way of creating an instance of an object besides using the *CreateObject* function.

When you use the *CreateObject* function, you must first declare an object variable and then use the Set statement to assign the object instance to the object variable. If you use *New* when declaring an object variable, you don't have to do that. Once an object is declared in a Dim statement that includes the keyword *New,* a new instance of the object is created on the first reference to it in code.

Note The *New* keyword can be used to declare only object variables and not any other data type such as String, Integer, or Long.

Create a New Application Object

1. In the Visual Basic Editor of Excel, in the same code module, add and run the following procedure:

```
Sub UsingKeywordNew()
    Dim appPPT As New PowerPoint.Application
    MsgBox appPPT.Path
End Sub
```

Visual Basic creates a new instance of the PowerPoint *Application* object using this syntax, but it's not visible. The message box line where you display the path of the PowerPoint application is the first reference to the PowerPoint *Application* object you declared in the second line.

After the Dim statement, you don't need the statement Set appPPT = CreateObject ("PowerPoint.Application"). The use of the *New* keyword in the Dim statement indicates that a new instance of the PowerPoint *Application* object is available but won't load until the first reference is made to it or to one of its members.

2. Click OK to close the message box.

Referencing an Existing Object with *GetObject*

In a couple of instances you need to use the *GetObject* function:

- When you want to access an instance of an object that's already loaded, such as an Excel *Application* object.

- When you want to start an application and load an existing file in a single step.

If neither one of these two scenarios is applicable, you'd use the *CreateObject* function or the *New* keyword in a declaration statement.

The function *GetObject* has the syntax GetObject(*pathname, class*). The *pathname* argument specifies the pathname and filename of a file located on your computer or on a drive on your network. If the pathname isn't included in the filename, Visual Basic looks in the current folder of the application containing the code that's running the *GetObject* function. If *pathname* is omitted, the *class* argument is needed.

The *class* argument has the same syntax as the *CreateObject* function: *ApplicationName.ObjectType*. *ApplicationName* is the name of the application providing the object you want to create, and *ObjectType* is the type or class of object to create. If you specify the filename but not the class, Visual Basic determines which application to start and which object to activate based on the filename you provide.

Access an Existing Application

The *GetObject* function is useful when you want to determine whether an application is already loaded. That way you can avoid loading a separate instance and perhaps confusing the user with multiple instances of an application.

1. In Excel, save the default workbook as Book1 in the Temp subfolder on your machine. For our purposes, we'll use C:\Temp. Later, you'll load the workbook in Excel by using the *GetObject* function.

2. Exit Excel and then start PowerPoint.

3. In the opening PowerPoint dialog box, select Blank Presentation, and then click OK. In the New Slide dialog box, choose any AutoLayout and click OK.

4. On the Tools menu, point to Macro and then click Visual Basic Editor on the submenu.

5. On the Tools menu, click References, select the Microsoft Word 9.0 Object Library from the list, and click OK.

6. On the Insert menu, click Module. In the inserted module, create a new procedure by typing **Sub GetExistingApp** and pressing ENTER.

7. Add the following procedure-level variable declaration to the *GetExistingApp* procedure:

```
Dim appWd As Word.Application
```

8. After the procedure-level variable declaration, add the following lines within the procedure:

```
On Error Resume Next
Set appWd = GetObject(, "Word.Application")
```

You add the line `On Error Resume Next` before the Set statement to tell Visual Basic that if an error occurs when it's running a line of code it should continue to the next line. If you omit the first argument, *pathname*, preceding the comma in the Set statement above from the *GetObject* function, as shown here, the function returns a currently active object of the specified class type. In this case, the class is the Word application. If no object of the specified type exists, an error occurs.

9. Add the following If...Then condition block:

```
If appWd Is Nothing Then
    Set appWd = CreateObject("Word.Application")
End If
```

The Visual Basic keyword *Nothing* is used with object variables and indicates whether an object variable has been assigned to an actual object in memory. When you declare an object variable, Visual Basic sets it to *Nothing* until you set it to an object by using the Set statement. The declaration of an object variable as a specific type tells Visual Basic what type of object that variable can be set to. In the preceding If...Then condition, if you didn't set the object variable *appWd* in the *GetObject* function, *appWd* still isn't assigned to a valid object and is set to *Nothing* instead. This means that an existing instance of the Word application wasn't found and you have to create a new one by using the *CreateObject* function.

10. Add the following as the last line in the procedure:

```
appWd.Visible = True
```

Setting the Visible property of the Word *Application* object to True displays the Word application window on the screen.

11. Place the cursor in the procedure and press F5 to run it. If Word isn't running, the procedure creates a new instance of the application. However, if Word is running, the *GetObject* function returns the current instance. If the instance of Word is running in the background, as it is when you use Word as your e-mail editor in Outlook, *GetObject* returns the instance of Word that's currently running in the background, which is not displayed to the user.

12. Exit PowerPoint without saving changes. Don't exit Word.

Load an Excel Workbook

When you use the *GetObject* function to start an application with a file that's already loaded, it's essentially the same as first using the *CreateObject* function to create an instance of an application, and then using an *Open* method of the document collection of the specific application to open the file. The *GetObject* function reduces the number of lines of code needed to do the same thing.

1. Switch to Word and open a new document. Open the Visual Basic Editor. On the Tools menu, click References, select Microsoft Excel 9.0 Object Library from the list, and click OK.

2. Insert a new code module, and then add the following module-level variable declaration:

```
Dim m_wbBook1 As Excel.Workbook
```

By adding a module-level declaration, you ensure that Excel won't automatically close the workbook that will be loaded by the *GetObject* function once you run all the lines of code in the procedure that you create in the next step.

3. Create a new procedure by typing **Sub UsingGetObject** and pressing ENTER.

Note Make sure you insert the new module into the project for the new document, not into the Normal project (Normal.dot). If you're not sure, open the Project Explorer window and see under which project the new module appears.

---

4. Type the following line within the procedure:

```
Set m_wbBook1 = GetObject("C:\Temp\Book1.xls")
```

You use the Set statement to assign the object returned by GetObject (an Excel *Workbook* object) to the module-level object variable *m_wbBook1*. The *pathname* argument specified in the *GetObject* function above assumes you have correctly saved an Excel file named Book1.xls to drive C in the Temp subfolder. If you saved to a different file location the Excel file in step 1 of "Access an Existing Application" earlier in this chapter, make sure that the *pathname* argument in the *GetObject* function reflects the correct location.

Note If an instance of Excel is already running, the *GetObject* function used in the code accesses and loads only the specified file in that instance of Excel. If Excel isn't running, the *GetObject* function creates and loads the specified file in a new instance of Excel.

---

5. Type the following two lines after the Set statement:

```
m_wbBook1.Windows(1).Visible = True
m_wbBook1.Application.Visible = True
```

When *GetObject* runs, it loads the Excel workbook invisibly. By default, each workbook contains at least one window. To make it visible, set its Visible property to True.

6. Place the cursor in the procedure and press F5 to run it. When this code runs, it starts the application associated with the specified pathname (Excel, in this case) and opens the object in the specified file (Book1.xls).

Disconnecting a Variable from an Object

When you use the *CreateObject* or *GetObject* function or the *New* keyword to assign a variable to an object, the object resides in your computer system's memory. Depending on your program's complexity, releasing certain objects from memory may speed up other parts of your program. To disconnect an object variable from an object in memory that you no longer need, set the object variable to the keyword *Nothing*. Once an object variable is set to *Nothing*, it no longer references an actual object in memory. If no other object variable refers to that object, it's removed from your system's memory.

Note If the object variable is declared as a procedure-level variable, Visual Basic will automatically set it to *Nothing* once Visual Basic finishes executing the procedure containing the procedure-level variable. Explicitly setting object variables to *Nothing* is common for public or module-level object variables.

All Office applications provide, as a member of the respective *Application* object, a *Quit* method that closes the application whether it's visible or not. Running the *Quit* method in Visual Basic is the same as clicking Exit on the File menu in an Office application. In some cases, running the *Quit* method doesn't release the reference to the actual object until you explicitly set the object variable to *Nothing* or until the object variable goes out of scope.

Quit Excel Using Visual Basic Code

1. Exit any running versions of Excel without saving changes.

2. In the *UsingGetObject* procedure you just created in Word's Visual Basic Editor, add the following message box statement and With...End block after the last line of the procedure and just before the End Sub statement:

```
MsgBox "Excel will now be closed."
With m_wbBook1.Application
    .DisplayAlerts = False
    .Quit
End With
```

The DisplayAlerts property of the Excel *Application* object indicates whether Excel displays a dialog box asking if you want to save changes (or any other alert dialog box Excel normally displays). If DisplayAlerts is set to False, no dialog boxes are displayed. Thus, when Visual Basic executes the *Quit* method of the Excel *Application* object, Excel won't display a dialog box asking whether you want to save changes to the workbook.

3. Place the cursor in the procedure and press F5 to run it. When you run the *UsingGetObject* procedure, Excel starts and the file, Book1.xls, is activated.

4. Switch to Word, but do nothing to Excel. Once Book1.xls is displayed, Word displays a message box indicating that Excel will now be closed. When you click OK in the Word message box, Word closes Excel, along with the Book1 workbook.

Creating a PowerPoint Presentation from a Word Document

After creating a report using Word, you may find that its breakdown of topics could easily be integrated into a PowerPoint presentation. Word enables you to send your active Word document to PowerPoint simply by pointing to Send To on the File menu and then clicking Microsoft PowerPoint on the submenu. Unfortunately, the result may not match your Word template's formatting. However, you can use Visual Basic for Applications to create your own Send To PowerPoint feature. This way, you can customize the output to meet your needs.

Note   The practice files for Chapter 7 already include a Word document that has the code needed to generate both a PowerPoint presentation and an Outlook e-mail message that the presentation is attached to. You can load the practice file, browse through the code in the Visual Basic project of the Word document, and run the code to see the results.

Create Source Information and Define Module-Level Variables

1. Switch to Word.

When you install Word, the Normal template that's attached to new blank documents contains a short list of predefined text styles: Heading 1 through Heading 9, Normal, and a few others. To see this list of text styles, click Style on the Format menu, and then select All Styles from the List drop-down list. In the Styles box, you should see a full list of the Word text styles defined in the Normal template. You can also see an abbreviated list by clicking the Style drop-down list on the Format toolbar.

2. In the default document (Document1 or a similar name), add a few one-line paragraphs and format each line as one of these text styles: Heading 1, Heading 2, Heading 3, and Heading 4. Use the following illustration as a guide. You can also copy these lines from the CreatePP.doc file.

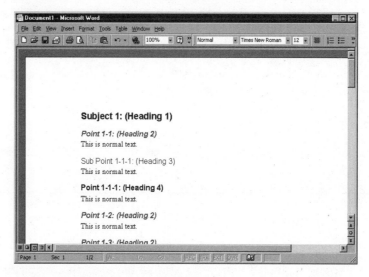

3. In the Visual Basic Editor of Word, insert a new code module.

4. On the Tools menu, click References, select the Microsoft PowerPoint 9.0 Object Library from the Available References list, and click OK.

5. In the declarations section (the top) of the code module, add the following module-level variable declarations:

```
Dim m_sldNew As PowerPoint.Slide
Dim m_paraItem As Paragraph
```

6. Add the following module-level constant declaration:

```
Const m_sPresFile As String = _
"C:\Temp\MyPres.ppt"
```

The module-level constant m_sPresFile is set equal to the filename given to the slide presentation that you will create. Save the presentation to your hard disk so that you'll be able to use the file as an attachment in an Outlook e-mail message (as you'll do later in this chapter).

Write the Code to Examine the Headings

1. Create a new procedure in the code module by typing **Sub Main** and pressing ENTER, and then add the following declarations and a Set statement within the procedure:

```
Dim appPPT As New PowerPoint.Application
Dim pres As PowerPoint.Presentation
Dim sStyle As String

Set pres = appPPT.Presentations.Add(WithWindow:=msoFalse)
```

Note the use of the keyword *New* in the first object variable declaration. The first time you use the variable *appPPT* in code, the program creates a PowerPoint Application object and implicitly sets it to the object variable *appPPT*.

The last line represents the first time that *appPPT* is referenced in code. Thus, the PowerPoint Application object is automatically created. You use the *Application* object to access the *Presentations* collection object, which consists of the list of presentations currently open in PowerPoint, whether or not they're visible to the user. The *Add* method of the *Presentations* object creates a new presentation.

2. Add the following With...End block containing the For Each...Next loop:

```
With ActiveDocument.Range
    For Each m_paraItem In .Paragraphs
    Next m_paraItem
End With
```

You'll use this loop to iterate through each paragraph in the active Word document.

3. Just after the line `For Each m_paraItem In .Paragraphs`, add the following code as the first line in the For Each...Next loop:

```
sStyle = m_paraItem.Style
```

The Style property of the *Paragraph* object in Word returns a string that represents the name of the text style used in the paragraph. The string is assigned to the variable *sStyle*.

4. Add the following Select Case block:

```
Select Case sStyle
Case "Heading 1"
    Set m_sldNew = pres.Slides _
        .Add(pres.Slides.Count + 1, ppLayoutText)
    SetText ppTitleStyle, 1
```

```
Case "Heading 2"
    SetText ppBodyStyle, 1
Case "Heading 3"
    SetText ppBodyStyle, 2
Case "Heading 4"
    SetText ppBodyStyle, 3
End Select
```

The Select Case block examines the value of the string variable *sStyle*. If the value of *sStyle* is Heading 1, it creates a new slide in the PowerPoint presentation. The *Add* method of the *Slides* collection object accepts two arguments. The first argument is the index position of the newly added slide in the presentation, and the second is the slide layout type. In this case, you always create a slide with Title and Body placeholders and add it to the end of the *Slides* collection. The text of a paragraph in Word with the text style Heading 1 is used as the slide title in the first newly created slide.

For each case in the above Select Case block, you call the *SetText* procedure and pass it two arguments: an integer (an enumeration value in the form of a built-in PowerPoint constant) representing the text style and an integer representing the paragraph indent level in the body-text placeholder of a PowerPoint slide. Heading 1 represents a slide title; Heading 2 represents a first-level paragraph in the body-text placeholder; Heading 3 represents a second-level paragraph in the body-text placeholder; and Heading 4 represents a third-level paragraph in the body-text placeholder.

Generate a Correctly Formatted PowerPoint Slide from Word Text

1. Below the *Main* procedure, create a new procedure by typing **Sub SetText (iTextStyle As Integer, iIndentLevel As Integer)** and pressing ENTER.

This procedure places the text from the Word document in the appropriate slide placeholder in the PowerPoint presentation. The code between the parentheses declares the arguments to the procedure. Note that the way you declare arguments is similar to the way you declare variables.

2. Add the following declaration within the procedure:

```
Dim txtTitle As TextRange
```

3. Create the first half of an If...Then...Else statement by adding the following lines of code:

```
If iTextStyle = ppTitleStyle Then
    Set txtTitle = m_sldNew.Shapes.Title _
        .TextFrame.TextRange
    With txtTitle
        .Text = m_paraItem.Range
        .Text = .TrimText
    End With
```

The If...Then statement determines the value of the Integer variable *iTextStyle*, which was passed as an argument to the *SetText* procedure from the *Main* procedure. The program uses the text style in the Word document to determine the value of *iTextStyle*. If the text style of the paragraph in the Word document is Heading 1, it sets the equivalent text style to the title style of a PowerPoint slide.

The program sets the object variable *txtTitle* to the text range of the title shape on the PowerPoint slide. The With...End block following the Set statement sets the actual text in the title shape to the text in the paragraph in the Word document. The *TrimText* method of the *TextRange* object in PowerPoint removes any spaces, carriage returns, or linefeeds from the text.

4. Complete the If...Then...Else statement by adding the following lines of code:

```
Else
    m_sldNew.Shapes.Placeholders(2).TextFrame _
        .TextRange.InsertAfter(m_paraItem.Range) _
        .IndentLevel = iIndentLevel
End If
```

If the text style of the paragraph in the Word document isn't Heading 1, the program adds the paragraph's text to the body shape in the PowerPoint slide. The second placeholder for a slide with the Bulleted List layout (specified by the constant ppLayoutText in Visual Basic code) represents the body shape. The program inserts the paragraph from the Word document into the body shape's text range after the body shape's last paragraph.

The IndentLevel property of the *TextRange* object in PowerPoint determines how many times to indent the bulleted point in the shape. The program passes the value of the Integer variable *iIndentLevel* as an argument to the *SetText* procedure from the *Main* procedure, and the value is determined by the text style in the Word document.

5. Finally, add the following With...End block to the end of the *Main* procedure:

```
With appPPT
    If .Visible = msoTrue Then
        pres.NewWindow
    Else
        .Visible = msoTrue
    End If
    pres.SaveAs m_sPresFile
    .Activate
End With
```

The If...Then...Else condition block sets the PowerPoint application window to Visible if it's not currently displayed. If the application window is currently visible, the new presentation is displayed using the *NewWindow* method. The line after the If...Then...Else condition block saves the presentation to the location specified by the module-level string constant m_sPresFile. This constant was previously set to "C:\Temp\MyPres.ppt." You may have specified a different file location in the declaration of the constant. The final line activates the PowerPoint application window and puts it in front of all the windows on the screen.

6. Place the cursor in the *Main* procedure and press F5 to run it.

After iterating through the Word document and determining the text style of each paragraph in the document, your program uses the text to create a new PowerPoint presentation that should look like the following:

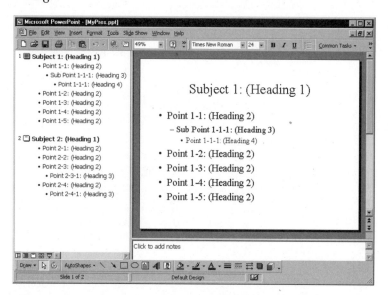

7. Exit PowerPoint. (Changes have already been saved.)

Send Your Presentation in E-Mail

Once you've automatically created your PowerPoint presentation, you might want to send it automatically to a specific audience. Using the Outlook object library, you can easily extend your program to create an Outlook e-mail message that contains the presentation as an attachment.

Note   In the following example, the e-mail message you create with Visual Basic for Applications uses Outlook and doesn't work for any other e-mail client. You also need to be connected to a network or the Internet to actually send e-mail. As long as you have Outlook installed on your computer, however, you can still run the code in this example without sending the e-mail message you create.

---

1. In the same Visual Basic for Applications project, in the Visual Basic Editor of Word, click References on the Tools menu, select the Microsoft Outlook 9.0 Object Library from the Available References list, and click OK.

2. Below the *SetText* procedure, create a new procedure by typing **Sub SendMail** and pressing ENTER.

3. In the *SendMail* procedure, add the following two declarations:

```
Dim oOutlook As Outlook.Application
Dim oMessage As Outlook.MailItem
```

You could use the New keyword in the declaration of the object variable *oOutlook* just as you did when you created the PowerPoint *Application* object. When you don't use the New keyword, you have to explicitly set the *oOutlook* object variable using the *CreateObject* function.

4. Just below the added declarations, add the following Set statement with the *CreateObject* function:

```
Set oOutlook = CreateObject("Outlook.Application")
```

You've now created an Outlook *Application* object and you're ready to work with it.

5. Just below the Set statement with the *CreateObject* function, add the following:

```
Set oMessage = oOutlook.CreateItem(olMailItem)
```

You declared the object variable *oMessage* as an Outlook *MailItem* object and, using the Set statement, assigned the *oMessage* object to a newly created mail item that you're ready to work with. The *CreateItem* method is a member of the Outlook *Application* object. *CreateItem* accepts one of seven possible values, each represented by an enumeration value (in the form of a built-in Outlook constant), which is a predefined name for an Integer or Long value.

6. Add the following With...End block:

```
With oMessage
    .To = "Executive Committee"
    .Subject = "New Sales Report"
    .Body = "The following presentation reflects" & _
        " the final sales figures for Q2." & vbCrLf
End With
```

The With...End block allows you to set properties of the mail item without having to continuously prefix each property of the *MailItem* object with *oMessage*. This both improves performance (because Visual Basic needs to determine what *oMessage* is just once) and improves your code's readability. The first line in the With...End block sets the To property of the *MailItem* object to equal the e-mail alias "Executive Committee." (Of course, you should set this to a valid e-mail alias on your e-mail system.) The subject of the e-mail message is set using the Subject property, and the body text of the mail item is set using the Body property. The constant vbCrLf is a Visual Basic constant representing a "carriage return and linefeed" in the text you specify.

7. At the end of the With...End block, add the following line just before the line End With:

```
.Attachments.Add m_sPresFile, , , "Q2 Sales"
```

The *MailItem* object provides an *Attachments* collection to which you can add items or iterate through the attachments already contained in the mail item. In this case, you'll add the PowerPoint presentation you previously created. The third argument in the *Add* method of the *Attachments* object, called the *Position* argument, indicates to the *Add* method after which character position within the body text it should add the attachment. By default, if nothing is specified (as in the above line), the *Add* method adds the attachment after the last character in the MailItem.Body text. The fourth argument, *DisplayName,* represents the text used with the icon of the attachment. By default, the program uses the filename of the attachment. Here, you explicitly set it to "Q2 Sales."

8. Just after the method to add attachments, add the following line before End With:

```
.Display
```

The *Display* method of the *MailItem* object displays the mail item you created.

9. Now add the following line as the last line in the With...End block:

```
.Send
```

The *Send* method of the *MailItem* object sends the newly created e-mail message automatically. However, instead of sending the item now, you'd probably prefer to store it in your Outlook Drafts folder until you're ready to send it manually.

10. If you want to store the e-mail item in Outlook, replace .Send with the following line:

```
.Close (olSave)
```

The *Close* method then closes the mail item, so you no longer see it on the screen. The olSave constant specified in the argument of the *Close* method saves the mail item to the item type's Outlook default folder. In this case, it's saved to the Drafts folder in your Outlook mailbox.

Now that you've created your e-mail procedure, you need to call the procedure that creates and sends the mail item from the same code that automatically generates the PowerPoint presentation.

11. In the *Main* procedure, add the following line just before End Sub:

SendMail

12. Place the cursor in the *Main* procedure and press F5.

In the *Main* procedure, once the code finishes creating the PowerPoint presentation based on your Word document, it saves the presentation file to your hard disk and then calls the *SendMail* procedure. The *SendMail* procedure creates a new mail item in Outlook and adds the generated presentation as an attachment, as shown here:

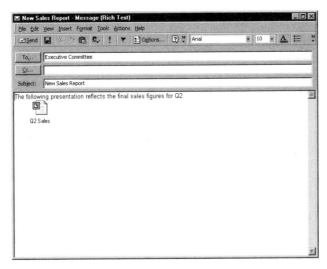

13. Exit all Office applications. Save the changes to Word if you like.

Chapter Summary

Creating (or starting) a new instance of an Office application or accessing an application that is running allows you to create new documents and content or retrieve data from another application. By creating a link between two applications to exchange data, you can present data and information in more than one way, depending on your audience and how they want to view the data.

Chapter 8

Developing an Integrated Office Solution

Estimated time: 90 minutes

- Develop an integrated Microsoft Office solution using data and forms in a Microsoft Access database.

- Retrieve data in a database from Access or any other Office application.

- Produce a report in Microsoft Word from database information.

- Create a Microsoft Excel worksheet and chart from database information.

- Present an Excel chart in Microsoft PowerPoint.

- Send Office documents in a Microsoft Outlook e-mail message.

When you develop Microsoft Visual Basic for Applications programs for Office, you often apply functionality and tools across the Office suite. Building integrated solutions helps you keep the core of your information centralized and easy to manage, while allowing you to communicate that information in ways that best suit your users' needs.

In this chapter you'll create an integrated Office solution. You'll begin with an Access database containing a form that lets users interact with your program. The custom form provides options for creating a Word report for management and customers, an Excel worksheet for data analysis, and a PowerPoint presentation for meetings and sales demonstrations. It also has the ability to use Outlook to automatically send the documents your program generates through e-mail. The code you'll add in the Access database file drives the automatic generation of all these documents.

Tip The full solution for this chapter is provided in the Chapter 8 practice folder in the file Energy.mdb. Open the Energy.mdb file and press ALT+F11 to display the Visual Basic Editor and the code in the database. You can then use this chapter as a step-by-step guide for each line of code in the project.

Creating an Access Database

The integrated Office solution you're about to create involves a fictitious set of data representing an energy usage log for a computer lab in your company. The solution is called "Energy Management," and it tracks a lab's energy use over a one-month period so that management can do a cost assessment and determine ways of reducing energy costs.

The Access database that stores the energy usage data consists of three main elements. The first element is the table containing the data. The second is the user interface, or dialog box, where you select the document items you want to automatically generate. The third is the code, contained in the various code modules, that creates the selected document items. The steps in this chapter show you how to create all three elements of the database.

Import Data into an Access Database Table

1. Start Access. In the opening Access dialog box, select the Blank Access Database option button and click OK.

2. In the File New Database dialog box, select the Chapter 8 practice folder; in the File Name text box, type **MyEnergy** and click Create. The Database window is displayed.

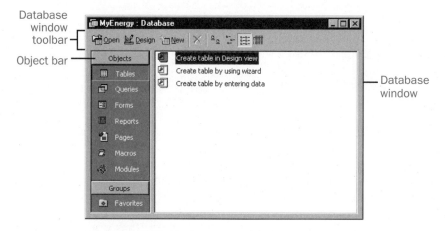

Database window toolbar

Object bar

Database window

3. In the Database window, click Tables in the Objects bar, and then click New on the Database window toolbar. Select Import Table in the New Table dialog box and click OK.

4. In the Import dialog box, select Text Files in the Files Of Type drop-down list. In the Chapter 8 practice folder, select LabEnerg.txt and click Import.
   In this fictitious solution, a digital meter connected to a computer automatically generated the text file. The hardware and software associated with the meter automatically fed the data to the text file.

5. In the Import Text Wizard dialog box, click Next five times until you reach the final step in the wizard, and then type **LabEnergyUsage** in the Import To Table text box.

    Because you're importing a comma-delimited text file containing data that was automatically generated by the tools connected to the circuits, you should accept the default settings in each step of the wizard.

6. In the Import Text Wizard dialog box, click Finish.

7. When the Import Text Wizard displays the message box indicating that Access has finished importing the data file, click OK.

8. Select the LabEnergyUsage table and click Design on the Database window toolbar.

9. In the Field Name column, double-click in the second row, which currently contains the text "Field1."

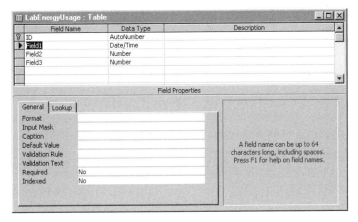

10. In the Field Name column, clear the text and type **Date and Time**.

11. In the Field Name column, double-click in the third row, which currently contains the text "Field2." Clear the text and type **Lighting**.

12. In the Field Name column, double-click in the fourth row, which currently contains the text "Field3." Clear the text and type **Computer Network**.

13. Close the Table Design View window by clicking the lower Close Window button in the upper-right corner of the Table Design View window.

Close Window

14. When Access asks if you want to save changes to the design of table LabEnergyUsage, click Yes.

    The table is now ready for exporting data to Word, Excel, and PowerPoint, and you can start creating the dialog box that will display your document options.

Quick Guide: Using Code to Retrieve Data from the Database

Before exporting data to other Office applications, you can create a simple code procedure within the database file that retrieves data from the table you just created and prints the data values to the Immediate window in the Visual Basic Editor in Access. This procedure can be used as a basis for any procedure that accesses data from a standard Access database. In the integrated Office solution created in this chapter, you'll use the following procedure as a basis for the *GetDatabaseInfo* procedure.

After you use the following example, the steps in the Quick Guide "Retrieve Data in a Database from Another Office Application" show how you can use the same procedure in another Office application to achieve the same result.

1. Use the keyboard shortcut ALT+F11 to display the Visual Basic Editor in Access.

2. On the Tools menu, click References to display the References dialog box. If the item Microsoft ActiveX Data Objects 2.1 Library is cleared, select the item and click OK.

   Although you're ensuring here that this reference exists, a reference to the ActiveX Data Objects (or ADO) object library is automatically set for any new database files created in Access 2000, so you should not need to perform this step every time.

3. Click Module on the Insert menu to insert a new code module and type the following procedure.

```
Sub RetrieveDataFromTable()
    Dim rstEnergy As New ADODB.Recordset

    rstEnergy.Open "LabEnergyUsage", _
        CurrentProject.Connection, adOpenStatic
    With rstEnergy
        Do While Not .EOF
            Debug.Print .Fields("Id")
            Debug.Print .Fields("Date and Time")
            .MoveNext
        Loop
        .Close
    End With
End Sub
```

4. On the View menu, click Immediate Window to display the Immediate window.

(continued)

5. Click in the *RetrieveDataFromTable* procedure and press F5. The *RetrieveDataFromTable* procedure iterates through each row in the LabEnergyUsage table and the value in the Id and the Date and Time fields are printed to the Immediate window in the Visual Basic Editor in Access.

The use of the *Open* method on the Recordset sets the *rstEnergy* object variable and assigns the records from the LabEnergyUsage table to the *rstEnergy* object. The Do…Loop moves through each record (or row) in the table. As the loop iterates through each record, the EOF property indicates whether the current record position is after the last record in a Recordset object. The *MoveNext* method is then used to sequentially access each record in the table. The *Close* method after the Do…Loop closes the Recordset object, *rstEnergy*, to free any associated system resources.

Quick Guide: Retrieve Data in a Database from Another Office Application

You can also use the *RetrieveDataFromTable* procedure to access the database from another Office application, by adding three lines of code and changing one other line. (Changes to the *RetrieveDataFromTable* procedure are highlighted in bold text in the code that follows.) You also need to ensure there is a reference to the Microsoft ActiveX Data Objects 2.1 Library at the point where the following code is executed. You set this reference in the project in the Visual Basic Editor of the other Office application.

1. Start the Windows Explorer and display the Chapter 8 practice folder. In the Chapter 8 practice folder, copy the Energy.mdb file to the folder C:\Temp.

    If you copy the database file to a different folder, be sure to change the path of the filename specified in the *ConnectionString* argument of the *Open* method in the procedure listed in step 5.

2. Start Word, Excel, PowerPoint, or Outlook and display the Visual Basic Editor.

3. In the Visual Basic Editor, on the Tools menu, click References to display the References dialog box.

4. Scroll through the Available References list box, select Microsoft ActiveX Data Objects 2.1 Library and click OK.

5. Click Module on the Insert menu to insert a new code module and then type the procedure on the following page.

(continued)

**Quick Guide: Retrieve Data in a
Database from Another Office Application** *(continued)*

```
Sub RetrieveDataFromFile()
    Dim rstEnergy As New ADODB.Recordset
    Dim cnnEnergyUsage As New ADODB.Connection

    cnnEnergyUsage.Open ConnectionString:= _
        "Provider=Microsoft.Jet.OLEDB.4.0;" & _
        "Data Source=" & "C:\Temp\Energy.mdb"

    rstEnergy.Open "LabEnergyUsage", cnnEnergyUsage, _
        adOpenStatic
    With rstEnergy
        Do While Not .EOF
            Debug.Print .Fields("Id")
            Debug.Print .Fields("Date and Time")
            .MoveNext
        Loop
        .Close
    End With
    cnnEnergyUsage.Close
End Sub
```

6. On the View menu, click Immediate Window to display the Immediate window.

7. Click in the *RetrieveDataFromFile* procedure and press F5.

   The *RetrieveDataFromFile* procedure iterates through each row in the LabEnergyUsage table in the database file Energy.mdb. The values in the Id and the Date and Time fields are printed to the Immediate window in the Visual Basic Editor of the application you started in step 2.

   In the *RetrieveDataFromFile* procedure, there are three differences from the *RetrieveDataFromTable* procedure in the previous Quick Guide. The first is the additional line that sets the *cnnEnergyUsage* variable, and the second is the use of the same variable in the *Open* method on the *RecordSet* object. The third is the last line in the procedure, which closes the connection to the data source.

   The *ConnectionString* argument of the *Open* method contains the information used to establish a connection to a specified data source. The data source in this example is the Energy.mdb database. When you access data from a database file with the extension .mdb, the data provider as specified in the *ConnectionString* argument is Microsoft Jet. In cases such as where you access data from a source through a file with the extension .adp (new to Access 2000), the data is provided through the Microsoft OLE DB Provider for SQL Server.

Create a Form in Access

1. In the Database window, click Forms in the Objects bar, and then click New on the Database window toolbar.

2. In the New Form dialog box, select Design View and click OK. The form is now in Design view, and you can start adding controls to it.

3. Click the *Check Box* control in the Toolbox and then click anywhere on the form to insert a check box control. Repeat these actions three more times to create a total of four check boxes.

Check Box control

4. Click the *Command Button* control in the Toolbox and then click anywhere on the form to insert a command button control. When the Command Button Wizard appears, click Cancel. Repeat this step to create a total of two command buttons.

Command Button control

5. Click the *Label* control in the Toolbox and then click anywhere on the form to insert a label control. Immediately after inserting the *Label* control to replace the label's default text, type **Generate the following documents:**. You need to add a caption immediately or the control will disappear.

Label control

6. Click the *Image* control in the Toolbox and then click anywhere on the form to insert an image control. In the Insert Picture dialog box that's displayed automatically once you insert the *Image* control, change to the Chapter 8 practice folder, select Logo.wmf, and click OK.

7. Move and resize the controls and the form so that they appear similar to those shown in the following illustration:

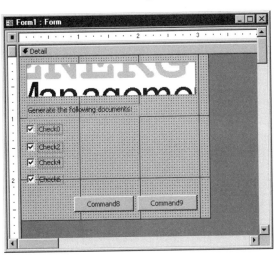

8. If the Properties window isn't displayed, on the View menu in Access, click Properties. In the Properties window, click the All tab to see a full list of properties, and then set the following values for the controls. To set the properties in the table on the following page, select each control and set the value listed in the table in the Properties window.

Note Unlike the *CheckBox* control in the UserForm of the Visual Basic Editor, which has a Caption property, the label associated with a *Check Box* control in an Access form is listed as a separate control in the Properties window. Select the label of the check box to set its properties.

Control	Property	Value
Check0	Name	chkWord
Label1	Name	lblWord
Label1	Caption	Microsoft Word report
Check2	Name	chkExcel
Label3	Name	lblExcel
Label3	Caption	Microsoft Excel workbook
Check4	Name	chkPowerPoint
Label5	Name	lblPowerPoint
Label5	Caption	Microsoft PowerPoint presentation
Check6	Name	chkOutlook
Label7	Name	lblOutlook
Label7	Caption	Microsoft Outlook e-mail message
Command8	Name	cmdOK
Command8	Caption	OK
Command9	Name	cmdCancel
Command9	Caption	Cancel
Command9	Cancel	Yes
Label10	Name	lblGenerate
Image11	Name	imgLogo
Image11	Size Mode	Stretch

9. To display the progress of your solution while it's running, add four Label controls just above the OK and Cancel buttons. Add the following captions consecutively: **Number of records read:** , **#**, **of**, **#**. When you insert each Label control, add the caption immediately or the control disappears.

10. In the Properties window, set the following properties:

Control	Property	Value
Label12	Name	lblProgress
Label13	Name	lblCurrentRecord
Label14	Name	lblOf
Label15	Name	lblTotalRecords

In the Form Design window, click anywhere outside the form design area to display the list of properties for the form. (You may have to scroll down in order to display the area below the form design area.)

11. In the Properties window, set the following values for the form:

Property	Value
Caption	Energy Management
Record Selectors	No
Navigation Buttons	No
Dividing Lines	No
Border Style	Dialog
Shortcut Menu	No

12. Click the form window's title bar and Press F5 to display the dialog box. Try selecting and clearing the check boxes. Notice that the Form Design window creates forms just like UserForms in the Visual Basic Editor of Word, Excel, and PowerPoint does.

13. Click the Close Window button to close the form. When Access asks if you want to save changes to form *Form1*'s design, click Yes. In the Save As dialog box, type **frmMain** in the Form Name text box and click OK.

Close Window

Before adding code, you may want to click the Design button and move or resize the controls to resemble the preceding illustration. Press F5 to display the form, click the Close Window button to close it, and then save your changes.

Add Code Behind the Form

1. In the MyEnergy: Database window, click Forms in the Objects bar, select the item *frmMain,* and then click Design on the Database window toolbar.

2. On the View menu, click Code to display the code module behind the form *frmMain.* You'll see the Visual Basic Editor for Access.

3. In the Object drop-down list of the Code window, select *cmdOK.* By default, the Click event procedure is displayed in the Code window.

4. In the event procedure *cmdOK_Click*, add the following lines of code:

```
Dim bReport As Boolean, bSheet As Boolean
Dim bPres As Boolean, bEmail As Boolean

If Me.chkWord.Value = True Then bReport = True
If Me.chkExcel.Value = True Then bSheet = True
If Me.chkPowerPoint.Value = True Then bPres = True
If Me.chkOutlook.Value = True Then bEmail = True

modMain.Main bReport, bSheet, bPres, bEmail
DoCmd.Close acForm, "frmMain", acSaveNo
```

The first two lines contain declarations of the Boolean variables *bReport, bSheet, bPres,* and *bEmail.* By default, the Boolean variables are set to False when they're declared. The four If...Then condition statements that follow check the value of each check box in the form *frmMain* and set the appropriate Boolean variable. The Me keyword represents the form in which the code you're writing resides. Once you set all the Boolean variables, the program calls the *Main* procedure in the code module modMain, which you'll create next. The Boolean variables are passed as arguments to the *Main* procedure.

5. In the Object drop-down list of the Code window, select *cmdCancel.*
By default, the click event procedure is displayed in the code window.

6. In the event procedure *cmdCancel_Click*, add the following line of code:

```
DoCmd.Close acForm, "frmMain", acSaveNo
```

Close Window

You can specify three arguments in the *Close* method of the *DoCmd* object in Access. The first argument is the object type you want to close, the second is the name of the object you want to close, and the third sets whether to save changes to the object when it's closed. In the line of code you just added, you close the Access form *frmMain* without saving changes to the form in the database.

Save

7. Click the Save button on the Standard toolbar in the Visual Basic Editor to save changes to the code.

You've now completed the dialog box your users will interact with to generate their required Office documents from the data in the database. You now have to add code to create each of the Office documents listed in your custom dialog box.

Add Code to the Database to Create an Office Document

1. In the Visual Basic Editor, click Module on the Insert menu to create a new code module.

2. In the Visual Basic Editor, on the Tools menu, click References to display the References dialog box.

3. Select the following items in the Available References list box and click OK when you finish: Microsoft Word 9.0 Object Library, Microsoft Excel 9.0 Object Library, Microsoft PowerPoint 9.0 Object Library, and Microsoft Outlook 9.0 Object Library.

   You're going to write code that accesses all of these object libraries so that you can create each type of document.

4. Add the following declarations to the code module:

```
Public g_sgTotalCost As Single
Public g_iTotalHours As Integer
Public g_sDBProjectPath As String

Public Const g_sCircuit As String = "Computer Network"

Const m_sgCost As Single = 1.075
Const m_iWattage As Integer = 560
```

   The first two declarations are public variables used to total the data in the database. The public constant g_sCircuit is set to "Computer Network," the circuit that the procedure will analyze. Later you can reset it to "Lighting" so you can analyze the lighting data. You declare the public variable, *g_sDBProjectPath,* as a string; you'll use it to assign the file path of the MyEnergy database.

   In this solution you'll use a supporting file, a Word template, to help create a report in Word. To keep the code of this solution from being complex, the Word template file should be copied to the same folder as the MyEnergy database, because the path to the database file can then easily be retrieved in code. In addition, the path to the database also specifies where to save the Word, Excel, and PowerPoint files created by this example. The two module-level constants, m_sgCost and m_iWattage, are values used to calculate the energy cost.

Note After you complete the steps in this chapter and you want to move or copy the MyEnergy.mdb file created in this chapter to another disk folder, you also need to copy the file EnerRpt.dot from the Chapter 8 practice folder to the new disk location. If you do not, and you run the form in the MyEnergy.mdb database to create a Word report, an error will occur, because the EnerRpt.dot template file used to create the Word document will not be found.

---

5. After the variable declarations, add the following *Main* procedure:

```
Sub Main(bReport As Boolean, bSheet As Boolean, _
    bPres As Boolean, bEmail As Boolean)
    g_sDBProjectPath = Application.CurrentProject.Path & "\"
End Sub
```

   The Click event procedure for the cmdOK command button that you added to the form *frmMain* will call the *Main* procedure. The four Boolean variables passed into the *Main* procedure indicate which check boxes were selected in the form *frmMain*. You set the Boolean values in the Click event procedure of cmdOK.

This procedure assigns the *g_sDBProjectPath* variable to the Path property. In this example, the Path property returns a string value that is the pathname to the disk location of the Access database MyEnergy.mdb.

6. After the line of code that sets the *g_sDBProjectPath* variable, add the following If...Then condition blocks:

```
If bReport = True Then
    modWord.CreateWordDocument
End If
If bSheet = True Or bPres = True Then
    modExcel.CreateExcelSheet
End If
```

If the Boolean variable *bReport* is passed into the *Main* procedure with a value of True, the program calls the procedure *CreateWordDocument*, located in the code module modWord. If the Boolean variable *bSheet* or the Boolean variable *bPres* is passed into the *Main* procedure with a value of True, the program calls the procedure *CreateExcelSheet*, located in the code module modExcel. In order to create a presentation with the data in a chart, you first have to create the chart in Excel. You'll create the procedures *CreateWordDocument* and *CreateExcelDocument* later in this chapter. These two procedures create a document and a worksheet ready for the database information.

7. After the two If...Then condition blocks, add the following call to the *GetDatabaseInfo* procedure:

```
GetDatabaseInfo bReport, bSheet, bPres, True
```

The *GetDatabaseInfo* procedure retrieves the information from the database and sends it to Word and Excel. The Boolean variables *bReport*, *bSheet*, and *bPres* are passed to the procedure so that you can check whether you need to pass the data to Word or Excel.

The last argument in the *GetDatabaseInfo* procedure indicates whether the Access form, *frmMain*, should be updated. Because the line of code above calls the *GetDatabaseInfo* procedure from within the *Main* procedure, and the *Main* procedure is only called when clicking OK on the form *frmMain*, this value is always set to True. As you'll see later in this chapter, when you test your code for creating the Word, Excel, and PowerPoint documents, this argument is set to False because running the procedure you'll use to test your code does not require the form to be displayed.

8. Add the following If...Then condition blocks after the line of code added in the previous step:

```
If bReport = True Then
    modWord.AddTotalRow
End If
```

```
If bSheet = True Or bPres = True Then
    modExcel.CreateChart
End If
If bPres = True Then
    modPowerPoint.CreatePowerPointPres
End If
If bEmail = True Then
    modOutlook.SendEmail bReport, bSheet, bPres
End If
```

If the Boolean variable *bReport* is True, the procedure adds the row containing the total cost and energy usage to the report. If the Boolean variable *bSheet* or *bPres* is True, it creates an Excel chart. If the Boolean variable *bPres* is True, the procedure also creates a PowerPoint presentation that uses the Excel chart created in the procedure *CreateChart*. If the Boolean variable *bEmail* is True, it creates an Outlook e-mail message.

You've now completed the *Main* procedure, which is the heart of the program. Now you need to create the supporting procedures that you called.

Retrieve Data from the Database

1. Click beneath the procedure *Main* and then create a new procedure called *GetDatabaseInfo* by adding the following code:

```
Sub GetDatabaseInfo(bReport As Boolean, bSheet As Boolean, _
        bPres As Boolean, bUpdateForm As Boolean)
    Dim sID As String, sDateTime As String
    Dim sComputer As String
    Dim sgPeriodkWh As Single, sgCost As Single
    Dim iCounter As Integer
    Dim rstEnergy As New ADODB.Recordset
    rstEnergy.Open "LabEnergyUsage", CurrentProject.Connection, _
        adOpenStatic
End Sub
```

The first two lines of the *GetDatabaseInfo* procedure declare variables that are set to the data in the database. The variable *rstEnergy* is declared as the type *Recordset* defined in the ActiveX Data Objects (ADO) object library. You use the *Recordset* object to assign data in a database table. Following the Recordset declaration, the variable *rstEnergy* is set to the recordset found in the table LabEnergyUsage in the MyEnergy.mdb database.

2. Below the line using the Open method in the code added in the previous step, add the following With...End block containing a Do...Loop:

```
With rstEnergy
    If bUpdateForm Then
        Forms("frmMain").Controls("lblTotalRecords") _
            .Caption = .RecordCount
    End If
```

```
        Do
            sID = .Fields("Id")
            sDateTime = .Fields("Date and Time")
            sComputer = .Fields("Computer Network")
            If bUpdateForm Then
                Forms("frmMain").Controls("lblCurrentRecord") _
                    .Caption = .Fields("Id")
                DoEvents
            End If
            .MoveNext
        Loop Until .EOF = True
        .Close
    End With
```

The For...Next loop iterates through the recordset, setting the value in each field (*Id, Date and Time,* and *Computer Network*) to the declared variables. The last line in the Do...Loop moves to the next record in the recordset, making that record the current record. When the recordset is first opened, the first record in the recordset is, by default, the current record. When the last record is the current one, the EOF property is set to True and the Do...Loop exits. After the Do...Loop exits, the recordset closes.

The two lines within the With...End block that manipulate the *Label* controls on the form *frmMain* are used to update the captions of the *Label* controls. This way you have a visual representation of the loop's progress. The keyword DoEvents is a built-in Visual Basic function used to make sure that the screen is updated to reflect the changes in the form and in the *Label* controls.

3. Within the Do...Loop, just before the line moving to the next recordset, .MoveNext, add the following mathematical assignment statements:

```
sgPeriodkWh = m_iWattage * Int(sComputer) / 1000
sgCost = sgPeriodkWh * m_sgCost
g_sgTotalCost = g_sgTotalCost + sgCost
g_iTotalHours = g_iTotalHours + Int(sComputer)
```

4. Just below the lines you added in step 3 and above the line moving to the next recordset, .MoveNext, add the following two If...Then condition blocks:

```
If bReport = True Then
    modWord.AddToTable sID, _
        sDateTime, sComputer, sgPeriodkWh, sgCost
End If
If bSheet = True Or bPres = True Then
    modExcel.AddToSheet sID, _
        sDateTime, sComputer, sgPeriodkWh, sgCost
End If
```

Once the data is set to the variables *sID*, *sDataTime*, and *sComputer* and the appropriate calculations are made, the two condition blocks above determine whether the data is written to the Word report, the Excel workbook, or both. The second If…Then condition block also checks the value of *bPres*, because to create a presentation in PowerPoint you first have to send the data to Excel so that you can create a chart. After that, you copy the chart into the presentation.

5. In the Properties window in the Visual Basic Editor, change the Name property of the code module to **modMain**.

6. Click the Save button on the Standard toolbar in the Visual Basic Editor to save changes to the code.

The code module modMain contains the procedure *Main*, which is called by the Click event procedure of the cmdOK command button on the form *frmMain*. The module modMain contains all the code that pertains to opening and retrieving information from the database, as well as the code that determines which Office document to create. In the following sections, you'll create code modules that allow you to create each Office document.

Creating a Word Report from Database Information

Most company reports are based on a customized template containing predefined text styles and formatting. In our example, the Access database generates a report by creating a new Word document based on a formatted Word template. (This template, EnerRpt.dot, can be found in the Chapter 8 practice folder.) As you'll see, the Energy Report template is a one-row table with preset headers. As you retrieve each row of data from the database, you add a new row containing the database information and some calculated entries to the table. When you've imported all the data to the table, a final row containing the totals from two columns in the table is automatically added.

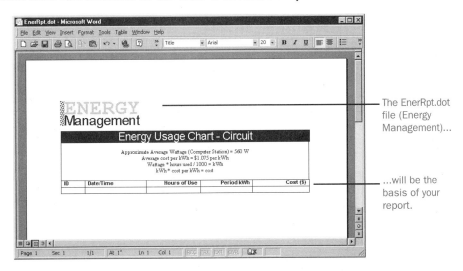

The EnerRpt.dot file (Energy Management)…

…will be the basis of your report.

Produce a Word Document from Access Data

1. In the Visual Basic Editor, click Module on the Insert menu to create a new code module.

2. Add the following declarations to the code module:

```
Dim m_appWd As New Word.Application
Dim m_docReport As Word.Document
```

The first declaration declares the module-level variable *m_appWd* as a new instance of the Word Application object. The use of the keyword New in the declaration statement indicates that the first time you use the variable *m_appWd* in code, a new instance will be created. Consequently, you won't need to use the CreateObject function. The *m_appWd* variable is a module-level variable because it's used in the procedure *AddTotalRow* to set the Visible property of the Word application window to True once you generate the report. You'll create the *AddTotalRow* procedure in the section of this chapter titled "Format the Final Row in the Word Table."

The second declaration declares the module-level variable *m_docReport* as a Word Document object, which is used by each of the procedures created in the current code module.

3. Add the following *CreateWordDocument* procedure after the variable declarations:

```
Sub CreateWordDocument()
    Set m_docReport = m_appWd.Documents.Add(Template:= _
        g_sDBProjectPath & "EnerRpt.dot", NewTemplate:=False)
    With m_docReport
        .BuiltinDocumentProperties("Subject").Value = g_sCircuit
        .Fields.Update
    End With
End Sub
```

The *CreateWordDocument* procedure sets the module-level variable *m_docReport* to the newly added Word Document object. You base the new Word document on the template EnerRpt.dot, which is found in the Chapter 8 practice folder. The first line within the With...End block in the *CreateWordDocument* procedure sets the built-in document property Subject to the circuit under investigation. In the code module modMain, you set the public variable *g_sCircuit* to "Computer Network." You can easily add new circuits to the investigation in the future. The second line (.Fields.Update) in the With...End block updates all of the fields in the Word document. One field, named *Circuit*, was added to the Energy Report template, EnerRpt.dot, beside the title "Energy Usage Chart"; this field contains the Subject document property.

Add Rows and Entries to a Word Table

1. Click beneath the procedure *CreateWordDocument* and create a new procedure called *AddToTable* by adding the following code:

```
Sub AddToTable(sID As String, sDateTime As String, _
    sComputer As String, sgPeriodkWh As Single, _
    sgCost As Single)

    With m_docReport.Tables(1)
        With .Rows.Last
            .Cells(1).Range.Text = sID
            .Cells(2).Range.Text = sDateTime
            .Cells(3).Range.Text = sComputer
            .Cells(4).Range.Text = sgPeriodkWh
            .Cells(5).Range.Text = Format$(sgCost, "###0.00")
        End With
        .Rows.Add
    End With
End Sub
```

Five arguments are passed to the *AddToTable* procedure. You set the values of the arguments in the *GetDatabaseInfo* procedure in the code module modMain. You use the With…End block added within the *AddToTable* procedure to access the first (and only) table in the Word document created in the *CreateWordDocument* procedure.

This code's With…End block adds values to each cell in the last row of the Word table. Each cell in a row in a table has a text range, represented by the *Range* object. The *Range* object allows you to access the Text property so that you can assign a text string to the cell. In the last line within the With…End block, you format the text string assigned to the cell text by using the built-in Visual Basic function *Format$*. The *Format$* function formats a string according to the second argument in the function. This is similar to formatting cells in Excel.

After data from the database is added to the cells of the last row in the table, the line *.Rows.Add* adds a new row to the table in the Word document. That way, data from the next record in the database can be added to the table. Your code should match that in the following illustration:

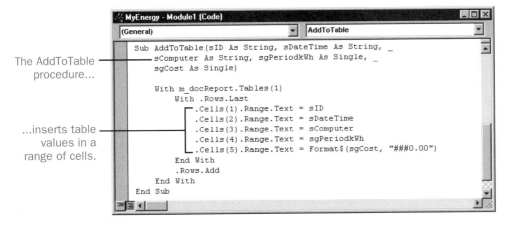

The AddToTable procedure…

…inserts table values in a range of cells.

Format the Final Row in the Word Table

1. Click beneath the procedure *AddToTable* and create a new procedure called *AddTotalRow* by adding the following code:

```
Sub AddTotalRow()
    With m_docReport.Tables(1).Rows.Last
        .Range.Bold = True
        .Range.Font.Size = 12
        .Borders.Item(wdBorderTop) _
            .LineStyle = wdLineStyleDouble
    End With
End Sub
```

The *AddTotalRow* procedure contains a With...End block that formats the last row in the Word table. The text range in the cells of the last row are made bold and set to a font size of 12 point. The procedure also sets the border style at the cells' top edge to double lines.

2. Above the End With statement, in the *AddTotalRow* procedure, add the following code:

```
.Cells(1).Range.Text = "Total"
.Cells(3).Range.Text = g_iTotalHours
.Cells(5).Range.Text = Format$(g_sgTotalCost, "###0.00")
```

The text of the first cell in the table's last row is "Total." You set the third cell's text to the total number of hours the stations in the computer network were turned on. The fifth cell indicates the total energy cost for the period under investigation. The public variables *g_iTotalHours* and *g_sgTotalCost* are calculated in the *GetDatabaseInfo* procedure in the code module modMain.

3. After the With...End block, above End Sub, add the following two lines to save the document with the filename "Report," and to display the Word application window:

```
m_docReport.SaveAs g_sDBProjectPath & "Report.doc"
m_appWd.Visible = True
```

4. In the Properties window in the Visual Basic Editor, change the Name property of the code module to **modWord**.

5. Click the Save button on the Standard toolbar in the Visual Basic Editor to save changes to the code.

You've now added all the code for creating a Word document based on a predefined template and for adding values to the table within the document.

Save

1. Copy the Word template file EnerRpt.dot from the Chapter 8 practice folder on the CD for this book to the same folder as the MyEnergy database. If this file is already located in this folder, you can skip this step.

2. Double-click the modMain project item in the Project Explorer to make the code window active.

3. In the modMain code module, add the following procedure.

```
Sub TestCreatingWordDocument()
    g_sDBProjectPath = Application.CurrentProject.Path & "\"
    modWord.CreateWordDocument
    GetDatabaseInfo bReport:=True, bSheet:=False, _
        bPres:=False, bUpdateForm:=False
    modWord.AddTotalRow
End Sub
```

Note the values of the arguments passed to the *GetDatabaseInfo* procedure. You set the first argument, *bReport,* to True in order to create a report in Word. You set the second and third arguments, *bSheet* and *bPres,* to False because an Excel spreadsheet and chart and a PowerPoint presentation are not required. You set the last argument, *bUpdateForm,* to False because the Access form is not displayed.

When you run the procedure above, the document should appear as follows:

Note If the Option Explicit statement appears at the top of the modMain module, running the TestCreatingWordDocument procedure will result in an error. Procedures called from modMain have not been created, or defined, and therefore, a runtime error occurs. Before running the TestCreatingWordDocument procedure, add an apostrophe to the beginning of the Option Explicit statement. Remember to remove the apostrophe before running the final integrated Office solution at the end of the chapter so that you can find coding errors more easily.

Creating an Excel Worksheet and Chart

Excel worksheets make it easy to filter data for analysis and to create charts for further study. Adding data to an Excel worksheet is similar to adding values to the cells of a table in Word. Once you populate (or fill in) your worksheet, you can add an AutoFilter with just one line of Visual Basic code. Adding an Excel chart involves a few more steps, but it's also fairly simple. The Excel chart serves two purposes: to complement the data in the worksheet and to perform in a PowerPoint presentation.

Create an Excel Worksheet

1. In the Visual Basic Editor, click Module on the Insert menu to create a new code module.

2. Add the following declarations to the code module:

```
Public g_chtUsage As Excel.Chart
Dim m_appXl As New Excel.Application
Dim m_shUsageData As Excel.Worksheet
Dim m_wbEnergy As Excel.Workbook
```

The first declaration declares the public variable *g_chtUsage* as an Excel Chart object. You declare the variable *g_chtUsage* as public because it's used in the code module that creates a PowerPoint presentation. The second declaration declares the module-level variable *m_appXl* as a new instance of the Excel Application object.

You use the keyword New in the declaration statement to indicate that the first time the variable *m_appXl* is used in code, a new instance will be created. Thus, you don't need to use the CreateObject function. The *m_appXl* variable is a module-level variable that's used in the *CreateChart* procedure to set the Visible property of the Excel application window to True once the worksheet and chart have been generated. You'll add the *CreateChart* procedure in the section of this chapter titled "Create a chart in Excel."

3. After the variable declarations, add the following *CreateExcelSheet* procedure:

```
Sub CreateExcelSheet()
    Set m_wbEnergy = m_appXl.Workbooks.Add
    Set m_shUsageData = m_wbEnergy.Worksheets(1)
End Sub
```

The *CreateExcelSheet* procedure sets two variables to Excel objects. It sets the first, *m_wbEnergy,* to an Excel Workbook object, which is added to the *Workbooks* collection of the newly created instance of the Excel Application object, *m_appXl.* Unless the setting in the Options dialog box on the Tools menu in Excel indicates otherwise, the procedure adds three Worksheet objects to a newly created Workbook object. You set the first worksheet to the module-level variable *m_shUsageData.*

4. After the two Set statements in the *CreateExcelSheet* procedure, add the following With...End block:

```
With m_shUsageData.Rows(1)
    .Font.Bold = True
    .Cells(, 1).Value = "ID"
    .Cells(, 2).Value = "Date/Time"
    .Cells(, 3).Value = "Computer Network"
    .Cells(, 4).Value = "Period kWh"
    .Cells(, 5).Value = "Cost"
End With
```

Within the With...End block, the font in the first row of the worksheet is set to bold. The next five lines add headers to the first five cells in the first row. The Cells property takes two arguments. The first argument is the row index, and the second is the column index. Because the procedure accesses the Cells property from the first row object, you don't need to specify the row index, but only the second argument, the column index.

You've created a new Excel workbook and formatted the first worksheet. The worksheet is now ready to accept data from the database.

Add Entries in an Excel Worksheet

1. Click beneath the procedure *CreateExcelSheet* and create a new procedure called *AddToSheet* by adding the following code:

```
Sub AddToSheet(sID As String, sDateTime As String, _
    sComputer As String, sgPeriodkWh As Single, _
    sgCost As Single)
End Sub
```

The procedure passes five arguments to the *AddToSheet* procedure. The values of the arguments are set in the *GetDatabaseInfo* procedure in the code module modMain.

2. Add the following With...End block and code above the End Sub statement:

```
With m_shUsageData.Rows(Int(sID) + 1)
    .Cells(, 1).Value = sID
    .Cells(, 2).Value = sDateTime
```

```
     .Cells(, 3).Value = sComputer
     .Cells(, 4).Value = sgPeriodkWh
     .Cells(, 5).Value = Format$(sgCost, "###0.00")
End With
```

The With…End block adds values to each cell in the next available row in the Excel worksheet. Each cell in a row in a worksheet has a value, represented by the Value property. In the last line within the With…End block, you format the text string assigned to the cell text by using the built-in Visual Basic function *Format$*, as you did when you added the same value to the Word table you created earlier in this chapter.

Create a Chart in Excel

1. Click beneath the procedure *AddToSheet* and create a new procedure called *CreateChart* by adding the following code:

```
Sub CreateChart()
    Set g_chtUsage = m_wbEnergy.Charts.Add
    With g_chtUsage
        .ChartType = xlAreaStacked
        .SetSourceData _
            Source:=m_shUsageData.Range("C2:C63,E2:E63"), _
            PlotBy:=xlColumns
        .Location Where:=xlLocationAsNewSheet, Name:= _
            "EnergyUsage-" & g_sCircuit
    End With
End Sub
```

The first line of the *CreateChart* procedure sets the variable *g_chtUsage* to a newly created chart in the Excel workbook. The procedure then uses the variable in the With…End block to set the chart type, the data source for the chart, and where the chart is to be added in the workbook. The *Where* argument of the Location method of the *Chart* object indicates that Excel should add the chart to a newly created chart sheet in the workbook. The tab name of the new sheet will be "EnergyUsage-Computer Network." The data sources are the computer network usage column (Column C) and the cost column (Column E) in the workbook's first worksheet.

2. Within the With…End block, after the *Location* method and above End With, add the following lines of code:

```
.HasTitle = True
.ChartTitle.Characters _
    .Text = "Energy Usage - " & g_sCircuit
```

```
With .Axes(xlCategory, xlPrimary)
    .HasTitle = True
    .AxisTitle.Characters.Text = "Index"
End With
With .Axes(xlValue, xlPrimary)
    .HasTitle = True
    .AxisTitle.Characters.Text = "Cost ($)"
End With
```

These lines add formatting to the newly created chart. The first two lines add the title "Energy Usage - Computer Network" to the chart. The two following With...End blocks add a label to the chart's *x* axis and *y* axis, respectively.

3. Immediately following the last With...End block you just added in the *CreateChart* procedure, above the End Sub statement, add the following two With...End blocks:

```
With m_shUsageData.Range("A:F")
    .Columns.AutoFit
    .AutoFilter
End With

With m_appXl
    .DisplayAlerts = False
    m_wbEnergy.SaveAs _
        g_sDBProjectPath & "DataAnalysis", xlNormal
    .Visible = True
    .UserControl = True
End With
```

Once you add AutoFilters to the Excel worksheet, the program saves the workbook with the name "DataAnalysis" and displays the Excel application window. The DisplayAlerts property of the Excel Application object is set to False so that no message box is displayed if the *SaveAs* method detects that an Excel file with the same filename already exists. The UserControl property of the Excel Application object is set to False when the Excel Application object is created through Visual Basic. (If the user started Excel, UserControl would be set to True.)

By setting the UserControl property to True, you're giving control of the Excel Application object you created through Visual Basic to the user. Consequently, the Excel application window remains visible on the screen once the Visual Basic code finishes running. When the Visible property of the respective Application object is set to True, the Word, PowerPoint, and Outlook application windows also remain visible.

4. In the Properties window in the Visual Basic Editor, change the Name property of the code module to **modExcel**.

5. Click the Save button on the Standard toolbar in the Visual Basic Editor to save changes to the code.

You've now added all the code needed to create an Excel worksheet and chart.

Test Your Code

1. Double-click the modMain project item in the Project Explorer to make the code window active.

2. In the modMain code module, add the following procedure.

```
Sub TestCreatingExcelWorkbook()
    g_sDBProjectPath = Application.CurrentProject.Path & "\"
    modExcel.CreateExcelSheet
    GetDatabaseInfo bReport:=False, bSheet:=True, _
        bPres:=False, bUpdateForm:=False
    modExcel.CreateChart
End Sub
```

Note the values of the arguments passed to the *GetDatabaseInfo* procedure. You set the first argument, *bReport,* to False because a report created in Word is not required. You set the second argument, *bSheet,* to True in order to create an Excel spreadsheet and chart. You set the third argument, *bPres,* to False because a presentation created in PowerPoint is not required. You set the last argument, *bUpdateForm,* also to False because the Access form is not displayed.

When you run the procedure above, the worksheet with AutoFilters should appear as follows:

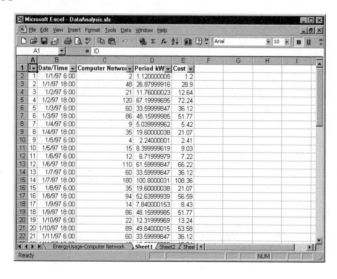

The Excel chart that's created simultaneously should look like this:

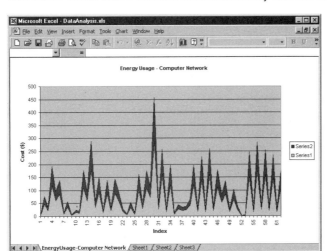

Presenting Results in PowerPoint

You use slide presentations to communicate information to an audience, and PowerPoint presentations are especially effective because they organize information in screen-size segments that audiences can absorb quickly. When you add the Excel chart to the presentation, you convey data results in an easy-to-understand format.

Create a Presentation

1. In the Visual Basic Editor, click Module on the Insert menu to create a new code module.

2. Add the following *CreatePowerPointPres* procedure:

```
Sub CreatePowerPointPres()
    Dim appPPT As New PowerPoint.Application
    Dim presEnergy As PowerPoint.Presentation
    Dim sldUsage As PowerPoint.Slide
    Dim sgBottom As Single
End Sub
```

The first declaration defines the variable *appPPT* as a new instance of the PowerPoint Application object. The use of the keyword New in the declaration statement indicates that the first time you use the variable *appPPT* in code, you create a new instance. The second and third declarations define a *Presentation* object and a *Slide* object, respectively. The final declaration in the *CreatePowerPointPres* procedure defines the variable *sgBottom* as a Single data type, which is set to the bottom coordinate of the first slide's title shape.

3. Add the following Set statements and With…End block after the declarations in the *CreatePowerPointPres* procedure:

```
Set presEnergy = appPPT.Presentations.Add
Set sldUsage = presEnergy.Slides.Add(1, ppLayoutTitleOnly)
With sldUsage.Shapes.Placeholders(1)
    With .TextFrame.TextRange
        .Text = "Energy Usage - " & g_sCircuit
        .Font.Bold = True
        .ChangeCase ppCaseUpper
    End With
    sgBottom = .Top + .Height
End With
```

You add the new presentation to the PowerPoint Application object in the first Set statement, and you add a new slide to the new presentation in the second Set statement. The new slide has the Title Only layout, which contains only a Title placeholder and no other preset shapes. The With…End block following the two Set statements accesses the properties of the Title placeholder to set the text, make the font bold, and change the case to uppercase. The last line in the With…End block sets the variable *sgBottom* to the sum of the top coordinate of the Title placeholder plus its height.

4. After the With…End block you added in the previous step, add the following With…End block. This will add the Excel chart to the first slide in the presentation:

```
g_chtUsage.ChartArea.Copy
With sldUsage.Shapes.Paste
    .Top = sgBottom + 20
    .Height = sldUsage.Master.Height - sgBottom + 20
    .Left = sldUsage.Master.Width / 2 - .Width / 2
End With
```

In order to add the Excel chart to the PowerPoint presentation, you copy the chart area to the Clipboard and paste it into the *Shapes* collection of the first slide in the presentation. The With…End block then sets the top and left coordinates and the height of the newly pasted chart shape.

5. After the With…End block, above End Sub, add the following two lines to save the presentation with the filename "EnergyPres," and to display the PowerPoint application window:

```
presEnergy.SaveAs g_sDBProjectPath & "EnergyPres"
appPPT.Visible = True
```

6. In the Properties window in the Visual Basic Editor, change the Name property of the code module to modPowerPoint.

7. Click the Save button on the Standard toolbar in the Visual Basic Editor to save changes to the code.

You've now added all the code needed to create a PowerPoint presentation.

Test Your Code

1. Double-click the modMain project item in the Project Explorer to make the code window active.

2. In the modMain code module, add the following procedure.

```
Sub TestCreatingPowerPointPresentation()
    g_sDBProjectPath = Application.CurrentProject.Path & "\"
    modExcel.CreateExcelSheet
    GetDatabaseInfo bReport:=False, bSheet:=False, _
        bPres:=True, bUpdateForm:=False
    modExcel.CreateChart
    modPowerPoint.CreatePowerPointPres
End Sub
```

Note the values of the arguments passed to the *GetDatabaseInfo* procedure. You set the first argument, *bReport,* to False because a report created in Word is not required. You set the second argument, *bSheet,* also to False. However, because you set the third argument, *bPres,* to True, an Excel spreadsheet and chart are created in order to copy the chart to the presentation created in PowerPoint. You set the last argument, *bUpdateForm,* to False because the Access form is not displayed.

When you run the procedure above, the slide should appear as follows:

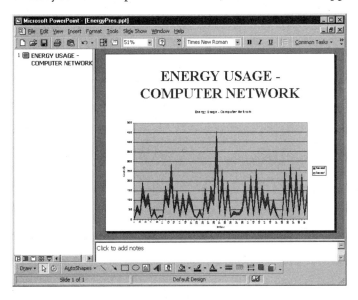

Sending E-mail in Outlook

Once all of the Office documents selected in the form *frmMain* are automatically generated, you can send them as an e-mail message created in Outlook. This link gives you a convenient way to update people about a project.

Create an Outlook E-mail Message

1. In the Visual Basic Editor, click Module on the Insert menu to create a new code module.

2. Add the following *SendEmail* procedure:

```
Sub SendEmail(bReport As Boolean, bSheet As Boolean, _
        bPres As Boolean)
    Dim appOL As New Outlook.Application
    Dim itemUsageEmail As Outlook.MailItem

    Set itemUsageEmail = appOL.CreateItem(olMailItem)
End Sub
```

The three Boolean variables you pass into the *SendEmail* procedure indicate which check boxes were selected in the form *frmMain*. You use these variables to determine which file attachments should be added to the e-mail message. Within the *SendEmail* procedure, you declare two variables. The first, the variable *appOL*, is the declaration of a new instance of the Outlook Application object. You use the keyword New in the declaration statement to indicate that the first time the variable *appOL* is used in code, you create a new instance. The second, the variable *itemUsageEmail*, declares the variable as an Outlook MailItem object, which you set in the Set statement following the declaration.

3. After the Set statement in the *SendEmail* procedure, add the following With...End block:

```
With itemUsageEmail
    .To = "Energy Committee"
    .Subject = "New energy usage documents"
    .Body = "The following documents reflect" & _
        " the energy usage for the circuit: " & _
        g_sCircuit & "." & vbCrLf
    .Display
End With
```

The With...End block sets the main properties of the e-mail message and then displays the message on the screen. If you want to send the e-mail message automatically, you can replace the Display method with the Send method in the last line of the With...End block. The message will go to the alias "Energy Committee."

4. Before the line used to display the Outlook message, add the following
If...Then condition blocks to add attachments to the message:

```
If bReport = True Then
    .Attachments.Add g_sDBProjectPath & "Report.doc"
End If
If bSheet = True Then
    .Attachments.Add g_sDBProjectPath & "DataAnalysis.xls"
End If
If bPres = True Then
    .Attachments.Add g_sDBProjectPath & "EnergyPres.ppt"
End If
```

The three If...Then condition blocks evaluate the Boolean values
representing the items selected in the form *frmMain*. If an item is selected
and the appropriate Office document is generated, the document is
attached to the e-mail message.

5. In the Properties window in the Visual Basic Editor, change the Name
property of the code module to **modOutlook**.

6. Click the Save button on the Standard toolbar in the Visual Basic Editor
to save changes to the code.

You've now added all the code needed to create an Outlook e-mail message.
Later, when you run the integrated Office solution and select the item to cre-
ate an Outlook e-mail message along with the other Office documents, the
Outlook e-mail message should look like this:

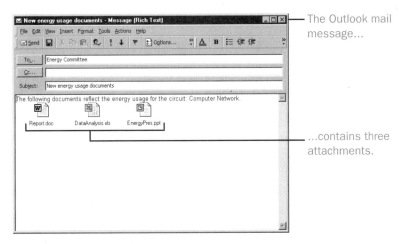

The Outlook mail
message...

...contains three
attachments.

Note   Before running the integrated solution, remove the apostrophe at the
beginning of the Option Explicit statement in the modMain module if you previously
added an apostrophe. The Option Explicit statement will enable you to find coding
errors more easily (if any exist).

See the Solution in Action

1. In the MyEnergy: Database window, click Forms in the Objects bar, select the item frmMain, and then click Open on the Database window toolbar. You'll see the custom Energy Management form.

2. Select all four check boxes in the Energy Management form and click OK. Depending on your computer system's hardware and software configuration, it may take a few minutes to iterate through the data in the Access database and generate each Office document. You can watch the progress by reading the Number Of Records Read indicator in the dialog box. Once the *Main* procedure finishes running, you'll see the new Word report, the Excel worksheet and chart, the PowerPoint presentation, and the Outlook e-mail message with the Office documents attached. Each window displayed on your screen should look similar to the graphic shown at the end of the example that created that particular Office document.

Tip   If your code has errors you can't easily resolve, or if you didn't have time to complete this chapter, you can run the solution from the Energy.mdb file provided in the Chapter 8 folder of the practice files. This file contains the complete working code for all the sections in this chapter.

3. Close the Energy database and exit Access.

4. After examining the generated contents in Word, Excel, and PowerPoint, close each application without saving any changes.

Chapter Summary

This chapter describes how to build an Access database and automatically generate a Word document, an Excel workbook, a PowerPoint presentation, and an Outlook message from the database information. You can use the procedure that iterates through the records in a table in the database as a basis for any program that needs to access data in an Access database. You can also use this procedure to access the database from any Office application. Therefore, you can, for example, develop add-ins for any Office application that can retrieve data from a database. With your solutions, you might want to provide a menu item that when clicked retrieves data from a database and uses it to insert or manipulate document content.

Preview of the Next Chapter

The next chapter describes how to determine the type of object contained in the current selection in a Word, Excel, or PowerPoint document window. In other chapters, you'll use code that determines the type of selection to satisfy scenarios such as determining when the selection changes and appropriately updating custom menu items and toolbar buttons based on the type of selection.

Working with Active Window Content

Chapter 9

Retrieving and Setting Active Content

Chapter Objectives   Estimated time: 60 minutes

- Establish what document is contained in the top-most document window displayed to the user.

- Understand how to work with the Selection property and objects in order to retrieve and change the selection.

- Determine whether the selection contains text, cells, shapes or any other content that can be inserted into a Word, Excel, or PowerPoint document, or whether the selection contains mail, appointment, or any other folder item in a Microsoft Outlook folder.

- Have any content in an open Word, Excel, or PowerPoint document scroll into view so that it's visible on the user's screen.

- Locate content such as text, a cell, or a shape in relation to the top-left position on the user's screen in order to position custom dialog boxes relative to specific content.

No matter how many documents you may have open, you can interact with only one at a time. That single document is referred to as the *active* document, and it's contained in the *active* window. In most cases, a current selection is within the active window. This selection can be anything from a range of text characters selected in Microsoft Word to a range of cells selected in Microsoft Excel to a set of shapes selected in Microsoft PowerPoint.

As you work with a Microsoft Office document, you use a number of menu and toolbar commands to operate on the active document, the active window, or the current selection (the selection in the active window). Commands on the File menu, like Save, Save As, Close, and Print, act on the active document that's displayed to the user. On the Edit menu, the Cut and Copy commands act on the current selection. On the Formatting toolbar, the Font drop-down list sets the font of the current text selection and the Bold button sets the text to bold.

A number of commands set the active document or selection. For example, the Window menu lists all the documents currently open. Each item you click on the Window menu becomes the active document. When you use the spelling checker or the Find and Replace functionality on a text string, the application scrolls and sets the selection to the text string that is to be corrected or replaced.

The majority of commands in the command bar set act on the current document or current selection. Similarly, you'll develop programs that need to retrieve, set, or act upon the active document or current selection. This chapter discusses the ways you use Word, Excel, PowerPoint, and Outlook to retrieve, set, and manipulate the active content.

ActiveDocument and ActiveWindow

When you work with documents in any Office application, you interact with only one document at a time. Although you may see two or more document windows open, just one window—and one window's title bar—is active. The active window always contains the active document.

Quick Guide

If every window has a document and one window is always active, there will always be an active document (unless all documents are closed and only the application window is visible). You have two ways to get to the active document. In each application, a specific property is defined that allows you to return the active document. You can also get to the active document through the active window. Each *Window* object in Word and Excel (and the equivalent object, *DocumentWindow*, in PowerPoint) contains a property that allows you to return the document in the window.

In the Immediate window of the Visual Basic Editor for each application listed in the following table, type a question mark (?) followed by the code and press RETURN. Each line of code, with the exception of the code for Outlook, reveals how to return the name of the document in the active window, and indicates the properties you can use to return the active content.

Application	Syntax to return the active document
Word	`ActiveWindow.Document.Name` `ActiveDocument.Name`
Excel	`ActiveWindow.ActiveSheet.Parent.Name` `ActiveWorkbook.Name`
PowerPoint	`ActiveWindow.Presentation.Name` `ActivePresentation.Name`

Outlook	`ActiveWindow.Caption`
	`ActiveExplorer.Caption`
	`ActiveInspector.Caption`

(continued)

Quick Guide *(continued)*

In Outlook, the Explorer object represents the main Outlook window. When you first start Outlook, the window that displays the list of Outlook folders or the Outlook bar, along with the items in a folder or in a calendar, is referred to as an *Explorer*. In Outlook you can display more than one Explorer window at a time. Each time you click the Microsoft Outlook icon on the Programs menu, accessed from the Windows Start menu, you display a new Outlook Explorer window. When you open an individual mail item or appointment, the window displayed is referred to as an *Inspector*. Because you can have more than one mail or other folder item open, you can display more than one Inspector window.

Note The ActiveWindow property in Word and Excel returns the *Window* object, and the ActiveWindow property in PowerPoint returns the *DocumentWindow* object. The *Window* object and the *DocumentWindow* are conceptually the same thing. PowerPoint gives this object a more specific name in order to distinguish a window that contains an editable document from a slide-show window, which displays a document (presentation) for electronic slide shows. Both the *Window* and *DocumentWindow* objects are windows that contain a document. You'll often see a reference to the "document window." This just refers to a window that contains a document and not necessarily to the active window or active document.

When would you use ActiveWindow rather than ActiveDocument? That is, why wouldn't you just use `ActiveWindow.Document` instead of `ActiveDocument`? Using the ActiveDocument in code usually signifies that your code acts on the document, but using the ActiveWindow indicates that you need to determine something about (and do something with) the selection.

Selection

The most common selection that you'll see is text selected in a Word document or in an e-mail message. The text appears inverted as you select its characters. You can tell that a shape or an object is selected by the sizing handles that appear at the corners and along the edges of the shape's or object's rectangle. In Excel, a thick black border around the range of cells tells you that a range of cells is selected. You work with selections every day. For example, you select a cell in a worksheet and add a formula or a text value. You select a word in a document and make it bold. You select a shape in PowerPoint and set its background fill to yellow.

The user selects content and applies some formatting to it by clicking on a menu item or toolbar button. Solutions often use the current user selection in order to format the selection or send it to some other document or application. At other times, solutions set the selection to draw the user's attention to that content. The following section tells you how to determine and manipulate what the selection is and how to set the selection for cases like the spelling checker or the Find and Replace functionality.

Retrieving the Selection

You can retrieve the selection from the active window. In fact, you can retrieve it from any window, whether it's in view or not. Depending on the application, the window remembers the selection; so when you navigate from one window to another, the selection becomes visible when the window is activated. Selection is window-based, not document-based.

Quick Guide

In the Immediate window of the Visual Basic Editor for each application listed in the following table, type a question mark (?) followed by the code and press RETURN. Each line of code reveals how to return the selected text in the active window. In Word, if the selection is text (that is, text is highlighted), the line of code returns the text. In Excel, if the selection is one cell only, the line of code in the following table returns the text contents of the active cell. If multiple cells containing text are selected, this line of code returns Null, indicating that more than one cell is selected. In this case, you can iterate through each of the cells in the selected range and retrieve the text of the cell. See the sample code listed for Excel under the heading "Retrieve the Text and Value From a Range of Selected Cells," later in this chapter.

In PowerPoint, if the selection is text in a shape or just the shape itself, the line of code in the following table returns the highlighted text or the text in the shape. In Outlook, if a mail item is selected in the Inbox (or any folder that contains a mail item), the line of code returns the text of the mail message that's selected. If a mail item is opened in its own window and text is selected, the line of code returns a run-time error. The line of code works only when an item in an Outlook folder is selected.

Application	Code to return the selected text
Word	`ActiveWindow.Selection.Text`
Excel	`ActiveWindow.Selection.Text`
PowerPoint	`ActiveWindow.Selection.TextRange.Text`
Outlook	`ActiveExplorer.Selection.Body`

Word

The most common selection in Word is text. For example, you select a paragraph to indent it an inch. Or you select a word and click the Underline button on the Formatting toolbar. A selection can also exist when you see the cursor only in between two characters or at the end of a line. Word understands this selection as an insertion point (IP). When you select a row in a table, Word also understands this as a row selection and not just a selection of text.

You may also select a shape or picture, and Word again sees this as a different selection. In this case, Word indicates the selection by placing sizing handles around the shape or picture (instead of highlighting the text). Because a document may have different content types, Word has different types of selections. For example, when you select a word in a document, you'll see the Bold and Italic buttons enabled. But when you select a picture, the Bold and Italic buttons are disabled. Word can't apply the bold and italic attributes to a picture, only to text. So just as Word determines what the selection type is in order to update its menus and toolbars, you also need to determine what the selection is.

When you determine what the selection is, you can use the Type property of the *Selection* object. The Type property returns one of the WdSelectionType constant values. The following procedure shows a Select Case statement that contains all of the possible values that the Type property can return. Based on the type of selection, your code will do different things.

```
Sub GetSelectionInWord()
    Dim oSel As Word.Selection
    Set oSel = ActiveWindow.Selection
    Select Case oSel.Type
        Case wdNoSelection '0
        Case wdSelectionIP '1
        Case wdSelectionNormal '2
        Case wdSelectionFrame '3
        Case wdSelectionColumn '4
        Case wdSelectionRow '5
        Case wdSelectionBlock '6
        Case wdSelectionInlineShape '7
        Case wdSelectionShape '8
    End Select
End Sub
```

The table on the following page indicates when the selection types listed in the above procedure or in the WdSelectionType constant in the Object Browser in the Microsoft Visual Basic Editor are returned.

Word selection type	It's returned when...
wdNoSelection	No selection exists.
wdSelectionIP	A blinking cursor resides anywhere in text between two characters, or at the beginning or end of a line, including text in a table cell or shape.
wdSelectionNormal	A contiguous range of text is selected. This is the most common selection type. It's also returned when a combination of table and text is selected.
wdSelectionFrame	A frame is selected. (Frames were commonly used in versions of Word prior to Word 97.)
wdSelectionColumn	A column in a table is selected. It's also returned when one or more than one cell is selected in a table. If more than one cell is selected, this value is returned whether the cells are in the same row or in the same column.
wdSelectionRow	A row in a table is selected (it has to be a full row, as when the user clicks to the left of the row). It's also returned when the full table is selected.
wdSelectionBlock	When the user holds down the ALT key and uses the mouse to select text. The user can block only text, not a table.
wdSelectionInlineShape	The shape within the text is an inline shape. If a shape like a picture is inline, the "In line with text" wrapping style is highlighted on the Layout tab in the Format Picture dialog box.
wdSelectionShape	The shape is over or under the text. In the Format AutoShape dialog box, on the Layout tab, the "In front of text" wrapping style is highlighted.

Format the Text Selection to Bold

When you want to format text in a document, several selections may indicate that text is actually selected or the cursor exists within text characters. Just determining whether the selection is of type wdSelectionNormal won't handle all the cases where the user may have text selected. Text exists within a block selection or within a table cell, column, or row. The following procedure uses a Select Case statement to handle selection types that indicate that text is contained within the selection. The commas used within the *Case* expression indicate that the selection type can be any of the types listed in the *Case* expression.

```
Sub ApplyFormatToTextSelection()
    Select Case ActiveWindow.Selection.Type
        Case wdSelectionIP, wdSelectionNormal, _
            wdSelectionBlock, wdSelectionColumn, wdSelectionRow
            ActiveWindow.Selection.Font.Bold = True
```

```
        Case Else
            MsgBox "Please select range of text."
    End Select
End Sub
```

Note With the exception of the line of code that sets the font to **Bold**, this is a generic procedure that's applicable to any scenario in which you need to determine if the selection is text and therefore, if you can apply text methods and properties to the selection. This procedure is used as the basis for the sample in Chapter 10 under the heading "Set Up the WindowSelectionChange Event in Word."

Insert a New Paragraph Before the Text Selection

The following procedure adds a new paragraph by first inserting a new paragraph before the current selection and then setting the text range of the newly inserted paragraph. The selection must be either an insertion point or a normal text selection in the active document. This also means that if the insertion point exists in a table cell or if a set of characters is selected in a table cell, the procedure inserts a new paragraph in the table cell.

```
Sub InsertNewParagraph()
    Select Case ActiveWindow.Selection.Type
        Case wdSelectionIP, wdSelectionNormal
            With ActiveWindow.Selection.Paragraphs(1)
                .Range.InsertParagraphBefore
                .Previous.Range = "New paragraph." & Chr(13)
            End With
        Case Else
            MsgBox "Please select range of text."
    End Select
End Sub
```

As discussed in Chapter 6 under the heading "Determining Where Text Belongs," you can use the Paragraphs property of the *Range* object to return the first paragraph of the selected text. For example, if one word is selected, `ActiveWindow.Selection.Paragraphs(1)` returns the paragraph that contains the selected word. In the preceding procedure, a new paragraph is inserted before the first paragraph of the selected range of text. Then, using the Previous property on the *Paragraph* object, the newly inserted paragraph is returned and its text is set to "New paragraph," followed by a carriage return. The carriage return character is represented by using the built-in language function *Chr* and passing into the function the value of 13.

Excel

The most common selection in Excel is a range of cells. For example, you select a cell and enter a formula or value into it. Or you select a range of cells and use their data to build a new chart. If you select one cell, a set of contiguous cells, or a discontiguous range of cells, Excel returns the type of selection as a *Range* object. Like Word and PowerPoint, Excel never mixes the type of content in a selection. For example, you can't select a cell and a shape at the same time. You select either a drawing shape, a chart element on a chart sheet, or a range.

Unlike Word and PowerPoint, however, Excel doesn't have a *Selection* object. Excel does consistently have a Selection property on the *Window* object, but in Excel the Selection property returns a specific object based on the selection and not a *Selection* object as in Word and PowerPoint. What does this mean? In Word and PowerPoint, you'd use the Type property on the *Selection* object to determine the selection type. In Excel, neither a *Selection* object nor an equivalent for the selection Type property exists. However, you can use the built-in Visual Basic for Applications function called *TypeName* to determine what type of object Excel returns from the ActiveWindow.Selection property.

In the following procedure, you use the *TypeName* function in the Visual Basic for Applications language to determine what type of object is returned by ActiveWindow.Selection. Essentially, the result is similar to using the Type property on the *Selection* object in Word and PowerPoint, except that the *TypeName* function returns a string of the name of the object type, whereas the Type property returns a constant value defined by Word and PowerPoint.

```
Sub GetSelectionInExcel()
    Dim oSel As Object
    Set oSel = ActiveWindow.Selection
    Select Case TypeName(oSel)
        Case "Range"
        Case "Picture"
        Case "OLEObject"
        Case "ChartArea"
        Case "ChartTitle"
        Case "PlotArea"
        Case "Series"
        Case "Point"
        Case "Gridlines"
        Case "Axis"
        Case "AxisTitle"
        Case "Legend"
        Case "LegendEntry"
        Case "DataTable"
        Case "DataLabel"
        Case "DataLabels"
        Case "Nothing"
        Case Else
    End Select
End Sub
```

In this procedure, the *Case* expression "Nothing" indicates that the active sheet in Excel is a chart but no object on the chart is selected. The *Case Else* expression indicates that every other selection is a drawing shape or a picture. Each drawing shape returned by ActiveWindow.Selection returns a specific drawing object. For example, a rectangle returns an object of type *Rectangle*.

Note When the cursor is in a cell or in the text of a shape, no commands from the object model can be executed. Excel is in a *modal* state. In this state Excel prevents any property or method executed in Visual Basic from accessing or modifying any part of the Excel application or any workbook or content. In this case, if the Visual Basic Editor is displayed, you cannot click within the editor's window. When the cursor is not in a cell or in the text of a shape, the Excel application and any workbook or content can be accessed or modified through Visual Basic code.

The following table indicates when the object types are returned from the *TypeName* function.

Excel selection type	It's returned when...
Range	Any single cell or adjacent or nonadjacent range of cells on any worksheet is selected.
Picture	A picture inserted on a worksheet or chart is selected.
OLEObject	An embedded object inserted with the Insert Object dialog box is selected.
ChartArea; ChartTitle; PlotArea; Series; Point; Gridlines; Axis; AxisTitle; Legend; LegendEntry; DataTable; DataLabel; DataLabels	Anything on a chart sheet or on a chart on a worksheet is selected.
Line, Rectangle, Oval, TextBox	A drawing shape is selected.

Set the Font Color of Cells to Red

In Excel you usually manipulate a selection over a range of cells. To manipulate a range of cells, you use the Selection property on the *Window* object to return an object of type *Range*. The following procedure uses a Select Case statement to handle the type name of the object returned by the Selection property. If the type name is *Range*, the font color of the cell is set to red. In this procedure, ActiveWindow.Selection returns a *Range* object. The Font property is on the *Range* object and it returns the *Font* object, whose Color property is used to set the color.

```
Sub SetCellFormatting()
    Select Case TypeName(ActiveWindow.Selection)
        Case "Range"
            ActiveWindow.Selection.Font _
                .Color = RGB(255, 0, 0)
        Case Else
            MsgBox "Please select a range."
    End Select
End Sub
```

Set the Text of Selected Cells

If you'd like to display the Auto List Members drop-down list as you work with the selection, you should declare a variable of the type of object you'll use in your code. For example, in the following procedure, after you type the word **rngSel** and press the period key, the procedure will display the Auto List Members drop-down list, showing the methods and properties of the *Range* object.

```
Sub SetCellText()
    Dim rngSel As Excel.Range
    Select Case TypeName(ActiveWindow.Selection)
        Case "Range"
            Set rngSel = ActiveWindow.Selection
            rngSel.Value = "New text."
        Case Else
            MsgBox "Please select a range."
    End Select
End Sub
```

Retrieve the Text and Value From a Range of Selected Cells

In the previous example, you first select more than one cell and run the procedure. After execution is complete, the string *New Text* appears in every cell in the range. With the same cells selected, you can retrieve the value from the range of selected cells. First, you need to determine if the selection does contain more than one cell. If so, the *IsArray* function provided by the Visual Basic for Applications language returns a value of True after evaluating the *rngSel* object variable.

```
Sub GetTextFromRangeSelection()
    Dim rngCell As Range, rngSel As Range

    If TypeName(ActiveWindow.Selection) <> "Range" Then Exit Sub
    Set rngSel = ActiveWindow.Selection

    If IsArray(rngSel) Then
        For Each rngCell In rngSel
            Debug.Print rngCell.Text
            Debug.Print rngCell.Value
        Next rngCell
    End If
End Sub
```

A For Each...Next loop then iterates through each cell in the selection. The Value property returns the cell value. The property can also be used to assign a new value to the cell, as the previous example reveals. The Text property returns the cell text. Unlike the use of the Text property in Word and PowerPoint, you can use the Text property in Excel only to retrieve cell text, not to set the cell's text. You use the Value property instead to set text.

PowerPoint

The most common selection in PowerPoint is a shape. For example, you select a shape and set the background fill color to green or add a border. Whether you have one shape selected or more than one, PowerPoint interprets the selection as a shape range selection. If text is selected in a shape, PowerPoint interprets the selection as a text range selection. You can never have both a text range and a shape range selected, just one or the other. You also can have no selection when you're working with a slide. If you click a slide in Slide view or Normal view (new in PowerPoint 2000), no shape or text is selected. PowerPoint also provides other views of the content in the presentation, such as Outline view and Slide Sorter view (both of which also have different selection types).

As in Word, when you determine what the selection is in PowerPoint, you can use the Type property of the *Selection* object. The Type property returns one of the values from the constant PpSelectionType. However, PowerPoint has fewer selection types than Word. The following procedure shows a Select Case statement that contains all of the possible values that the Type property can return. Based on the type of selection, your code will do different things.

```
Sub GetSelectionInPowerPoint()
    Dim oSel As PowerPoint.Selection
    Set oSel = ActiveWindow.Selection
    Select Case oSel.Type
        Case ppSelectionNone '0
        Case ppSelectionSlides    '1
        Case ppSelectionShapes '2
        Case ppSelectionText '3
    End Select
End Sub
```

The following table indicates when the selection types listed in the above procedure or in the PpSelectionType constant in the Object Browser in the Visual Basic Editor are returned.

PowerPoint selection type	It's returned when the selection is...
ppSelectionNone	• In Slide view or Normal view (PowerPoint 2000 only) and no shape or text is selected. • In Slide Sorter view and no slide preview is selected; just a blinking cursor between slide previews is displayed. • In Notes Page view and nothing is selected. In Normal view, if the active slide in the view changes, the selection Type property will return ppSelectionNone.
ppSelectionSlides	• In Slide Sorter view and slide preview is selected.
ppSelectionShapes	• In a slide, Notes Page or Handout view and handles around a shape appear.

(continued)

(continued)

PowerPoint selection type	It's returned when the selection is...
ppSelectionText	• In a shape where the adjust handles and a shaded selection rectangle appear around the shape. • In Outline view or in the notes pane in Normal view (PowerPoint 2000 only). In either of these cases, this selection type constant is returned only when one or more text characters are selected. If an insertion point exists (that is, a blinking cursor exists in between two text characters), the selection type constant returned in this case is ppSelectionNone, or the value of 0.

Set the Font Name of Selected Text or All Text in a Shape

When you want to format text in a shape, the selection type should be ppSelectionText. When you can manipulate a range of text, the Selection property on the *DocumentWindow* object in PowerPoint will return ppSelectionText. The following procedure uses a Select Case statement to handle the selection type, and if the selection type is text, the font name is set to Arial.

```
Sub SetFontFormatting()
    Select Case ActiveWindow.Selection.Type
        Case ppSelectionText
            ActiveWindow.Selection.TextRange _
                .Font.Name = "Arial"
        Case Else
            MsgBox "Please select a shape or text."
    End Select
End Sub
```

Set the Font Name of Selected Shapes That Can Contain Text

In the above procedure, the *Case ppSelectionText* expression indicates that the selection must be text. In PowerPoint, even though you may have selected a shape, you can still access the text of the shape using the TextRange property of the *Selection* object. If you do have a shape selected that can contain text (shapes like a picture can't contain text), you can use the same code to change the font name, just as if the selection *had* been text. But what if your selection contained one shape that can contain text and another that couldn't (like a line, a picture or a WordArt shape)? In the first procedure on the facing page, you add a new *Case* expression explicitly to handle just the shape selection type. Within the *Case* expression that handles the value of ppSelectionShapes, the procedure *SetFontNameOfShapes* is called.

In the second procedure, you use a For...Each loop to iterate through the shapes in the selection. The statement Shp.HasTextFrame in the If...Then statement determines whether each shape in the selection contains a text frame. For any shape that does, the font name of the shape is set to Arial; for any shape that doesn't, the loop continues to the next shape in the selection.

```
Sub SetFontFormattingForAllShapesSelected()
    Select Case ActiveWindow.Selection.Type
        Case ppSelectionText
            ActiveWindow.Selection.TextRange _
                .Font.Name = "Arial"
        Case ppSelectionShapes
            SetFontNameOfShapes
        Case Else
            MsgBox "Please select a shape or text."
    End Select
End Sub


Sub SetFontNameOfShapes()
    Dim shp As PowerPoint.Shape
    For Each shp In ActiveWindow _
        .Selection.ShapeRange

        If shp.HasTextFrame Then
            shp.TextFrame.TextRange _
                .Font.Name = "Arial"
        End If
    Next shp
End Sub
```

A number of shapes don't contain a text frame. For example, a line, a picture, a WordArt shape, and any OLE object inserted on the slide—such as a Chart, a Word document, or a sound—do not have a text frame.

Set the Font Name of Text in a Table

Add the following If...Then statement just after the End If line in the above *SetFontNameOfShapes* procedure. Use the If...Then statement to determine if the shape in the selection range is of the type msoTable. Each shape in Word, Excel, and PowerPoint has a Type property. The Type property returns a value from the MsoShapeType constant defined in the Microsoft Office 9.0 Object Library. If the shape type is msoTable, the two For...Next loops iterate through each cell in the table. Each cell in a table is ultimately just a shape in PowerPoint. Once your code accesses a specific cell in a table, you can use the *Shape* object to manipulate the formatting and content of the cell.

```
If shp.Type = msoTable Then
    Dim i As Integer, j As Integer
    For i = 1 To shp.Table.Columns.Count
        For j = 1 To shp.Table.Rows.Count
            shp.Table.Columns(i).Cells(j) _
                .Shape.TextFrame.TextRange _
                .Font.Name = "Arial"
        Next j
    Next i
End If
```

Outlook

In Outlook, the selection is based on the different types of items that Outlook stores. If you look through your Mailbox, you'll see the breakdown by the types of folders that are displayed after you install Outlook. You have an Inbox that contains mail items, a calendar with meeting requests and appointments, a Notes folder containing notes, a Contacts folder, and a couple of other folders. If you want to programmatically determine what the selected item is in Outlook, you can use the following procedure. Like Excel, Outlook doesn't have a *Selection* object. You have to use the built-in Visual Basic for Applications function called *TypeName* to determine what type of item object Outlook returns from the ActiveExplorer.Selection property.

The following procedure shows a Select Case statement that contains all of the possible string values that the built-in Visual Basic for Applications function *TypeName* can return when evaluating the expression *ActiveExplorer.Selection*. Depending on the type of selection, your code will do different things. The TypeName string returns similar values that are listed in the OlItemType. In most cases it's obvious when the string values are returned. A *MailItem* object is returned from ActiveExplorer.Selection.Item(1) when the first selected item is a mail message.

```
Sub GetItemSelectionInOutlook()
    If ActiveExplorer.Selection.Count < 1 Then Exit Sub
    Select Case TypeName(ActiveExplorer _
        .Selection.Item(1))
        Case "MailItem"
        Case "AppointmentItem"
        Case "ContactItem"
        Case "JournalItem"
        Case "NoteItem"
        Case "TaskItem"
        Case "PostItem"
        Case "DistributionListItem"
    End Select
End Sub
```

Open All E-Mail Messages Selected

In Outlook, the selection can contain many selected items. You need to use the *Item* method to iterate through the selected items. If a folder in your Mailbox contains multiple item types such as mail, contact, and task items, the following procedure iterates through each item in the selection and determines if the object returned is of type *MailItem*. If it is, the procedure opens the mail item and displays it on screen. Declaring the variable *oMailItem* as `Outlook.MailItem` and setting it to the generically declared *oItem* allows you to use the Auto List Members drop-down list when you're coding with the *MailItem* object. This step may be redundant, but if you were using the *MailItem* object extensively, having the Auto List Members drop-down list available as you type your code would improve your efficiency without greatly increasing your program's size.

```
Sub OpenMailItemsInSelection()
    Dim oItem As Object
    Dim oMailItem As Outlook.MailItem

    For Each oItem In ActiveExplorer.Selection
        Select Case TypeName(oItem)
            Case "MailItem"
                Set oMailItem = oItem
                oMailItem.Display
        End Select
    Next oItem
End Sub
```

Setting the Selection

When you click Find in the Edit menu in Word, Excel, or PowerPoint, the Find dialog box is displayed. You can then enter the string you want to find in the Find What text box. When you click the Find or Find Next button in the dialog box and the application finds a string in the document that matches the find criteria in the Find dialog box, it will scroll through the document to the string and select it. With the Find and even the spell checking functionalities, the application conducts three actions. First, it navigates to the content; second, it scrolls until the content is in view; third, it actually selects the content.

Navigating to content and scrolling until it's in view is discussed later in this chapter in the section titled "Finding Content on the Screen." You use the *Select* method to achieve the last action, selecting content. You'll find the *Select* method throughout the suite of Office object libraries. Depending on the application, however, in order to select content you have to ensure that the content is visible in the active window. If it's not, the *Select* method will fail. For example, if you select cell D21 on the second worksheet in an Excel workbook and the first worksheet is currently displayed, the *Select* method generates an error. That's why navigating to the content and ensuring that it's in the active window in some cases is the first step to selecting content.

Quick Guide

In the Immediate window of the Visual Basic Editor for each application listed in the following table, type the code and press RETURN. A question mark (?) is not required before the line since the code executes a method rather than retrieving a property. Each line of code reveals how to set the selection in the active window. For all cases using the code in the following table, the current selection is deselected and the text, cell, or shape is selected.

In Word, the code in the following table sets the selection to a range of text. In Excel, the code sets the selection to a specific cell. In PowerPoint, the code sets the selection to a shape.

Application	Code to select text or an item...
Word	`ActiveWindow.Document.Paragraphs _` `    .First.Range.Select`
Excel	`ActiveWindow.ActiveSheet _` `    .Range("A1").Select`

PowerPoint	`ActiveWindow.View.Slide.Shapes _`
	`    .Placeholders(1) _`
	`    .TextFrame.TextRange.Select`

Word

In Word, the *Select* method exists for a number of objects, including the *Range, Table, Cell, Row, Bookmark, Field, Shape,* and *InlineShape* objects. You'll see a number of features that select the text range. The Find dialog box selects a text string that matches the search criteria, and the spelling and grammar checker selects the text string that's misspelled or contains incorrect grammar. You can use the *Select* method on any text range in the document, including text in headers and footers.

You also can use the *Select* method on any content element, such as a shape in the document. Unlike Excel and PowerPoint, Word lets you set the selection in any window regardless of whether that window is active. As you'll see in Excel and PowerPoint, before selecting the content you need to make the workbook or presentation active, along with the worksheet or slide.

Select the First Paragraph in the Document

The following procedure selects the range that represents the first paragraph in the active window. You use the *ScrollIntoView* method after the *Select* method so the user can see the selection. In "Using the *ScrollIntoView* Method" later in this chapter, you'll read more about the *ScrollIntoView* method so you can scroll the selection—or any object that's not selected—into view.

```
Sub SetSelection()
    Dim rngText As Word.Range
```

```
    Set rngText = ActiveWindow.Document _
        .Paragraphs.First.Range
    rngText.Select
    ActiveWindow.ScrollIntoView rngText
End Sub
```

Select the Whole Paragraph of the Current Insertion Point or Selection

Word allows you to determine which paragraph in any range of text contains the text range. For example, if you had a character selected (or just an insertion point in a paragraph), you could use properties on the *Range* object to return the word in which the character or insertion point were contained. You can also determine which sentence or paragraph contains the character or insertion point. A useful scenario for this type of capability is an electronic document reader that starts reading a document from the current selection. If the document reader reads a paragraph at a time and starts reading with the first paragraph containing the selection, it can easily identify the paragraph, select it, and send it to a program that can read the text back to you.

The following procedure determines whether the selection is an insertion point or a normal text selection. If it's either one, the procedure selects the first paragraph containing the selection and scrolls to display it. You can also use rngSel.Words(1).Select or rngSel.Sentences(1).Select, respectively, to select the first word or sentence in the selection (where rngSel represents a text range). To see this, create a new Word document, insert two paragraphs of text, and place the cursor in the middle of the first paragraph. Run the following procedure to select the paragraph containing the selection.

```
Sub SelectWholeParagraph()
    Dim rngSel As Word.Range
    Select Case ActiveWindow.Selection.Type
        Case wdSelectionIP, wdSelectionNormal
            Set rngSel = ActiveWindow.Selection.Range
            rngSel.Paragraphs(1).Range.Select
            ActiveWindow.ScrollIntoView rngSel
    End Select
End Sub
```

Determine What Page the Current Selection Is On

You can use the Information property on the *Range* object to determine information about a range of text. This information includes whether the range of text is in a table, in an endnote or footnote area in Print Layout view, or in an endnote or footnote pane in Normal view. The most common information you can retrieve about a range of text, especially selected text, is the information you see in the status bar at the bottom left of the document window.

You can get information like the page number, section number, number of pages, line number, and column number wherever the current selection exists. In the following procedure, the constant value wdActiveEndPageNumber retrieves the page number where the end of the selection exists. If the selection or range of text spanned two pages, the wdActiveEndPageNumber value would return the page number at the end of the selection.

```
Sub GetPageNumberOfSelection()
    Select Case ActiveWindow.Selection.Type
        Case wdSelectionIP, wdSelectionNormal
            MsgBox "End of selection is on page " & _
                ActiveWindow.Selection.Range _
                .Information(wdActiveEndPageNumber)
    End Select
End Sub
```

Excel

In Excel, the *Select* method exists on all objects that the ActiveWindow.Selection property returns. See the "Excel" part of "Retrieving the Selection" earlier in this chapter for the list of all the objects returned by ActiveWindow.Selection. The main thing to remember when using the *Select* method in Excel is, unlike in Word, you can't set the selection unless the content the *Select* method acts on is in view in the active window. For example, when two workbooks are open and the second is the active workbook, if you want to set the selection in the first document you first have to make its window active and then set the selection. (Note that you not only have to make the workbook active, but have to make the *worksheet* active as well.)

Select a Specific Cell on the Active Worksheet

The following procedure makes an arbitrary cell active. The code first ensures that the active sheet is a worksheet (not a chart), and then selects cell H10 in the active window. The procedure scrolls the selection into view so the user can see it. In the case where the user changes the active sheet, you might want to programmatically move the active cell to A1 (or any specific cell), for example:

```
Sub SetSelection()
    Dim rngCell As Excel.Range
    If TypeName(ActiveSheet) = "Worksheet" Then
        Set rngCell = ActiveSheet.Range("H10")
        rngCell.Select
        ActiveWindow.ScrollIntoView rngCell.Left, _
            rngCell.Top, rngCell.Width, rngCell.Height
    End If
End Sub
```

In scenarios where you know the workbook and worksheet you want to work with and select content on, you first need to activate the workbook and worksheet and then set the selection on the range of cells. Once you know the worksheet and workbook, you can use the following procedure. The same holds true if you need to select content on a chart sheet: you first need to activate the chart sheet and then set the selection. To see the following procedure work, start Excel, create two workbooks, make the second workbook active, and then run the procedure.

```
Sub ActivateSheetAndSelect()
    Workbooks(1).Worksheets(1).Activate
    Workbooks(1).Worksheets(1).Range("H10").Select

    With ActiveWindow.Selection
        ActiveWindow.ScrollIntoView.Left, _
            .Top, .Width, .Height
    End With
End Sub
```

If you comment out the first line, make the second workbook active again, and then run the procedure, you'll get the error "Select method of Range class failed" and Visual Basic for Applications will break on the line of code containing the *Select* method.

PowerPoint

In PowerPoint, the *Select* method exists on either the *TextRange, Shape, ShapeRange, Slide,* or *SlideRange* objects and the table objects *Cell, Column,* and *Row* (in PowerPoint 2000 only). When you want to select either text in a shape or the shape itself, you need to ensure that either the shape containing the text or just the shape itself exists on the slide currently displayed in the active window.

The following procedure selects the title placeholder on the slide in the active window. The If...Then statement within the With...End block uses the HasTitle property on the *Shapes* collection of a slide to determine if a title placeholder exists. If it does, the title placeholder is selected.

```
Sub ActivateWindowSetSelection()
    With ActiveWindow.View.Slide.Shapes
        If .HasTitle Then .Placeholders(1).Select
    End With
End Sub
```

> ## Select a Specific Shape on a Specific Slide and Presentation

In scenarios where you know the presentation and slide you want to work with and select content on, you first need to activate the presentation, go to the slide, and then set the selection. To see the following procedure work, start PowerPoint, create a presentation with a few slides, and then save the presentation as "MyPres.ppt". Create a new presentation, and then run the following procedure. This procedure does several things. It activates the first document window belonging to the presentation "MyPres"; it changes the view to Normal; it activates the slide pane; it determines the number of slides in the presentation using Slides.Count; it uses the *GotoSlide* method on the *View* object to navigate to the last slide; and it selects the title placeholder (if the slide has one).

```
Sub SetTitleSelection()
    Dim oWindow As DocumentWindow
    Dim oSlide As Slide, nSlides As Integer
    Dim oPres As Presentation

    Set oPres = Presentations("MyPres")
    Set oWindow = oPres.Windows(1)
    With oWindow
        .Activate
        .ViewType = ppViewNormal
        .Panes(2).Activate
        nSlides = oPres.Slides.Count
        .View.GotoSlide nSlides
        Set oSlide = .View.Slide
        If oSlide.Shapes.HasTitle Then
            oSlide.Shapes.Placeholders(1).Select
        End If
    End With
End Sub
```

Finding Content on the Screen

Office provides a rich set of objects, methods, and properties that allow developers to return and set content within an Office document. For example, in Word, solutions can parse through a document and retrieve such information as the number of words, the text styles, and the font formatting. Until Office 2000 was created, there was no programmatic way for developers to determine where the document content was displayed on the user's monitor. The developer could obtain text from a paragraph in a Word document but couldn't determine where that text was on the screen—or if it was even visible to the user.

Why would you care? There are a number of scenarios in which you'll find that capability useful. The most common one is the Find and Replace functionality in Word, Excel, or PowerPoint. When you start a search for a text string, every time the application finds a matching text string, it displays and highlights the text. Note also that the Find and Replace dialog box is repositioned so that it never covers the highlighted text. The Spelling and Grammar dialog box also behaves like the Find and Replace dialog box.

Quick Guide

To use functionality like the Find and the Spelling and Grammar dialog boxes, Word, Excel, and PowerPoint 2000 provide a set of methods and properties that enable you either to easily determine with your solutions where document content is visible on the user's screen, or to make it visible. The scenarios that the properties and methods enable are described in the following table.

Method/Property	Scenario
ScrollIntoView	Scroll document content into view on the user's screen.
PointsToScreenPixelsX, PointsToScreenPixelsY GetPoint (in Word)	Determine where content such as text, cells, or shapes are located with respect to the top-left position on the screen.
RangeFromPoint	Conduct "hit testing"; that is, return a document content object in Word, Excel, or PowerPoint given a specified set of (x, y) screen coordinates.

Using the *ScrollIntoView* Method

When the spelling checker in Word, Excel, or PowerPoint finds an incorrect word, the application automatically highlights and displays the word (that is, the selection becomes visible on the screen). For example, suppose you have a three-page document loaded in Word and the page in view is the first. If the spelling checker finds a word spelled incorrectly on page three, the word is highlighted and Word scrolls down until the highlighted word is visible.

In addition, as a user you use the vertical scroll bar at the side of the window until you find the word you want to see. In order to add functionality to your solutions that allow you to either mimic the spelling checker or to scroll through the window as a user does, you can use the *ScrollIntoView* method in Word, Excel, or PowerPoint. The *ScrollIntoView* method scrolls through the document window so that a specified object, whether it's text, a cell, or a shape, is displayed in the active window. One common scenario that might use *ScrollIntoView* is a document reader that scrolls through the text as it reads the text selection, passing the text selection to a text-to-speech engine on your machine.

Word

The *ScrollIntoView* method in Word is a member of the *Window* object, and two arguments are passed into it. The first argument, named *obj*, is defined as type Object. This means you can pass an object of either type *Range* or type *Shape*. More generically, you can pass either text or a shape (such as an AutoShape or a Picture). The second argument, named *Start*, defined as type Boolean, is optional.

This argument specifies which corner of the bounding rectangle of the text range or shape takes viewing precedence when the bounding rectangle is bigger than the physical size of the window on screen. A value of True indicates that the top left of the bounding rectangle should be scrolled into view so that it appears at the top left of the window. If the value passed as the *Start* argument is False, the window should be scrolled so that the bottom right of the rectangle appears at the window's bottom right. If the rectangle is larger than the screen, the Start Boolean will determine which part of the rectangle will be in view.

```
ActiveWindow.ScrollIntoView _
    obj:=ActiveDocument _
        .Paragraphs.Last.Range, _
    Start:=True
```

Scroll the Last Paragraph Into View

1. Open any Word document that has a lot of text and scroll up through the document so that the last paragraph isn't visible on the screen.

2. Add the following procedure in a code module in the Visual Basic Editor and run it:

```
Sub ScrollToSelection()
    Dim rngText As Word.Range
    Set rngText = ActiveWindow.Document _
        .Paragraphs.Last.Range
    rngText.Select
    ActiveWindow.ScrollIntoView rngText
End Sub
```

In this procedure, the last paragraph of the document is selected and the active window scrolls to view it. If the text selection bounds fit into the visible window, the *ScrollIntoView* method will scroll the text selection so that all of it is visible. Even if part of the selection isn't visible when the procedure starts (that is, a paragraph is selected but only the first line or two is visible at the bottom of the window), using the *ScrollIntoView* method will scroll the window until all of the text is visible (unless the text bounds of the paragraph are larger than the window).

Excel

The *ScrollIntoView* method in Excel is a member of the *Window* object, but instead of taking two arguments (*obj* and *Start*), as Word does, it takes five. The first four arguments represent the coordinates and size of the object. In this 0regard, PowerPoint is like Excel.

So what's the difference between Word and Excel/PowerPoint? The coordinates and size of the object passed into Word's *ScrollIntoView* method are called implicitly for you. In Excel and PowerPoint, you explicitly pass in the coordinates and size of the object you want to scroll into view. Word's method is more efficient when it comes to the amount of code you have to write.

The *ScrollIntoView* method in Excel is a member of the *Window* object as well as a member of the *Pane* object. In Excel, you can split the window into multiple panes, and most of the members of the *Window* object are also a member of the *Pane* object (because the *Pane* acts like a window in the window). The first four arguments passed into the *ScrollIntoView* method are *Left, Top, Width,* and *Height* and are defined as type *Long*.

```
ActiveWindow.ScrollIntoView Left:=0, Top:=0, _
    Width:=100, Height:=100, Start:=True
```

The *Left* argument represents the left value of the bounding rectangle in points along the horizontal of the worksheet window. The *Top* argument is the top value of the bounding rectangle, expressed in points along the vertical of the worksheet window. The *Width* argument is the width of the bounding rectangle, expressed in points along the horizontal of the window. And the *Height* is the height value of the bounding rectangle, expressed in points along the vertical of the window.

Finally, the fifth and last argument of the *ScrollIntoView* method is the same as the second argument in Word's *ScrollIntoView* method. It's named *Start*; it's declared of type Boolean; and it specifies which end of the bounding rectangle is important. The default value is True, indicating that the top left of the rectangle scrolls so that it appears at the top left of the window. If the value of False is passed into the Start argument, the window scrolls so that the bottom right of the rectangle appears at the bottom right of the window. If the rectangle is larger than the screen, the Start Boolean will determine which part of the rectangle will be in view.

Scroll the Range of Selected Cells Into View

1. Load an Excel workbook, select a range of cells, and scroll the window so that you can't see your selection.

2. Add the following procedure in a code module in the Visual Basic Editor and run it:

```
Sub ScrollSelection()
    With ActiveWindow.Selection
        ActiveWindow.ScrollIntoView .Left, .Top, _
            .Width, .Height, True
    End With
End Sub
```

Excel will scroll into view the selected cells, whether they constitute a contiguous selection of cells or not. Note that this sample code also works if you have a shape such as an AutoShape or Picture selected.

PowerPoint

In PowerPoint, the *ScrollIntoView* method is defined as it is in Excel. That is, there are five arguments passed to it. The first four are the coordinates and the size of the object, and the fifth is the Start Boolean. You can use the *ScrollIntoView* method only in a view that can contain a shape selection.

Scroll the First Shape of a Shape Selection Into View

1. Load a blank PowerPoint presentation and add a rectangle AutoShape anywhere on the first slide.

2. Select the shape and scroll the one shape selection (using the scroll bars) so that only the top of the rectangle is visible at the bottom of the PowerPoint document window in Normal view.

3. Add the following procedure in a code module in the Visual Basic Editor and press F5 to run it:

```
Sub ScrollSelection()
    If ActiveWindow.Selection _
        .Type = ppSelectionShapes Then
        With ActiveWindow.Selection.ShapeRange(1)
            ActiveWindow.ScrollIntoView .Left, .Top, _
                .Width, .Height
        End With
    End If
End Sub
```

This code works when only one shape is selected. If the shape selection bounds fit into the visible window, the *ScrollIntoView* method will scroll the shape selection so that all of it is visible.

Screen Position

When you use the spelling checker in a document, an application like Word will display the Spelling and Grammar dialog box the first time the spelling or grammar checker finds an incorrect fragment of text. When the dialog box is displayed, the text fragment is scrolled into view and selected, and the Spelling and Grammar dialog box is positioned so that it doesn't overlap the selection.

In some cases, you may need to move a custom dialog box so it doesn't cover the text selection. In order to position a dialog box, you need to determine where content such as text, a cell, or a shape is located with respect to the top-left position on the screen. Note that the Left and Top property values of a dialog box in Visual Basic 6.0 or UserForms in the Visual Basic Editor are specified with respect to the top-left of the screen. Thus, knowing where content in a Word, Excel, or PowerPoint document is with respect to the top-left of the screen helps position custom dialog boxes around content visible to the user.

Word

To determine where content in the active document window is in Word, you need to use the *GetPoint* method on the *Window* object. The *GetPoint* method takes five arguments. The first four are variables declared as *Long*, which represent the left coordinate, top coordinate, width, and height of the content on the screen. You declare the coordinate variables, and after the *GetPoint* method is executed, Word fills in the variables with the return values.

The last argument is the object that represents content in the document of a window. The object must be of type Range or Shape. So you can pass in either an object representing text in the document in the active window or a shape floating on top of and below text. If the content is visible on the screen, *GetPoint* returns in units of pixels the screen coordinates of the content. If the content passed into the last argument of the *GetPoint* method is a text range, the coordinates of the virtual, rectangular bounding box around the text is returned.

Position a Userform over the Selection

Of the following two procedures, the first, *GetSelection,* determines the selection type in the active window. If the selection is one of the types listed in the Case statement, the range or shape (depending on the selection) is passed to the second procedure, called *MoveAssistant.* The *GetPoint* method in the second procedure returns the position of the text range or shape with respect to the top-left of the screen. The If…Then statement checks to see if the object's left or top coordinate is off the screen, and thus, not all the content is visible. If this isn't the case, the procedure moves the position of the Office Assistant closer to the top-left coordinates of the content.

Add the following procedures to a module in the Visual Basic Editor and switch back to Word. Press ALT+F8 to display the Macros dialog box, select the *GetSelection* procedure and then click Run. The left and top position of the Office Assistant will be close to the top-left position of the selection.

```
Sub GetSelection()
    Select Case ActiveWindow.Selection.Type
        Case wdSelectionNormal, wdSelectionShape, _
            wdSelectionIP
            MoveAssistant ActiveWindow _
                .Selection.Range
    End Select
End Sub

Sub MoveAssistant(objSel As Object)
    Dim lLeft As Long, lTop As Long
    Dim lWidth As Long, lHeight As Long

    On Error Resume Next
    ActiveWindow.GetPoint lLeft, lTop, _
        lWidth, lHeight, objSel
```

```
        If lLeft < 0 Or lTop < 0 Then
            Debug.Print "Content not fully visible."
        Else
            With Application.Assistant
                .Visible = True
                .Move lLeft, lTop
            End With
        End If
End Sub
```

Excel and PowerPoint

In Excel and PowerPoint, developers can use the PointsToScreenPixelsX and PointsToScreenPixelsY properties to determine where text, cells, or shapes are located on the screen. These properties convert units of points (document coordinates) to screen pixels. They are members of the *Window* object in Excel and the corresponding *DocumentWindow* object in PowerPoint. The associated *GetPoint* method in Word is a member of the *Window* object. The PointsToScreenPixelsX and PointsToScreenPixelsY properties require that the text, cell, or shape in question be located on the active slide in PowerPoint or on the active sheet in Excel.

The following procedures are similar in function to the ones in Word. In the *MoveAssistant* procedure, the *GetPoint* method is replaced with the two PointsToScreenPixel methods. The *MoveAssistant* procedure is exactly the same in Excel and PowerPoint. The only difference between Excel and PowerPoint is the code in the *GetSelection* procedure, as listed below, to retrieve the current selection.

1. Add the following procedures to a module in the Visual Basic Editor and switch back to Excel or PowerPoint.

2. Press ALT+F8 to display the Macros dialog box, select the *GetSelection* procedure and then click Run. The left and top position of the Office Assistant will be close to the top-left position of the selection.

```
' For EXCEL only
Sub GetSelection()
    Select Case TypeName(ActiveWindow.Selection)
        Case "Range"
            MoveAssistant ActiveWindow _
                .Selection
    End Select
End Sub
```

```
' For POWERPOINT only
Sub GetSelection()
    Select Case ActiveWindow.Selection.Type
        Case ppSelectionShapes
            MoveAssistant ActiveWindow _
                .Selection.ShapeRange.Item(1)
    End Select
End Sub


' For EXCEL and POWERPOINT
Sub MoveAssistant(objSel As Object)
    Dim lLeft As Long, lTop As Long

    On Error Resume Next
    With ActiveWindow
        lLeft = .PointsToScreenPixelsX(objSel.Left)
        lTop = .PointsToScreenPixelsY(objSel.Top)
    End With

    If lLeft < 0 Or lTop < 0 Then
        Debug.Print "Content not fully visible."
    Else
        With Application.Assistant
            .Visible = True
            .Move lLeft, lTop
        End With
    End If
End Sub
```

Chapter Summary

The *Selection* object in Word and PowerPoint, along with the Selection property in Excel and Outlook, allows you to determine what content is currently selected in the active window. The next chapter shows you how to use this understanding of what type of content is selected to appropriately update custom menu commands and toolbar buttons. In addition, being able to navigate to specific content and position a custom dialog box around content visible on the user's screen allows you to develop functionality similar to that built into the Office applications—for example, how the Find and the Spelling and Grammar dialog boxes scroll.

Chapter 10

Handling Window and Content Interaction Events

Chapter Objectives   Estimated time: 60 minutes

- Update menus and toolbars based on the selection.

- Display custom shortcut menus based on the selection.

- Display custom dialog boxes based on the selection.

- Enable or disable custom menu commands and toolbar buttons depending on whether or not a Microsoft Office document is in the active window.

A developer can think of documents in two ways. First, there's the content—the text, tables, charts, shapes, pictures, and so on. Second, there's how the user interacts with the content using the mouse, the keyboard, and the tools on the menus and toolbars when a document is displayed in a window. When you start an Office application and open a document, you see the document in a window. You navigate to a specific part of the document, click where you want to add or remove content using the mouse, and then use the keyboard to type text or click buttons on a toolbar to format the content, for example.

When you interact with content through the mouse and keyboard, you trigger, or "fire" events in the background. Each Office application tracks the interaction, determining what document is displayed and what you've selected, clicked, right-clicked, or double-clicked. Once it determines the specific content you're interacting with, the application updates its menus and toolbars, displays a specific dialog box or shortcut menu, or updates a status bar.

As a developer, you can handle the same events the application does, and thus you can customize what happens when the user interacts with the content. This chapter describes the events that the Office application fires; common scenarios that you can address in your solution with them; and ways you can customize the user's experience with custom dialog boxes, shortcut menus, and menu and toolbar customizations.

Quick Guide: Setting Up an Event to Track User Interaction

This quick guide explains how to connect to the Application-level events provided by an Office application to track user interaction with content. What events can you handle? This chapter describes the selection change, double-click, right-click, and the window activate and window deactivate events. As you'll see throughout this chapter, these events enable scenarios like those listed below.

- Display custom dialog boxes (cancel the default behavior) after double-clicking a selection

- Display custom context menus when right-clicking a selection

- Update command bar controls based on a given selection

- Start or stop electronic document readers based on document window activation

- Update command bars based on document type (Web versus binary)

- Show or hide components (such as the Office Assistant)

Note All the events described in this chapter are triggered whether the event occurs in the user interface or programmatically through the object model (using Microsoft Visual Basic for Applications).

Set Up an Event

The following steps show a simple tip for debugging and testing your solution and determining exactly when an event procedure is called. Always remember to create a new class module and declare an object of type Application before using the application's events.

1. Start Microsoft Word, Microsoft Excel, Microsoft PowerPoint, or Microsoft Outlook and press ALT+F11 to start the Visual Basic Editor. This example uses Word.

2. Click Class Module on the Insert menu, add the following code in the class module, and then press ENTER.

```
Public WithEvents App As Application
```

Once you press ENTER, the new *App* object, declared with events, appears in the Object drop-down list in the class module. When you select the new object in the Object drop-down list, the Procedure drop-down list shows the events for the *Application* object.

3. Select the new object *App* in the Object drop-down list in the class
module and then select *WindowSelectionChange* in the Procedures drop-
down list. Add the following lines within the event procedure:

```
Static i As Integer
i = i + 1
Debug.Print "EventProcedureName: " & i
```

These three lines are great for debugging your solution and determining
exactly when the event procedure is called. After everything is set up in
step 5, the event should fire every time you manipulate the content. You
use the static integer variable *i* so when the text from the code line
Debug.Print is printed to the Immediate window in the Visual Basic
Editor, you can see a change from line to line in the printed text.

You should change the text "EventProcedureName" to the procedure
name of the event you selected from the Procedures drop-down list in
step 2. In this example, the text would be replaced with "Window-
SelectionChange."

4. Click Module on the Insert menu and add the following code in the
standard code module:

```
Dim AppEvents As New Class1

Sub InitEvents()
    Set AppEvents.App = Application
End Sub
```

Before an event procedure will run, you must connect the declared
object *App* in the class module to the Application object. Note that the
class name "Class1" stated just after the *New* keyword in the declaration
statement should be the name of the class module that you declared the
App variable to be in step 2. By default, the class module inserted in step
2 is Class1, but you can change the name of the class module to anything
you like.

5. Place the cursor in the *InitEvents* procedure and press F5 to run the project.
After you run the *InitEvents* procedure, the *App* object in the class module
points to the Word *Application* object, and the event procedures in the
class module will run when the events occur.

6. Position the Office application window so you can see the Immediate
window in the Visual Basic Editor, and then start clicking around in the
Word document, inserting new content and selecting the text and
shapes.

In the Immediate window, you should see the text "WindowSelection-
Change" followed by a number. Each time an action occurs such that the
selection changes in the active document window in Word, the number
following the text "WindowSelectionChange" is changed by one.

No matter what event you write code for, you should use this technique to help you debug and test your solutions. It also helps you determine exactly when an event is fired. Later in this chapter you'll learn more about each event that's fired as a result of a user's interaction with and manipulation of the active document's content. You can either use the lists from each of the descriptions for each event or use the technique described in this example to determine when an event fires.

The Selection Change Event

When you're manipulating content in a document or in your mailbox in Outlook, many things are happening under the covers in Office to reflect the current state of selected content. As discussed in the section of the previous chapter entitled "Selection," the most common selection you see is selected text. The text appears inverted as you select the characters of the text. You can tell that a shape or an object is selected by the sizing handles that appear at the corners and along the edges of the rectangle when it is selected.

In Excel, a thick black border around a range of cells represents the selection of that range of cells. Finally, in Outlook, the highlighted items in a folder in your mailbox represent a selection. Whenever you change where the selection handles appear, what text is inverted, what cells are selected in Excel, or what items are selected in your mailbox in Outlook, a selection change event occurs.

Word, Excel, PowerPoint, and Outlook each provide an event that handles a selection change. The chart below shows the different names used for the event procedure.

Office Application	Selection change event procedure
Word	WindowSelectionChange
Excel	SheetSelectionChange
PowerPoint	WindowSelectionChange
Outlook	SelectionChange

Differences Between Word, Excel, PowerPoint, and Outlook

For each Office application—Word, Excel, PowerPoint, and Outlook—a list under the heading "When the Selection Change Event Triggers," indicates when the selection change event fires and discusses any differences among the applications. The most obvious difference among the selection change events in each application is the prefix used in the name of the event procedure. However, the events in each application all work towards the goal of trapping when the selection of content changes in the active document (or Explorer window in Outlook). In Word and PowerPoint, one argument—an instance of the *Selection* object—is passed to the event procedure in each application. Using the *Selection* object, you can determine what type of object is contained within the selection. The selection may be text or a shape, for example.

In Excel, two arguments are passed into the selection change event. The second argument is always a *Range* object. The selection change event in Excel fires only when the range of cells selected changes. In Outlook, no arguments are passed to the selection change event: you use the Selection property to determine the set of items selected in the active mailbox folder. Items can consist of mail, notes, appointments, or any other mailbox item found in Outlook.

Selection Change Scenario

One of the most common scenarios that the selection change event allows you to handle is the updating of the command bar controls based on selection. The classic example is the Bold button on the Formatting toolbar in Word, Excel, and PowerPoint. Whenever the active selection contains text that is all bold, the Bold button is in the depressed position. If the text isn't all bold, the button is in the up position. The Bold button is also disabled when the selection can't contain text, and it's enabled when the selection can contain text.

Update Your Controls Based on a Selection Change

In this section, you'll create a custom Bold button and add it to the Standard toolbar in Word, Excel, and PowerPoint. The custom Bold button will mimic the behavior of the built-in Bold button on the Formatting toolbar—based on the current selection, it will appear in the depressed or up position and be disabled or enabled.

For each step under the descriptions of the selection change event in Word, Excel, and PowerPoint, you need to complete the following steps first. The code is generic because it uses the *CommandBar* object model and, as a result, works identically in Word, Excel, and PowerPoint.

1. In whatever application you're working with, Word, Excel, or PowerPoint, display the Visual Basic Editor and insert a new class module by clicking Class Module on the Insert menu. Add the following declaration:

   ```
   Public WithEvents App As Application
   ```

2. Insert a new standard code module by clicking Module on the Insert menu. Add the following declaration and procedure to the top of the module:

   ```
   Dim AppEvents As New Class1

   Sub InitEvents()
       Set AppEvents.App = Application
   End Sub
   ```

   As noted in the Quick Guide at the beginning of the chapter, you should use the class name "Class1," stated just after the *New* keyword in the declaration statement, as the name of the class module you added in the previous step. By default, the class module inserted is Class1, but you can change the name of the class module to anything you like.

3. After the *InitEvents* procedure, add the following procedure:

```
Sub InsertCustomBoldButton()
    With Application.CommandBars("Standard") _
        .Controls.Add(msoControlButton)
        .Caption = "&CustomBold"
        .Tag = "CustomBold"
        .FaceId = 113
    End With
End Sub
```

In Word, Excel, and PowerPoint, you use this procedure to insert a custom Bold button at the end of the Standard toolbar. Note that the Tag property is set to "CustomBold" so your code can easily search for all instances of this control using the FindControls method. The FaceId property is set to the value of 113, which is the same FaceId value for the built-in Bold button. Your control will look exactly the same as the built-in Bold button on the Formatting toolbar.

4. Add the following procedure to the standard code module:

```
Sub SetButtonState( _
    iButtonState As MsoButtonState, _
    bEnabled As Boolean)

    Dim ctlItem As CommandBarControl
    Dim ctlColl As CommandBarControls

    Set ctlColl = Application.CommandBars _
        .FindControls(Tag:="CustomBold")

    If Not ctlColl Is Nothing Then
        For Each ctlItem In ctlColl
            ctlItem.State = iButtonState
            ctlItem.Enabled = bEnabled
        Next ctlItem
    End If
End Sub
```

You set the search criterion for the FindControls method to search for the tag "CustomBold" and use the FindControls method to return all instances of the custom bold button. Thus, as in the following steps, no matter how many times the custom bold button is copied to other places in the command bar set, the button state will always be applied to all instances of the control. That is, the For Each...Loop iterates through each instance of the custom Bold button and sets its state appropriately.

This procedure was copied from the steps "Searching for All Instances of a Built-In Control" in the "FindControls Method" section of Chapter 11. Its name is changed here from *RenameBuiltInCommand* to *SetButtonState*. The arguments *iButtonState*, declared as MsoButtonState, and *bEnabled*, declared as Boolean, were added within the Sub statement of the *SetButtonState* procedure.

5. Place the cursor in the procedure *InsertCustomBoldButton* and press F5 to run it.

6. Switch back to Word, Excel, or PowerPoint and note the custom Bold button at the end of the Standard toolbar. Click Customize on the Tools menu to get into command bar customization mode.

7. Holding down the CTRL key, click and drag a copy of the custom Bold button right beside the original copy of the custom Bold button. Repeat the same click-and-drag process to copy the button to any visible toolbar or to somewhere else on the Standard toolbar.

Now you're ready for Word, Excel, or PowerPoint to update a custom (or built-in) command bar control, based on the selection change. Once you complete the steps under the Word, Excel, and PowerPoint sections below and on the following pages, the selection change will cause the state of each instance of the custom Bold button to be up or down, enabled or disabled.

Word

The previous chapter discussed how a selection in Word is defined as an insertion point in the text, highlighted text, or selection handles around any shape. A good way for you to visually determine if the selection has changed is by looking at the value of Col in the status bar at the bottom of the document window. The Col label is to the right of the "At" and "Ln" (Line) labels and indicates the column of text where the left side of a selection starts or ends. The size of the highlight of text or the presence of selection handles are other visual indicators. The following lists show when you can expect the selection change event to trigger and when you can expect the selection change event to *not* trigger.

When the Selection Change Event Triggers

- Selecting text with the mouse pointer and clicking between text. The event triggers when you let go of the left mouse button after selecting some text or clicking between text.

- Moving the insertion point (IP) with the arrow keys. The insertion point is the bar that is positioned either in between text or at the end of a line of text where you are about to type text.

- Double-clicking to select text. This causes the selection change event to trigger twice. The first click causes the event to trigger because it places the IP directly under the mouse pointer. The second click causes the event to trigger again because it causes the word containing the IP to be highlighted. When you double-click, the WindowBeforeDoubleClick event is also fired after the WindowSelectionChange event. See the section, "The Double-Click Event," later in this chapter for details.

- Right-clicking nonhighlighted text. A right click places the IP directly under the mouse pointer. Right-clicking highlighted text doesn't fire the event, because the selection doesn't change.

- Holding down the SHIFT key or CTRL key and pressing the arrow keys on your keyboard. Each time the text highlight is extended, the event triggers.

- Selecting a drawing shape.

- Deleting a floating shape.

- Selecting more than one shape. Each time you hold down the SHIFT key and select another shape, the event triggers.

When the Selection Change Event Does *Not* Trigger

- Typing text in Word. Unlike in PowerPoint, the event doesn't trigger when you type text, even though the cursor and Col value is changing. In PowerPoint, the selection change event triggers each time you enter a new character.

- Grouping or ungrouping shapes.

- Formatting text.

Set Up the WindowSelectionChange Event in Word

Before completing the following steps, complete the steps in the section "Update Your Controls Based on a Selection Change."

1. In the Visual Basic Editor started from Word, double-click the Class1 project item in the Project Explorer to make it the active window.

2. Click *App* from the Object drop-down list and then select *Window-SelectionChange* from the Procedures drop-down list in the class module. In the *WindowSelectionChange* event procedure, add the following code so that the procedure appears as follows:

```
Private Sub App_WindowSelectionChange( _
    ByVal Sel As Selection)
```

```
      Select Case Sel.Type
          Case wdSelectionIP, wdSelectionNormal, _
              wdSelectionBlock, wdSelectionColumn, _
              wdSelectionRow

              If Sel.Font.Bold = True Then
                  SetButtonState msoButtonDown, True
              Else
                  SetButtonState msoButtonUp, True
              End If

          Case Else
              SetButtonState msoButtonUp, False
      End Select
End Sub
```

One argument is passed to the WindowSelectionChange event in Word. As in PowerPoint, the argument is defined as type Selection. Using the *Selection* object in Word (and in PowerPoint), you can determine whether the selection is text, a shape, or any other selection type, as described in the previous chapter in the section entitled "Selection."

The Select Case statement in the *WindowSelectionChange* event procedure evaluates the selection type of the *Sel* object passed into the event procedure. If the selection is an insertion point, a continuous text selection, or a block, column, or row of text, an If...Then statement evaluates whether the selected text is bold. If it is, the *SetButtonState* procedure is called to set the custom Bold button to an enabled, depressed state. If the selection doesn't contain text, the custom Bold button is disabled and the state is set to "up."

Note The elements of the Select Case block have been copied from the section "Format the Text Selection to Bold" in the previous chapter. You should use this Select Case block whenever you want to determine if the selection contains text.

---

3. Double-click the standard code module project item, Module1, in the Project Explorer to make it the active window. Place the cursor in the procedure *InitEvents* and press F5 to run the project.

4. Switch back to Word, add some text, shapes, and so forth, and format some text to bold in the active document.

5. Click the document's content, such as bold text, text without bold formatting, or a shape.

As you click around the content, the custom Bold button on the Standard toolbar—as well as any other place you copied the button—should toggle between the up and down (depressed) state and between enabled and disabled. The state of the custom Bold button should parallel the behavior of the built-in Bold button on the Formatting toolbar.

Excel

The selection change event in Excel is just about the easiest to understand. It fires only when the range of selected cells on the active worksheet changes. In most cases, the range contains only one cell. However, the selection change event is slightly limited in Excel, given that there's no way you can determine if the selection has changed from a cell to a shape, a chart, or any other object that floats on top of the cells in a worksheet.

When the Selection Change Event Triggers

- Changing the active cell. See the Name Box drop-down list at the top left of the Excel worksheet window (just below the toolbars).

- Using the black square at the bottom right of the range to expand or contract the size of the active range.

When the Selection Change Event Does *Not* Trigger

- Changing the selection from a cell to a shape. The SheetSelectionChange event fires only when the range of cells in the selection changes, as previously explained.

- Changing the selection from a shape back to a cell. This doesn't cause the event to trigger if you select the same cell you chose before selecting the shape. If the selected cell is different, the event triggers.

- Switching from sheet to sheet or window to window. You have to trap the SheetActivate or the WindowActivate events and then determine the selection in those events (or call the selection change event explicitly from the other event handlers). Even though the Name Box drop-down list is changing, it's constant for each sheet.

Excel has two events that allow the developer to determine if the selection change has happened and what content was changed, and it also has an event to determine if the active sheet has changed. The events are SheetSelection-Change, WindowActivate, and SheetActivate. The section "The Window Activate and Deactivate Events" later in this chapter describes how to use all three to update command bar customizations based on the current selection.

Set Up the SheetSelectionChange Event in Excel

Before completing the following steps, complete the steps in the section "Update Your Controls Based on a Selection Change."

1. In the Visual Basic Editor started from Excel, double-click the Class1 project item in the Project Explorer to make it the active window.

2. Click *App* from the Object drop-down list and then select *SheetSelection-Change* from the Procedures drop-down list in the class module. In the *SheetSelectionChange* event procedure, add the following code so that the procedure appears as follows:

```
Private Sub App_SheetSelectionChange( _
    ByVal Sh As Object, ByVal Target As Range)

    If Target.Font.Bold = True Then
        SetButtonState msoButtonDown, True
    Else
        SetButtonState msoButtonUp, True
    End If
End Sub
```

In Excel, the second argument of the *SheetSelectionChange* event procedure is always a *Range* object. The selection change event in Excel fires only when you change the range of cells selected. The second argument in the *SheetSelectionChange* event procedure is a range of selected cells. If all of the cells contain text that is all bold, *SetButtonState* is called to set all instances of the custom Bold button to enabled and depressed.

3. Double-click the standard code module project item, Module1, in the Project Explorer to make it the active window. Place the cursor in the procedure *InitEvents* and press F5 to run the project.

4. Switch back to Excel, add some text to a cell, add shapes, and format the text in any cell that contains text to bold.

5. Click the workbook's content such as the bold text, text without bold formatting, or a shape.

    As you click around the content, the custom Bold button on the Standard toolbar, as well as any other place you copied the button, should toggle between the up and down (depressed) state. The state of the custom Bold button should parallel the behavior of the built-in Bold button on the Formatting toolbar.

Note   The SheetSelectionChange event doesn't fire in Excel when the selection changes from a cell to a shape. Therefore, the custom Bold button does not disable when you click a shape.

PowerPoint

In PowerPoint, the selection can consist of text, shapes, slides, or nothing. When you change the selection from any of these types or extend or reduce the selection of one type, the selection change event triggers. One of the main differences between PowerPoint and Word's WindowSelectionChange event is that the event in PowerPoint is triggered every time you type a new character. This functionality can enable scenarios where you want to track the text that you enter. If you find a particular word, you can add "AutoCorrect" type functionality.

When the Selection Change Event Triggers

- Selecting text in Outline view with the mouse pointer or the arrow keys.

- Holding down the SHIFT key or the CTRL key and pressing the arrow keys to extend the text selection.

- Typing text or pressing ENTER when in text. Unlike Word, the selection change event fires when you type text.

- Switching slides in Normal view using the vertical scroll bar. Because the WindowSelectionChange event fires when you switch between slides, you can use the event to determine when the active slide has changed.

- Inserting a new slide in Normal view. This is a direct result of the previous bulleted item.

- Switching views.

- Clicking a slide icon in Outline view.

- Moving a slide icon to another position in Outline view.

- Clicking in any inactive pane in Normal view.

- Selecting multiple shapes on a slide.

- Letting the left-mouse button go when drag-selecting shapes or text.

- Selecting a slide image in Slide Sorter view or selecting in-between slide images.

- Selecting multiple slide images in Slide Sorter.

When the Selection Change Event Does *Not* Trigger

- Grouping or ungrouping shapes.

- Formatting text.

- Switching between presentations. To determine the selection when a presentation window is activated, you should set up the *WindowActivate* event procedure, as described towards the end of this chapter. In the *WindowActivate* event procedure, you can explicitly call the *WindowSelectionChange* event procedure. Here's how the WindowActivate event procedure would appear:

```
Private Sub App_WindowActivate( _
    ByVal Pres As Presentation, _
    ByVal Wn As DocumentWindow)

    PpApp_WindowSelectionChange Wn.Selection
End Sub
```

This procedure is described in full and used later in this chapter in the description for the WindowActivate event.

Set Up the WindowSelectionChange Event in PowerPoint

Before completing the following steps, complete the steps in the section "Update Your Controls Based on a Selection Change."

1. In the Visual Basic Editor started from PowerPoint, double-click the Class1 project item in the Project Explorer to make it the active window.

2. Click *App* from the Object drop-down list and then select *WindowSelectionChange* from the Procedures drop-down list in the class module. In the *WindowSelectionChange* event procedure, add the following code so that the procedure appears as follows:

```
Private Sub App_WindowSelectionChange( _
    ByVal Sel As Selection)

    Select Case Sel.Type
        Case ppSelectionShapes
            If Sel.ShapeRange.HasTextFrame Then
                If Sel.ShapeRange _
                    .TextFrame.TextRange _
                    .Font.Bold = msoTrue Then
                    SetButtonState msoButtonDown, True
                Else
                    SetButtonState msoButtonUp, True
                End If
            Else
                SetButtonState msoButtonUp, False
            End If
```

```
Case ppSelectionText
    If Sel.TextRange _
        .Font.Bold = msoTrue Then
            SetButtonState msoButtonDown, True
    Else
            SetButtonState msoButtonUp, True
    End If

Case Else
    SetButtonState msoButtonUp, False

    End Select
End Sub
```

One argument is passed to the WindowSelectionChange event in PowerPoint. As in Word, the argument is defined as type Selection. Using the *Selection* object in PowerPoint, you can determine whether the selection is text, a shape, a slide, or nothing.

The Select Case statement in the *WindowSelectionChange* event procedure evaluates the selection type of the *Sel* object passed into the event procedure. If the selection is a range of shapes, the first If...Then statement evaluates whether the shape range has a text frame. The shape range can contain any number of shapes on a slide, a notes page, or a master slide. You can query properties on the entire shape range to determine if they all share the same property setting. If none of the shapes in the shape range can contain text (specifically, the property HasTextFrame is False), the custom Bold button is disabled and its state set to "up."

If the shapes can contain text (that is, the property HasTextFrame is True), the If...Then statement contained within the first If...Then statement evaluates whether all the text across the range of selected shapes is bold. If all the text is bold, the *SetButtonState* procedure is called to set the custom Bold button to an enabled, depressed state. If the text is not bold, the custom Bold button is enabled, but the state is set to "up." The last If...Then statement works the same way, and is evaluated when the selection is text.

3. Double-click the standard code module project item, Module1, in the Project Explorer to make it the active window. Place the cursor in the procedure *InitEvents* and press F5 to run the project.

4. Switch back to PowerPoint, add some text and shapes, and format some text to bold in any shape.

5. Click the presentation's content, such as the bold text, text without bold formatting, or a shape.

As you click around the content, the custom Bold button on the Standard toolbar, as well as any other place you copied the button, should toggle between the up and down (depressed) state and between enabled and disabled. The state of the custom Bold button should parallel the behavior of the built-in Bold button on the Formatting toolbar.

Outlook

In Outlook, the selection change event is set up using an *Explorer* object and not the *Application* object as in Word, Excel, and PowerPoint. When you start Outlook, the first window you see is an *Explorer* object. It's the window that displays the folders in your mailbox as well as the contents in each folder. The selection change event is named SelectionChange, and it's triggered when the selection in the active explorer window changes.

In Outlook, unlike in Word, Excel, or PowerPoint, the selection isn't passed into the selection change event procedure. You need to query the Selection property in Outlook to determine what items are contained in the *Selection* collection object. The *Selection* object contains the items selected in the active mailbox folder. Items can consist of mail, notes, appointments, or any other mailbox items found in Outlook.

When the Selection Change Event Triggers

- Selecting one or more items in your Inbox, Notes, Sent Items, Tasks, or any other folder.

When the Selection Change Event Does *Not* Trigger

- Having a file-system folder be the current folder in view.

- Changing the selection when Outlook Today is displayed.

Set Up the SelectionChange Event in Outlook

The following steps show you how to set up a mode-less form that floats on top of the active explorer window (containing your mailbox folders and items) in Outlook. The contents of a text box in the form are updated with the mail item that's first in the collection of selected items. This behavior is exactly the same as that of Outlook's Preview Pane. You can display the Preview Pane by clicking Preview Pane on the View menu.

1. Start Outlook and display the Visual Basic Editor.

2. Insert a UserForm and from the control Toolbox, add a *TextBox* control and two labels. Set the properties on the controls and userform, as shown in the table on the following page.

Control	Property	Setting
Label1	Caption	Selected item:
Label2	Name	lblItemType
Label2	Caption	(Item type)
TextBox1	Name	txtItemBody
TextBox1	Multiline	True
TextBox1	WordWrap	True
TextBox1	ScrollBars	2 - fmScrollBarsVertical
UserForm1	Name	frmPreview
UserForm1	Caption	Selected Outlook Item
UserForm1	ShowModal	False

The userform should appear as follows:

3. Click Code on the View menu or press F7 to display the userform's code module. Add the following code to the top of the module:

```
Dim OlEvents As New OutlookEvents

Private Sub UserForm_Initialize()
    Set OlEvents.expWindow = ActiveExplorer
End Sub

Private Sub UserForm_Terminate()
    Set OlEvents.expWindow = Nothing
End Sub
```

The class name "OutlookEvents" stated just after the *New* keyword in the declaration statement should be the name of the class module you add in the next step. If you change the name of the class added in the next step, you must also change the class name after the *New* keyword in the above declaration. When the userform is loaded, the Initialize event sets the *Explorer* object defined in the class containing the *SelectionChange* event (set up in the next step) to the active *Explorer* object. You can then use the explorer's *SelectionChange* event once the userform loads.

4. Insert a Class module, name it OutlookEvents, and add the following code:

```
Public WithEvents expWindow As Explorer

Private Sub expWindow_SelectionChange()
    If Not frmPreview Is Nothing Then
        If expWindow.Selection _
            .Count > 0 Then GetBodyText
    End If
End Sub
```

The first If...Then block in the event procedure determines if the mode-less userform frmPreview is loaded. Because the userform is mode-less, the user may have closed the userform. The If...Then block is provided so that even if the userform is not loaded, the *SelectionChange* event procedure can still execute other code.

As previously mentioned, unlike in Word, Excel, and PowerPoint, no arguments are passed into the *SelectionChange* event procedure in Outlook. You need to use the Selection property on the *Explorer* window object to determine if any items are selected. If the count of items in the *Selection* collection object is greater than zero, the *GetBodyText* procedure, added in the next step, is called.

5. Below the *SelectionChange* procedure in the class module, add the following procedure:

```
Sub GetBodyText()
    Dim oItem As Object, sItemType As String
    Set oItem = expWindow.Selection.Item(1)
    Select Case TypeName(oItem)
        Case "MailItem"
            sItemType = "Mail"
        Case "AppointmentItem"
            sItemType = "Appointment"
        Case "NoteItem"
            sItemType = "Note"
        Case "TaskItem"
            sItemType = "Task"
    End Select
    With frmPreview
        .txtItemBody.Text = oItem.Body
        .lblItemType = sItemType
    End With
End Sub
```

The *GetBodyText* procedure retrieves the first item in the *Selection* collection object. As in the Preview pane in Outlook, the contents in only the first item in the selection are displayed. The Select Case block determines the item type by using the built-in *TypeName* function in the Visual Basic for Applications language. Once the item is known, the label lblItemType is set to the string describing the item type and the text box txtItemBody is set to the body of the selected Outlook item.

6. Double-click the frmPreview project item in the Project Explorer in the Visual Basic Editor to make the userform the active window. Press F5 to run the userform.

7. In the Outlook explorer window, select a mail item in your Inbox, switch to the Notes folder and select a note item, or display any other folder and select an item.

   If the folder is a mail, appointment, note, contacts, or task folder, you'll see the contents of the body of the first selected item in the userform's text box, just as the Preview pane displays the same text.

The Double-Click Event

When you double-click content in a Word, Excel, or PowerPoint document, the action that follows depends on the content. For example, when you insert and double-click an *ActiveX* control, the Visual Basic Editor is displayed by default. Some developers want to write code for users so that instead of displaying the Visual Basic Editor, the default action is cancelled and a wizard or custom property dialog box appears.

In Word, Excel, and PowerPoint, the document's content below the double-click is viewed as a selection. When you double-click most parts of a document's content, you trigger the double-click event. The event occurs before the default double-click action that's built into the application. This action may be to display a dialog box, select text, or enter into text edit mode. This depends on whether the double click occurs in Word, Excel, or PowerPoint, and on the nature of the content that's double-clicked.

In all three applications, as the use of the word 'Before' in the name of the event implies, you can prevent (that is, cancel) the default behavior from occurring. As a result, you can customize the experience of double-clicking for any document content. The following chart shows the different names used for the double-click event procedure:

Office Application	Double-click event procedure
Word	WindowBeforeDoubleClick
Excel	SheetBeforeDoubleClick
PowerPoint	WindowBeforeDoubleClick

Differences Between Word, Excel, and PowerPoint

The main difference between the double-click events in Word, Excel, and PowerPoint is the argument passed into the event procedure. In Word and PowerPoint, two arguments—an instance of the *Selection* object and the Cancel Boolean—are passed to the event procedure in each application. Using the *Selection* object, you can determine what type of object is below the double click and perform a specific action. The selection may be text or a shape, for example. In Excel, three arguments are passed into the double-click event. The second argument is always a *Range* object.

The second argument in Word and PowerPoint and the third argument in Excel is the Cancel Boolean. You can set the Cancel Boolean to True if you want to cancel the built-in default action.

Cancel the Default Action Based on the Selection Beneath a Double Click

You can perform many different actions when you double-click content. The actions, as previously mentioned, depend on the type of content that's double-clicked. Your double-click event procedures will normally contain a Select Case or an If…Then block that determines the type of content beneath the double click and performs a specific action. The following examples in Word, Excel, and PowerPoint show three different customizations of the double-click action.

1. In whichever application you're working with (Word, Excel, or PowerPoint), display the Visual Basic Editor and insert a new class module by clicking Class Module on the Insert menu. Add the following declaration.

```
Public WithEvents App As Application
```

2. Insert a new standard code module by clicking Module on the Insert menu. Add the following declaration and procedure to the top of the module:

```
Dim AppEvents As New Class1

Sub InitEvents()
    Set AppEvents.App = Application
End Sub
```

The class name "Class1" stated just after the *New* keyword in the declaration statement should be the name of the class module you added in the previous step. If you've changed the name of the class module, you must also change the class name after the *New* keyword in the above declaration.

Now you're set up for either Word, Excel, or PowerPoint to customize the double-click action, based on the selection.

Word

The double-click event in Word triggers whenever you double-click any part of the document in the active window. Word takes different actions depending on the content you double-click. For example, when you double-click a shape like a rectangle, you see the Format AutoShape dialog box (as you do in Excel and PowerPoint). When you double-click a word, Word selects the entire word. If you insert a symbol (which is just a text character) through the Symbol dialog box, double-clicking the symbol results in the display of the Symbol dialog box. Since the *WindowBeforeDoubleClick* event procedure provides a *Cancel* argument, you can cancel any one of these built-in behaviors and customize the result of a double click.

When the Double-Click Event Triggers

- Double-clicking a word. Setting the *Cancel* argument in the *WindowBeforeDoubleClick* event procedure to True results in the word not being fully selected.

- Double-clicking the margin of a paragraph to select the paragraph.

- Double-clicking a row in a table.

- Triple-clicking. The double-click event triggers after the first two clicks of a triple click.

- Double-clicking the upper corners of a page in Print Layout view. Double-clicking here normally brings up the Page Setup dialog box.

When the Double-Click Event Does *Not* Trigger

- Double-clicking in the Document Map pane.

Set Up the WindowBeforeDoubleClick Event in Word

When you click the Symbol menu item on the Insert menu, you see the Symbol dialog box. When you select a symbol, click the Insert button, click Close to dismiss the Symbol dialog box, and then double-click the symbol character in the document's text, you see the Symbol dialog box. The following steps show how to mimic the same type of functionality. Your code will determine if you clicked on a dollar sign, and if you did, it will display a message box. You can replace the call to display a message box with a call to show a userform.

Before completing the following steps, complete the steps in the section "Cancel the Default Action Based on the Selection Beneath a Double Click."

1. In the Visual Basic Editor started from Word, double-click the Class1 project item in the Project Explorer to make it the active window.

2. Click *App* from the Object drop-down list and then select *WindowBeforeDoubleClick* from the Procedures drop-down list in the class module.

In the *WindowBeforeDoubleClick* event procedure, add the following code so that the procedure appears as follows:

```
Private Sub App_WindowBeforeDoubleClick( _
    ByVal Sel As Selection, Cancel As Boolean)

    If Sel.Type = wdSelectionIP Then
        If Trim$(Sel.Text) = "$" Then
            Cancel = True
            Sel.Words(1).Select
            MsgBox "MySymbol"
        End If
    End If
End Sub
```

The If...Then statement evaluates the type of the selection that is passed into the *WindowBeforeDoubleClick* event procedure through the *Sel* argument. If the type of the selection is an insertion point (IP), a nested If...Then expression determines if the text of the selection is the dollar sign ($). In the evaluation, you use the built-in Visual Basic for Applications language function *Trim$* to remove any spaces before and after the dollar sign. If the text under the double click is a dollar sign, the text is selected, as would normally happen during a double click, and the message box is displayed.

You should note that when you double-click to select a word of text, the *WindowBeforeDoubleClick* event procedure is called just before Word expands the selection to the word. (Before you double-click, only an insertion point exists in the text.) If you cancel the default behavior, the word isn't selected; if you don't cancel, you get the built-in behavior of expanding the selection to the word. In this example, you can get the whole word where the insertion point exists. The code Sel.Words(1) returns the word that the insertion point is contained in and where the text is selected.

3. Double-click the standard code module project item, Module1, in the Project Explorer to make it the active window. Place the cursor in the procedure *InitEvents* and press F5 to run the project.

4. Switch back to Word and type the dollar sign ($) in the active document.

5. Double-click the dollar sign. You'll see the message box displaying the text "MySymbol." You can expand this solution to do anything, depending on what the selection is under the double click. As you'll see later in the PowerPoint example, you can prevent (cancel) the default dialog box from being displayed and display your own message or userform.

Excel

The double-click event in Excel fires when you double-click a cell in the active worksheet. If you double-click a cell that is not in edit mode, Excel's built-in behavior is to enter edit mode so that you can type text or a formula into the cell. The double-click event in Excel does not provide a way for you to determine if the user has double-clicked on a shape or any other object that floats on top of the cells in a worksheet.

Set Up the SheetBeforeDoubleClick Event in Excel

In the following example, you use the *SheetBeforeDoubleClick* event to prevent a cell from being edited when it's double-clicked; instead, the cell displays a message box. You can take this example and, as another option, display a custom userform that has a custom functions dialog box. Before completing the following steps, complete the steps in the section "Cancel the Default Action Based on the Selection Beneath a Double Click."

1. In the Visual Basic Editor started from Excel, double-click the Class1 project item in the Project Explorer to make it the active window.

2. Click *App* from the Object drop-down list and then select *SheetBefore-DoubleClick* from the Procedures drop-down list in the class module. In the *SheetBeforeDoubleClick* event procedure, add the following code so that the procedure appears as follows:

```
Private Sub App_SheetBeforeDoubleClick( _
    ByVal Sh As Object, ByVal Target As Range, _
    Cancel As Boolean)

    If Target.Address = "$A$1" Then
        Cancel = True
        MsgBox "Display custom function form"
    End If
End Sub
```

The If...Then statement evaluates the address of the cell beneath the double click. If the address of the cell is A1, the *Cancel* argument passed into the event procedure is set to True, thereby canceling the default behavior of entering the cell into edit mode. You then see the message box.

Of course, this doesn't prevent the user from using the arrow keys on the keyboard to move the active cell to the A1 cell and pressing F2 to enter edit mode in the cell. In other scenarios, you can modify the double-click behavior on a cell to display a custom dialog box that, for example, allows the user to modify the formula of the cell.

3. Double-click the standard code module project item, Module1, in the Project Explorer to make it the active window. Place the cursor in the procedure *InitEvents* and press F5 to run the project.

4. Switch back to Excel and double-click the cell A1 on the active worksheet or any worksheet in the workbook.

You won't be able to enter edit mode in cell A1 by double-clicking. The message box appears with the text, "Display custom function form." As previously mentioned, you can extend this example so that the *SheetBeforeDoubleClick* event procedure analyzes the cell formula, and if it's one that your code recognizes, a custom dialog box will be displayed. You can use the Formula property on the *Range* object to determine a cell's formula. The code in the evaluation of the If...Then statement above would start with Target.Formula = "=MyFunction(2+2)."

PowerPoint

The double-click event in PowerPoint triggers whenever you double-click a shape's border or a slide image in Slide Sorter view. As in Word, you can customize the action that takes place when the user double-clicks a specific shape type. For example, double-clicking an *ActiveX* control will by default display the Visual Basic Editor. Double-clicking an AutoShape displays the Format AutoShape dialog box. In any case, you can cancel the default action and display custom dialog boxes instead.

When the Double-Click Event Triggers

- Double-clicking the border of a shape in Normal view, Notes Page view, or a Master view.

- Double-clicking a slide image in Slide Sorter view. By default, this action changes the view in the active window to Normal view and displays the slide that was double-clicked in Slide Sorter view.

- Double-clicking an embedded object. You can cancel the in-place activation resulting from double-clicking an embedded object by setting the *Cancel* argument in the WindowBeforeDoubleClick event to True.

When you double-click a slide preview in PowerPoint Slide Sorter view, the selection type should be ppSelectionSlides. Note that when you double-click a slide preview in Slide Sorter view, PowerPoint will go to Normal view. However, you can cancel this action by setting the *Cancel* argument to True. You can double-click the slide preview in Notes Page view. In this case, the selection type is ppSelectionShape and the *Cancel* argument allows you to cancel the PowerPoint action that changes the view from Notes Page view to Normal view.

When the Double-Click Event Does *Not* Trigger

- WindowBeforeDoubleClick is not called in any situation where the double-click doesn't perform an operation, such as double-clicking an area of a slide where no shape is underneath the mouse pointer. Note, however, that if you right-click in the same place, you see a shortcut menu.

- Double-clicking text. Unlike in Word, double-clicking text doesn't trigger the double-click event.

Set Up the WindowBeforeDoubleClick Event in PowerPoint

The following steps cancel the default action of displaying the Visual Basic Editor when you double-click an *ActiveX* control. Before completing the following steps, complete the steps in the section "Cancel the Default Action Based on the Selection Beneath a Double Click."

1. In the Visual Basic Editor started from PowerPoint, double-click the Class1 project item in the Project Explorer to make it the active window.

2. Click *App* from the Object drop-down list and then select *WindowBefore-DoubleClick* from the Procedures drop-down list in the class module. In the *WindowBeforeDoubleClick* event procedure, add the following code so that the procedure appears as follows:

```
Private Sub App_WindowBeforeDoubleClick( _
    ByVal Sel As Selection, Cancel As Boolean)

    Dim shpSel As Shape
    If Sel.Type <> ppSelectionShapes Then Exit Sub

    Set shpSel = Sel.ShapeRange(1)
    If shpSel.Type = msoOLEControlObject Then
        Select Case TypeName(shpSel.OLEFormat.Object)
            Case "CommandButton"
                MsgBox "CommandButton"
                Cancel = True
            Case "Label"
                MsgBox "Label"
                Cancel = True
        End Select
    End If
End Sub
```

The first If...Then statement evaluates the selection type. If the selection isn't a shape, the *WindowBeforeDoubleClick* event procedure is exited. Otherwise the second If...Then statement determines the shape type. If it's an *ActiveX* control, the embedded Select Case block determines the type name of the control. If the control is a command button or label, a message box is displayed and the default action of displaying the Visual Basic Editor is canceled.

3. Switch back to PowerPoint. Right-click a toolbar and from the shortcut menu click Control Toolbox to display the Control Toolbox toolbar.

4. In the Control Toolbox toolbar, click and drag a command button, a label, and a list control onto the active slide. Insert some other drawing shapes.

5. Switch to the Visual Basic Editor. Double-click the standard code module project item, Module1, in the Project Explorer to make it the active window. Place the cursor in the procedure *InitEvents* and press F5 to run the project.

6. Switch to PowerPoint. Double-click the borders of the drawing shapes as well as the three controls.

When you double-click the command button and label, you see a message box. When you double-click the list, you see the Visual Basic Editor, because that's the default action. When you double-click the border of a drawing shape, you see the Format AutoShape dialog box.

The Right-Click Event

Microsoft Windows 95 introduced the widespread use of right-clicking. You can right-click almost anything in Windows and most applications. When you right-click, you see a shortcut menu containing a list of items to select. Usually, the list contains the most common actions that pertain to the object you right-clicked. When you right-click content in a Word, Excel, or PowerPoint document, you do see a shortcut menu; what items it lists depends on the content below the right click.

The document's content below the right click is viewed as a selection in Word, Excel, and PowerPoint. You should note that the right-click event occurs only when any part of a document's content is right-clicked. It doesn't happen when you right-click a command bar. In Word, Excel, and PowerPoint, the right-click event occurs before the default right-click action, which is to display a built-in shortcut menu.

In all three applications, as the use of the word "Before" in the name of the event implies, you can cancel the display of the default shortcut menu and, therefore, you can display your own custom shortcut menu for any document content. The chart below shows the different names used for the right-click event procedure.

Office Application	Right-click event procedure
Word	WindowBeforeRightClick
Excel	SheetBeforeRightClick
PowerPoint	WindowBeforeRightClick

Differences Between Word, Excel, and PowerPoint

The main difference between the right-click events in Word, Excel, and PowerPoint is the argument that's passed into the event procedure. In Word and PowerPoint, two arguments—an instance of the *Selection* object and the Cancel Boolean—are passed to the event procedure in each application. Using the *Selection* object, you can determine what type of object is below the right click and display a specific custom shortcut. The selection may be text or a shape, for example. In Excel, three arguments are passed into the right-click event. The second argument is always a *Range* object.

The second argument in Word and PowerPoint and the third argument in Excel is the Cancel Boolean. You can set the Cancel Boolean to True if you want to cancel the display of the built-in, default shortcut menu. In the following example, a custom shortcut menu is displayed and the display of the built-in shortcut menu is canceled.

Display a Custom Shortcut Menu Based on the Selection Beneath a Right Click

The most common scenario that the right-click event allows you to handle is the display of a custom shortcut menu based on the content that the user right-clicked. In the following sections, you'll create a custom shortcut menu in Word, Excel, and PowerPoint. The custom shortcut menu that's displayed will be based on the type of the current selection.

For each procedure under the descriptions of the right-click event in Word, Excel, and PowerPoint, you need to complete the following steps first. The code in the following steps is generic, because it uses the *CommandBar* object model and, hence, works identically in Word, Excel, and PowerPoint. Note that if you started with the steps from the sections "The Selection Change Event" or "The Double-Click Event," you've most likely completed the first two steps already.

1. In whichever application you're working with (Word, Excel, or PowerPoint), display the Visual Basic Editor and insert a new class module by clicking Class on the Insert menu. Add the following declaration.

```
Public WithEvents App As Application
```

2. Insert a new standard code module by clicking Module on the Insert menu. Add the following declaration and procedure to the top of the module:

```
Dim AppEvents As New Class1

Sub InitEvents()
    Set AppEvents.App = Application
End Sub
```

The class name "Class1" stated just after the *New* keyword in the declaration statement should be the name of the class module you added in the previous step. If you've changed the class module's name, you must also change the class name after the *New* keyword in the above declaration.

3. After the *InitEvents* procedure, add the following procedure:

```
Sub InsertShortcut()
    Dim cmbNewShortcut As CommandBar

    Set cmbNewShortcut = Application _
        .CommandBars.Add(Name:="NewShortcut", _
        Position:=msoBarPopup, Temporary:=True)
    With cmbNewShortcut.Controls
        With .Add
            .Caption = "&ShortcutItem 1"
        End With
        With .Add
            .Caption = "&ShortcutItem 2"
        End With
    End With
End Sub
```

This procedure is copied from the procedure *InsertShortcutMenu* from the "Add a Shortcut Menu" section in the next chapter. The procedure adds a custom shortcut menu named NewShortcut to the command bar collection. The custom shortcut menu contains two menu items. You can use this procedure in all applications.

In the Add method of the *CommandBars* collection object, you specify the *Position* and the *Temporary* arguments. As discussed in the next chapter, which describes working with the CommandBar objects, methods and properties, you need to specify the *Position* argument in order to create a shortcut menu. Setting the *Temporary* argument to True indicates that the shortcut menu will be removed when the Office application is exited.

4. Place the cursor in the procedure *InsertShortcut* and press F5 to insert the custom shortcut menu.

Now you're set up for either Word, Excel, or PowerPoint to display a custom shortcut menu, based on the selection. Once you complete the steps under the following Word, Excel, and PowerPoint sections, a right click will result in the display of a custom shortcut menu rather than the application's built-in, default shortcut menu.

Word

The right-click event in Word triggers whenever you right click any part of a document in the active window.

Before completing the following steps, complete the steps in the section "Display a Custom Shortcut Menu Based on the Selection Beneath a Right Click."

1. In the Visual Basic Editor started from Word, double-click the Class1 project item in the Project Explorer to make it the active window.

2. Click *App* from the Object drop-down list and then select *WindowBefore-RightClick* from the Procedures drop-down list in the class module. In the *WindowBeforeRightClick* event procedure, add the following code so that the procedure appears as follows:

```
Private Sub App_WindowBeforeRightClick( _
    ByVal Sel As Selection, Cancel As Boolean)

    Application.CommandBars("NewShortcut") _
        .ShowPopup
    Cancel = True
End Sub
```

3. Double-click the standard code module project item, Module1, in the Project Explorer to make it the active window. Place the cursor in the procedure *InitEvents* and press F5 to run the project.

4. Switch back to Word and right-click in the active document. You'll see the custom shortcut menu. You can extend the *WindowBeforeRightClick* event procedure to filter the content type in the selection beneath the right click and display shortcut menus based on the content.

Excel

The right-click event in Excel fires when you right-click a range of cells on the active worksheet. In most cases, the range contains only one cell. The right-click event in Excel does not provide a way for you to determine if the user has right-clicked a shape or any other object that floats on top of the cells in a worksheet.

Before completing the following steps, complete the steps in the section "Display a Custom Shortcut Menu Based on the Selection Beneath a Right Click."

1. In the Visual Basic Editor started from Excel, double-click the Class1 project item in the Project Explorer to make it the active window.

2. Click *App* from the Object drop-down list and then select *SheetBefore-RightClick* from the Procedures drop-down list in the class module.

In the *SheetBeforeRightClick* event procedure, add the following code so that the procedure appears as follows:

```
Private Sub App_SheetBeforeRightClick( _
    ByVal Sh As Object, ByVal Target As Range, _
    Cancel As Boolean)

    Application.CommandBars("NewShortcut") _
        .ShowPopup
    Cancel = True
End Sub
```

3. Double-click the standard code module project item, Module1, in the Project Explorer to make it the active window. Place the cursor in the procedure *InitEvents* and press F5 to run the project.

4. Switch back to Excel and right-click in the active document. You'll see the custom shortcut menu. You can extend the *SheetBeforeRightClick* event procedure to filter the content in the target range and display shortcut menus based on the content.

PowerPoint

The right-click event procedure is called when you right-click a shape, text, or a slide in any view, including a master view and Notes Page view. This event is triggered after the right mouse button returns to the up position after being pressed down. The cancel behavior prevents (cancels) only the context menu from appearing.

Set Up the WindowBeforeRightClick Event in PowerPoint

Before completing the following steps, complete the steps in the section "Display a Custom Shortcut Menu Based on the Selection Beneath a Right Click."

1. In the Visual Basic Editor started from PowerPoint, double-click the Class1 project item in the Project Explorer to make it the active window.

2. Click *App* from the Object drop-down list and then select *WindowBefore-RightClick* from the Procedures drop-down list in the class module. In the *WindowBeforeRightClick* event procedure, add the following code so that the procedure appears as follows:

```
Private Sub App_WindowBeforeRightClick( _
    ByVal Sel As Selection, Cancel As Boolean)

    Application.CommandBars("NewShortcut") _
        .ShowPopup
    Cancel = True
End Sub
```

3. Double-click the standard code module project item, Module1, in the Project Explorer to make it the active window. Place the cursor in the procedure *InitEvents* and press F5 to run the project.

4. Switch back to PowerPoint and right-click in the active document.

   You'll see the custom shortcut menu. You can extend the *Window-BeforeRightClick* event procedure to filter the content type in the selection beneath the right click and display shortcut menus based on the content.

The Window Activate and Deactivate Events

When you switch between windows in Windows, one window becomes the active window while the window you're moving away from becomes inactive. You can see the difference by the change in color of the window's title bar. When you switch between documents in Word, Excel, and PowerPoint, the same behavior occurs. Knowing when a document window becomes active or inactive allows you to develop solutions that address scenarios like the following:

- Start or stop text-to-speech document readers based on when a document window is activated or deactivated.

- Update command bar customizations to reflect the current selection in the active window.

- Show or hide components. This is similar to the way Office shows and hides the Office Assistant when you navigate to and from an Office application or a document window.

Differences Between Word, Excel, and PowerPoint

The names of the window activate and deactivate events are the same in Word, Excel, and PowerPoint: WindowActivate and WindowDeactivate. Like the other events described in this chapter, they apply at the application level, so you can determine when any document window becomes active or inactive. In all three applications, two arguments are passed to each event. The first is the document in the window that's being activated or deactivated, and the second is the document window.

The main difference between Word, Excel, and PowerPoint is that in Word and PowerPoint, when you navigate to and from a window that doesn't belong to the application, the window activate and deactivate events will be triggered for the application's document windows. In Excel, the window activate and deactivate events will be triggered only when you navigate between Excel document windows.

If you navigate from an Excel document window to Notepad, for example, the window deactivate event doesn't get triggered. Conversely, navigating from Notepad to an Excel document window doesn't trigger the window activate event. When you navigate to and from Notepad to a document window in Word or PowerPoint, however, the window activate and deactivate events trigger each time a document window becomes active and inactive respectively.

Word

When you switch between document windows in Word, the selection change event doesn't get triggered. Since each window in Word maintains its own selection, as in PowerPoint, the selection doesn't change when you switch between document windows. Thus, you use the window activate event to determine when the active document window has changed and, therefore, to determine what the active selection is in order to update any command bar customizations. In the following steps, the selection change event procedure is explicitly called from the window activate event so that the same code in the selection change event procedure doesn't have to be repeated in the window activate event. This example continues the scenario of updating custom command bar controls that was started with the selection change event procedure at the beginning of this chapter.

When the Window Activate
and Deactivate Events Trigger

- Navigating between Word document windows.

- Navigating between a Word document window and a window that doesn't belong to Word. When you navigate from a document window to another window such as Notepad, the window deactivate event fires for the Word document window only. When you navigate back to the Word document window, the window activate event fires.

When the Window Activate
and Deactivate Events Do *Not* Trigger

- Navigating to and from a document to a mode-less balloon displayed by the Office Assistant. If you press F1 while in Word, Excel, or PowerPoint, you see the Office Assistant with a balloon that allows you to enter a question. The balloon in this case is mode-less, because you can navigate to and from the Office Assistant's balloon without having to click anything in it.

Set Up the WindowActivate Events in Word

Before completing the following steps, complete the steps in the section "Update Your Controls Based on a Selection Change" and the Word-specific steps just after that section.

1. In the Visual Basic Editor started from Word, double-click the Class1 project item in the Project Explorer to make it the active window.

2. Click *App* from the Object drop-down list and then select *WindowActivate* from the Procedures drop-down list in the class module. In the *Window-Activate* event procedure, add the following code so that the procedure appears as follows:

```
Private Sub App_WindowActivate( _
    ByVal Doc As Document, ByVal Wn As Window)

    App_WindowSelectionChange Wn.Selection
End Sub
```

The window selection change event in Word takes one argument, the *Selection* object. In the *WindowActivate* event procedure, the *Wn* argument represents the active window. You use the Selection property on the *Wn* object to return the active selection object, which is passed to the *WindowSelectionChange* event procedure.

3. Double-click the standard code module project item, Module1, in the Project Explorer to make it the active window. Place the cursor in the procedure *InitEvents* and press F5 to run the project.

4. Switch back to Word, add some text to the document, add shapes, and change the style of some of the text to bold.

5. Click the document's content, such as the bold text, not-bold (lightface) text, or a shape.

6. Create a new document and insert some content along with more text. Format some text to bold.

7. Switch between the document windows. The selection is maintained between windows, but the WindowActivate event is called when you switch between windows, and the custom Bold button still toggles between the up and down (depressed) state and between enabled and disabled.

Excel

When you switch between document windows in Excel, the selection change event doesn't get triggered. Because in Excel each sheet in the window maintains its own selection, the selection doesn't change when you switch between document windows and sheets within a window. Thus, you use the window activate event *and* the sheet activate event to determine when the active document window and sheet have changed. With the combination of these two events, you can determine what the active selection is in order to update any command bar customizations. In the following steps, the selection change is explicitly called from the window activate and sheet activate events, so that the same code in the selection change event procedure doesn't have to be repeated in other event procedures.

When the Window Activate and Deactivate Events Trigger

- Navigating between Excel document windows.

When the Window Activate and Deactivate Events Do *Not* Trigger

- Navigating between an Excel document window and a window that doesn't belong to Excel.

- Navigating to and from a document to a mode-less balloon displayed by the Office Assistant.

Set Up the WindowActivate Events In Excel

Before completing the following steps, complete the steps in the section "Update Your Controls Based on a Selection Change" and the Excel-specific steps just after that section.

1. In the Visual Basic Editor started from Excel, double-click the Class1 project item in the Project Explorer to make it the active window.

2. Click *App* from the Object drop-down list and then select *WindowActivate* from the Procedures drop-down list in the class module. In the *WindowActivate* event procedure, add the following code so that the procedure appears as follows:

```
Private Sub App_WindowActivate( _
    ByVal Wb As Workbook, ByVal Wn As Window)

    App_SheetSelectionChange _
        Wn.ActiveSheet, Wn.Selection
End Sub
```

The window selection change event in Excel takes two arguments, the active sheet in the activated window and the *Range* object. In the *WindowActivate* event procedure, the *Wn* argument represents the active window. You use the Selection property on the *Wn* object to return the object in the active selection, which is passed to the *SheetSelectionChange* event procedure.

3. From the Procedures drop-down list in the class module, click *SheetActivate* and add the following code to the event procedure so that the procedure appears as follows:

```
Private Sub App_SheetActivate(ByVal Sh As Object)
    If TypeName(Sh) = "Worksheet" Then
    App_SheetSelectionChange _
        Sh, ActiveWindow.Selection
    End If
End Sub
```

   In the *SheetActivate* event procedure, the *Sh* argument represents the active sheet in the activated window.

4. Double-click the standard code module project item, Module1, in the Project Explorer to make it the active window. Place the cursor in the procedure *InitEvents* and press F5 to run the project.

5. Switch back to Excel, add some text to a cell, add shapes, and format the text to bold in any cell that contains text.

6. Click the workbook's content, such as the bold text, not-bold (lightface) text, or a shape.

7. Create a new workbook, and insert some content, along with more text. Format some text to bold.

8. Switch between the document windows and sheets within a window. The selection is maintained between windows and between sheets. However, the WindowActivate and the SheetActivate events are called when you switch between windows and sheets, respectively. The custom Bold button therefore toggles between the up and down (depressed) state.

PowerPoint

When you switch between document windows in PowerPoint, the selection change event procedure doesn't get triggered. Because each window in PowerPoint maintains its own selection, as in Word, the selection doesn't change when you switch between document windows. Thus, you use the window activate event procedure to determine when the active document window has changed and, therefore, to determine what the active selection is in order to update any command bar customizations. In the following steps, the selection change is explicitly called from the window activate event procedure so that the same code in the selection change event procedure doesn't have to be repeated in the window activate event procedure.

When the Window Activate and Deactivate Events Trigger

- Navigating between PowerPoint document windows.

- Navigating between a PowerPoint document window and a window that doesn't belong to PowerPoint.

When the Window Activate and Deactivate Events Do *Not* Trigger

- Switching to a Slide Show window. The window activate event doesn't get triggered when you switch to a Slide Show window, and the window deactivate event doesn't get triggered when a Slide Show window becomes inactive.

- Navigating to and from a document to a mode-less balloon displayed by the Office Assistant.

Set Up the WindowActivate Events in PowerPoint

Before completing the following steps, complete the steps in the section "Update Your Controls Based on a Selection Change" and the PowerPoint-specific steps just after that section.

1. In the Visual Basic Editor started from PowerPoint, double-click the Class1 project item in the Project Explorer to make it the active window.

2. Click *App* from the Object drop-down list, and then select *WindowActivate* from the Procedures drop-down list in the class module. In the *Window-Activate* event procedure, add the following code so that the procedure appears as follows:

```
Private Sub App_WindowActivate( _
    ByVal Pres As Presentation, _
    ByVal Wn As DocumentWindow)

    On Error GoTo Error_Handler
    App_WindowSelectionChange Wn.Selection

Error_Handler:
    Debug.Print Err.Description
End Sub
```

The window selection change event in PowerPoint takes one argument, the *Selection* object. In the *WindowActivate* event procedure, the *Wn* argument represents the active window. You use the Selection property on the *Wn* object to return the active selection object, which is passed to the *WindowSelectionChange* event procedure.

3. Double-click the standard code module project item, Module1, in the Project Explorer to make it the active window. Place the cursor in the procedure *InitEvents* and press F5 to run the project.

4. Switch back to PowerPoint, add some text to a cell, add shapes, and format the text to bold in any cell that contains text.

5. Create a new presentation and insert some content along with more text. Format some text to bold.

6. Switch between the document windows.

The selection is maintained between windows. However, the Window-Activate event is called when you switch between windows and the custom Bold button still toggles between the up and down (depressed) state and between enabled and disabled.

Advanced Scenarios

This chapter has so far discussed a common scenario in which you update your custom command bar controls based on the current selection. Because it depends on what is selected and the current view, the state of the command bars is updated constantly in each of the Office applications. With the combination of the selection change and window activate events, you can mimic the behavior of built-in command bar controls with your own control customizations.

Tracking Documents and Active Windows Using a Custom Window Menu

The Window menu contains a list of active document windows; this not only allows the user to switch between document windows, but also shows which window is the active one. A combination of events is used to update the Window menu in Word, Excel, and PowerPoint.

On the CD-ROM version of this book, the file WndMenu2.xls shows how you can use a combination of events such as window activate, window deactivate, and command bar control clicks to build your own custom window menu. Open the WndMenu2.xls file in Excel and click ALT+F11 to display the Visual Basic for Applications project for this workbook.

When the workbook WndMenu2.xls is opened, the *Workbook_Open* event procedure in the ThisWorkbook project item of the workbook is executed. The custom *Init* procedure in the Main code module is called, where the Excel event procedures are set up. The *InsertMenu* procedure is called from within the *Init* procedure and it creates the custom window menu called Window2. The *InsertMenu* procedure also sets up the button Click event for any custom command added to the Window2 menu.

As you open and close workbooks, each workbook's name is either added to or removed from the Window2 menu. When each window is activated, a check mark appears in the Window and Window2 menu adjacent to the name of the workbook that is then active. The WindowActivate and WindowDeactivate events in Excel update where the check mark appears in the custom Window2 menu.

Finally, when a custom command is clicked on the Window2 menu, the button Click event procedure within the *CmdBarEvents* event class is called. The event procedure determines which workbook should be activated and adds a check mark on the custom command that was clicked. When the workbook is closed, the *Workbook_BeforeClose* procedure in the ThisWorkbook class module is called. In this procedure, the *Uninit* procedure in the Main code module is called and the Window2 menu is deleted. The lists in the built-in Window menu and the custom Window2 menu will look identical, as the following figures reveal.

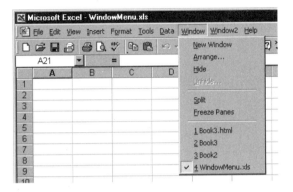

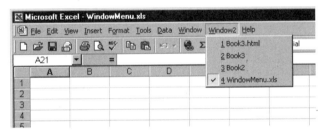

Chapter Summary

When you change the content you select in a document window, you can use the selection change event in Word, Excel, and PowerPoint to update custom menu commands and toolbar buttons. This is similar to how built-in commands and buttons are updated each time the selection changes. The Bold button on the Formatting toolbar, for example, is a command that is updated based on whether the selected text is bold or not.

You also can use the *WindowBeforeDoubleClick* and *WindowBeforeRightClick* events in Word and PowerPoint, or the *SheetBeforeDoubleClick* and *SheetBeforeRightClick* events in Excel, to cancel built-in behavior such as displaying a dialog box or shortcut menu. By canceling the built-in behavior, you can display a custom dialog box or a shortcut menu, or change the double-click or right-click behavior to a specific action that's dependent on what's clicked. Finally, by using the *WindowActivate* and *WindowDeactivate* events in combination with events such as the document Open and document Close event, you can develop programs that mimic built-in functionality, such as the Window menus in Word, Excel, and PowerPoint.

Preview of the Next Chapter

The next chapter describes how to create custom menus and toolbars. In addition, you'll learn how to create custom controls on menus and toolbars similar to built-in controls like the Zoom controls on the Standard toolbar in Word, Excel, and PowerPoint. Because the objects, methods, and properties required to create custom menus, toolbars, and controls are in the shared Microsoft Office 9.0 Object Library, the code in the next chapter can be used without modification in any Office application.

Chapter 11

Creating Menus and Toolbars

Estimated time: 90 minutes

- Add and remove new top-level menus, shortcut menus, submenus, and toolbars to any Microsoft Office 2000 application.

- Add new menu commands, toolbar buttons, and combo boxes.

- Set up event procedures that are executed when the user clicks a menu command or toolbar button, or selects a value listed in a combo box.

- Add menu and toolbar customizations similar to built-in Office functionality, such as toggling the state of a toolbar button, adding a separator bar between menu commands, or adding the Zoom control on the Standard toolbar in Microsoft Word, Microsoft Excel, or Microsoft PowerPoint.

- Find all copies of a menu command or toolbar button in the menus and toolbars set.

To use most of Microsoft Office's tools and access much of its functionality, you typically need to click an item on a menu, click a button, or make selections from a drop-down list on a toolbar. Menus and toolbars are the interfaces between you and the Office tools, just as they'll be between your users and the custom Microsoft Visual Basic for Applications programs that you develop. Internally, Office makes no distinction between menus and toolbars. Office refers to all menus, including submenus and shortcut menus, and all toolbars as *command bars*. Anything that contains a command that the user clicks or interacts with is considered a *command bar control* and it exists on a command bar. The command bar can appear as either a menu, a toolbar, or a combination of both. Menus and submenus can exist on a toolbar; buttons can exist on the menu bar.

You can modify any built-in menu bar or toolbar, and you can create and modify custom toolbars, menu bars, and shortcut menus to include in your Visual Basic application. You present the features of your application as individual buttons on toolbars or as groups of command names on menus. Because toolbars and menus are both command bars, you use the same kind of controls on both. For example, the New, Open, and Save commands on the File menu in Word, Excel, and PowerPoint are also displayed, by default, as the first three buttons on the Standard toolbar.

The *CommandBar* object model represents both menus and toolbars in all Office applications. Consequently, a toolbar or menu may be referred to as a command bar within the context of Visual Basic programming. Every toolbar and menu bar available to you in an Office application is considered a *CommandBar* object. Depending on what items you place on it, the command bar may appear as a menu bar, a toolbar, or a hybrid. You can easily reuse any code you write that accesses and manipulates menus and toolbars within Word, Excel, PowerPoint, Microsoft Access, or Microsoft Outlook, because the *Command-Bar* object model resides in the shared Microsoft Office 9.0 Object Library.

Basic Elements of Menu Items and Toolbar Buttons

Menu items, toolbar buttons, combo boxes, and edit controls on a command bar consist of two main elements:

- The group of properties (such as a caption, a tooltip, an image, or an accelerator key) specific to the menu item, button, combo box, or other control types.

- The item's response to an event, such as the user clicking the menu item or button, or changing the selected item in a drop-down list.

As might be inferred by the first element above, when you add a command bar control to a command bar, you set control properties such as caption, style, and tag. The second element of a command bar control, the response to an event that has occurred on the control, is determined by the control itself. For example, if the control is a menu item or a toolbar button, it responds to the click event. If the control is a combo box or edit control, it responds to the change event that occurs when the user selects an item in the drop-down list or enters a value in the box.

Basic Menu Item and Toolbar Button

Whether you add a simple menu item or a toolbar button, the code is the same. A menu item is just a button, but the button's caption is always displayed. In some cases, the menu item can contain an image next to the caption. When a menu item is copied onto a toolbar, the button style, by default, is set so that the user sees only the image, and not both image and caption.

Add a Simple Menu Item

The following procedure contains the most basic code you use to create a menu item. The code in the procedure can actually be written in one line, but the With...End block is used because this code could easily be extended to add more properties to the newly inserted menu item or toolbar button. This procedure works in all Office applications, because they all display a Tools menu. (In Outlook, you need to add *.ActiveExplorer* after *Application* in the first line.) To change the code so that it applies to a menu other than Tools menu, change the string "Tools" to the name of that other menu.

```
Sub InsertMenuItem()
    With Application.CommandBars("Tools").Controls.Add
        .Caption = "&Basic MenuItem"
    End With
End Sub
```

Because the item's position in the menu isn't indicated in the Controls.Add method, the procedure will add the menu item to the end of the menu. If you want to place the menu item in a specific position, you can specify the optional *Before* parameter in the *Add* method of the *CommandBarControls* collection object. The first line from the procedure above would appear as follows if you specify the *Before* parameter and set it to the integer value of 1. The menu item control will be added as the first item in the menu.

```
With Application.CommandBars("Tools") _
    .Controls.Add(Before:=1)
```

How Does the Code for a Toolbar Button Appear?

As described on the previous page, the code for a toolbar button is exactly the same as the code for a menu item. By changing the string specified as the argument in the CommandBars property from "Tools" to "Standard," the command bar control that you add will be displayed as a toolbar button at the end of the Standard toolbar in Word, Excel, or PowerPoint. In the Visual Basic Editor in Word, Excel, or PowerPoint, click Module on the Insert menu, add the following code, and run the procedure.

```
Sub InsertButton()
    With Application.CommandBars("Standard") _
        .Controls.Add(msoControlButton)

        .Caption = "&Basic Button"
    End With
End Sub
```

To execute this procedure in a standard code module in the Visual Basic Editor in Access, change the string "Standard" to "Database." Access doesn't have a toolbar named "Standard." You also need to add a reference to the Microsoft Office 9.0 Object Library. Click References on the Tools menu and select Microsoft Office 9.0 Object Library from the Available References list box.

A Menu Item's Caption Property and the Accelerator Key

The Caption property is the most commonly set property of a command bar button or command bar control. When the Caption property is set, it'll also be used, by default, as the tooltip text—if the TooltipText property of a command bar control isn't set. When you're in customize mode for command bars, the Caption property is the same as the text entered in the Name edit control. When you're in customize mode and you right-click a control, the shortcut menu will display the properties for the control. You also use the caption when directly accessing a control in the controls collection of a command bar.

Tip   If clicking a menu item will display a dialog box, you should add an ellipsis (...) to the end of the menu item's caption string. (Microsoft Windows user interface guidelines indicate that you should use an ellipsis whenever clicking a menu item displays a dialog box.) The ellipsis tells a user that the menu item displays a dialog box instead of performing an action directly. The Save As command on the File menu in any of the Office applications, for instance, contains an ellipsis in the caption string and displays the Save As dialog box. The Copy command on the Edit menu, on the other hand, doesn't contain an ellipsis and copies the contents of the current selection to the Windows clipboard. For more information about user interface guidelines, see *The Windows Interface Guidelines for Software Design* (Microsoft Press, 1995).

You also use the Caption property to set the *accelerator key* for the control. The accelerator key is the character in the caption that's underlined when it's displayed on a menu or toolbar. When the user presses the ALT key plus the underlined character (the accelerator key), the focus is moved to that control. It's important to set the accelerator key so it can be employed by users who do not or cannot use a mouse. To set the accelerator key, in the caption string you need to include an ampersand (&) immediately preceding the character you want to set as the accelerator key for the control. In the procedure on the previous page (the one that inserted a menu item on the Tools menu), the first capital "B" is designated as the accelerator key.

Note   Assigning a distinct accelerator in the caption for a menu command in a built-in menu, such as the Tools menu in each Office application, often is not possible. For example, if you create a custom menu command on the Tools menu in Word with the caption "New Menu Item" and you assign the accelerator to the letter "N," you will have assigned the same accelerator as that in the caption of the Online Collaboration command. If there are more than one of the same accelerator values in a menu, pressing the accelerator multiple times will cycle through the menu items. You then have to press ENTER once you've found the menu item you're interested in.

Although command bars exhibit the ability to create custom menus and toolbars and add common controls such as buttons and combo boxes, there are a number of controls you can't add and some functionality you can't replicate. One common functionality you can't replicate is a shortcut key. Shortcut keys are used throughout Office and Windows, as shown in the following figure. Common built-in shortcut keys are CTRL+C to copy a selection (equivalent to clicking the Copy command on the Edit menu), CTRL+V to paste contents from the Windows clipboard, and CTRL+S to save the active document.

Quick Guide: Setting Up the Button Click Event

Once you've created the user interface elements, you need to provide a *hook* that connects a command bar control such as a toolbar button, menu item, or drop-down list to code that is executed when the user clicks or selects an item in the control. The following four steps explain what you need to do to connect a custom button on the Standard toolbar with an event procedure containing code that is executed when the button is clicked.

1. Add the following procedure to a standard code module and add the declaration to the top of the same code module:

```
Dim CmdBarEvents As New Class1

Sub InsertButtonAndConnectEvent()
    Dim ctlBtn As Office.CommandBarButton
    Set ctlBtn = CommandBars("Standard").Controls.Add
    With ctlBtn
        .Caption = "&Custom Button"
        .FaceId = 2950
        .Tag = "BrButton"
        Set CmdBarEvents.BtnCtrl = ctlBtn
    End With
End Sub
```

If you try to run this procedure, you'll get an error on the Set statement, or the last line in the procedure. If you just want to add a button on a toolbar, you should comment out the Set statement line of code by adding an apostrophe (') at the beginning of the line. The last line in the procedure, the Set statement, will be used to connect the click event of the button to a Click event procedure. You set up the Click event procedure after the first step.

2. Insert a new class module. By default, the name will be Class1.

```
Public WithEvents BtnCtrl As Office.CommandBarButton

Private Sub BtnCtrl_Click(ByVal Ctrl As _
    Office.CommandBarButton, CancelDefault As Boolean)
    MsgBox Ctrl.Caption & " was clicked"
End Sub
```

3. Remove the apostrophe (if one was added in step 1) and run the procedure *InsertButtonAndConnectEvent*.

4. Switch to the Office application and click the custom button.

(continued)

Quick Guide: Setting Up the Button Click Event *(continued)*

At the top of the Class1 class module, you declare with events the variable *BtnCtrl* as a *CommandBarButton*. Using the *WithEvents* keyword of the Visual Basic for Applications language in a class module indicates that the *BtnCtrl* object variable will be used to respond to events triggered by a button. A *CommandBarButton* control in Office has only one event—a Click event, which is used when the user clicks a toolbar button or menu command.

At the top of the standard code module where you added the procedure for inserting the control (in step 1), you added the declaration line `Dim CmdBarEvents As New Class1`. The variable *CmdBarEvents* declares a new instance of the class Class1, which contains the event procedure for the command bar control you've declared with events. The declaration also ties in the line `Set CmdBarEvents.BtnCtrl = ctlBtn`, added at the end of the procedure in step 1. When you click the custom button, the code in the *BtnCtrl_Click* procedure (added in step 2) executes.

Responding to CommandBar Events

When the user clicks a menu item or toolbar button or selects an item from a drop-down list on a toolbar, specific code is executed, depending on the control, in order to respond to the event. An *event* is something that takes place, such as a click or a change, that causes an object to react. In the case of menus and toolbars, the Click event is triggered when the user clicks a menu item or toolbar button, and the Change event is triggered when the user selects an item in a drop-down list or changes the text in an edit control. You write code that connects to these events and processes them in one way or another.

The Click and Change events are new members of the *CommandBar* object model in Microsoft Office 2000. Events allow you to connect an event procedure to an action, such as a click on a command bar button or a change in the item selected in a drop-down list. Because most menu and toolbar controls are buttons (whether they display both an image and text, or text or an image only), the Click event on the *CommandBarButton* object is the most common event. In a Click event procedure, you commonly place code that displays a custom dialog box when a command bar button is clicked.

The Change event on the *CommandBarComboBox* object is the next most common event. In addition to a menu item or toolbar button, you'll commonly see drop-down list or combo box controls in the toolbar set. These controls can take the form of an edit list, a combo box, or just a drop-down list. On the Standard toolbar in Word, Excel, and PowerPoint, you'll find the *Zoom* control, while on the Formatting toolbar you'll find the Font and Font Size combo boxes.

> **Note** The third and final addition to the *CommandBar* object model events in Office 2000 is the OnUpdate event, which is used less frequently. It fires whenever there's an update to some part of the *CommandBar* object model. The Office application could fire this event a lot.

Setting the Tag Property

Before setting up the event procedure, you also need to set the Tag property on the custom command to a unique string you define. In the Quick Guide "Setting Up the Button Click Event" at the beginning of this chapter, you set the Tag property to "BrButton." Setting the Tag property ensures that no matter how many copies of a custom control exist in a command bar set, the Click or Change event procedure will always be executed. As long as your code connects to one copy of the custom control, Office uses the Tag property to uniquely identify the control and connect the control to the appropriate event procedure.

For example, after your code creates a custom menu command with the Tag property set to a unique string you've defined, the user can click Customize on the Tools menu so that the Office application is in Command Bar Customize mode. Holding the CTRL key, the user can copy your custom control to another menu or toolbar. Because the Tag property uniquely identifies all copies of the control, setting up an event procedure to just one copy of the control ensures the event procedure is always executed, no matter which copy of the control is clicked or changed.

> **Note** Setting the Tag property is important when the custom command is created in Word. A unique Tag property ensures that the event procedure will always be executed. However, if more than one document window is displayed in Word and if the Tag property is not assigned a unique string, the Click event procedure, in particular, may not be called.

The Tag property is also useful when you want to search for all copies of a custom menu command or toolbar button or any other command bar control you can add through code. The last section of this chapter discusses how to use the *FindControls* method and why the Tag property is important when using the *FindControls* method.

Canceling Existing Built-In Command Behavior

You can cancel the built-in behavior of a command like the Open command on the File menu and bring up your own dialog box. The Open command is in two places in the command bar set in Word, Excel, PowerPoint, and Access. You can connect to just one copy of the Open command and always get the event no matter which command the user clicked. This is the same way custom commands behave. That is, Office uses the built-in Id property of the command to sink an event. Then no matter where the button is clicked, if it has the associated Id, Office will execute the command's event sink. By setting the *CancelDefault* argument passed into the Click event procedure to True, you cancel a built-in command's default behavior. To do this, follow the steps below.

1. Add the following procedure to a standard code module and add the declaration to the top of the same code module.

```
Dim CmdBarEvents As New Class1


Sub OverrideButton()
    Dim ctlBtn As Office.CommandBarButton
    Set ctlBtn = _
        CommandBars("File").FindControl(Id:=23)
    Set CmdBarEvents.OpenBtnCtrl = ctlBtn
End Sub
```

The *FindControl* method (not to be confused with the *FindControls* method, described at the end of this chapter) returns a control that fits the search criteria. In this case, the search criteria passed into the *FindControl* method is set to find the control with the built-in identifier value of 23. This represents the Open control.

Note   To determine the Id of a control in the command bar set in an Office application, type code with the following syntax in the Immediate window in the application's Visual Basic Editor:

```
?Application.CommandBars("File").Controls("Open").Id
```

This code may generate an error. In some cases, you have to use "&Open..." as the argument passed for the index in the Controls property; this depends in which application you run the code. If you change the word "File" to "Standard," the code works correctly as is. To avoid this confusion, use the *FindControl* method and pass the Id of the control.

---

2. Insert a new class module and add the following code. Make sure you enter the declaration of the public-level variable *OpenBtnCtrl* at the top of the class module.

```
Public WithEvents OpenBtnCtrl As _
    Office.CommandBarButton


Private Sub OpenBtnCtrl_Click(ByVal Ctrl As _
    Office.CommandBarButton, CancelDefault As Boolean)
    CancelDefault = True
    MsgBox Ctrl.Caption & " was cancelled"
End Sub
```

If you are inserting this code in one of the examples listed earlier in this chapter, the default name of the inserted class module will be Class2. You need to ensure that the name of this class module is the same as the data type name in the *CmdBarEvents* variable declaration entered in step 1. For example, if the inserted class module is named Class2, change the declaration entered in step 1 to:

```
Dim CmdBarEvents As New Class2
```

3. Run the procedure *OverrideButton*, switch to the Office application, and click the Open button on the File menu or the Standard toolbar.

When you click the Open command on the File menu in Word, Excel, or PowerPoint, you see the Open dialog box. However, in the event procedure added in step 3, you set CancelDefault to True. Clicking the Open button on the File menu or Standard toolbar therefore will first display the message box "&Open was cancelled" and then nothing else happens; the Open dialog box isn't displayed. To prevent the event procedure from executing and canceling the built-in behavior of the Open command, switch to the Visual Basic Editor and click Reset on the Run menu.

Adding and Removing Custom Menus and Toolbars

Sometimes your solution requires a set of custom menu commands. Adding a set of custom commands to an existing menu may expand the menu so much that it contains too many items. Introducing a new menu may be a good alternative. The Microsoft Office 9.0 Object Library provides an object model that allows you to manipulate any of the menus or toolbars provided by an Office application and to add custom menus and toolbars.

Creating your own toolbars by using Microsoft Visual Basic allows you to add elements to the user interface that, in turn, allow your customers to access the functionality in your programs. For example, if you develop a wizard that guides a user through the process of creating a specific type of Word document, you'll want to add a toolbar button or menu item that, when clicked, displays the custom wizard.

Note   The naming convention used in this chapter and throughout the rest of this book for command bar variables and command bar control variables is the following:

Command bar = *cmbX*
Command bar control = *ctlY*

X and *Y* represent names that indicate what each control variable represents.

The Quick Guide on the next page provides a quick reference to creating the most common elements of a command bar set. These include adding a new menu, a submenu, a shortcut menu, a menu item, and a toolbar. The Quick Guide also describes how to write code to remove a toolbar. The section "Creating a Toolbar, Step by Step" later in this chapter explains the details of adding a new toolbar.

Quick Guide: Before You Start

As you experiment with adding new controls and menus to existing toolbars and menu bars, you can quickly reset built-in menus and toolbars or delete custom menus and toolbars. To reset a menu bar, in the Immediate window in the Visual Basic Editor, type the following line of code and press ENTER. Change the string to "Worksheet Menu Bar" when running the code in the Immediate window through Excel's Visual Basic Editor. Because the following line of code executes a method, the question mark (?) is not required before the beginning of the line.

```
Application.CommandBars("Menu Bar").Reset
```

If you want to reset just one menu on the menu bar, type the following line of code in the Immediate window and press ENTER. Change the string from "Tools" (or any other menu) to "Standard" (or any other toolbar) to reset a toolbar.

```
Application.CommandBars("Tools").Reset
```

To delete a custom menu or toolbar, type the following line of code in the Immediate window and press ENTER. Change the string from "MyMenu" to the name of a custom menu or toolbar you've created by using code already given in this chapter.

```
Application.CommandBars("MyMenu").Delete
```

Iterate Through the Command Bars Collection

The following procedure reveals two ways of iterating through a command bar collection. The first uses a For Each...Next loop, and the second uses a regular For...Next loop. In the Visual Basic Editor in any Office application, click Module on the Insert menu, add the following code, and run the procedure. The procedure provides two different For...Next loops to iterate through the CommandBars collection object and print the name of each command bar to the Immediate window. You can use this procedure to determine if a specific command bar exists in the collection.

```
Sub IterateCommandBarCollection()
    ' For Each...Next loop
    Dim cmbItem As CommandBar
    For Each cmbItem In Application.CommandBars
        Debug.Print cmbItem.Name
    Next cmbItem
' OR
    'For...Next loop
    Dim i As Integer
```

```
    For i = 1 To Application.CommandBars.Count
        Debug.Print Application.CommandBars(i).Name
    Next i
End Sub
```

Add a Menu

To create a custom menu on the menu bar alongside the built-in menus in Word, Excel, PowerPoint, and other programs, you need to add a pop-up command bar control on the menu bar. The following procedure adds a new menu in between the File and Edit menus. But you can add menus to any toolbar, not just the main menu bar. If you change the string "Menu Bar" in the CommandBars property to "Standard," the new menu appears on the Standard toolbar with a drop-down arrow at the side of the caption. The Draw menu on the Drawing toolbar in Word, Excel, or PowerPoint is an example of a menu located on a toolbar.

Note When running the following code in Excel, change the string "Menu Bar" to "Worksheet Menu Bar" in the CommandBars property:

```
Set cmbNewMenu = Application _
    .CommandBars("Worksheet Menu Bar")
```

In Outlook, you access the *CommandBars* collection through an Explorer or Inspector object:

```
Set cmbNewMenu = Application _
    .ActiveExplorer.CommandBars("Menu Bar")
```

An *Explorer* object is the window where you see folders such as the Inbox, Sent Items, and Deleted Items. An *Inspector* object is a window where you see items such as e-mail messages, meeting requests, and contact information.

In the Visual Basic Editor in any Office application, click Module on the Insert menu, add the following code, and run the procedure. To run the procedure in Excel or Outlook, make sure you change the code as indicated in the previous note. The procedure produces a custom menu with the caption "NewMenu" and two menu items.

```
Sub InsertMenu()
    Dim cmbNewMenu As CommandBar
    Dim ctlPopup As CommandBarPopup

    Set cmbNewMenu = Application.CommandBars("Menu Bar")
    With cmbNewMenu.Controls
        Set ctlPopup = .Add(Type:=msoControlPopup, _
            Before:=2)
        With ctlPopup
            .Caption = "&NewMenu"
            With .Controls.Add
                .Caption = "&Item 1"
            End With
```

```
            With .Controls.Add
                .Caption =  "&Item 2"
            End With
        End With
    End With
End Sub
```

Your new menu should appear as follows:

The Menu Bar, which is itself represented by a CommandBar object, contains a *Controls* collection object that represents all of the pop-up menus, including File, Edit, View, Insert, and so on. The Set ctlPopup statement near the bottom of the previous page adds a new pop-up control to the Menu Bar command.

The *Before* argument of the *Add* method of the *Controls* collection object indicates the index position within the *Controls* collection where the menu is to be placed. In this case, a value of "2" places the new menu to the right of the File menu. To change the position of the new menu, change the integer value set to the *Before* argument. The *Before* argument is optional, so if the *Before* argument isn't specified, the new menu is added to the end of the menu (after the Help menu). In this case, the Set ctlPopup statement on the previous page would appear as:

```
Set ctlPopup = .Add(Type:=msoControlPopup)
```

Add a Submenu

Adding a submenu is the same as creating a menu on the main menu bar. Examples of a submenu are the Macro submenu on the Tools menu and the Toolbars submenu on the View menu in all Office applications. To create a submenu, just change the string "Menu Bar" in the CommandBars property to any menu that exists on the menu bar or some other command bar. For example, if you change "Menu Bar" to "Tools," you create a submenu named "New Menu" containing the submenu at the second position of the Tools menu.

```
Sub InsertSubmenu()
    Dim cmbMenu As CommandBar
    Dim ctlPopup As CommandBarPopup

    Set cmbMenu = Application.CommandBars("Tools")
    Set ctlPopup = cmbMenu.Controls _
        .Add(Type:=msoControlPopup)
    With ctlPopup
        .Caption = "&Submenu"
        With .Controls.Add
            .Caption = "Su&bmenuItem 1"
        End With
```

```
        With .Controls.Add
            .Caption = "S&ubmenuItem 2"
        End With
    End With
End Sub
```

Your new submenu should appear as follows:

You should note that you can't create a "tear-off" submenu. An example of a tear-off menu is the AutoText submenu on the Insert menu in Word. It contains a small title bar that you can click and drag to create a floating or docked toolbar.

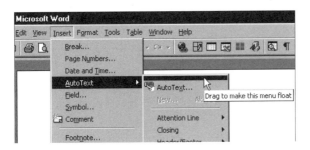

Add a Shortcut Menu

The following procedure inserts a new shortcut menu named NewShortcut. Like any menu, you can add any number of menu items that are of the command bar control type *msoControlButton*. In the Visual Basic Editor in any Office application, click Module on the Insert menu, add the following code, and run the procedure.

```
Sub InsertShortcutMenu()
    Dim cmbNewShortcut As CommandBar

    Set cmbNewShortcut = Application.CommandBars.Add( _
        Name:="NewShortcut", Position:=msoBarPopup)
    With cmbNewShortcut.Controls
        With .Add
            .Caption = "&ShortcutItem 1"
        End With
        With .Add
            .Caption = "&ShortcutItem 2"
        End With
    End With
End Sub
```

You use the *ShowPopup* method to display shortcut menus. In the same code module where you typed the *InsertShortcutMenu* procedure, add the following code and run the *DisplayPopup* procedure. The shortcut menu NewShortcut, containing two items, is displayed wherever the mouse pointer is located on screen. If you switch back to the Office application, press ALT+F8 to display the Macros dialog box, and click DisplayPopup, the shortcut menu appears on top of the Office application window.

```
Sub DisplayPopup()
    Application.CommandBars("NewShortcut").ShowPopup
End Sub
```

You can display a shortcut menu in response to a right-click event in Word, Excel, or PowerPoint. Word, Excel, and PowerPoint all support assigning an event procedure to the user action of right-clicking in any document. Chapter 10 describes how to set up the right-click event in Word, Excel, and PowerPoint.

To quickly delete the shortcut menu created by the procedure *Insert-ShortcutMenu,* type the following line of code in the Immediate window and press ENTER. Because the following line of code executes a method, the question mark (?) is not required before the beginning of the line.

```
Application.CommandBars("NewShortcut").Delete
```

Add a Menu Item

Although adding a menu item is discussed at the beginning of this chapter, the procedure below is given for the sake of completeness to explain how to insert a new menu item at the top of the Tools menu. You'll set the menu item's style to display both the icon and caption—although not all menu items have or require an icon. The FaceId property sets the icon, and the value of 2950 isn't used by any built-in controls in Office, but reserved for custom use. In most cases, a FaceId value won't be set and an icon image won't be added to the control. The section later in this chapter entitled "Add an Image to a Control" describes more details and issues about adding images to command bar controls.

```
Sub InsertMenuItem()
    With Application.CommandBars("Tools") _
        .Controls.Add(Type:=msoControlButton, _
            Before:=1)
        .FaceId = 2950
        .Caption = "&MenuItem"
        .Tag = "MyCustomTag"
        .Style = msoButtonIconAndCaption
    End With
End Sub
```

Add a Toolbar

To create a custom toolbar like the Standard or Formatting toolbar in Word, Excel, PowerPoint, or Outlook, you need to add a command bar to the *CommandBars* collection. The following procedure adds a new custom command bar and positions (or *docks)* the command bar below the Standard and Formatting toolbars. You add only one control, as specified in the With...End With block. You can add any number of controls to the new command bar by adding more Set statements that add controls to the command bar, and adding a With...End With block that sets the properties of the new controls.

```
Sub InsertToolBar()
    Dim cmbNewBar As CommandBar
    Dim ctlBtn As CommandBarButton

    Set cmbNewBar = CommandBars.Add(Name:="NewBar")
    With cmbNewBar
        Set ctlBtn = .Controls.Add
        With ctlBtn
            .Style = msoButtonIconAndCaption
            .BeginGroup = True
            .Caption = "&Button"
            .TooltipText = "ToolTip"
            .FaceId = 59
        End With
        .Protection = msoBarNoCustomize
        .Position = msoBarTop
        .Visible = True
    End With
End Sub
```

Your new toolbar should appear as follows:

Remove a Command Bar

The easiest way to remove your toolbar with Visual Basic code is to add this line of code to a procedure: `Application.CommandBars("NewBar").Delete`, and then execute the procedure. However, if the toolbar doesn't exist, an error results when the line is executed. In order to ensure that the toolbar is deleted if it exists and that no error arises if it does not, you can write code in one of two ways. (You can also include both methods.)

Remove a Command Bar by Trapping Errors

The following procedure traps the error that's generated when a line of code attempts to delete a command bar that doesn't exist. The first line in the procedure indicates that if an error occurs, execution of the procedure should skip to the line starting with the word "Error_Handler." (You can change the text "Error_Handler" to anything you want, as long as the colon (:) appears at the end of the line. If you do change the text, make sure to do so in both places in the procedure.) If no error occurs when the *Delete* method is executed, the procedure is exited. If the Exit Sub line didn't exist, execution of the procedure's lines of code would continue into the Error_Handler, even if no error occurred.

```
Sub DeleteCommandBarByErrorTrapping()
    On Error GoTo Error_Handler
    Application.CommandBars("NewBar").Delete
    Exit Sub

Error_Handler:
    ' command bar does not exist
    ' Debug.Print Err.Description
End Sub
```

Remove a Command Bar by Iteration

To delete a command bar if it exists and ensure that no error arises if it doesn't exist, you can use a For Each...Next loop to iterate through the command bars in the *CommandBars* collection. In the procedure below, the If...Then statement within the For Each...Next loop evaluates the name of each existing command bar. If the name of any command bar in the collection matches the name of your new command bar, the procedure deletes the first command bar and exits the loop.

Because the name of a command bar is unique within the *CommandBars* collection, only one command bar with the name you want to delete will exist. Exiting the loop after the command bar is deleted improves the performance of your code, because the loop doesn't need to continue looping through the collection. The only exception is in Word, where two command bars with the same name can exist; thus, you should remove the Exit For line from the procedure.

```
Sub DeleteCommandBarByIteration()
    Dim cmbItem As CommandBar
    For Each cmbItem In Application.CommandBars
        If cmbItem.Name = "NewBar" Then
            cmbItem.Delete
            Exit For
        End If
    Next cmbItem
End Sub
```

Creating a Toolbar, Step by Step

Each Office application provides a collection of toolbars, and each toolbar helps you perform a set of common functions. For example, the Formatting toolbar consists of a set of buttons and drop-down lists that help you format text in your document, worksheet, or slide. You'll see the list of toolbars available in any particular Office application in the Toolbars tab of the Customize dialog box.

To access the Customize dialog box, on the Tools menu in any Office application, click Customize; or, on the View menu in Word, Excel, PowerPoint, or Access, point to Toolbars and then click Customize on the submenu. You can also right-click any toolbar and then click Customize on the shortcut menu. The Toolbars list displays all available toolbars, and the check box beside each item indicates whether or not that toolbar is visible.

Customize a Toolbar

1. Start Word, Excel, or PowerPoint, open the Visual Basic Editor, and insert a new, standard code module.

2. In the code module, type **Sub InsertToolbarStepByStep** and press ENTER.

3. Type the following declaration lines in the procedure:

```
Dim cmbNewBar As CommandBar
Dim ctlBtn As CommandBarButton
```

You're declaring the object variable *cmbNewBar* as the object type CommandBar. (Every toolbar and menu bar available to you in an Office application is considered a CommandBar object. Depending on what items you place on the command bar, it may appear as a menu bar, a toolbar, or a hybrid.) The second declaration is for a button control you're going to add to the newly created command bar.

4. Add a command bar by typing the following line after the declaration of cmbNewBar and ctlBtn:

```
Set cmbNewBar = Application.CommandBars.Add
```

Each Application object in any Office application except Outlook provides access to the *CommandBars* collection object. The *CommandBars* collection object allows you to add a command bar to, or access an individual command bar from, the collection. In this case, the *Add* method of the *CommandBars* collection object returns a CommandBar object, which you assign to the object variable *cmbNewBar*.

5. Below the Set statement in which you added a new CommandBar object to the collection, add the following line to name the newly created command bar:

```
cmbNewBar.Name = "My CommandBar"
```

Each newly created CommandBar object is given a default name. Before you assign a name to a new command bar, the name appears with the syntax "Custom *number*," where *number* represents the next available integer. (The name of a floating command bar is the name that appears on its title bar; a *floating* command bar isn't docked to any side of an application window.) The name of a command bar also appears in the Toolbars list in the Toolbars tab of the Customize dialog box.

6. To add a button to your custom command bar, add the following With...End block below the name assignment line:

```
With cmbNewBar
    Set ctlBtn = .Controls.Add(msoControlButton)
End With
```

Each CommandBar object contains a Controls collection object that represents all of the buttons, drop-down lists, pop-up menus, and other controls available on the command bar. When you create a command bar, however, no controls yet exist in the Controls collection: the Set statement above adds a button control. Note that the *Add* method of the Controls collection object accepts up to five parameters, with the first one representing the type of control to add. You can specify the types of parameter to be *msoControlButton, msoControlEdit, msoControlDropdown, msoControlComboBox,* or *msoControlPopup*.

7. Set the properties of the newly created button by adding the following With...End block just after the Set statement that adds a new button control to the Controls collection object:

```
With ctlBtn
    .Style = msoButtonIconAndCaption
    .BeginGroup = True
    .Caption = "&Button"
    .FaceId = 59
    .TooltipText = "ToolTip"
End With
```

You can set a number of properties for a button on a command bar, but you have already set five of the main ones. The first is the button style, which allows you to represent a button as a combination of an icon and a caption (to the right of the icon), or an icon or a caption alone. To change the style of either of the latter choices, assign to the Style property the value msoButtonIcon or msoButtonCaption, respectively.

Because you've specified both an icon and a caption in the above procedure, both the Caption property and the FaceId property are set. More than 1,000 face Ids are built into Office. Most of them are the buttons on the toolbars that you see in the application window (such as New, Save, or Print). You use the TooltipText property to set the text of the ToolTip that appears when the mouse is over the button on the command bar.

8. Add the following lines to the procedure, just after the `End With` line of the With...End block added in the previous step:

```
.Protection = msoBarNoCustomize
.Position = msoBarTop
.Visible = True
```

The Protection property is set to the constant msoBarNoCustomize, indicating that the command bar is protected from user customization. The Protection property can be set to be one or more of the MsoBar-Protection constants. When the constant msoBarNoCustomize is assigned to the command bar, the user can neither add nor remove a command bar control to or from the command bar.

You can explicitly set the position of a command bar by using the Position property. You can set the Position property to one of the five values in the enumeration MsoBarPosition. Setting the property to msoBarTop docks the command bar at the top of the document window, while msoBarLeft, msoBarRight, and msoBarBottom dock the command bar at the left, right, and bottom, respectively. The Position property is set to the enumeration value msoBarFloating by default.

When you add a new command bar, you can also set its position. Note that the *Add* method of the CommandBars collection contains the optional *Position* parameter. However, if you don't specify the *Position* parameter in the *Add* method or explicitly set the Position property, a newly added command bar floats. Also note you can't use the enumeration value msoBarPopup to set the Position property. You can use it only when you add a command bar first. (If you specify the *Position* parameter in the *Add* method of the CommandBars collection as *msoBarPopup*, the command bar is added as a context menu.)

When you add a command bar, it's not visible by default; you have to explicitly set the command bar to Visible. The last line in the procedure above does so. The complete procedure for adding a command bar is as follows:

```
Sub InsertToolBarStepByStep()
    Dim cmbNewBar As CommandBar
    Dim ctlBtn As CommandBarButton

    Set cmbNewBar = Application.CommandBars.Add
    cmbNewBar.Name = "My CommandBar"
    With cmbNewBar
        Set ctlBtn = .Controls.Add(msoControlButton)
        With ctlBtn
            .Style = msoButtonIconAndCaption
            .BeginGroup = True
```

```
                .Caption = "&Button"
                .TooltipText = "ToolTip"
                .FaceId = 59
            End With
            .Protection = msoBarNoCustomize
            .Position = msoBarTop
            .Visible = True
        End With
End Sub
```

9. Place the cursor in the procedure and press F5.

The final toolbar should look like the following graphic, containing just one button displaying an icon and a caption. When you move the cursor over the button, you see the ToolTip.

Adding Customizations
Similar to Built-In Controls

If you've used any of the Office applications, you've noticed a wide array of controls on the toolbars. Besides the basic buttons and menus, you see controls such as an edit combo box like the *Zoom* control and a split button pop-up like the *Font Color* control on the Formatting toolbar. You can use the Type property on the *CommandBarControl* object to determine the type of a control. The Type property returns an MsoControlType constant. The following table shows a summary of the types of controls you can create.

Control type	Control
msoControlButton	
msoControlComboBox	
msoControlDropdown	

(continued)

(continued)

Control type	Control
msoControlEdit	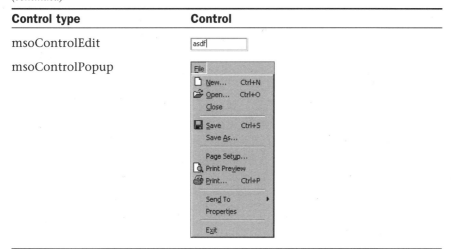
msoControlPopup	

If the control type doesn't appear in the list, you unfortunately can't create it. For example, you can't create the control type msoControlSplitButton, even though it appears several times across the Office applications. You can't create the Font Color split button control (shown here) on the Formatting toolbar in Word, Excel, and PowerPoint, either.

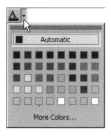

Quick Guide: Before You Add Customizations

The examples in this section modify built-in menus and toolbars. The following lines of code are similar to the code to reset a menu or toolbar, also seen under the heading "Adding and Removing Custom Menus and Toolbars" in the Quick Guide, "Before You Start."

To reset a menu or toolbar to the default setting defined by the Office application, type the following line of code in the Immediate window and press ENTER.

```
Application.CommandBars("Tools").Reset
```

This line is useful if you know a menu or toolbar doesn't have any customizations from another add-in. After you test your code to ensure that your command bar customizations were made correctly, the line of code above quickly resets the state of the command bar.

(continued)

To delete a specific control from a menu or toolbar, type the following line of code in the Immediate window and press ENTER.

```
Application.CommandBars("Tools") _
    .Controls("CaptionOfMenuItem").Delete
```

Add Controls After a Separator Bar

In any menu or toolbar in the Office applications, a separator bar exists between both groups of menu items and groups of buttons. The separator bar is used to logically group menu items or toolbar buttons that are, in most cases, functionally related. For example, on the Edit menu, Cut, Copy, Paste, and Paste Special are grouped between two separator bars. You can display a separator bar between any two menu items or toolbar controls (including buttons, drop-down lists, edit controls, and so forth) by using the BeginGroup property. This property is found on the *CommandBarButton, CommandBarCombobox,* and *CommandBarControl* objects.

In the Visual Basic Editor in any Office application, click Module on the Insert menu, add the following code, and run the procedure. The procedure adds a new menu item to the File menu. The new menu item, with the caption "After Separator," is listed as the fourth item from the top in the File menu, and a separator bar is added before the item. For this procedure to work in Outlook, you need to add `ActiveExplorer.` before `CommandBars` in the following code:

```
Sub InsertControlAfterSeparator()
    With CommandBars("File").Controls
        .Item(4).BeginGroup = False
        With .Add(Before:=4)
            .Caption = "&After Separator"
            .BeginGroup = True
        End With
    End With
End Sub
```

In Word, Excel, and PowerPoint, the File menu appears as seen in the following graphic.

You can set the BeginGroup property on any command bar control, no matter where it's located, unless the control is at the beginning of a toolbar, where the drag handles are, or at the top of a menu. Consequently, the separator bar is not a control but just a property of the control directly below it. If you wanted a new control to appear below a particular separator bar, you'd first have to do the following:

1. Set to False the BeginGroup property of the control directly under the current separator bar.

2. Add your custom control, as in the procedure on the previous page.

3. Set the BeginGroup property to True on the control you added.

In this procedure, before the new menu item is added to the fourth position on the File menu, the BeginGroup property of the menu item that currently exists in the fourth position is set to False. In Word, Excel, and PowerPoint, the Save menu item exists in the fourth position on the File menu.

Toggle the Caption and State of a Button

When you add and select different shapes from the Drawing toolbar in Word, Excel, and PowerPoint, both the caption of the last item on the Format menu in Word and PowerPoint and the first item on the Format menu in Excel change, depending on the type of shape selected. The caption cycles between Format Object, Format AutoShape, and Format Picture, among others. Similarly, depending on the selection, you may style the text contents of a selection to be bold, italics, or underline. If you apply one of these formats to the selection's text, the respective Bold, Italics, or Underline button on the Formatting toolbar in Word, Excel, and PowerPoint changes to a depressed state—that is, it toggles. The following procedure mimics these buttons by toggling the state of the button, as well as toggling the caption.

1. In the Visual Basic Editor in Word, Excel, or PowerPoint, insert a new class module and set its name to CmdBarToggleEvent in the Properties window. At the top of the class module, add the following declaration; add the procedure anywhere in the class module.

```
Public WithEvents CmdTgglCtrl As Office.CommandBarButton

Private Sub CmdTgglCtrl_Click(ByVal Ctrl As _
    Office.CommandBarButton, CancelDefault As Boolean)
    If Ctrl.State = msoButtonDown Then
        Ctrl.State = msoButtonUp
        Ctrl.Caption = "Button Up"
        ' do something when button is up
    Else
        Ctrl.State = msoButtonDown
        Ctrl.Caption = "Button Down"
        ' do something when button is depressed
    End If
End Sub
```

2. Add the following procedure to a standard code module. Make sure the declaration below is added to the top of the standard code module.

```
Dim ToggleEvent As New CmdBarToggleEvent


Sub InsertToggleButton()
    Dim ctlBtn As CommandBarButton
    Set ctlBtn = CommandBars("Standard") _
        .Controls.Add(msoControlButton)
    With ctlBtn
        .Caption = "Button Up"
        .State = msoButtonUp
        .Tag = "tgglButton"
        .Style = msoButtonCaption
    End With
    Set ToggleEvent.CmdTgglCtrl = ctlBtn
End Sub
```

3. Run the procedure InsertToggleButton, switch back to the application, and click the button with the caption "Button Up" on the Standard toolbar.

Keep clicking the button, and you'll see the state of the button toggle between the down and up states, while the caption also toggles between the strings "Button Up" and "Button Down."

If you don't want to do anything besides toggle the state of the control, you can just add the following line of code. This code uses the Visual Basic for Applications keyword *Not* to flip the value of the State property of the control. If the State property equals msoButtonDown, it has the integer value of -1. If the State value is msoButtonUp, it has the integer value of 0. The *Not* keyword will flip a value of 0 to a value of -1 (and vice-versa) and a value of True to a value of False (and vice-versa).

```
Ctrl.State = Not Ctrl.State
```

Create a Menu Item with a Check Mark

You also can create menu items that have a check mark next to them. You can do this only for menu items that don't have an icon image. Examples of built-in controls that have a check mark next to them when clicked are the Window menus in Word, Excel, and PowerPoint, and the Ruler command in Word. The steps and code to create a menu item with a check mark are identical to the steps and code in the previous section.

However, instead of adding the custom button control to the Standard toolbar, change the string "Standard" to "Tools." Click the custom control with the caption "Button Up" at the bottom of the Tools menu. The caption of the menu item will change and a check mark will appear and disappear as the menu item is clicked, as shown in the figure on the following page. The check mark is equivalent to the down state (msoButtonDown) of a button on a toolbar, and the absence of a check mark is equivalent to the up state (msoButtonUp) of a button on a toolbar.

Insert a Combo Box Like the Zoom Control

You find a *Zoom* control on the Standard toolbar in Word, Excel, and PowerPoint, and you'll probably find it on most productivity software applications. The *Zoom* control lets the user enlarge or shrink the content on the screen. It also allows the user to choose between a list of predefined magnifications or to type in a custom magnification. In most applications that support a *Zoom* control, if you enter a magnification that the application can't support, the application will either display an alert indicating that the entered value is out of range, or just set the magnification to the closest supported value.

In Word, in Print Layout view, if you enter a value greater than 500% in the *Zoom* control on the Standard toolbar, you get an alert indicating that you can enter only values between 10% and 500%. In PowerPoint, on the other hand, if you specify a magnification value of greater than 400% (its upper limit), PowerPoint automatically sets the value of the control to the highest supported value (400%). At the other end of the scale, if the magnification value is smaller than the supported lower limit, PowerPoint sets the magnification to the lowest supported value (10%).

The following code inserts a combo box control at the end of the Standard toolbar. Six predefined values are added to the list in the combo box. If you add the control as type msoControlComboBox, the user can select from the list of items in the drop-down portion of the combo box, or enter a custom value in the edit portion of the combo box. The second procedure in this code handles the event that occurs when the value of the combo box changes.

1. In the Visual Basic Editor in Word, Excel, or PowerPoint, in a standard code module, add the following procedure:

```
Sub InsertComboBox()
    Dim ctlCombo As CommandBarComboBox
    Set ctlCombo = CommandBars("Standard") _
        .Controls.Add(msoControlComboBox)
    With ctlCombo
        .AddItem "50%"
        .AddItem "60%"
        .AddItem "66%"
```

```
                    .AddItem "75%"
                    .AddItem "85%"
                    .AddItem "100%"
                    .Caption = "Size"
                    .DropDownWidth = 52
                    .ListIndex = 3
                    .Visible = True
                    .Width = 55
                End With
                Set CmdBarEvents.ZoomCtrl = ctlCombo
            End Sub
```

Note If you try to run the previous procedure, you'll get an error on the Set statement, the last line in the procedure. If you just want to add a combo box on a toolbar, you should comment out the Set statement line of code. The last line, the Set statement, will be used to connect the change event of the combo box to a Change event procedure. (You set the Change event procedure after the first step.)

The variable *ctlCombo* is declared as a *CommandBarComboBox* object, and the second line inserts the combo box control on the Standard toolbar in Word, Excel, or PowerPoint, depending on where you run the procedure. The *AddItem* method adds the specified string to the drop-down list of the combo box. Note that it's possible for you to insert an item at a specific position in the list by specifying the optional second argument of the *AddItem* method. For example, to insert 55% as the second item, enter the line of code `.AddItem "55%", 2` anywhere in the With ctlCombo...End With section.

The Width property is the width of the combo box control that's visible on the toolbar. The DropDownWidth is the width of the drop-down list that appears when the user clicks the arrow at the right of the control.

2. Insert a new class module and in the Properties window set the name to CmdBarCtrlEvents.

3. At the top of the CmdBarCtrlEvents class module, add the following declaration:

```
Public WithEvents ZoomCtrl As _
    Office.CommandBarComboBox
```

The *ZoomCtrl* variable is declared with events as a *CommandBar-ComboBox*. The use of the *WithEvents* keyword of the Visual Basic for Applications language in a class module indicates that the *ZoomCtrl* object variable will be used to respond to events triggered by the combo box. A *CommandBarComboBox* control in Office exposes only a Change event, and this is the event that's used to handle the event that occurs when the user has changed the value in the combo box.

4. When you entered the declaration with events in the previous step, the item ZoomCtrl was added to the Object drop-down list of the class module. If you select the ZoomCtrl item and then click the Procedure drop-down list, the Change event is the only event listed. Select the Change event and add the following code. (If you clicked the Change event in the Procedure drop-down list, you won't need the first two lines below; your action automatically inserted the *Sub* procedure definition for you.)

```
Private Sub ZoomCtrl_Change(ByVal Ctrl As _
        Office.CommandBarComboBox)
    Static sCurValue As String, sEnteredText As String

    With Ctrl
        sEnteredText = .Text
        If Right$(sEnteredText, 1) = "%" Then
            sEnteredText = Left$(sEnteredText, _
                Len(sEnteredText) - 1)
        End If
        If IsNumeric(sEnteredText) Then
            Select Case CInt(sEnteredText)
                Case Is > 125
                    .Text = "125%"
                Case Is < 10
                    .Text = "10%"
                Case Else
                    .Text = sEnteredText & "%"
            End Select
            sCurValue = .Text
            ' call procedure that manipulates content
            ActiveWindow.View.Zoom = CLng(Left$( _
                sCurValue, Len(sCurValue) - 1))
        Else
            .Text = sCurValue
        End If
    End With
End Sub
```

Office calls this procedure when the user changes the value of the combo box. When the event is triggered, Office passes into the Change event procedure an instance of the command bar combo box control where the event triggered. The first If...Then block removes the "%" sign from the text value of the combo box control, if it exists.

You use the built-in Visual Basic for Applications function *IsNumeric* to determine if the string entered by the user is a number. If it isn't, the text of the control is reset to the value that was there before the user changed it. If the text *is* a number, the procedure converts the value to an integer using the *CInt* function (built-in Visual Basic for Applications function), and then the procedure determines whether the value is above or below the specified bounds.

5. If you typed the code in Excel, before running the *InsertComboBox* procedure in step 1 change the line setting the Zoom property to the following:

```
ActiveWindow.Zoom = CLng(Left$(sCurValue, _
    Len(sCurValue) - 1))
```

The only difference between this line in Excel and the same line for Word and PowerPoint is that the Zoom property is accessible from the *Window* object in Excel, while in Word and PowerPoint, the Zoom property is accessible on the *View* object.

6. At the top of the standard code module where the procedure in step 1 was added, insert the following line:

```
Dim CmdBarEvents As New CmdBarCtrlEvents
```

The variable *CmdBarEvents* declares a new instance of the class CmdBarCtrlEvents, which contains the event procedures for any command bar controls you've declared with events, as done in step 3 previously. This declaration also ties in the line `Set CmdBarEvents .ZoomCtrl = ctlCombo` added at the end of the procedure in step 1.

7. Run the procedure in step 1, switch to the application, click any item in the drop-down list of the newly inserted combo box (or enter a custom value) and press ENTER.

The code in the *ZoomCtrl_Change* procedure is executed and, depending on the value entered, the value is either displayed or set to the minimum or maximum supported value. Try entering values like 5 and 500 to see the execution of the code that handles limits.

The combo box in this example mimics the behavior of the built-in *Zoom* control on the Standard toolbar in Word, Excel, and PowerPoint in terms of how the combo box handles string versus numeric input, and whether the input is greater or less than a predefined value. The line of the *ZoomCtrl_Change* procedure that assigns the value to the Zoom property, `ActiveWindow.View.Zoom`, actually changes the zoom in the active window in Word and PowerPoint. If you modified the code for Excel in step 5, the zoom in the active window in Excel will be changed similarly. (The built-in Visual Basic for Applications function *CLng*, used in steps 4 and 5 on the previous page, converts the string value in the variable sCurValue to a value of type Long.)

Add a Noneditable Drop-Down List

A noneditable drop-down list control looks the same as a combo box control except for the fact that you can't type a value in the control. The user must select an item in the drop-down list and can't enter a custom value in the control, as can be done in a combo box control.

1. Add the following procedure to a standard code module. Make sure the declaration below is added to the top of the standard code module.

```
Dim CmdCombo As New CmdBarDropdownEvents

Sub InsertDropDown()
    Dim ctlCombo As CommandBarComboBox
    Set ctlCombo = CommandBars("Standard") _
        .Controls.Add(msoControlDropdown)
    With ctlCombo
        .BeginGroup = True
        .AddItem "Item 1"
        .AddItem "Item 2"
        .AddItem "Item 3"
        .AddItem "Item 4"
        .Caption = "List Items"
        .DropDownWidth = 117
        .ListIndex = 3
        .Width = 120
        .Tag = "ItemList"
    End With
    Set CmdCombo.CmdListCtrl = ctlCombo
End Sub
```

2. Create a new class module and name it CmdBarDropdownEvents. At the top of the class module, add the following declaration and then add the procedure anywhere in the class module.

```
Public WithEvents CmdListCtrl As _
    Office.CommandBarComboBox

Private Sub CmdListCtrl_Change(ByVal Ctrl As _
        Office.CommandBarComboBox)
    Dim sListItemText As String
    Dim iPosnInList As Integer
```

```
With Ctrl
    sListItemText = .List(.ListIndex)
    iPosnInList = .ListIndex
    Select Case sListItemText
        Case "Item 1"
            Debug.Print "1"
        Case "Item 2"
            Debug.Print "2"
        Case "Item 3"
            Debug.Print "3"
        Case "Item 4"
            Debug.Print "4"
    End Select
End With
End Sub
```

The code can do two things to evaluate what the selected item is in the drop-down list. The first is to evaluate the string of the selected item; the second is to evaluate the position of the selected item in the drop-down list. In either case, you use a Select Case statement to evaluate the property you've chosen. In the previous procedure, for example, you can use the *sListItemText* or *iPosnInList* variables in the Select Case statement as expressions to evaluate the selected item.

You use the ListIndex property of the *CommandBarComboBox* object to return the numeric position of the selected item. You also use this property when retrieving the string of the selected item. You do this former evaluation by using the List property of the *CommandBarComboBox* object and passing in an integer value in the List property. The integer value represents the position of the item in the drop-down list.

Because you are interested in retrieving the selected item and the ListIndex property returns the position of the selected item in the list, you pass the value of ListIndex directly into the List property. Note the use of the With...End block. The expression in the With...End block is the *CommandBarComboBox* control, so `.List(.ListIndx)` really represents `Ctrl.List(Ctrl.ListIndex)`.

3. Display the Immediate window in the Visual Basic Editor.

4. Run the *InsertDropDown* procedure added in the first step, switch back to the application, and click the drop-down list.

To see the values being printed to the Immediate window in the Visual Basic Editor, position the Office application so that the Immediate window is visible behind the application window.

Add an Image to a Control

Unfortunately there's no simple way to assign an image to a toolbar button or menu item. There are, however, a number of workarounds, all of which have one thing in common: you need to get an image onto the clipboard. Once it's there, you use the *CommandBarControl.CopyFace* method to copy the image from the clipboard to the control. The crux lies in somehow copying the image to the Windows clipboard *before* using the *CopyFace* method.

If you plan on creating an add-in for any Office application, Chapters 13 and 14 describe how to do so using the new COM add-in model introduced in Office 2000. Microsoft Visual Basic 5.0 and newer versions allow developers who create COM add-ins to use a resource file and directly store images for command bar controls in a COM add-in.

In Visual Basic 6.0, for example, you can use the function LoadResPicture to retrieve an image resource from a resource file stored in your COM add-in. Thereafter, you can use the Clipboard object to set the image onto the Windows clipboard. The online Microsoft Visual Basic Help file describes the LoadResPicture and Clipboard functions as well as how to insert a resource file into your project. Your code would look similar to the following. The value of "100" used in the LoadResPicture function would represent an image in a resource file stored in your project.

```
With CommandBars("Tools").Controls.Add
    .Caption = "&MenuItem With Image"
    .Style = msoButtonIconAndCaption
    Clipboard.SetData LoadResPicture("100", vbResBitmap)
    .PasteFace
End With
```

Change the Cursor when the Menu Item Is Clicked

Often when the user clicks a menu item or toolbar button, code is executed that will retrieve data from a data source (rather than display a dialog box) and then format the data and insert it into the active document. This process may take a while, depending on whether the data source is local or on the network and on how much data is being retrieved. In these scenarios, you may want to change the cursor to an hourglass (or the equivalent wait pointer) on the user's system. This tells the user that something is happening behind the scenes and, when the cursor changes back to the normal selection pointer, the process is complete.

1. Add the following code to a standard code module in any Office application. In Access, change "Standard" to "Database." Also, in Access you must load the Microsoft Office 9.0 Object Library, using the References command on the Tools menu, since it is not loaded by default.

```
Dim CmdBarEvents As New Class1

Sub InsertButton()
    Dim ctlBtn As Office.CommandBarButton
    Set ctlBtn = CommandBars("Standard").Controls.Add
    With ctlBtn
        .Caption = "&Custom Button"
        .FaceId = 2950
```

```
            .Tag = "BrButton"
               Set CmdBarEvents.BtnCtrl = ctlBtn
        End With
    End Sub
```

2. Add the following code in a class module named Class1. All lines before
the BtnCtrl_Click procedure must be placed at the top of the class
module.

```
Private Declare Function SetCursor Lib "User32" _
    (ByVal hCursor As Long) As Long
Private Declare Function LoadCursor Lib "User32" _
    Alias "LoadCursorA" (ByVal hInstance As Long, _
    ByVal lpCursorName As Any) As Long
Private Declare Sub Sleep Lib "kernel32" ( _
    ByVal dwMilliseconds As Long)
Const IDC_WAIT As Long = 32514

Public WithEvents BtnCtrl As Office.CommandBarButton

Private Sub BtnCtrl_Click(ByVal Ctrl As _
    Office.CommandBarButton, CancelDefault As Boolean)
    Dim Start As Long

    SetCursor LoadCursor(0, IDC_WAIT)
    ' get current time and loop for 1 second
    Start = Timer
    Do While Timer < Start + 1
    Loop
    ' use Sleep Windows API to sleep for 1 second more
    Sleep 1000
    ' do something here
    SetCursor LoadCursor(0, 0&)
End Sub
```

The Click event procedure uses the *SetCursor* function declared at the
top of the class module to set the cursor to the wait pointer. You then use
the Do...Loop to simulate the delay of some process, like retrieving data.
The execution loops through the Do...Loop for one second and then exits
the loop. After the Do...Loop, a value of 1000 is passed to the Sleep function.
Since a thousand milliseconds equals one second, the code does not
continue to the next line until one second has passed. The *SetCursor*
function then resets the mouse pointer to the default pointer.

The three declarations, SetCursor, LoadCursor, and Sleep, are Windows
application programming interfaces (or Win32 APIs). You can find more

information about Win32 APIs at *http://msdn.microsoft.com/* or any other Microsoft Developer Network source.

3. Run the InsertButton procedure added in the first step, switch back to the application, and click the button with the caption "Custom Button" at the end of the Standard toolbar.

   When you click the button, the cursor changes to an hourglass for two seconds before changing back to the default cursor. When you add this code to your add-in, instead of adding code that pauses execution for two seconds, you could, for example, add code that retrieves data from a database.

Finding and Removing Controls

Once you have created command bar customizations, you usually have to do one of two things with them. Either you need to find them and reconnect their event procedures, or you need to find them and remove them. (You may need to find and remove command bar customizations when the user unloads an add-in or when the application is unloaded and the customizations are to be removed.) The best way to find a set of customizations is by using the *FindControls* method. However, there are actually two ways to find a customization. Either iterate through the controls on a specific menu or toolbar or use the *FindControls* method. So when should you use one technique over the other? The new *FindControls* method included in Office 2000 allows you to mimic built-in command bar control behavior.

Shortcut to Removing Command Bar Controls

The fastest and easiest way to remove a toolbar control from a visible toolbar or remove a menu control from the menu bar is to hold down the ALT key, click the control with the mouse, and drag the control off of the toolbar. When you click the control while holding down the ALT key, the mouse pointer changes to a button-drag image. (The border of the control also changes to a thick black line.) You can also use this technique to move controls and menus around the menu bar and visible toolbars.

If the Protection property of a command bar is set to msoBar-NoCustomize, the command bar is protected from user customization. Therefore, you can neither add a command bar control to, nor remove a command bar control from, the command bar. For more on the Protection property, see the section "Creating a Toolbar, Step by Step" earlier in this chapter, or consult the online Office Visual Basic for Applications Help file.

The *FindControls* Method

What if there is more than one instance of your command on the command bar or somewhere else on some other menu or toolbar? The *FindControls* method allows you to find all instances of your control. The *FindControls* method thus handles the case in which the user has moved your custom command from its original position or has copied the custom command to another menu. Built-in controls could also be copied many times in a command bar set. For example, the built-in Save command is on both the File menu and the Standard toolbar, by default. Nonetheless, the *FindControls* method finds all instances of a built-in or custom control and can manipulate them accordingly, or assign them to an event procedure.

You can specify any combination of the four optional parameters of the *FindControls* method to narrow the control search. However, you'll usually use the *Id* or the *Tag* parameter. You should specify the *Id* parameter when searching for built-in controls. Each built-in command bar control, such as the Save or Open command, has a unique built-in identifier, or Id, in Office. When you're searching for all built-in controls with a specific Id, you should specify the *Id* parameter of the *FindControls* method only. When you're searching for custom controls, you should specify the *Tag* argument. (The Id property for all custom controls is 1.) As described near the beginning of this chapter in the section entitled "Setting the Tag Property," you should always set the Tag property for any command bar controls you add.

Searching for All Instances of a Built-In Control

The following procedure finds all instances of the Save command and changes the caption from the default "Save" to "Save Document." You can also use the procedure to reset all built-in instances of a control. In the procedure, place a comment at the beginning of the line that sets the Caption property and remove the comment from the line below that resets the command bar control to its built-in state. In the Visual Basic Editor in any Office application, insert a standard code module, add the following code, and run the procedure.

```
Sub RenameBuiltInCommand()
    Dim ctlItem As CommandBarControl
    Dim ctlColl As CommandBarControls

    Set ctlColl = Application.CommandBars.FindControls(Id:=3)

    If Not ctlColl Is Nothing Then
        For Each ctlItem In ctlColl
            ctlItem.Caption = "&Save Document"
            'ctlItem.Reset
        Next ctlItem
    End If
End Sub
```

Tip To determine the Id of a built-in control quickly, execute a line like the following in the Immediate window in the Visual Basic Editor. Just change the name of the command bar where the control exists and the name of the control.

```
?Application.CommandBars("File").controls("&Save").Id
```

To reset the Save command to its default characteristics as defined by Office, remove the apostrophe (') from the beginning of the line ctlItem.Reset and add an apostrophe at the beginning of the line setting the Caption property.

How the *FindControls* Method Works

The *FindControls* method, defined as FindControls([Type], [Id], [Tag], [Visible]), returns a CommandBarControls collection object. If no controls are found that fit the criteria specified by the arguments of the *FindControls* method, FindControls is set to the Visual Basic for Applications keyword *Nothing*. Don't confuse the new *FindControls* (plural) method with the *FindControl* (singular) method that has existed since Office 97.

The *FindControl* method works a lot like the new *FindControls* method in Office 2000. However, if the *CommandBars* collection contains two or more controls that fit the search criteria, the *FindControl* method returns only the first control that's found. Therefore, if the user customized the command bar set and copied your custom control to a new location, the *FindControl* method isn't robust enough to find all instances of your custom control. With the new *FindControls* method, if the *CommandBars* collection contains two or more controls that fit the search criteria, the *FindControls* method returns a CommandBarControls collection. Your code would then iterate through the CommandBarControls collection, manipulating each control in the collection as appropriate.

Search for All Instances of a Custom Control

1. Start the Visual Basic Editor in Word, Excel, or PowerPoint, add the following procedure in a standard code module, and press F5.

```
Sub InsertNewButton()
    With Application.CommandBars("Standard") _
        .Controls.Add(Type:=msoControlButton)
        .Caption = "&Button1"
        .FaceId = 2141
        .Tag = "MyCustomTag"
    End With
End Sub
```

A new custom button, with the FaceId set to 2141, is added to the end of the Standard toolbar.

2. Switch back to the Word, Excel, or PowerPoint application window and click the Customize command on the Tools menu. This displays the Customize dialog box and puts the command bars in customize mode.

3. Hold down the control key, click the custom button added by the procedure in the first step, and drag the control to any other toolbar or menu that's currently displayed. Repeat this for the same custom button as many times as you like.

   You now have multiple copies of your custom button control on the command bar set.

4. For any of the custom buttons copied, or even the first custom button added by the procedure in the first step, change the image or the name of the control by right-clicking the control and making the appropriate changes on the context menu.

   This step will reveal that the *FindControls* method will find all instances of a custom control, regardless of what customizations have been made to it.

5. Click the Close button on the Customize dialog box to exit the command bar customize mode.

6. Switch back to the Visual Basic Editor and below the procedure added in the first step, add the following procedure and press F5.

```
Sub DeleteControlUsingFindControls()
    Dim ctlItem As CommandBarControl
    Dim ctlColl As CommandBarControls

    Set ctlColl = Application.CommandBars _
        .FindControls(Tag:="MyCustomTag")

    If Not ctlColl Is Nothing Then
        For Each ctlItem In ctlColl
            ctlItem.Delete
        Next ctlItem
    End If
End Sub
```

7. Switch back to the Word, Excel, or PowerPoint application window.

   All instances of your custom button control that you copied to existing toolbars and the menu bar should have been removed. (The code in step 6 removes all instances of the custom command bar control you added in steps 1 and 3.) The search is conducted by using the *FindControls* method and specifying the *Tag* argument. Because in step 6 you set the *Tag* argument to the string "MyCustomTag," which is the same Tag value set in the *InsertNewButton* procedure, the If...Then loop in step 6 finds all instances.

Reconnecting an Event Procedure to a Control

When you create add-ins, as described in chapters 13 and 14, you need a way to connect an event procedure to a custom command bar control that already may exist in the command bar set when the add-in is loaded. In the procedure that's called when an add-in is loaded, code should exist to find any custom controls that the add-in works with. If the custom control doesn't exist, you should add code to your add-in to recreate it. Otherwise, your code connects the custom control to its event procedure. The basic structure of your code would appear similar to the following procedure. However, this topic is described in full in chapter 14.

```
Sub SomeAddInInitialization()
    Dim ctlColl As CommandBarControls
    Set ctlColl = Application.CommandBars _
        .FindControls(Tag:="MyCustomTag")
    If ctlColl Is Nothing Then
        ' Add command bar controls.
    Else
        ' Reconnect controls to event procedures.
    End If
End Sub
```

You assign the *ctlColl* variable in the Set statement to the collection returned by the *FindControls* method. You use the If...Then...Else block to determine if the collection is *Nothing*. If it is, it means that no custom controls with the tag specified exist and your code would call a procedure that adds the custom command bar controls. Otherwise, at least one copy of the custom control exists somewhere in the command bar set and the first item in the collection returned by the *FindControls* method is assigned to the button object that handles the events.

Iterating Through a Command Bar to Find a Control

Sometimes you may not be concerned that a command bar set has multiple copies of a command bar control. Instead, you may be concerned with just one instance of a control on a specific command bar. When you iterate through the command bar controls collection on a command bar, you're not addressing the fact that the control you're interested in may have been copied or moved to another location, and that all your code is set up to address a control on a specific command bar only.

One way to rectify this would be, in the Visual Basic Editor in any Office application, to insert a standard code module, add the following code, and run the procedure below. The procedure iterates through the controls on the Tools menu. If the caption of a control in the Tools menu is set to the string "&MenuItem," the control is deleted.

```
Sub DeleteControlByIteration()
    Dim ctlItem As CommandBarControl
    For Each ctlItem In Application _
        .CommandBars("Tools").Controls
        If ctlItem.Caption = "&MenuItem" Then
            ctlItem.Delete
        End If
    Next ctlItem
End Sub
```

However, iterating through a command bar controls collection to find a control by comparing the caption is *not* recommended. It can easily bring complications. For example, if you didn't have the accelerator in the Caption string, the correct control wouldn't be found. Also, the user may have changed the caption of the control when in command bar customize mode. The caption can also be specific to a locale, so your code would need to understand what locale the solution and Office are running in and what the locale-specific name of the control may be.

A better iteration approach involves using the Tag property to find a control in the command bar controls collection. This approach is safer and better because the user can't change the Tag property. In the procedure above, change the expression in the If...Then statement to evaluate the Tag property. This line would appear as `If ctlItem.Tag = "MyCustomTag" Then`.

Remove a Command Bar Control by Trapping Errors

In the section "Remove a Command Bar by Trapping Errors" earlier in this chapter, the procedure *DeleteCommandBarByErrorTrapping* attempts to delete a specific command bar. If the command bar does not exist, an error would occurs when the *Delete* method tries to delete a nonexistent command bar. Execution in the procedure then skips to the line starting with the word "Error_Handler." Similarly, the following procedure traps the error that's generated when a line of code attempts to delete a command bar that doesn't exist.

The first line in the procedure indicates that if an error occurs, execution in the procedure should skip to the line starting with the word "Error_Handler." (You can change the text "Error_Handler" to anything you want, as long as the colon (:) appears at the end of the line. If you do change the text, make sure to do so in both instances of it in the procedure.) If no error occurs when the *Delete* method is executed, the procedure is exited. Note that if the Exit Sub line didn't exist, execution of the procedure's lines of code would continue into the Error_Handler, even if no error occurred.

```
Sub DeleteControlByErrorTrapping()
    On Error GoTo Error_Handler
    Application.CommandBars("Tools") _
        .FindControl(Tag:="MyButton").Delete
    Exit Sub

Error_Handler:
    MsgBox "The command button does not exist"
End Sub  .
```

In the Visual Basic Editor in any Office application, insert a standard code module, add the preceding code, and run the procedure. The procedure attempts to delete the control with the Tag "MyButton." This example uses the *FindControl* method, similar to the *FindControls* (plural) method to return the control that has the Tag assigned to the string "MyButton." If the control does not exist, the *Delete* method produces an error, and code execution skips to the line starting with the word "Error_Handler."

Chapter Summary

Inserting and manipulating menus and toolbars in any Office application is a common task performed by an add-in. Custom menu commands and toolbar buttons allow a user access to functionality provided by any add-in. This chapter describes how to create custom menus and toolbars using the objects, methods, and properties provided by the CommandBars object model in the Microsoft Office 9.0 Object Library. Using the CommandBars object model, along with the selection change events in Word, Excel, PowerPoint, and Outlook described in Chapter 10, you can add menu and toolbar controls that mimic the state and behavior of built-in controls such as the Bold, Zoom, and Ruler commands.

Chapter 12

Working with the Office Assistant

Estimated time: 50 minutes

- Set the characteristics and functions of custom balloons displayed by the Assistant.

- Work with the elements of the Assistant's balloon, including the heading, labels, buttons, and check boxes.

- Set text attributes such as color and underlining in the balloon's heading, labels, and check boxes.

- Understand the similarities between the Assistant's *Balloon* object and the *MsgBox* function built into the Microsoft Visual Basic for Applications language.

- Determine if the Assistant is on and visible and learn when to display a message box instead of the Assistant.

- Place a button on a custom dialog box that displays the Office Assistant—one that's similar to many of Microsoft Office's built-in dialog boxes, such as the toolbar Customize dialog box. (The *custom dialog box* is a file search dialog box based on the use of Office's *FileSearch* object.)

The Office Assistant provides a common interface for displaying Help information and tips to users who are working with any Office application. To allow Visual Basic for Applications solutions to use the Office Assistant as well, each Office application provides an Assistant property on the *Application* object. This property returns a reference to the *Assistant* object, as defined in the shared Microsoft Office 9.0 Object Library. By using the Assistant in your custom solution, you can provide Help tips that explain how to use your custom dialog box or wizard. You can also display a set of ways to get more information. Since the objects, methods, and properties associated with the Office Assistant are defined in the Microsoft Office 9.0 Object Library, you can write code that can be shared among, and executed in, all the Office applications without having to tailor the code to each one.

This chapter describes the *Assistant* and *Balloon* objects, along with their associated methods. It also contains an example that shows you how to create a custom dialog box with a button similar to the ones in wizards and in dialog boxes across the Office suite of applications that display the Office Assistant. This would be a button like the one at the bottom left of the Customize dialog box, which you access by clicking Customize on the Tools menu in any Office application. You build the functionality of the custom dialog box by using the *FileSearch* object, methods, and properties, which are also defined in the Microsoft Office 9.0 Object Library. The *FileSearch* object allows your code to return a list of files from a search with specific criteria.

Quick Guide: Elements of the Assistant's Balloon

The Office Assistant displays or gathers information through the Assistant's balloon. The balloon can display message text as well as numbered or bulleted list items, check boxes, bitmaps, and buttons. Each of these items lets the user get information or select an item from a set of choices. The following diagram shows the main elements of the Assistant's balloon. You use the methods and properties associated with these elements to set a balloon's display and purpose.

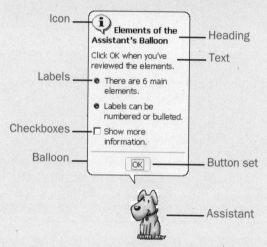

The following code is the procedure that generated the characteristics of the Assistant's balloon in the diagram above. The With…End block contains the properties on the *Balloon* object that you use to set the balloon's appearance.

```
Sub ShowBalloon()
    Dim bln As Office.Balloon
    Set bln = Assistant.NewBalloon
    With bln
        .Icon = msoIconAlertInfo
        .Heading = "Elements of the Assistant's Balloon"
        .Text = "Click OK when you've reviewed the elements."
        .Labels(1).Text = "There are 6 main elements."
```

(continued)

Quick Guide: Elements of the Assistant's Balloon *(continued)*

```
        .Labels(2).Text = "Labels can be numbered" & _
            "or bulleted."
        .Checkboxes(1).Text = "Show more information."
        .BalloonType = msoBalloonTypeButtons
        .Mode = msoModeModal
        .Button = msoButtonSetOK
        .Show
    End With
End Sub
```

The following table lists each element of the Assistant's balloon and describes the property associated with it. The descriptions summarize those given in this chapter's step-by-step examples. You can assign text to the Heading and Text properties and to each label and check box in the *BalloonLabels* and *BalloonCheckboxes* collections. As you'll see in the "Setting Text Attributes in the Assistant's Balloon" section of this chapter, you can set attributes like underlining and color to any text in the balloon.

Balloon Element	Property Description
Heading	Use the Heading property for bold text displayed at the top of the balloon.
Icon	You can set the Icon property to one of the MsoIconType constants. These icons are like those you see when you use the *MsgBox* function built into the Visual Basic for Applications language. The icon appears at the upper-left side of the Assistant's balloon, just to the left of the heading. If you don't want to display an icon, set the Icon property to msoIconNone.
Text	Use the Text property for text that's displayed just below the heading but isn't bold. This text is displayed above any labels or check boxes.
Labels	Use the Labels property to return the *BalloonLabels* collection object. Using the *Item* method of the *BalloonLabels* object, or the shortcut syntax Labels(index), you can specify up to five labels in a balloon. You don't need to explicitly add a label. A label in the collection of five appears when you assign a value to the label's Text property.

(continued)

Quick Guide: Elements of the Assistant's Balloon *(continued)*

Balloon Element	Property Description
Check boxes	Use the Checkboxes property, similar to the Labels property, to return the *BalloonCheckboxes* collection object. Using the *Item* method of the *BalloonCheckboxes* object or the shortcut syntax Checkboxes(index), you can specify up to five check boxes in a balloon. You don't need to explicitly add a check box. A check box in the collection of five appears when you assign a value to the Text property of the check box.
Balloon type	The BalloonType property of the Balloon object indicates whether the labels specified by the Label property appear as a numbered list, a bulleted list, or a list with circular buttons. You specify the numbered list with msoBalloonTypeNumbers, the bulleted list with msoBalloonTypeBullets, and the button list with msoBalloonTypeButtons. By default, if you don't set the ButtonType property, msoBalloonTypeButtons is used.
Button set	Use the Button property to display the set of buttons that appear at the bottom of the Assistant's balloon. You can assign the Button property to one of the following MsoButtonSetType constants:
	msoButtonSetAbortRetryIgnore
	msoButtonSetBackClose
	msoButtonSetBackNextClose
	msoButtonSetBackNextSnooze
	msoButtonSetCancel
	msoButtonSetNextClose
	msoButtonSetNone
	msoButtonSetOK
	msoButtonSetOkCancel
	msoButtonSetRetryCancel
	msoButtonSetSearchClose
	msoButtonSetTipsOptionsClose
	msoButtonSetYesAllNoCancel
	msoButtonSetYesNoCancel
	msoButtonSetYesNo
	By default, if you don't set the Button property, msoButtonSetOK is used.

Displaying a Custom Balloon

In the following example you'll create a balloon in the Assistant to display Help information. The balloon's function is very similar to that of the *MsgBox* function built into the Visual Basic for Applications language. This example also explains the difference between the procedure you create here and the one that displays a functionally equivalent message box using the *MsgBox* function.

1. Start any Office application, open the Visual Basic Editor, and insert a new code module.

2. In the Properties window, change the name of the newly added code module to modAssistant.

3. Create a new procedure in the code module modAssistant by typing **Sub DisplayOfficeAssistant**.

4. Type the following declaration as the first line:

```
Dim bln As Office.Balloon
```

You declare the variable *bln* as type Office.Balloon, and in the following step you'll set it to a new Balloon object returned by the *NewBalloon* method. When you typed the word Office and then typed a period (.), you should have seen the Auto List Members drop-down list display the Balloon item. By default, Microsoft Word, Microsoft Excel, Microsoft PowerPoint, and Microsoft Outlook automatically reference the Microsoft Office 9.0 Object Library, which contains the Assistant and Balloon objects. In Microsoft Access, you need to set a Reference to the Microsoft Office 9.0 Object Library using the References dialog box in the Visual Basic Editor.

Note If you didn't see the Auto List Members drop-down list, you may not have the Office Object Library referenced, or the Auto List Members feature may not be selected in the Options dialog box. To reference the Office Object Library, on the Tools menu in the Editor, click References, and then select the check box next to the Microsoft Office 9.0 Object Library item in the list. To turn on the Auto List Members feature, on the Tools menu, click Options, and then select Auto List Members on the Editor tab.

---

5. To assign the object variable *bln* to a balloon object, type the following Set statement:

```
Set bln = Assistant.NewBalloon
```

The *NewBalloon* method of the *Assistant* object returns a *Balloon* object, which is assigned to the *bln* object variable.

6. After the Set statement, type the following With...End block:

```
With bln
End With
```

7. Within the With...End block, type the following lines to set the Heading and Text properties of the newly created Assistant Balloon object:

```
.Heading = "File Search"
.Text = "To conduct a file search, " & _
    "follow the steps outlined below."
```

You use the Heading property for the bold text displayed at the top of the balloon. The Text property is assigned to text that's displayed just below the heading, but isn't bold.

8. To set the type of buttons that will appear at the bottom of the balloon, type the following before the End With statement added in step 6:

```
.Button = msoButtonSetOK
```

You can set the Button property to a wide range of predefined buttons and combinations of buttons. They include OK, Cancel, Yes, No, Next, Previous, and others. In this case, you set the Button property to the OK button. (To see the full list of button combinations you can set to the Button property, scroll down the Auto List Members drop-down list that you see after you type the equal sign (=), or refer to the Balloon Elements table at the beginning of this chapter.)

9. After setting the Button property, type the following before the End With statement to set the balloon mode:

```
.Mode = msoModeModal
```

The Assistant's balloon can be in one of three modes:

- **Modal** indicates that the balloon must be closed before you can continue working in the application or UserForm.

- **AutoDown** indicates that the balloon closes once you click anywhere on the screen.

- **Modeless** allows you to continue working with the application or UserForm but continues to display the balloon until you close it, either programmatically through Microsoft Visual Basic or by pressing a button in the balloon.

When you specify that the balloon is Modeless (by setting the Mode property to msoModeModeless), you must set a value for the Callback property. The *Callback property value* is the name of a procedure that's called just after you close the balloon. By default, if you don't explicitly set the Mode property, msoModeModal is used.

Important   You can't create a modeless balloon with a COM add-in. If you create a COM add-in, which is described in Chapters 13 and 14, you can display only a modal balloon that requires the user to close it before continuing to work with the Office application or the COM add-in form.

---

10. To display the balloon on the screen, type the following *Show* method
before the `End With` statement:

`.Show`

11. Place the cursor in the *DisplayOfficeAssistant* procedure and press F5 to
run it. You'll see the Assistant along with a balloon containing a heading,
text, and a button.

The complete procedure for displaying this custom balloon is as follows:

```
Sub DisplayOfficeAssistant()
    Dim bln As Office.Balloon
    Set bln = Assistant.NewBalloon
    With bln
        .Heading = "File Search"
        .Text = "To conduct a file search, " & _
            "follow the steps outlined below."
        .Button = msoButtonSetOK
        .Mode = msoModeModal
        .Show
    End With
End Sub
```

The procedure for displaying a functionally equivalent message box is as
follows:

```
Sub DisplayMessageBox()
    Dim sHeading As String, sText As String
    sHeading = "File Search"
    sText = "To conduct a file search, " & _
        "follow the steps outlined below."
    MsgBox Prompt:=sText, Buttons:=vbOKOnly, Title:=sHeading
End Sub
```

To make the message box code easier to read, you declare the variables *sHeading* and *sText* as being assigned to the *Title* and *Prompt* parameters, respectively, of the *MsgBox* function. The Heading, Text, and Button properties of the Assistant's *Balloon* object are equivalent to the *MsgBox* function's Title, Prompt, and Buttons parameters. Setting the Icon property of the *Balloon* object, described later in this chapter, is equivalent to assigning a value like vbInformation, vbCritical, vbExclamation, or vbQuestion to the *Buttons* parameter of the *MsgBox* function. The *Buttons* parameter allows you to set both the button set and icon displayed in the message box:

```
Buttons:=vbOKOnly + vbInformation
```

On the other hand, in the Assistant's *Balloon* object, you specify the button set and icon separately, with two different properties (Button and Icon).

Determine Whether to Display the Assistant or a Message Box

You can use the combination of the *Assistant* object's Visible and On properties to determine if the Assistant is both turned on and visible. Office uses the Assistant's visible and on state in order to determine whether an alert should be displayed through the Assistant's balloon or a message box.

- If the Assistant is turned off (or not installed), Office displays a message box.

- If the Assistant is turned on and visible, Office uses the Assistant's balloon to display messages.

- If the Assistant is turned on but hidden, Office displays a message box.

A user's right-clicking the Assistant, clicking Options from the shortcut menu, or clearing "Use The Office Assistant" on the Options tab can turn off the Assistant. If the user turns it off, clicking the "Show the Office Assistant" command on the Help menu of any Office application will turn it back on. To hide the Assistant but not turn it off, the user clicks the "Hide the Office Assistant" command on the Help menu.

The following procedure allows you to mimic this Office functionality in your Visual Basic programs by using an If...Then...Else condition block to determine whether you should have the program display a given message with the Assistant or a message box. (Using a Boolean to store the state of the Assistant may be useful, but you should note that the state of the Assistant may change if the user decides to turn the Assistant on or make it visible.) Your code might look similar to the following:

```
Sub CheckIfAssistantIsVisible()
    If Assistant.On And Assistant.Visible Then
        ' Display Office Assistant
    Else
        ' Display message box
    End If
End Sub
```

Using a Generic Function to Display Messages

An efficient way to structure your code is to create a single custom function that displays messages to the user, whether it's through the Assistant's balloon or the *MsgBox* function. Every time you need to display a message, your code calls the generic function, which then determines how the message is displayed. For example, the following *TestDisplay-OKMessage* procedure calls the custom function *Display-OKMessage*.

```
Sub TestDisplayOKMessage()
    DisplayOKMessage "TIP", "Use a generic function."
End Sub

Function DisplayOKMessage(sHeading As String, _
        sText As String)
    If Assistant.On And Assistant.Visible Then
        Dim bln As Office.Balloon
        Set bln = Assistant.NewBalloon
        With bln
            .Heading = sHeading
            .Text = sText
            .Button = msoButtonSetOK
            .Show
        End With
    Else
        MsgBox Prompt:=sText, Buttons:=vbOKOnly, _
            Title:=sHeading
    End If
End Function
```

You can call the *DisplayOKMessage* function anywhere in your code without duplicating the functionality of checking whether the Assistant is on and visible. This custom function is very simple, although it doesn't handle the case where the button that's set in the Assistant's balloon or message box can be something other than an OK button.

However, you can expand this custom function to include the most common button sets. You'll need to write a custom function that maps the Assistant's MsoButtonSetType constants to button constants that are supported in the *MsgBox* function built into the Visual Basic for Applications language. In the Chapter 12 practice folder, the file modAssnt.bas contains the custom function *DisplayMessage* along with the custom function *ButtonSet* that maps an MsoButtonSetType constant to the equivalent VbMsgBoxStyle constant used in the Buttons argument of the *MsgBox* function. Use the *TestDisplayMessage* procedure to test the custom functions.

Determining Which Button Gets Clicked

Both the *MsgBox* function and the *Show* method of the *Balloon* object return a value that depends on the button set that's defined. In the following two procedures, you declare the variable *lReturn* as type Long and assign it to the value returned by the *MsgBox* function and *Show* method, respectively. The first procedure displays a message box that's functionally equivalent to the Assistant's balloon displayed in the second procedure.

```
Sub DisplayMessageBoxWithOKCancelButtons()
    Dim lReturn As Long
    lReturn = MsgBox(Prompt:="Test", Buttons:=vbOKCancel)
    Select Case lReturn
        Case 1
            Debug.Print "OK"
        Case 2
            Debug.Print "Cancel"
    End Select
End Sub

Sub DisplayOfficeAssistantWithOKCancelButtons()
    Dim lReturn As Long
    With Assistant.NewBalloon
        .Text = "Test"
        .Button = msoButtonSetOkCancel
        lReturn = .Show
    End With
    Select Case lReturn
        Case msoBalloonButtonOK
            Debug.Print "OK"
        Case msoBalloonButtonCancel
            Debug.Print "Cancel"
    End Select
End Sub
```

The return value of the *Show* method is one of the MsoBalloonButtonType constants:

msoBalloonButtonAbort	msoBalloonButtonCancel
msoBalloonButtonIgnore	msoBalloonButtonNo
msoBalloonButtonOK	msoBalloonButtonRetry
msoBalloonButtonSnooze	msoBalloonButtonYes
msoBalloonButtonBack	msoBalloonButtonClose
msoBalloonButtonNext	msoBalloonButtonNull

msoBalloonButtonOptions   msoBalloonButtonSearch

msoBalloonButtonTips   msoBalloonButtonYesToAll

These values represent the possible buttons that can be displayed in the balloon, depending on the value assigned to the Button property.

Setting Text Attributes in the Assistant's Balloon

A new feature in Microsoft Office 2000 is the capability of letting you set attributes to any text in the Assistant's balloon. You can assign text to the Heading and Text properties and to each label and check box in the BalloonLabels and BalloonCheckboxes collections. The following procedure shows a combination of underlining and setting of the color of the text in a balloon.

```
Sub UnderliningAndColorText()
    With Assistant.NewBalloon
        .Heading = "{cf 252}{ul}Underlining and Text Colors"

        .Text = "This balloon shows a mixture of color " & _
            "text, like {cf 249}Red{cf 0} text, and some " & _
            "underlined {cf 252}{ul 1}Blue{ul 0}{cf 0} text."

        .BalloonType = msoBalloonTypeButtons
        .Labels(1).Text = "{cf 253}{ul}Text " & _
            "is all underlined.{cf 249}{ul 0}"
        .Labels(2).Text = "No underlined or colored text."
        .Labels(3).Text = "Some {ul 1}words underlined."

        .Show
    End With
End Sub
```

In this example, you set the text of the balloon heading to blue and underlined. The balloon's body text contains a mix of single words that are colored, along with a single word that's underlined. The three labels displayed in the balloon show three kinds of text: underlined, not underlined and at the same time set with the default text color, and with two words underlined.

You should add the syntax {cf *number*} to set the text's color. In the syntax {cf *number*}, "number" represents one of the 16 system palette colors listed in the table on the next page. By default, text in the Assistant's balloon is black. If you use a number other than a value listed in the following table in the syntax {cf *number*}, the text will also be black. To display underlined text, you use the syntax {ul} or {ul 1}. You use the syntax {ul 0} after text where underlining should be turned off. If you don't specify {ul 0} to terminate underlining in a text string, underlining continues to the end of the text string (as the text assigned to the third label in the preceding procedure reveals).

System color number	Color	System color number	Color
0	Black	248	Medium gray
1	Dark red	249	Red
2	Dark green	250	Green
3	Dark yellow	251	Yellow
4	Dark blue	252	Blue
5	Dark magenta	253	Magenta
6	Dark cyan	254	Cyan
7	Light gray	255	White

Adding Label and Check Box Controls to Balloons

The *Assistant* object model provides two types of controls you can display in the Assistant balloon—up to five *Label* controls and up to five *Check Box* controls; when you specify the text of either a label or a check box, it's displayed in the balloon. However, you can't position the controls within the balloon: the set of labels is always displayed before the set of check boxes.

Displaying Labels

1. Within the With...End block added in the example in the section "Displaying a Custom Balloon" earlier in this chapter, add the following set of lines just before the *Show* method so that the procedure appears as follows. The new set of lines added to the procedure start on the line beginning with .BalloonType = msoBalloonTypeNumbers and end with the line starting .Labels(3).Text.

```
Sub DisplayOfficeAssistant()
    Dim bln As Office.Balloon
    Set bln = Assistant.NewBalloon
    With bln
        .Heading = "File Search"
        .Text = "To conduct a file search, " & _
            "follow the steps outlined below."

        .BalloonType = msoBalloonTypeNumbers
        .Labels(1).Text = "Specify a file extension in " & _
            "the text box next to the label 'Enter a " & _
            "file extension'."
```

```
        .Labels(2).Text = "Click the Search button."
        .Labels(3).Text = "To display these steps again, " & _
            "click the Assistant button."

        .Button = msoButtonSetOK
        .Mode = msoModeModal
        .Show
    End With
End Sub
```

The BalloonType property of the *Balloon* object indicates whether the labels specified by the Label property appear as a numbered list, a bulleted list, or a list with circular buttons. You specify the numbered list with msoBalloonTypeNumbers, the bulleted list with msoBalloonTypeBullets, and the button list with msoBalloonTypeButtons. Because you're listing a set of steps, you want to set the button type to a numbered list. Because you specified the text of three of the five *Label* controls, three items will be in the numbered list.

2. Place the cursor in the *DisplayOfficeAssistant* procedure and press F5 to run it. You'll see the Assistant displayed with a numbered list:

Displaying Check Boxes

The following procedure displays the Assistant's balloon with three check boxes added. Because the Mode property isn't set and by default the mode is set to msoModeModal, the balloon is displayed in a modal state. Thus, when you execute this procedure, code doesn't execute after the *Show* method is executed until the user dismisses the balloon. Once the balloon is closed, the lines following the *Show* method are executed, which allows your code to query the state of the check boxes.

```
Sub DisplayCheckboxes()
    Dim i as Integer
    With Assistant.NewBalloon
        .Heading = "Using Check Boxes"
        .Text = "Check any check box."
```

```
          For i = 1 To 3
              .Checkboxes(i).Text = "Item " & i
          Next
          .Show
          If .Checkboxes(1).Checked Then
              Debug.Print "Checkbox 1 is checked."
          End If
          If .Checkboxes(2).Checked Then
              Debug.Print "Checkbox 2 is checked."
          End If
          If .Checkboxes(3).Checked Then
              Debug.Print "Checkbox 3 is checked."
          End If
      End With
  End Sub
```

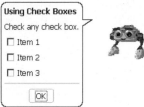

Place the cursor in the *DisplayCheckboxes* procedure and press F5 to run it. Select one or more check boxes and click OK. The three If...Then statements after the Show method of the Balloon object evaluate the checked state of the check box. If the user selected the check box, text is printed to the Immediate window indicating the box is checked.

Adding Icons and Bitmaps to Balloons

In the Assistant balloon, you can add bitmaps (.bmp files), Microsoft Windows metafiles (.wmf files), or built-in icons within the heading or body text. Icons and bitmaps make the information and tips within a balloon more interesting.

1. Within the same With...End block you modified in the steps in the "Displaying Labels" section, add the following line just before the line that sets the BalloonType property:

```
.Icon = msoIconTip
```

You can set the Icon property to one of the following MsoIconType constants: msoIconAlert, msoIconAlertCritical, msoIconAlertInfo, msoIconAlertQuery, msoIconAlertWarning, msoIconNone, or msoIconTip. Tip, specified by msoIconTip, is an image of a light bulb, and Alert, specified by msoIconAlert, is an image of an exclamation mark (!).

The icon appears at the upper-left side of the Assistant's balloon, just to the left of the balloon heading. If you don't want to display an icon, set the Icon property to msoIconNone.

2. Switch to the Windows Explorer and navigate to the Chapter 12 practice file. Copy the file Assistnt.bmp to the C:\ folder.

3. Assign a string variable to reference the location of a bitmap by adding the following line above the With...End block:

```
sBitmapFile = "{bmp C:\Assistnt.bmp}"
```

To specify a bitmap, use the syntax {bmp *<filename>*}, where *<filename>* represents a valid filename of an existing bitmap file. (If you want to specify a Windows metafile instead, change "bmp" to "wmf" in the syntax above and specify a valid filename to an existing Windows metafile.) This picture syntax is represented by a string, and you can assign it to a string variable or add it directly to a string within the Assistant balloon.

Important When you include a bitmap in an Assistant's balloon, you must give the bitmap a filename and pathname with no spaces. If the filename or pathname contains spaces, the Assistant's balloon may not be displayed.

Also, the filename specified above assumes that you have installed the practice files in that particular folder. If you installed them in a different folder, set the filename above to the correct location. You can set the filename to any valid bitmap file on your computer. If the filename isn't correct, the Assistant isn't displayed when you run the *DisplayOfficeAssistant* procedure.

---

4. Declare the string variable *sBitmapFile* at the beginning of the *DisplayOfficeAssistant* procedure where the other variables are declared:

```
Dim sBitmapFile As String
```

5. To add the bitmap in the Assistant's balloon, concatenate the text of the third label (added in step 1 of the section "Displaying Labels") with the string variable *sBitmapFile*. You do this by typing **& sBitmapFile** at the end of the .Labels(3).Text assignment statement. The revised line looks like this:

```
.Labels(3).Text = "To display these steps again, " & _
    "click the Assistant button. " & sBitmapFile
```

Note To *concatenate* means to join two or more separate groups of characters into one string using an ampersand (&).

---

6. Place the cursor in the *DisplayOfficeAssistant* procedure and press F5 to run it. You'll see the Assistant with an icon beside the balloon heading, and a bitmap in the third item of the numbered list.

7. In the *DisplayOfficeAssistant* procedure, change the line setting the Text property to the following and rerun the procedure:

```
.Text = "To conduct a file search, " & sBitmapFile & _
    "follow the steps outlined below."
```

You can add the specified bitmap to any text within the Assistant's balloon. Simply concatenate any string specified anywhere in the *DisplayOfficeAssistant* procedure with the string variable *sBitmapFile*.

8. Place the cursor in the *DisplayOfficeAssistant* procedure and press F5 to run it again. The balloon should appear as shown in the following illustration:

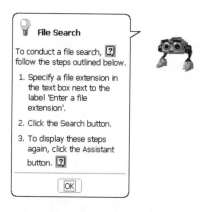

Note   The bitmap file needs to remain in the C:\folder as long as your program contains the line sBitmapFile = "{bmp C:\Assistnt.bmp}." If you commented out or removed this line, the program will work correctly and the Assistant's balloon will be displayed. Otherwise, if the line above was executed but you removed the bitmap file from its folder on your hard drive, the Assistant's balloon won't be displayed.

Displaying the Assistant from a Custom File Search Dialog Box

The Open dialog box in Word, Excel, PowerPoint, and Access, which you display by clicking Open on the File menu, provides a set of drop-down lists and text boxes that allow you to filter certain files. If you click Find on the Tools menu at the upper-right of the Open dialog box, you'll see the advanced Find dialog box.

With the advanced Find dialog box, you can search for files by specific file properties; the equivalent functionality is represented in Visual Basic by the *FileSearch* object model in the Office object library. You access the *FileSearch* object from the *Application* object in Word, Excel, PowerPoint, and Access. The *Application* object in Outlook doesn't support access to the *FileSearch* object.

Create a Dialog Box for File Search Results

1. Start Excel.

2. In the Visual Basic Editor, on the Insert menu, click UserForm.

3. If you don't see the Toolbox window, in the Visual Basic Editor, on the View menu, click Toolbox.

4. In the Toolbox, click the *Label* control, and then click near the upper-left corner of the UserForm.

5. Add a *TextBox* control and place it adjacent to Label1.

6. Add two *CommandButton* controls. Place the first control in the upper-right corner of the UserForm and place the second just below the first. UserForm1 should now look like the following illustration:

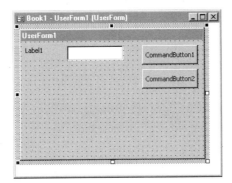

7. Add a second *Label* control below Label1, and add a *ListBox* control below Label2.

Note   This example works the same way in Word and PowerPoint, and gives exactly the same results, as it does in Excel. You may prefer to enter your code in those programs instead.

---

8. Below ListBox1, add a third *Label* control, and then add a fourth *Label* control to the right of the third. Use the following illustration as a guide to moving and sizing the controls.

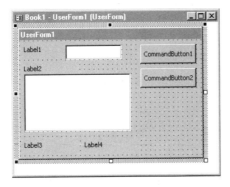

9. If you don't see the Properties window, then on the View menu in the Editor, click Properties Window; or press F4 as a shortcut. In the Properties window, set the following values:

Control	Property	Value
UserForm1	Name	frmSearch
UserForm1	Caption	File Search
Label1	Name	lblFileExt
Label1	Caption	File extension to search:
TextBox1	Name	txtFileExt
CommandButton1	Name	cmdSearch
CommandButton1	Accelerator	S
CommandButton1	Caption	Search
CommandButton2	Name	cmdClose
CommandButton2	Accelerator	C
CommandButton2	Caption	Close
Label2	Name	lblResults
Label2	Caption	Results:
ListBox1	Name	lstResults
Label3	Name	lblTotal
Label3	Caption	Total number of files found:
Label4	Name	lblTotalNumber
Label4	Caption	(Remove the caption string so there's no text in the label.)

10. Resize and move the controls on the UserForm so that they look like the following:

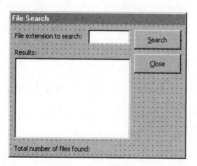

Now you're ready to add code behind the controls of the custom File Search dialog box.

Add File Search Code

1. In the UserForm frmSearch that you just created, double-click the *cmdSearch* control and type the following in the *cmdSearch_Click* procedure:

```
FileSearch
```

You'll create a procedure called *FileSearch* in step 3, and you'll want to keep the *file search* procedure and functionality separate so that you can easily use, or call, the procedure from another procedure or project.

2. Double-click the *cmdClose* control in the frmSearch UserForm, and then type the following in the *cmdClose_Click* procedure:

```
Unload frmSearch
```

Note If the UserForm window is behind the Code window, display it by clicking frmSearch (UserForm) on the Window menu.

The Unload statement removes a UserForm from the screen and from memory. In this case, the parameter you specify in the Unload statement is the frmSearch *UserForm* object. When you click the Close button, the Unload statement closes the dialog box and unloads it from memory. Because no other code is run after the Unload statement, your program will end.

Tip In the Unload statement, you can use the Visual Basic keyword *Me* in place of the parameter *frmSearch*. In this case, the keyword *Me* represents the UserForm in which the code is currently executing. (The *Me* keyword behaves like an implicitly declared variable, so you are setting *Me* to the object *frmSearch*.)

---

3. At the bottom of the frmSearch code module, create a new procedure by typing **Sub FileSearch**.

4. In the *FileSearch* procedure, add the following declaration and two lines to initialize the controls *lstResults* and *lblTotalNumber* on the frmSearch UserForm:

```
Dim i As Integer
lstResults.Clear
lblTotalNumber.Caption = ""
```

The *Clear* method of the *ListBox* control object, *lstResults,* removes all items in the drop-down list simultaneously. When you set the Caption property of the *Label* control object, *lblTotalNumber,* to an empty string (""), the label is displayed without any text. Every time you conduct a new search, the contents of the drop-down list and the caption of the *lblTotal-Number* control will therefore clear before the search begins.

5. Add the following With...End block:

```
With Application.FileSearch
End With
```

You access the *FileSearch* object from the *Application* object in Word, Excel, or PowerPoint.

6. Type the following as the first line in the With...End block created in the previous step:

```
.NewSearch
```

Before you can conduct a file search, you have to reset the search criteria to the default settings by using the *NewSearch* method.

7. Just after the line containing the *NewSearch* method of the *FileSearch* object, type the following to set the file search properties:

```
.LookIn = "C:\"
.SearchSubFolders = True
```

The LookIn property of the File Search dialog box allows you to specify a string value that indicates in which folder on your hard disk to search for the specified file(s). The SearchSubFolders property indicates whether the search should iterate through the contents of subfolders in the folder specified by the LookIn property.

8. To set two more file search properties, type the following just after the line setting the SearchSubFolders property:

```
.FileName = "*." & txtFileExt.Text
.FileType = msoFileTypeAllFiles
```

You set the FileName property to the name of the file looked for during the file search. You can include two wildcard characters in the filename: * (asterisk) or ? (question mark). When you want to match *single* character, use the question mark; when you want to match a *number* of characters, use the asterisk.

You set the FileName property to type *.<*file extension*>, where <*file extension*> represents the text value entered in the txtFileExt *TextBox* control on the frmSearch UserForm. This syntax finds all files that have the specified extension.

You set the FileType property to the enumeration value msoFileType-AllFiles, which indicates that the search should include all types of files. Other values you could set it to are:

msoFileTypeWordDocuments	msoFileTypeExcelWorkbooks
msoFileTypePowerPointPresentations	msoFileTypeDatabases
msoFileTypeTemplates	msoFileTypeOfficeFiles
msoFileTypeBinders	

9. To start the search, type the following:

```
.Execute SortBy:=msoSortByFileType, _
    SortOrder:=msoSortOrderAscending
```

The *Execute* method of the *FileSearch* object starts the file search using the settings of the properties specified before the method runs. The first two arguments that the *Execute* method supports are *SortBy* and *SortOrder*, and in this example you set their values to msoSortByFileType and msoSortOrderAscending, respectively.

You can set the *SortBy* argument to one of the following: msoSortByFileName, msoSortByFileType, msoSortByLastModified, or msoSortBySize. These are the common types of sorts you can perform in the right pane of Windows Explorer. The second argument, *SortOrder*, can be msoSortOrderAscending or msoSortOrderDescending.

Fill a List Box with the File Search Results

Once the *Execute* method of the *FileSearch* object finishes searching, the code following the method runs. You can access the list of files that return with the *FoundFiles* collection object of the *FileSearch* object, and you can use this list to *populate* (fill in) a *ListBox* control on a UserForm.

1. Just after the *Execute* method added in the *FileSearch* procedure, type the following With…End block:

```
With .FoundFiles
End With
```

The complete list of files found is represented by the FoundFiles collection object, which you access by the FoundFiles property of the FileSearch object.

2. In the first line of the With…End block, type the following:

```
lblTotalNumber.Caption = .Count
```

Count is a property of the collection object *FoundFiles*. (The Count and Item properties are members of all the collection objects across Office.) The total number of files found will be listed in the FoundFiles collection object; you're setting the Caption property of the *lblTotal-Number* label control to that total.

3. Type the following For…Next loop just after the line setting the Caption property of the *lblTotalNumber* label control:

```
For i = 1 To .Count
    lstResults.AddItem .Item(i)
Next i
```

The For…Next loop starts the value of the Integer *i* at 1 and changes the value incrementally until the value reaches the number of files listed in the *FoundFiles* collection object; this total is in turn represented by the value of the Count property. During each loop, each item in the *FoundFiles* collection object is also added to the *lstResults* drop-down list control using the *AddItem* method of the *ListBox* control object. The following illustration shows the complete *FileSearch* procedure:

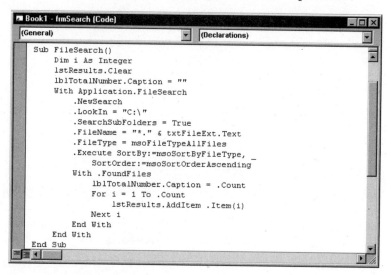

```
Book1 - frmSearch (Code)                                          _ □ ×
(General)                          ▼   (Declarations)                ▼

Sub FileSearch()
      Dim i As Integer
      lstResults.Clear
      lblTotalNumber.Caption = ""
      With Application.FileSearch
           .NewSearch
           .LookIn = "C:\"
           .SearchSubFolders = True
           .FileName = "*." & txtFileExt.Text
           .FileType = msoFileTypeAllFiles
           .Execute SortBy:=msoSortByFileType, _
                SortOrder:=msoSortOrderAscending
           With .FoundFiles
                lblTotalNumber.Caption = .Count
                For i = 1 To .Count
                     lstResults.AddItem .Item(i)
                Next i
           End With
      End With
End Sub
```

4. Press F5 to run the dialog box.

5. In the file extension text box adjacent to the label "File extension to search:," enter the file extension *txt* and click the Search button.

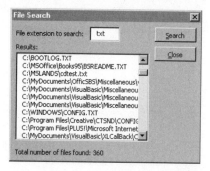

The lstResults *ListBox* control displays a filename list of all the files with the file extension *.txt* in the folder C:\ and all of the subfolders. The *lblTotalNumber* label control displays the total number of files found. Repeat the search by typing different file extensions in the File Search dialog box you created, or change the directory specified by the LookIn property of the *FileSearch* object.

6. Click the Close button. Then click the Save button and save your workbook as MyFileSearch in the Chapter 12 subfolder or any folder on your machine.

Save

**Connect the Custom File Search
Dialog Box to a Menu Command**

In the following steps, you'll add a menu item that when chosen displays the custom File Search dialog box. You can just as easily add a toolbar button that does the same thing when clicked.

1. In the Project Explorer, right-click MyFileSearch project and click Import File on the shortcut menu. In the Import File dialog box, navigate to the Chapter 12 practice folder, select the file modMenu.bas, and click Open.

2. In the *AddMenuItem* procedure, replace the first Set statement with the following:

```
Set ctlPopup = CommandBars("Worksheet Menu Bar") _
    .Controls("File")
```

   The main menu bar in Word and PowerPoint (and Access) is named Menu Bar; in Excel, it's named Worksheet Menu Bar.

3. In the *AddMenuItem* procedure, replace the With...End block with the following With...End block:

```
With ctlBtn
    .BeginGroup = True
    .Caption = "Fi&le Search"
    .OnAction = "ShowDialog"
End With
```

   There are a couple of differences between the two With...End blocks. First, the property values for Caption and OnAction are different. For instance, here you set the Caption property to "File Search" and specify the accelerator key as the letter "l." Additionally, when the menu item is chosen, the *ShowDialog* procedure is called and runs. (You'll add this procedure in the following step.) The other difference is that the With...End block immediately above adds the BeginGroup property. The BeginGroup property adds a separator between the File Search menu item and the preceding menu item.

4. Place the cursor beneath the *AddMenuItem* procedure and create a new procedure by typing **Sub ShowDialog**.

5. Add the following statement to the *ShowDialog* procedure:

```
frmSearch.Show
```

   The *Show* method of the frmSearch *UserForm* object loads the custom UserForm and displays it on screen.

6. Place the cursor in the *AddMenuItem* procedure that you revised in step 3 and press F5 to add the File Search menu item to the File menu in the Excel application window.

After the *AddMenuItem* procedure runs, the File menu appears as follows:

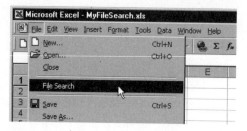

7. On the File menu in the Excel application window, click the custom File Search menu item.

The custom File Search dialog box is displayed each time you click File Search on the File menu. You no longer have to place the cursor in the *FileSearch* procedure in the Editor window to display it. Now both you and your users have access to your custom solution through the graphical user interface.

8. Close the File Search dialog box and save the changes to your workbook.

Hook the Office Assistant to the File Search Solution

Once you create code for the Office Assistant, you need to connect the procedure to an element in your custom UserForm so your users can access the Assistant.

1. Switch to the Visual Basic Editor in Excel, and in the Project Explorer window double-click the *frmSearch* form. (You may have to click the plus sign next to the Forms folder to see it.)

2. Click the *CommandButton* control in the Toolbox window and drag the control to the lower-right corner of the UserForm.

3. In the Properties window, set the following values:

Control	Property	Value
CommandButton1	Name	cmdAssistant
CommandButton1	Caption	(Remove the caption string so there's no text in the label.)
CommandButton1	Picture	Assistnt.bmp
CommandButton1	PicturePosition	12 – fmPicturePositionCenter

Note   You can't type the picture filename Assistnt.bmp in the Picture property in the Properties window. You have to click the button at the right of the Picture property value (the button label has three ellipsis points, or a series of three periods; see the illustration immediately below), which displays the Load Picture dialog box. In the dialog box, change to the Chapter 12 practice folder, select the Assistnt.bmp file, and then click OK.

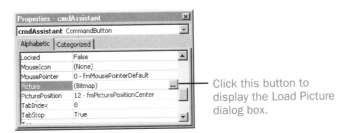

Click this button to display the Load Picture dialog box.

4. Click the UserForm and then click the Run Sub/UserForm button or press F5 to display the custom File Search dialog box. The custom File Search dialog box, frmSearch, should look like the following:

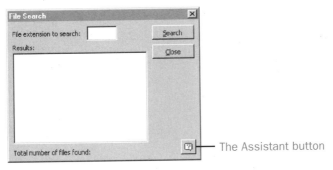

The Assistant button

5. Click the Close button and then double-click the *cmdAssistant* control in the UserForm frmSearch you added. Add the following within the *cmdAssistant_Click* procedure:

```
DisplayOfficeAssistant
```

6. Copy the *DisplayOfficeAssistant* procedure below the *cmdAssistant_Click* procedure. (You started to create the *DisplayOfficeAssistant* procedure in the section "Displaying a Custom Balloon" and completed it in the section "Displaying Labels" earlier in this chapter.)

7. On the File menu in the Excel application window, click the custom File Search menu item.

You'll see the custom File Search dialog box when you click File Search on the File menu. Click the Assistant button in the dialog box to display the Assistant and its balloon. Now your users can review the steps involved in conducting a file search.

8. Exit Excel and save your changes.

Chapter Summary

There are six elements in the Office Assistant's balloon in all Office applications: a heading, icons, text, labels, check boxes, and button sets. Using these elements, you can create custom balloons that look and function like balloons displayed by Office applications. In addition, if the Office Assistant is visible, you can use the Assistant's balloon to display messages rather than using the Visual Basic for Applications *MsgBox* function. This allows you to mimic Office behavior. Because the Assistant and Balloon objects are defined in the Microsoft Office 9.0 Object Library, you can write code once and reuse the code for multiple Office applications.

Preview of Next Chapter

The next chapter reveals how to develop COM add-ins. The COM add-in model provides a consistent way for developers to connect, disconnect, register, secure, and deploy an add-in for any Office application. Chapter 14 provides a more in-depth description of the COM add-in model, so that developers can continue to hone their skills and expand their add-ins to any Office 2000 application.

Developing COM Add-Ins for Office

Chapter 13

Developing COM Add-Ins

Estimated time: 60 minutes

- Get started quickly by learning how to create a simple COM add-in.

- Determine how to debug a COM add-in.

- Learn how to add and delete menu items and toolbar buttons from a COM add-in.

- Understand how to set up, in a COM add-in Office application, events such as selection changes.

- Use the Package and Deployment Wizard in Microsoft Visual Basic to prepare your COM add-in for distribution to your customers.

Add-ins are tools you can build to customize and extend any Microsoft Office 2000 application. Add-ins perform specific tasks and are usually accessed through a menu command or a toolbar button. Add-ins can also perform tasks in the background, responding to such events as selection changes in Microsoft Word or new mail items in Microsoft Outlook.

The most common, versatile way to customize and extend Office 2000 is by developing a Component Object Model (COM) add-in. A COM add-in is a .dll or .exe file that's registered on a user's machine. You can write code in any programming language, such as Visual Basic or Microsoft Visual C++, and use the same add-in code and file in any Office 2000 application. Once you know how to create a COM add-in, you'll be able to create an add-in for any Office 2000 application.

This chapter describes the most common features of add-ins and shows you how to build a COM add-in from start to finish.

Creating a COM Add-In

You can create a COM add-in for Office 2000 in any programming language that lets you create a COM .dll or COM .exe file. These languages include Microsoft Visual C++, Visual J++, Visual Basic version 5.0 or higher (Professional or Enterprise Edition), and the version of Visual Basic for Applications included in Microsoft Office 2000 Developer. The examples in this chapter use Visual Basic version 6.0.

Creating a COM Add-In with Visual Basic

To create a simple COM add-in for Office 2000 using Visual Basic version 6.0, complete the following steps:

ActiveX DLL

1. Start Visual Basic. In the New tab on the New Project dialog box, double-click the ActiveX DLL icon to create a new project. The Class1 class module is added by default.

2. In the Project Explorer, right-click the Class1 class module and select Remove Class1. Click No when prompted to save changes in Class1.

3. From the Project menu, click Components to display the Components dialog box for the current project.

4. Click the Designers tab and select Addin Class (if it's not already selected). This adds the menu item Add Addin Class to the Project menu.

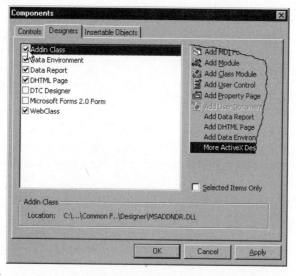

5. Click Add Addin Class from the Project menu. In the Properties window, change the Name property of the Designer project item from AddinDesigner1 to ConnectWord. Set the Public property to True and then click OK.

6. In the General tab of the ConnectWord window, enter or select the values listed in the following table. You may have to resize the Add-in Designer window in order to see the Initial Load Behavior drop-down list at the bottom of the General tab.

Property	Value
Addin Display Name text box	Type **Microsoft Office Basic COM Add-In for Word.**
Application drop-down list	Microsoft Word
Application Version drop-down list	Microsoft Word 9.0
Initial Load Behavior drop-down list	None

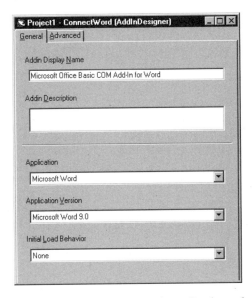

The COM add-ins dialog box displays the "friendly name" of the add-in, which is "Microsoft Office Basic COM Add-In For Word." The Application drop-down list contains the applications for which you can register your COM add-in. COM add-ins are supported in Office 2000 and later versions. If you have Office 2000 installed on your machine, each Office 2000 application will be listed. The Initial Load Behavior drop-down list at the bottom of the General tab allows you to set how your add-in loads. Chapter 14, in the section "COM Add-In Load Behavior Settings," describes the different load behaviors in more detail.

The default load behavior in the General tab is set to None; consequently, the add-in won't automatically load when you start Word. Instead, you have to load the add-in using the COM Add-Ins dialog box. The next section, "Test the COM Add-In," describes how to use the COM Add-Ins dialog box.

7. In the Project Explorer window, make sure you select the ConnectWord project item, and then click the View Code button or press F7. In the ConnectWord code window, select AddinInstance from the Object drop-down list. When you select AddinInstance, the *Sub* procedure *AddinInstance-_OnConnection* is automatically inserted, as shown in the figure below.

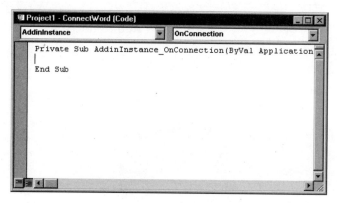

8. Add the following line to the *AddinInstance_OnConnection* procedure:

```
MsgBox "Add-in connected to: " & Application.Name
```

9. Select OnDisconnection from the Procedures drop-down list and add the following line to the *AddinInstance_OnDisconnection* procedure:

```
MsgBox "Add-in disconnected"
```

10. From the Project menu, click Project1 Properties. Type **BasicCOMAddIn** in the Project Name text box and then click OK.

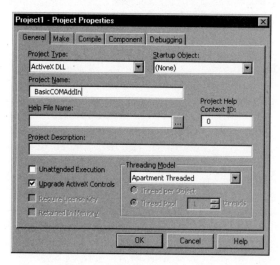

The project name represents the first part of the programmatic identifier (ProgID) of your COM add-in. The ProgID lets you uniquely identify your COM add-in.

Note   Programmatic identifiers are described in the next chapter.

11. On the File menu, click Save Project and save the project files under the names shown in the following table. Note that Visual Basic assigns the appropriate extension to each file.

File	File name	Extension
Add-in Designer	ConnectWord	.dsr
Project	BasicCOMAddIn	.vbp

Test the COM Add-In

The next step is for you to test your COM add-in.

1. Click the File menu, and then click Make BasicCOMAddIn.dll. In the Make Project dialog box, click OK.

When you compile the .dll, it's automatically registered in the Windows system registry. Because of the Add-in Designer, the add-in is registered where the Office application (such as Word) will know to load it.

2. Start Word. Click Customize on the Tools menu to display the Customize dialog box. Then click the Commands tab and select Tools from the Categories list box. Scroll down the Commands list box adjacent to the Categories list box until the COM Add-Ins command is in view.

In Word, the COM Add-Ins command is listed at the top of the Commands list box. However, the COM Add-Ins command is not listed in the same position in the Commands list box of every Office application, so you'll then need to scroll down the list.

3. Click COM Add-Ins and drag the command to the right end of the menu bar in Word, beside the Help menu.

4. Click the COM Add-Ins command to open the COM Add-Ins dialog box. Select the Microsoft Office Basic COM Add-In for Word check box, and then click OK.

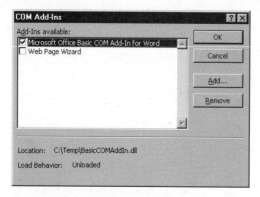

The following message box appears. Click OK to dismiss it.

5. Click COM Add-Ins again. Clear the Microsoft Office Basic COM Add-In for Word check box, and then click OK. Visual Basic displays a message box with the text, "Add-in disconnected." After you click OK on the message box, the add-in is disconnected.

The COM add-in you created is now compiled as a .dll file, registered, and available on your computer. When your add-in is fully developed and debugged, you'll need to *package* and *deploy* it—that is, make it available to other users. The last section of this chapter describes how to deploy your COM add-in so that you can register and install it on any user's machine.

Debugging Your COM Add-In

When errors occur or your add-in doesn't work as expected, you need to debug your code. To debug a COM add-in for Office in Visual Basic version 6.0, you simply place breakpoints in your code, put your Visual Basic project in run mode, and start the appropriate Office application.

Using the COM Add-Ins Dialog Box

Visual Basic lets you set breakpoints and go through your code line-by-line to detect and correct errors. To debug your code using the COM Add-Ins dialog box, complete the steps on the facing page.

1. In the Project Explorer, select the ConnectWord project and click the View Code button. Place the cursor in the line containing `Private Sub AddinInstance_OnConnection` and press F9 to add a breakpoint. Then press F5 or click Start on the Run menu to run your project. Click OK on the project Properties dialog box when it is displayed.

2. Restart Word. Click COM Add-Ins to display the COM Add-Ins dialog box. Select the Microsoft Office Basic COM Add-In for Word check box, and then click OK.

Note To learn how to find the COM Add-Ins command, see steps 2 and 3 in the section, "Test the COM Add-In."

Office loads the BasicCOMAddIn add-in into Word and calls the *OnConnection* procedure. Note that the add-in is actually running in the background in Visual Basic rather than as a compiled .dll on your computer. The breakpoint that you put in the *OnConnection* procedure stops code execution at the first line. The line is highlighted in yellow, indicating that your project is in break mode.

Note If nothing happens when you attempt to debug your add-in project, make sure you placed your project in run mode after you checked the add-in in the COM Add-Ins dialog box.

---

3. Press F8 to step into the *OnConnection* procedure and debug your add-in.

Note Adding breakpoints and stepping through each line of code to find errors is discussed in chapter 2, in the section, "Debugging Your Code." While debugging a COM add-in, the Visual Basic project is in break mode and Word is suspended (that is, the window appears "frozen"). To continue working in Word, you must take your project out of break mode, either by pressing F5 to put your Visual Basic project back in run mode or by stopping the Visual Basic project by clicking End from the Run menu.

---

4. Press F5 to put your project back in run mode. The message box with the text "Add-in connected to: Microsoft Word" appears. Click OK to close the message box.

Important When the line of code with the *MsgBox* function executes, you'll notice that the "Add-in connected to: Microsoft Word" message box appears in front of the Visual Basic window. This is very important to be aware of, because if your COM add-in project displays a message box or custom dialog box while your add-in project is in run mode in Visual Basic, the Office application may appear "frozen" after it loads the COM add-in. You need to switch to the Visual Basic window to interact with the message box or dialog box. (If your Visual Basic project is compiled into an add-in (.dll) and the Office application loads that compiled .dll file, *any* message box or custom dialog box will appear in front of the Office application window.)

Changing Code While in Break Mode

Visual Basic lets you fix errors in your code while in break mode. If your changes, however, affect the compiled state of the project, Visual Basic will display a message box, as shown below, telling you that the action will reset your project, and asking if you want to proceed anyway.

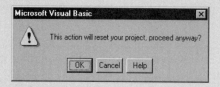

If you click OK, Visual Basic stops your project, but the Office application in which the add-in is loaded is not notified by Visual Basic that the add-in is no longer available. (You'll see that if you return to the Office application and display the COM Add-Ins dialog box, the add-in is still selected.) To reload the add-in, you must follow these steps:

1. Display the COM Add-Ins dialog box and clear the add-in check box. Click OK.

2. Switch to Visual Basic and run the project again by clicking Start from the Run menu.

3. Switch back to the Office application and display the COM Add-Ins dialog box.

4. Select the add-in check box and click OK.

The COM add-in's *OnConnection* procedure is executed again. If the *OnConnection* procedure isn't executed, exit and start the Office application again.

If you click Cancel in the message box, Visual Basic discards your changes and returns the project to break mode.

Stop the Project to Edit Your Code

1. Switch back to Word, click the COM Add-Ins command, and then *clear* the Microsoft Office Basic COM Add-In for Word item in the COM Add-Ins dialog box. Click OK.

2. Click the COM Add-Ins command, and then select Microsoft Office Basic COM Add-In for Word in the COM Add-Ins dialog box. Click OK.

The first line of the *OnConnection* procedure is highlighted in yellow, indicating that your project is in break mode. The following steps explain how to stop a project when you want to add or edit your code.

3. Click and drag the yellow arrow in the margin of the code module next to the line where code execution halts. Drag the arrow to the end of the procedure until it is adjacent to the line that contains the text End Sub.

4. Press F5 to put your project back in run mode.

5. In Word, click the COM Add-Ins command and then clear the Microsoft Office Basic COM Add-In for Word option in the COM Add-Ins dialog box. Click OK. Switch to the Visual Basic window. The *OnDisconnection* procedure runs.

   If there are errors, repeat steps 1 through 3. If there aren't, the add-in will be unloaded from the Office application. You can now safely stop your project.

6. In Visual Basic, click End on the Run menu.

Your project is back in design mode, where you can edit your code to fix errors or add new code to continue your project. When you need to debug your add-in, put your project back in run mode, return to the Office application, and select the appropriate add-in check box in the COM Add-Ins dialog box.

Note   If you find that your add-in isn't loading after you've selected the add-in check box in the COM Add-Ins dialog box, a connection between Office and your Visual Basic project may have been lost. Return to the COM Add-Ins dialog box, clear the add-in check box, and restart the Office application. When you display the COM Add-Ins dialog box again and select your add-in check box, the add-in should load.

Exposing Add-Ins Through Menus and Toolbars

After you set up the basic COM add-in project, you'll need to determine how the add-in will function in an Office 2000 application. Most add-ins will be *exposed*, or made available to the end user, through a custom menu or toolbar button. Generally, the add-in adds command bar customizations. The end user clicks on the customized menu or button, which executes some code in the add-in or displays a custom dialog box.

Other add-ins don't have a visible user interface like command bar customizations. Some add-ins will be loaded when the application is started and work in the background, handling events such as the opening, closing, or saving of documents. The examples in this section describe the code that allows your add-in to add a menu item that displays a custom dialog box . You can also set up your add-in to trap events from an Office application such as those described in chapters 5 and 10.

Activating Add-Ins Through Command Bar Customizations

When a COM add-in is loaded in an Office application, the first code that's executed is the code in the *OnConnection* event procedure. Each Office application initializes its menus and toolbars when the application's initialization sequence executes, and you should place code that customizes the application's command bars in the *OnConnection* procedure.

The following steps explain how to structure your code so that all command bar customization code is in one place, making the add-in project simpler, more readable, and easier to expand.

Adding a Menu Command When a COM Add-In Loads

When a COM add-in is loaded and the *OnConnection* procedure executes, your code should first ensure any command bar customizations previously added by your add-in exist. If they don't, the procedure given at the end of the following steps adds the specific customizations to the command bar set.

1. Switch to your COM add-in project in Visual Basic. On the Project menu, click References to display the References dialog box, then scroll down the list of Available References and select Microsoft Office 9.0 Object Library. Click OK to close the References dialog box.

   The Microsoft Office 9.0 Object Library defines the objects, methods, properties, and events that allow you to manipulate menus or toolbars, or to add custom menus and toolbars in an Office application. Chapter 11, "Creating Menus and Toolbars," provides a complete description of how to use the *CommandBars* collection object to customize menus and toolbars.

2. Click Add Module on the Project menu. In the Properties window, set the Name property of the class module to CmdBarInit.

3. At the top of the CmdBarInit code module, add the following declarations.

```
Public HostApp As Object
Dim HostCmdBars As Office.CommandBars
Dim CBEvents As New CmdBarEvents
Const m_sBtn1Caption As String = "Button1"
Const m_sBtn1Tag As String = "Button1"
```

   The first declaration declares the variable *HostApp* as the generic type Object; *HostApp* represents the Office application that the add-in is currently loaded into. (The *HostApp* variable will be set in the *OnConnection* procedure in a later step.)

The variable *HostCmdBars* is declared as the type CommandBars, which is defined in the Microsoft Office 9.0 Object Library. All Office applications access the *CommandBars* collection object. Here, the variable is used to store the *CommandBars* collection object of the Office application that the add-in is currently loaded into. The *HostCmdBars* variable will be set in the *InitCmdBarCustomizations* procedure, which is listed in the next step.

The *CBEvents* object variable references the class CmdBarEvents. For information on how to add this class, see the "Setting Up the Button Click Event Procedure" section following the current set of steps. The CmdBar-Events class contains command bar event procedures for each custom command bar button added.

The last two declarations are constants that are used to set the properties of the custom menu command that will be added. The strings are declared as constants at the beginning of the code module, so if they change, you need to change them only in one place in your code.

4. To determine if any command bar controls added by your add-in already exist, add the following *InitCmdBarCustomizations* procedure:

```
Sub InitCmdBarCustomizations()
    GetCommandBars
    If HostCmdBars.FindControls(Tag:=m_sBtn1Tag) _
        Is Nothing Then
        AddMenuCtrls
    Else
        Set CBEvents.CtlBtn1 = HostCmdBars _
            .FindControls(Tag:=m_sBtn1Tag).Item(1)
    End If
End Sub
```

The first line of the *InitCmdBarCustomizations* procedure calls the *Sub* procedure *GetCommandBars*, which will be added in the following steps. The *GetCommandBars* procedure sets the variable *HostCmdBars*. The If...Then...Else block uses the *FindControls* method on the *CommandBars* collection object to determine if any control in the command bar set has the custom string tag equal to the constant m_sBtn1Tag.

If the *FindControls* method doesn't find any controls that match the search criteria, it returns a value of Nothing. This causes the If...Then expression to evaluate to True and the function *AddMenuCtrls* is called. If the *FindControls* method returns one or more existing controls that match the search criteria, the Click event is set up for the existing control(s).

5. Add the following *AddMenuCtrls* procedure (in this example only one custom command bar control—namely, a button—is being added):

```
Sub AddMenuCtrls()
    Dim ctlBtn As CommandBarButton
    Set ctlBtn = HostCmdBars("Tools").Controls.Add
    With ctlBtn
        .Caption = m_sBtn1Caption
        .Tag = m_sBtn1Tag
        Set CBEvents.CtlBtn1 = ctlBtn
    End With
End Sub
```

6. Add the following function at the end of the CmdBarInit code module.

```
Sub GetCommandBars()
    Select Case HostApp.Name
        Case "Outlook"
            Set HostCmdBars = HostApp _
                .ActiveExplorer.CommandBars
        Case Else
            Set HostCmdBars = HostApp.CommandBars
    End Select
End Sub
```

This example assigns the *HostCmdBars* variable to the *CommandBars* collection object in an Office application. This lets you retrieve the collection once and store it globally for use by all the code in your add-in that manipulates the command bars. In Outlook, the *CommandBars* collection object can be retrieved through the active Explorer window (or any Explorer object). In all other Office applications, the *CommandBars* collection object is retrieved through the Application object.

7. In the Project Explorer, select the ConnectWord project item and click the View Code button. In the ConnectWord code module, add the following lines to the *OnConnection* procedure:

```
Set HostApp = Application
InitCmdBarCustomizations
```

When Office calls the *OnConnection* procedure, an instance of the *Application* object (of the application into which the add-in is being loaded) is *passed in*. The *Application* object is specified in the first argument of the *OnConnection* procedure. The name of the argument is *Application* and it is declared as the generic type Object.

The Set statement sets the public variable *HostApp*, which was declared in the CmdBarInit code module, to the *Application* object passed into the *OnConnection* procedure. The second line is the call to the *InitCmdBarCustomizations* procedure, which was added in the CmdBarInit code module.

Setting Up the Button Click Event Procedure

The following steps describe how to set up the Click event procedure. Once set up, the procedure will be called every time a specific command bar button is clicked by the user, allowing code you add in the Click event procedure to be executed.

1. On the Project menu, click Add Class Module. Then set the Name property of the class module to CmdBarEvents in the Properties window.

2. At the top of the CmdBarEvents class module, add the following declaration:

```
Public WithEvents CtlBtn1 As Office.CommandBarButton
```

3. In the Object drop-down list on the class module, click CtlBtn1.
    This inserts the Click event procedure for the command bar button.

4. Add the following line to the Click event procedure:

```
MsgBox Ctrl.Caption
```

5. On the File menu, click Make BasicCOMAddIn.dll.

6. Start Word. Select the Microsoft Office Basic COM Add-In for Word add-in check box in the COM Add-Ins dialog box, and then click OK.

7. Click OK to dismiss the message box with the text "Add-in connected to: Microsoft Word." On the Tools menu, click the custom button Button1. The message box with the caption "Button1" appears.

8. Click OK to dismiss the message box. Click Customize on the Tools menu. While in command bar custom-ization mode, hold down the CTRL key, and then click and drag Button1 on the Tools menu to any other visible toolbar or menu. Repeat this step, and then click Close on the Customize dialog. There are now a few copies of the custom button Button1 in the command bar set.

9. Click any instance of the custom button Button1 in the command bar set. No matter which copy is clicked, the same code is executed and a message box is displayed.

Displaying a Custom Dialog Box

If you scroll through the Insert, Format, or Tools menus on any Office application, you'll notice that a dialog box appears whenever you click a menu command that contains an ellipsis (...) in its caption string. To follow this standard Windows user-interface design guideline, in the following steps you add the code to the Click event procedure associated with the custom menu item that displays that dialog box. (That is, you add an ellipsis to the custom menu item added by the COM add-in.)

Add a Custom Dialog Box and Load It Through the Click Event

1. On the Project menu in the COM add-in project, click Add Form. The Add Form dialog box should appear. If the Add Form dialog box doesn't appear, click Options on the Tools menu and in the Options dialog box click the Environment tab. In the Show Templates For group, select the Forms check box and click OK. Then click Add Form on the Project menu again.

2. In the Add Form dialog box, click Dialog in the New tab and click Open. In order to make the new form represent a typical dialog box, the following properties are automatically set:

Property	Value
BorderStyle	3 – Fixed Dialog
MinButton	False
MaxButton	False
ShowInTaskbar	False
WhatsThisButton	False

3. Double-click the Dialog item in the Project Explorer to make the form active, and then double-click the OK button on the new form. In the code module, add the code **Unload Me** to the *OKButton_Click* event procedure.

4. In the Procedures drop-down list, click CancelButton and add the same code, **Unload Me**, in the *CancelButton_Click* procedure.

5. Double-click the CmdBarEvents item in the Project Explorer to make the code module active, and then add the following line to the *CtlBtn1_Click* procedure:

```
Dialog.Show Modal:=vbModal
```

The *Show* method takes two arguments. The *Modal* argument indicates whether a form should be displayed as *modal* or *modeless*. Dialog boxes are generally displayed as modal, which means that the user can't interact with the Office application until the dialog box has been dismissed.

Note Although the *Modal* argument in Visual Basic is optional and the default form display for the Show method is modal, you should explicitly set the *Modal* argument to vbModal when displaying a form from a COM add-in. If you don't explicitly set the argument, the form will be displayed as modeless and it will not appear in front of the Office application window. In this case, you need to set the parent window of the modeless to the Office application window.

6. In the CtlBtn1_Click procedure, add an apostrophe (') to the beginning of the line `MsgBox Ctrl.Caption` to prevent the message box from being displayed.

7. Double-click the CmdBarInit item in the Project Explorer to make the code module active and add an ellipsis to the string constant m_sBtn1Caption that was declared at the beginning of the module. The constant declaration should appear as follows:

```
Const m_sBtn1Caption As String = "Button1..."
```

8. Switch to Word and in the COM Add-Ins dialog box, clear the item Microsoft Office Basic COM Add-In for Word if it's selected. Click OK to dismiss the COM Add-Ins dialog box and click Exit on the File menu to exit Word.

9. Switch back to your Visual Basic project and on the File menu, click Save Project to save the new project items. On the File menu, click Make BasicCOMAddIn.dll, and in the Make Project dialog box, click OK.

10. Start Word. Select the Microsoft Office Basic COM Add-In For Word add-in check box in the COM Add-Ins dialog box, and then click OK.

11. Click Button1 on the Tools menu to display the custom dialog box.

    If you chose to run the project in Visual Basic rather than compile the project and then let the Office application load the compiled project, the resulting dialog box will be displayed in front of the Visual Basic window. This is similar to the custom dialog box behavior that occurs when you debug your Visual Basic code. If you compiled the add-in into a .dll without running the Visual Basic project, custom dialog boxes and message boxes will appear in front of the Office application.

Deleting Command Bar Customizations

When a COM add-in is loaded and the *OnConnection* procedure is executed, code that you added in the steps for "Adding a Menu Command When a COM Add-In Loads" determines if any command bar customizations added by your add-in already exist. If they don't, a procedure that adds the specific customizations to the command bar set is executed.

When an add-in is unloaded and the *OnDisconnection* procedure executes, your code conversely should determine whether command bar customizations should be removed. Notice that the following steps are similar to the steps for adding menu commands when a COM add-in loads.

1. In the Project Explorer window (with the ConnectWord project item selected), click the View Code button so the code module is active. In the *OnDisconnection* procedure, add the following code:

```
If RemoveMode = ext_dm_UserClosed Then
    DeleteMenuCtrls
End If
```

The first argument passed to the *OnDisconnection* event procedure is the *RemoveMode* value. The two values passed in are ext_dm_Host-Shutdown and ext_dm_UserClosed. The value of ext_dm_UserClosed is passed into the *RemoveMode* argument when you unload an add-in through the COM Add-Ins dialog box. When the add-in is cleared in the COM Add-Ins dialog box, the add-in is no longer available. Although the add-in is still registered, you should remove command bar customizations from the command bar set when the user unloads the add-in.

The value of ext_dm_HostShutdown is assigned to the RemoveMode argument when the Office application unloads the add-in while the application is exiting. In this case, you should retain command bar customizations. This way, the customizations will already be present the next time the Office application is started, without executing the code to add them. (In most cases, the application will unload add-ins when you exit it.)

2. Double-click the CmdBarInit item in the Project Explorer to make the code module active. Add the following *DeleteMenuCtrls* procedure at the CmdBarInit code module.

```
Sub DeleteMenuCtrls()
    Dim ctlItem As CommandBarControl
    Dim ctlColl As CommandBarControls

    Set ctlColl = HostCmdBars.FindControls(Tag:=m_sBtn1Tag)

    If Not ctlColl Is Nothing Then
        For Each ctlItem In ctlColl
            ctlItem.Delete
        Next ctlItem
    End If
End Sub
```

The *DeleteMenuCtrls* procedure uses the FindControls method to return all copies of the custom menu command in the command bar. The *FindControls* method allows you to support the scenario in which the user has moved your custom menu command from its original position or has copied the custom menu command to another menu. The section "The FindControls Method" in chapter 11 describes more about the *FindControls* method.

3. Switch to Word and in the COM Add-Ins dialog box, clear the item Microsoft Office Basic COM Add-In for Word if it's selected. Click OK to dismiss the COM Add-Ins dialog box and click Exit on the File menu to exit Word.

4. Switch back to your Visual Basic project, click Make BasicCOMAddIn.dll on the File menu and in the Make Project dialog box, click OK.

5. Start Word. Select the Microsoft Office Basic COM Add-In for Word check box in the Make Project dialog box, and then click OK. Display the COM Add-Ins again and clear the Microsoft Office Basic COM Add-In for Word check box in the COM Add-Ins dialog box. All instances of the custom menu command Button1 are removed.

Loading Add-Ins on Demand Through Command Bars

Add-ins that just add customizations to a command bar and execute code only when a custom menu item or toolbar is clicked don't need to be loaded when the Office application starts. Instead, you can have the add-in load *on demand*— that is, when the user clicks on a customization, the add-in loads into memory immediately following the click event.

To add your custom commands after your add-in is installed, you need to set the initial load behavior of the COM add-in so that it loads the next time the Office application starts. Office then sets the load behavior registered for the add-in so the custom command demand-loads the add-in the next time the Office application is started.

Because your add-in is loaded only on demand, it does not get loaded when the Office application is started, and thus does not affect the time it takes to start an Office application. Add-ins that *are* loaded when the Office application is started increase the time it takes to start the Office application.

Load an Add-In at Next Startup Only

1. In your COM add-in project, double-click the ConnectWord project item in the Project Explorer to make the Add-in Designer window active.

2. In the Initial Load Behavior drop-down list, select Load At Next Startup Only.

3. In the Project Explorer window, double-click the code module CmdBarInit to make it the active module. In the procedure *AddMenuCtrls*, add the following Select Case statement so that the procedure appears as follows:

```
Sub AddMenuCtrls()
    Dim ctlBtn As CommandBarButton
    Set ctlBtn = HostCmdBars("Tools").Controls.Add
    With ctlBtn
        .Caption = m_sBtn1Caption
        Select Case HostApp.Name
            Case "Microsoft Word"
                .OnAction = "!<BasicCOMAddIn.ConnectWord>"
        End Select
        .Tag = m_sBtn1Tag
        Set CBEvents.CtlBtn1 = ctlBtn
    End With
End Sub
```

When an add-in is set to load on demand, Office needs a way to associate a command bar control with a COM add-in. Office determines the association by evaluating the OnAction string assigned to the custom command bar control. In the Select Case statement above, the OnAction string is assigned to the programmatic identifier (or ProgID) of the COM add-in when it is loaded into Word. In the section "Adding Another Office Application to the Add-In" after the following steps, the ProgID will be BasicCOMAddIn.ConnectExcel and assigned to the OnAction property when the add-in is loaded into Excel. (The ProgID allows you to uniquely identify your COM add-in and distinguish it from other COM add-ins.)

4. Switch to Word and exit the application. On the File menu, click Make BasicCOMAddIn.dll. In the Make Project dialog box, click OK and then start Word. The COM add-in should be loaded and Button1 should be added to the Tools menu.

5. Display the COM Add-Ins dialog box and select Microsoft Office Basic COM Add-In for Word in the list. At the bottom of the dialog box you'll see the Load Behavior label and the current load status of the add-in. The load status will be "Load on Demand, (currently loaded)."

6. Click OK to dismiss the COM Add-Ins dialog box (do *not* clear the add-in in the list).

7. Click Button1 on the Tools menu to ensure that the click event is fired and displays the custom dialog box. Click OK.

8. Click Exit on the File menu and restart Word. Display the COM Add-Ins dialog box by clicking the COM Add-Ins command.

See steps 2 and 3 in the section "Test the COM Add-In" to learn how to find the COM Add-Ins command. In the COM Add-Ins dialog box, with Microsoft Office Basic COM Add-In for Word selected in the list, the load status will be "Load on Demand, (not currently loaded)."

9. Click OK to dismiss the COM Add-Ins dialog box. Click Button1 on the Tools menu. Office loads the add-in in Word, because this is the first time the add-in is needed. The add-in has now been loaded on demand and the custom dialog box is displayed.

10. Click OK to dismiss the custom dialog box, and then display the COM Add-Ins dialog box again.

With Microsoft Office Basic COM Add-In for Word selected in the list, the current load status will be "Load on Demand, (currently loaded)."

The user doesn't have to explicitly load the add-in through the COM Add-Ins dialog box. Once the add-in is set up on the user's machine, the next time the user starts Word, the COM add-in loads and Button1 is added. Thereafter, the next time the user starts the application, the add-in isn't loaded at startup, but only when the user clicks the custom command on the Tools menu.

Note For information on using the Package and Deployment wizard to deploy your add-in onto a user's machine, see the section "Packaging and Deploying Your COM Add-In" near the end of this chapter.

Adding Another Office Application to the Add-In

1. Click the Add Addin Class command on the Project menu. In the Properties window, change the Name property of the Designer project item from AddinDesigner1 to ConnectExcel. Set the Public property to True. When you set the Public property of the Add-in Designer to True, a message box is displayed. Click OK.

2. Add the following settings to the fields in the General tab of the ConnectExcel window:

Add-in Designer window	Setting
Addin Display Name edit box	Add the text "Microsoft Office Basic COM Add-In for Excel."
Application drop-down	Microsoft Excel
Application Version drop-down	Microsoft Excel 9.0
Initial Load Behavior drop-down	None

3. In the Project Explorer window, with the ConnectExcel project item selected, click the View Code button at the top left of the Project Explorer window. In the ConnectExcel code window, select AddinInstance in the Object drop-down list of the module.

4. In the *AddinInstance_OnConnection* procedure, which is added automatically after AddinInstance is selected in the Object drop-down list, add the following lines:

```
Set HostApp = Application
InitCmdBarCustomizations
```

5. In the Procedure drop-down list of the class module, select OnDisconnection. In the *AddinInstance_OnDisconnection* procedure, add the following code.

```
If RemoveMode = ext_dm_UserClosed Then
    DeleteMenuCtrls
End If
```

6. In the Project Explorer window, double-click the code module CmdBarInit to make it the active module. In the procedure *AddMenuCtrls*, add a new Case expression for Excel so that the Select Case statement appears as shown on the following page.

```
Select Case HostApp.Name
    Case "Microsoft Word"
        .OnAction = "!<BasicCOMAddIn.ConnectWord>"
    Case "Microsoft Excel"
        .OnAction = "!<BasicCOMAddIn.ConnectExcel>"
End Select
```

In the Select Case statement above, the OnAction string is assigned to the programmatic identifier (or ProgID) of the COM add-in when it is loaded into Excel. When the add-in is loaded into Excel, the ProgID is BasicCOMAddIn.ConnectExcel.

7. On the File menu, click Save Project to save the ConnectExcel project file. Name the file ConnectExcel.dsr.

8. Switch to Word and exit the application. On the File menu in the Visual Basic window, click Make BasicCOMAddIn.dll. In the Make Project dialog box, click OK.

9. Start Excel and click Customize on the Tools menu to display the Customize dialog box.

10. In the Customize dialog box, click the Commands tab and select Tools from the Categories list box. Scroll down the Commands list box next to the Categories list box until the COM Add-Ins command is in view.

11. Drag the COM Add-Ins command to the end of the main menu bar in Excel (to the right of the Help menu).

12. Click Close to dismiss the Customize dialog box. Click the COM Add-Ins command and in the COM Add-Ins dialog box select Microsoft Office Basic COM Add-In for Excel. Click OK. Button1 is added to the bottom of the Tools menu.

13. Click Button1 to display the custom dialog box.

14. Click OK, and then click the COM Add-Ins command again. Clear the Microsoft Office Basic COM Add-In for Excel option and click OK. The add-in is unloaded and the custom menu item Button1 is removed from the Tools menu. Exit Excel.

Trapping Events in an Add-In

Events are some of a developer's more powerful and useful tools. They allow you to create solutions that intercept double-clicking a cell in an Excel spreadsheet, the selection of a sentence in a Word document, a right-click on a shape on a PowerPoint slide, or a mail item opened in Outlook's Inbox. Events enable more solutions than any other aspect of the programming model that Microsoft Office 2000 provides. Events can be handled, or *trapped*, in a COM add-in just as easily as they can be from any VBA project in an Excel workbook, for example.

The following steps describe placing code to handle Excel events in a class module. The code is encapsulated in a separate class module; that way the code in the class module containing the *OnConnection* and *OnDisconnection* procedures is kept separate from the code that handles events in an application. If your COM add-in works for more than one Office application, this code separation makes the project simpler to follow and easier to read and expand.

Setting Up the SheetSelectionChange Event in Excel

1. On the Project menu, click Add Class Module. In the Properties window, set the Name property to ExcelEvents.

2. If a reference to the Excel object library isn't listed in your COM add-in project, click References on the Project menu and select the Microsoft Excel 9.0 Object Library entry in the Available References list. You'll know if there's no reference to Excel if "Excel" doesn't appear in the AutoList Members drop-down list after you type **As** in the declaration statement in the next step.

3. Add the following line of code to the top of the class module ExcelEvents:

```
Public WithEvents XlApp As Excel.Application
```

The *WithEvents* keyword specifies that variable *XlApp* is an object variable used to respond to events that Excel triggers. After the new object has been declared with events, it appears in the Object drop-down list in the ExcelEvents class module, and you can write event procedures for the new object. (When you select the new object in the Object drop-down list, the valid events for that object are listed in the Procedure drop-down list.)

4. Click XlApp in the Object drop-down list of the ExcelEvents class module.

5. Click the *SheetSelectionChange* event in the Procedure drop-down list to add the procedure to the ExcelEvents class module. Add the following code to the *SheetSelectionChange* procedure:

```
Private Sub XlApp_SheetSelectionChange( _
    ByVal Sh As Object, ByVal Target As Excel.Range)

    MsgBox "SheetSelectionChange"
End Sub
```

In the Procedure drop-down list, all of the Application-level events that Excel triggers are listed when *XlApp* is selected in the Object drop-down list. In this example, the *SheetSelectionChange* event procedure is set up.

The *SheetSelectionChange* event is triggered every time you change the active cell on the active worksheet. You can add any of the Application-level events by selecting any of the events listed in the Procedure drop-down list.

6. On the File menu, click Save Project to save the ExcelEvents project file. Name the file ExcelEvents.cls.

7. In the Project Explorer window, select the ConnectExcel item and click the View Code button at the top left of the Project Explorer window. Add the following line of code to the top of the ConnectExcel code module.

```
Dim XlEvents As New ExcelEvents
```

As described in the Visual Basic for Applications help file, the *New* keyword enables the implicit creation of an object. In this case a new instance of the ExcelEvents class module is created on first reference to it, so you don't have to use the Set statement to assign the object reference. The first reference to this class is made in the next step.

8. In the procedure *AddinInstance_OnConnection*, add the following line at the end of the procedure:

```
Set XlEvents.XlApp = Application
```

Before the event procedures will run, the declared object *XlApp* in the ExcelEvents class module must be connected with the *Application* object of Excel. This is done with the code `Set XlEvents.XlApp = Application` in the *OnConnection* procedure. After the *OnConnection* procedure is executed, the *XlApp* object in the ConnectExcel code module points to the Excel *Application* object, and the event procedures in the ExcelEvents class module will run when the Excel events occur.

9. Save the project, and on the Run menu, click Run or click Make Basic-COMAddIn.dll in the File menu. In the Make Project dialog box, click OK.

You can either put the project in run mode or compile it into a .dll file before loading the add-in into Excel to see how the SheetSelection-Change event is handled.

10. Start Excel, and in the COM Add-Ins dialog box, select Microsoft Office Basic COM Add-In for Excel. Click OK. Select any cell in the active worksheet.

Every time you select a different cell, you'll see a message box with the text *SheetSelectionChange*.

11. Click the COM Add-Ins command again. Clear the Microsoft Office Basic COM Add-In for Excel option and click OK.

Quick Guide: Setting Up an Event Procedure In a COM Add-in

You can easily set up your COM add-in to handle events from any Office application. To add code to handle events in an application, use the code structure defined in the previous example and follow this abbreviated list of steps (Word will be used here; to handle the events from another application, change the specific application where appropriate in the steps below):

Set up the WindowSelectionChange event in Word

1. On the Project menu, click Add Class Module. In the Properties window, set the Name property to WordEvents.

2. If a reference to the Word object library doesn't exist in your COM add-in project, add one by clicking References on the Project menu and selecting the Microsoft Word 9.0 Object Library entry in the Available References list.

3. Add the following line of code to the top of the class module WordEvents:

```
Public WithEvents WdApp As Word.Application
```

The variable *WdApp* appears in the Object drop-down list in the WordEvents class module.

4. Click WdApp in the Object drop-down list of the WordEvents class module. The events for the Word application are listed in the Procedure drop-down list.

5. Click any event in the Procedure drop-down list to add the procedure to the WordEvents class module. For example, click WindowSelectionChange in the Procedures drop-down list and add the following code in the inserted *WindowSelectionChange* event procedure:

```
MsgBox "WindowSelectionChange"
```

6. In the Project Explorer window, select the ConnectWord item and click the View Code button at the top left of the Project Explorer window. Add the following line of code to the top of the ConnectWord code module:

```
Dim WdEvents As New WordEvents
```

7. In the *AddinInstance_OnConnection* procedure, add the following line at the end of the procedure:

```
Set WdEvents.WdApp = Application
```

(continued)

Quick Guide: Setting Up an Event Procedure In a COM Add-in *(continued)*

> After the *OnConnection* procedure is executed, the *WdApp* object in the class module points to the Word *Application* object, and the event procedures in the WordEvents class module will run when the Word events occur.

8. Save the project, and then run or compile the project into a .dll file.

9. Start Word and load the add-in through the COM Add-Ins dialog box if the add-in is not currently loaded. Type in some text and select the text using the mouse pointer, or use the arrow keys to change the selection. You'll see a message box telling you that the event procedure in the COM add-in triggered and trapped the WindowSelectionChange event in Word.

Add-Ins That Handle Office Application Events Only

Add-ins don't necessarily have to have any visible user interface, such as command bar customizations. With the addition of a number of events in Office, some add-ins are loaded when the application is started and work in the background, handling events such as documents opening, closing, or being saved. Add-ins that handle the save event of any document, for example, may ascertain whether a document has certain properties (such as whether the author or title is filled out) before it's saved. If the document doesn't, the add-ins prompt the user to add properties that are listed in the Properties dialog box, which is accessed by clicking Properties in the File menu.

In a Word document, add-ins may also handle the double-click event to determine if text was selected by the double-click, and what the text is. If the text is a company's name, for example, a dialog box may be automatically displayed. This is functionally equivalent to inserting a symbol in a Word document and then double-clicking that symbol in the text: when you double-click the symbol, the Symbol dialog box is automatically displayed.

Setting the Load Behavior to Load at Application Startup

To set the basic COM add-in to load when Word starts up, complete the following steps. Once completed, the add-in monitors the selection change event in the background, evaluating the text of the selection to see if it contains the acronym "VBA." If it does, the add-in expands the acronym to "Visual Basic for Applications." This functionality behaves like Word's AutoCorrect, but it requires the user to select first before the text is "corrected."

1. In your COM add-in project, double-click the ConnectWord project item in the Project Explorer to make the Add-in Designer window active.

2. In the Initial Load Behavior drop-down list, select Startup.

3. Double-click the WordEvents item in the Project Explorer to make the code module active, and then add the following code in the *Window-SelectionChange* event:

```
If Sel.Type <> wdSelectionNormal Then Exit Sub
If UCase$(Trim$(Sel.Text)) = "VBA" Then
    Sel.Text = "Visual Basic for Applications"
End If
```

The one and only argument passed into the *WindowSelectionChange* event in Word is the *Sel* argument. The *Sel* argument is defined as the *Selection* object and represents the current selection in Word. If the selection type is not normal text, the *Sub* procedure is exited.

If it is text, the expression evaluated in the If...Then statement determines whether the selected text is equivalent to the acronym "VBA." The procedure makes the comparison by removing spaces from the string representing the selected text and converting the string to uppercase. If the expression is true, it changes the selected text to "Visual Basic for Applications."

4. Add a comment to the beginning of the line `MsgBox "WindowSelection-Change"` so the message box doesn't appear when the selection is changed.

5. Exit Word. On the File menu in Visual Basic, click Make BasicCOMAddIn.dll. In the Make Project dialog box, click OK.

6. Start Word. Type in some text and insert the acronym "VBA" anywhere. Select the text using the mouse pointer or use the arrow keys while holding down the SHIFT key.

Word converts the acronym "VBA" to "Visual Basic for Applications." The add-in is loaded when Word starts because the add-in is now registered to load at Word startup. The user doesn't have to explicitly load the add-in through the COM Add-Ins dialog box. As you'll see in the next section, you can use the Package and Deployment wizard to deploy your add-in onto a user's machine.

Once the add-in is set up on the user's machine, the next time the user starts Word, the add-in is available (assuming you set the initial load behavior to be either Startup or Load at Next Startup Only). The next chapter explains the different load behaviors of a COM add-in.

Packaging and Deploying Your COM Add-In

Users commonly interact with setup programs to install new applications and components on their computers. When your COM add-in is ready to be distributed to other users, you can use the Package and Deployment Wizard that's installed by Visual Basic 6.0 or Office 2000 Develper. The Package and Deployment Wizard allows you to create a setup program that you supply to your users so that they can install your add-in.

Depending on the initial load behavior of the add-in, the next rime a user starts an Office application that the add-in targets, the add-in will be available.

The following example steps through the use of the Package and Deployment Wizard in order to package the basic COM add-in created in this chapter.

Note Before you package and deploy your COM add-in, make sure the initial load behavior of your COM add-in is set appropriately; that is, according to the functionality the add-in provides.

Package the Basic COM Add-In

1. Load the Visual Basic project that represents your basic COM add-in. Exit Word and Excel if they running.

2. Click the File menu, and then click Make BasicCOMAddIn.dll. In the Make Project dialog box, click OK. (This step isn't necessary if you compiled your COM add-in project into a .dll.)

3. From the Windows Start menu, navigate to the Microsoft Visual Basic 6.0 folder in the Programs menu. Click Microsoft Visual Basic 6.0 Tools, and then click Package & Deployment Wizard. The Package and Deployment wizard is displayed.

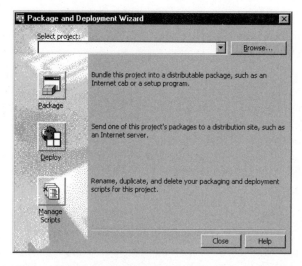

4. Click the Browse button next to the "Select project" text box and navigate to your COM add-in project. Click OK.

5. Click the Package button below the "Select project" text box. If you haven't compiled your project into a .dll, the wizard will display the dialog box on the following page, indicating that the project needs to be compiled. If necessary, click Compile.

   If the source files are newer than the previously compiled project, the wizard displays a dialog box indicating that the source files are newer and asks if you want to recompile. If you want the latest changes in your packaged solution, click Yes.

If a compiled file exists and is the most up-to-date, the Package and Deployment wizard displays another dialog box with a series of steps. The first step is selecting a package type.

6. In the Package Type list box, select Standard Setup Package. As described in the Description text box below the Package Type list box, this creates a package that will be installed by a setup.exe program.

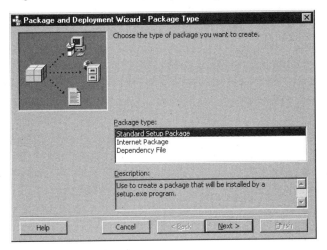

7. Click Next. In the Package Folder step, create a new folder or select a folder where the package will be assembled on your machine.

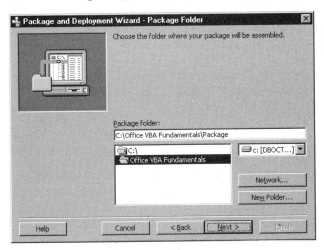

In most cases, the best place to place the package is in a subfolder named Package in the folder containing your compiled .dll and source files. The Package and Deployment wizard automatically selects this folder by default.

8. Click Next. In the Missing Dependency Information dialog box, click OK. For more information on the Missing Dependency Information dialog box, click the Help button in the dialog box. Clicking OK tells the wizard to proceed without the dependency information for the listed files.

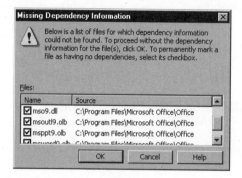

9. In the Included Files dialog box, make sure that only the following files are selected:

- BasicCOMAddIn.dll (or whatever the name of your compiled COM add-in .dll file is)

- Setup.exe

- Setup1.exe

- St6unst.exe

- Vb6stkit.dll

The file associated with the file listed as VB6 Runtime and OLE Automation is Msvbvm60.dll. You don't need to redistribute this file because Office always installs it. Its size is 1.3MB, and it will add to the size of the package that the wizard creates.

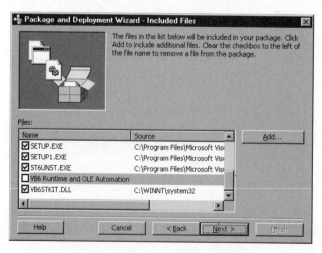

Often, other files listed in this dialog box are object libraries. If you made a reference to any of the Office object libraries, including any of the following, it will appear in the dialog box:

- Word (msword9.olb)

- Excel (excel9.olb)

- PowerPoint (msppt9.olb)

- Access (msacc9.olb)

- Outlook (msoutl9.olb)

- Office (mso9.dll)

If these files are listed, clear them. (Because they're part of the Office install, your package doesn't need to redistribute them.)

Note If you are using a service pack of Visual Basic 6.0 or a service release of Office 2000, you may find that your machine has a newer version of the VB6 Runtime file Msvbvm60.dll than your user's machine. The newer version of the VB6 Runtime file may have some fixes that your COM add-in requires. Make sure you fully test your add-in with the Office application. If you find that your add-in doesn't work for some reason on another user's machine (one that doesn't have Visual Basic 6.0 installed), package the VB6 Runtime from your installation of Visual Basic.

---

10. Click Next twice. In the Installation Title step, type in any name that you want to appear in the setup screen that's displayed when the user starts the setup.exe program. The Cab Options step is skipped. By default, it is set to package the COM add-in into a single CAB file.

11. Click Next twice. In the Install Locations step, add the text **\BasicCOM-AddIn** after the text $(ProgramFiles) in the *Install Location* field.

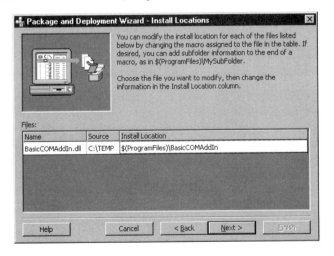

The string $(ProgramFiles) represents a token indicating the Program Files folder. Setup uses the token because the full path to the Program Files folder on the user's machine may differ. The subfolder information added to $(ProgramFiles) indicates that the subfolder BasicCOMAddIn will be created and the files will be copied to that location.

Note that the Start Menu Items step is skipped. This step allows you to list items that would appear on the Windows Start menu after setup is complete. But because your COM add-in is loaded only through Office, no items are required on the Start menu.

12. Click Next twice. In the Finish step, enter a name in the Script name text box and click Finish.

The script is a file that saves the settings made in the Package and Deployment wizard. The script is useful the next time you need to create a package containing the exact same files and settings—but with a newly compiled COM add-in .dll file.

13. In the Packaging Report dialog box, click Save Report, click Save, and then click Close.

The report saved is a text file containing information about where your package is found and about a batch file that allows you to recreate the cab file quickly when you make changes to some of the files.

14. Click Close to close the Package and Deployment wizard.

On the location specified in the Package folder step of the wizard, you'll find a CAB file, a Setup.exe file and Setup.lst. The Setup.exe program requires the LST file. The CAB file contains all of the files associated with your COM add-in, along with other files the setup program requires.

Installing the COM Add-In on Another Machine

1. Copy the three files onto another user's machine and run the Setup.exe program. The setup program begins like most other standard setup programs. Note that the installation title is displayed at the top left of the setup screen as well as in the caption of the first dialog box that's displayed. It's also displayed in the first paragraph in the dialog box, in the line beginning with "Welcome."

2. Click OK. Click the Click Here to Begin Setup button, as shown in the figure on the following page.

Most users won't change the default directory listed. This directory is the one you entered in the Install Locations step of the wizard.

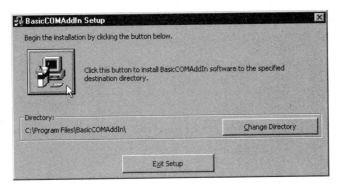

3. Click OK. Your COM add-in is now installed on the user's machine.

4. Start Word or Excel. A message box is displayed indicating that the add-in is connected and the custom menu item Button1 is added to the Tools menu. Your add-in has now been packaged and deployed onto a user's machine.

Chapter Summary

When you use COM add-ins to extend an Office application, the techniques you learn—to add and delete menu items and toolbar buttons, build a demand-loaded add-in, set up event procedures, and package and deploy your add-in—apply equally to all Office applications. This chapter describes the common tasks you'll need to develop COM add-ins. The next chapter describes in more depth these and a few other common tasks.

Chapter 14

Inside COM Add-Ins

Estimated time: 90 minutes

- Understand the basics of the COM add-in model in Microsoft Office 2000, including the advantages of developing a COM add-in instead of using the add-in capabilities that Microsoft Office 97 provides.

- Learn why you should use the COM add-in model and what design considerations to use.

- Develop, register, and load a COM add-in for more than one Office 2000 application.

- Determine how an Office application is loaded and distinguish between the applications that a COM add-in is loaded into.

- Answer frequently asked questions about COM add-ins.

In Office 97, the method of developing add-ins varies according to the application. What method you use depends on both the Office 97 application and the programming language it's developed with, such as Microsoft Visual Basic or Microsoft Visual C++. You have a total of nine ways to customize and extend the capabilities of Office 97 through add-ins, with each application, except Microsoft Outlook, having at least two ways to extend its capabilities through add-ins. However, the ways of connecting, disconnecting, registering, and deploying add-ins are quite different in each Office 97 application. Also, because each application has its own add-in model, you can't write code in one file and have it load the same way in any other Office 97 application.

The COM add-in model in Office 2000, however, is what an add-in model should be: one consistent way for developers to connect, disconnect, register, secure, and deploy an add-in for any Office application. In addition, the Office 2000 COM add-in model lets a developer transfer skills and add-ins developed for one Office application to any other. This chapter gives an overview of the COM add-in model. Once you understand the COM add-in model for Office 2000, you'll be able to hone your skills and expand your add-ins to any Office 2000 application and later versions of those applications.

Important   Existing add-ins created for Office 97 will continue to work in Office 2000 without modification. The COM add-in model for Office 2000 works side-by-side with the existing add-in model for each Office application. You should note, however, that COM add-ins created for Office 2000 won't work in Office 97. Because the architecture for COM add-ins in Office exists only in Office 2000 and later versions, Office 97 doesn't know how to connect a COM add-in.

In technical terms, a COM add-in is an in-process or out-of-process Automation server. The file extension is .dll or .exe, and you have to implement the interface IDTExtensibility2. You can create it in any programming language (like Visual Basic or Visual C++) that can create an Automation server. In simple terms, a COM add-in is one way for developers to build an add-in and plug it into any Office 2000 application.

Note This chapter assumes that you've read the previous chapter and that you have experience developing add-ins for Office. This chapter is the next step beyond the basic fundamentals of the COM add-in model and is meant to provide more insight into—and give more examples of—the COM add-in model.

Quick Guide: How To Write a COM Add-In With Visual Basic 6.0

Use the steps below as a starting point or as a reminder of what you need to get started quickly when you create a COM add-in using Visual Basic 6.0. The same steps are described more fully in the section of the previous chapter entitled "Creating a COM Add-In with Visual Basic."

1. Start with an ActiveX DLL project in Visual Basic 6.0.

2. On the Project menu, click Add Addin Class.

Note If the Add Addin Class menu item doesn't appear, click Components on the Project menu. In the Components dialog box, click the Designers tab and select Addin Class in the list box. Click OK. You should see the menu item Add Addin Class on the Project menu.

---

3. In the Properties window, change the Public property to True. Click OK after the message box is displayed.

4. On the General tab of the Add-in Designer, select the application that the add-in targets from the Application drop-down list and select Startup in the Initial Load Behavior drop-down list. If the add-in targets more than one application, repeat steps 2 through 4 for each application.

5. Press F7 to display the class module for the Add-in Designer. In the Object drop-down list at the top left of the class module window, select AddinInstance and write code in *OnConnection*, *OnDisconnection*, or in any other procedure listed in the Procedures drop-down list.

6. Compile the add-in (the act of compiling the .dll registers it in the system registry).

7. Start the Office 2000 application that the add-in targets.

Why Should You Develop COM Add-Ins?

If you buy a hair dryer in North America and you travel to Europe, you need to buy an adapter so you can plug it in and use it there. The hair dryer can't plug in and work in all areas of the world.

In Office 97, an add-in that plugs into Microsoft Word can't readily be plugged into Microsoft Excel or any other Office application. You need to develop an "adapter" to plug an add-in for one Office 97 application into another. In Office 2000, the COM add-in model provides the universal adapter to plug any add-in into any Office application.

The COM add-in model supersedes the capabilities of the add-in model provided by each Office 97 application. Because the COM add-in model supersedes Office 97 capabilities, if you've developed add-ins for Office 97, you'll have the option of using the COM add-in model in Office 2000 without sacrificing functionality.

Important   There's one exception where the COM add-in model doesn't supersede Office 97 capabilities. You can't use a COM add-in to extend the list of user-defined functions in Microsoft Excel 2000 that users can enter on worksheets and evaluate. In Excel 97 and Excel 2000, you can still use Visual Basic for Applications code in an XLA file or C/C++ code in an XLL add-in file to extend the list of user-defined functions. See the Microsoft Excel 97 Developer's Kit for more information about user-defined functions.

The Characteristics of an Add-In Model

The following table lists the characteristics that make an add-in model for Office successful. Each characteristic is available in the COM add-in model for Office 2000 and is not consistently available in Office 97. These characteristics all provide reasons why you should use the COM add-in model to create add-ins in Office 2000.

Characteristics of an Office Add-In Model	Remarks
Teaches you how to write an add-in once and apply skills to any application	Each Office 97 application, except Outlook, has at least two ways to extend its capabilities through add-ins. In Office 2000, when you learn how to create a COM add-in once, you've learned how to create it for any Office application.
Allows you to write code in one file and load it into any Office application	The registration of a COM add-in indicates which Office application the add-in file can be loaded into.
Add-ins are easily portable to other Office applications	Using the COM add-in model, you can add an additional Select Case statement where applicable to distinguish which application the add-in is loaded into.

(continued)

(continued)

Characteristics of an Office Add-In Model	Remarks
Allows you to use the programming language or developer tool you like	When Office loads a COM add-in, it doesn't know what programming language was used to build the add-in file. In Office 97, each application connects and disconnects an add-in in a different way based on the programming language the add-in is developed in.
Can set an add-in's connection to optimize performance	Word and Microsoft PowerPoint don't provide a way to load an add-in on demand (that is, when a menu or toolbar customization is clicked). Excel and Microsoft Access do, but in inconsistent ways. COM add-ins provide a consistent way to connect an add-in at application startup or when a user clicks a menu or toolbar customization.
Allows a registering of add-ins in the Microsoft Windows Registry that's consistent across applications	Each Office 97 application provides a different way and a different Windows Registry key to register an add-in. The keys to register a COM add-in are consistent in each Office 2000 application.
Provides a consistent and simple way to communicate between two add-ins PowerPoint's	In Office 97, Word, Excel, PowerPoint, and Access each provide the *Run* method on the *Application* object. However, method varies slightly. With COM add-ins, you can communicate between add-ins consistently using the Object property on the *COMAddIn* object.
Shows one way to learn how to package and deploy an add-in	The Package and Deployment Wizard, available in Visual Basic 6.0 or Microsoft Office 2000 Developer, provides a consistent way to package and deploy a COM add-in.
Can create add-ins that know if an Office application is started from the Windows Start menu or Windows Explorer, through Automation using *CreateObject,* or through an embedded object	A value from 1 to 3 is assigned to the first value of the custom() array argument passed into the *OnConnection* procedure in a COM add-in, indicating how the Office application is started. Add-ins in Office 97 don't provide a way to determine how the application is started.
Allows you to determine if an add-in is loaded when the application is started or after it's started	By using the *ConnectMode* argument passed into the *OnConnection* procedure in a COM add-in, you can determine when the add-in is loaded.

(continued)

(continued)

Characteristics of an Office Add-In Model	Remarks
Gives you the ability to create a template for use in any new add-in projects	You can create a template for Visual Basic 6.0 or Visual C++ to reuse every time you create a COM add-in.
Provides in each application a consistent add-ins dialog box that displays a list of available add-ins	You can access the add-ins dialog box by clicking the Add-Ins menu item or a related item on the Tools menu in each application. In Office 2000 you can access the COM Add-Ins dialog box from the COM Add-Ins command.

Although it'll take a little time to transfer your skills to the new COM add-in model, once you learn it you'll know how to create an add-in for any Office application. If you're an expert in developing add-ins for one Office application and you had plans on developing an add-in for another, you won't need to learn any details about connecting add-ins to another Office application when you use the COM add-in model.

Checklist for Developing COM Add-Ins

Your add-in's elements often determine how you should structure your code. For example, if your COM add-in is loaded when the application starts up, your code would search for your command bar customizations and either add them if they don't exist or set up the Click event procedures if they do exist. You need to build a checklist of what your COM add-in will do. The following table provides a list of the common items and associated tasks you'll need to address while building your COM add-ins.

Item	Tasks
❏ Connection	• Determine if the COM add-in is to be loaded at startup or after startup using the *ConnectMode* argument of the *OnConnection* procedure. • Set up code that handles Office application events. • Add command bar customizations.
❏ Disconnection	• Free memory and system resources by setting variables associated with an object to Nothing. • Remove command bar customizations if the user disconnects the add-in from the COM Add-Ins dialog box. Use the *RemoveMode* argument of the *OnDisconnection* procedure to determine if the add-in is to be unloaded when the application quits or if it will be unloaded through the COM Add-Ins dialog box.

(continued)

(continued)

Item	Tasks
❏ Managing command bar customizations	• Use the *FindControls* method to find all copies of a command bar customization. (See Chapter 11 for more information and for use of the *FindControls* method.) • Use the Protection property of the *CommandBar* object to indicate whether the command bar is protected from user customization. (See Chapter 11 for more information and for use of the *Protection* property.)
❏ Displaying custom dialog boxes (forms)	• Use the Show method of a form to display a custom dialog box or form. • If a custom Visual Basic 6.0 form is displayed from a command bar event procedure such as *Click* or *Change*, pass *vbModal* to the Modal argument in the Show method to ensure that the dialog box is properly displayed in front of the Office application window.
❏ Resources (strings, images)	• Use the Resource Editor in Visual Basic 6.0 to add resources to a COM add-in created in Visual Basic 6.0. You can access the Resource Editor by clicking Add-In Manager on the Add-Ins menu, selecting the VB 6 Resource Editor item in the Available Add-Ins list box, and then selecting the Load/Unloaded check box. • Use the Visual Basic 6.0 functions *LoadResString* and *LoadResPicture* to retrieve string and image resources.
❏ Performance	• Avoid writing a lot of code that gets executed when a COM add-in is first loaded. If a lot of code needs to be executed along with the initialization of other objects or Automation servers when an add-in is loaded, the start time of the Office application can be noticeably increased if the COM add-in is boot-loaded.
❏ Structuring code and resources for international use of an add-in	• Isolate resources that need to be translated to other languages in a resource file stored in the add-in so that there's no need to access the source code or recompile the add-in when strings are translated. • Alternatively, isolate resources that need to be translated in a resource file stored in another .dll file and accessed from the COM add-in. • Edit resources in a COM add-in .dll or .exe file using a software program like Visual C++ that allows you to translate resources without recompiling the add-in .dll/.exe.

An add-in that needs to be loaded when an Office application starts is called a boot-loaded add-in.

(continued)

(continued)

Item	Tasks
❑ Deployment	• Use the Package and Deployment Wizard installed by Visual Basic 6.0 or Office 2000 Developer to deploy COM add-ins. You can also use installation software from third-party vendors. The last section of the previous chapter steps through using the Package and Deployment Wizard. • Determine if your add-in will be registered under the HKEY_LOCAL_MACHINE or HKEY_CURRENT_USER branch of the Windows Registry. • Determine if the add-in will be installed on a machine where end-users have limited control over folders and subfolders.
❑ Security	• Apply for a certificate from a certificate authority. A certificate authority issues, manages, and revokes certificates. • Sign your COM add-in .dlls or .exes before you deploy them to your users.

The COM Add-In Model Overview

The basic elements of a COM add-in consist of connecting and disconnecting the add-in, exposing the add-in to Office through registration in the Windows Registry, and accessing the methods and properties in an Office application. Two main parts of the COM add-in model address the basic elements. The first is the IDTExtensibility2 interface. The second is how and where a COM add-in is registered in the Windows Registry. This section explains both the IDTExtensibility2 interface and the registration of COM add-ins.

IDTExtensibility2 Interface

From a technical perspective, when Office loads a COM add-in into an application, it determines if the interface IDTExtensibility2 exists in the COM add-in. Because using the Add-in Designer will keep you from understanding what it means to implement an interface, it won't be discussed here. Instead, this section discusses the five IDTExtensibility2 methods *OnConnection*, *OnAddInsUpdate*, *OnStartupComplete*, *OnBeginShutdown*, and *OnDisconnection* because Office calls them when a COM add-in is loaded or unloaded.

The description of each method tells you when it is called by Office and lists the information you can retrieve from the method. To a Visual Basic programmer, the methods of the IDTExtensibility2 interface act and behave like events. When you connect an add-in to Office, the *OnConnection* method is called automatically in an action that's similar to the execution of an event procedure. When you disconnect a COM add-in, the *OnDisconnection* method is called automatically. The methods of the IDTExtensibility2 interface are executed in the following sequence:

Execution order and Method	Description of when the procedure is called
1. *OnConnection*	Called when the add-in is loaded into the Office application.
2. *OnAddInsUpdate*	Called when the add-in is loaded into the Office application and after the *OnConnection* procedure is called. If other COM add-ins are also loaded, the *OnAddInsUpdate* procedure is called in the other COM add-ins sequentially.
3. *OnStartupComplete*	Called if the add-in is loaded when the application is started. This procedure is called after the *OnConnection* and *OnAddInsUpdate* procedures, when the application that loads the add-in is started.
4. *OnBeginShutdown*	Called when the application is exiting.
5. *OnDisconnection*	Called when the add-in is being unloaded by the application, either when the application is exiting or when the user clears the COM add-in item in the COM Add-Ins dialog box.

OnConnection

No matter how or when you load the add-in, the *OnConnection* procedure is always called. Use the *OnConnection* procedure to set a public variable representing the *Application* object of the application loading the add-in so that other procedures in your add-in can use this *Application* object.

Syntax

```
Private Sub IDTExtensibility2_OnConnection( _
    ByVal Application As Object, _
    ByVal ConnectMode As AddInDesignerObjects.ext_ConnectMode, _
    ByVal AddInInst As Object, custom() As Variant)
```

Argument	Description
Application	An object representing the *Application* object of the Office application that's loading the COM add-in.
ConnectMode	Can be one of the ext_ConnectMode constant values specified in the table on the facing page.
AddInInst	Represents the *COMAddIn* object defined in the Microsoft Office 9.0 Object Library. Specifically, the *AddInInst* object variable represents the COM add-in itself.
custom()	An array of variant expressions to hold user-defined data. Office sets the first element of the custom() array to a value that represents how the Office application is started.

The following table represents the ext_ConnectMode constant that Office will set the *ConnectMode* argument to in the *OnConnection* procedure. There are two other ext_ConnectMode constants, ext_cm_External and ext_cm_CommandLine, that Office never sets.

Constant	Value	Description
ext_cm_AfterStartup	0	Value returned if the add-in is loaded *after* the Office application starts. If an add-in is demand-loaded or if your add-in is loaded through the COM Add-Ins dialog box, this value will be set to the *ConnectMode* argument.
ext_cm_Startup	1	Value returned if the add-in is loaded *when* the Office application starts.

OnAddInsUpdate

The *OnAddInsUpdate* procedure is called when the load state of an add-in is changed. For example, when an add-in is loaded or unloaded, the *OnAddInsUpdate* procedure is called within the add-in that is being loaded or unloaded—and called in any other COM add-in that is currently loaded.

Syntax

```
Private Sub IDTExtensibility2_OnAddInsUpdate( _
    custom() As Variant)
```

OnStartupComplete

The *OnStartupComplete* procedure is called when the startup sequence of an Office application is complete. This procedure is called only in a boot-loaded add-in.

Syntax

```
Private Sub IDTExtensibility2_OnStartupComplete( _
    custom() As Variant)
```

So what's the difference between the *OnConnection* procedure and the *OnStartupComplete* procedure? The *OnConnection* procedure is the first procedure called when the Office application loads the COM add-in. The instance of the *Application* object of the Office application loading the COM add-in is passed to the *OnConnection* procedure.

You can store the instance of the *Application* object globally so you can use it throughout your COM add-in.

The *OnStartupComplete* procedure is called after the *OnConnection* procedure—but only when all COM add-ins loaded at startup are in memory. That is, first the *OnConnection* procedure is called for every COM add-in that is to be loaded. Once every add-in is loaded, the *OnStartupComplete* procedure is called for every COM add-in that's in memory.

OnBeginShutdown

The *OnBeginShutdown* procedure is called when the shut-down sequence of an Office application begins. This procedure is called only in add-ins that are loaded in memory when the application shuts down.

Syntax

```
Private Sub IDTExtensibility2_OnBeginShutdown( _
    custom() As Variant)
```

OnDisconnection

The *OnDisconnection* procedure is always called, no matter how or when you unload the add-in. You should use the *RemoveMode* argument in the *OnDisconnection* procedure in scenarios where the add-in needs to determine whether it should remove any command bar customizations that it made when it loaded. If the user disconnects an add-in through the COM Add-Ins dialog box, the add-in should remove any menu and toolbar customizations it added to the Office application.

Syntax

```
Private Sub IDTExtensibility2_OnDisconnection( _
    ByVal RemoveMode As AddInDesignerObjects.ext_DisconnectMode, _
    custom() As Variant)
```

The following table represents the ext_ DisconnectMode constant that Office will set the *RemoveMode* argument to in the *OnDisconnection* procedure.

Constant	Value	Description
ext_dm_HostShutdown	0	Value returned when the add-in is disconnected by the application during its shut-down sequence.
ext_dm_UserClosed	1	Value returned after the user clears the add-in item listed in the Available Add-ins list box in the COM Add-Ins dialog box.

COM Add-In Registration

Once you've written code in any of the *IDTExtensibility2* method procedures and throughout your COM add-in, two things need to happen so the COM add-in is recognized by an Office application as an available add-in. Both involve the Windows Registry. The first is to register the add-in on the end user's machine so that the system knows where it's located on the machine. The second is to register the add-in under an Office application key so that Office knows what add-ins are available and when it should be loaded.

In Visual Basic 6.0, when you click Make ProjectName.dll on the File menu and then click OK in the Make Project dialog box, Visual Basic automatically registers the COM add-in in the Windows system registry. The act of compiling the .dll registers it in the Windows system registry, and the system now knows where to locate the add-in. The Package and Deployment Wizard will also register a COM add-in so that the system on your end user's machine will know where to locate the add-in. Even though the add-in is registered on the machine, it still has to be registered where an Office 2000 application will know to load it.

Where COM Add-Ins are Registered for Office

You have two ways to register a COM add-in for use in an Office 2000 application: with a REG file or with the Microsoft Add-in Designer. If you use the Add-in Designer, you don't need a REG file. A REG file allows an add-in to be quickly registered for any Office 2000 application without adding the Addin Class to your COM add-in project in Visual Basic 6.0. A REG file's contents indicate where a COM add-in is registered for an Office 2000 application in the Windows Registry. In the section "How Do I…" later in this chapter, the example under the heading "…Create a COM Add-In Without Using the Add-In Designer" describes how to use a REG file for registering a COM add-in.

COM add-ins are registered under the following key in the Windows Registry:

```
[HKCU\Software\Microsoft\Office\<app>\AddIns\Prog.ID]
```

HKCU is the short form for the HKEY_CURRENT_USER key. The text *<app>* represents the name of any Office application. For example, *Word*, *Excel*, *PowerPoint*, *Access*, or *Outlook*, would replace *<app>*. The programmatic identifier, or ProgID, would replace the text "Prog.ID" for your COM add-in. The section "How Do I…?" later in this chapter describes how to determine and set the programmatic identifier of a COM add-in in Visual Basic 6.0. The following graphic shows how a COM add-in for Word would appear in the Windows registry.

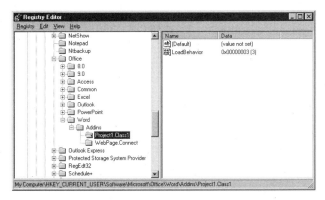

You can also register a COM add-in under the HKEY_LOCAL_MACHINE key. The structure of the key under the HKEY_CURRENT_USER key is exactly the same under the HKEY_LOCAL_MACHINE key. The Add-in Designer used in Visual Basic registers a COM add-in under the HKEY_CURRENT_USER key by default.

COM Add-In Load Behavior Settings

Under each COM add-in key, you need to add and set a LoadBehavior value. The LoadBehavior value determines how your add-in will be loaded. Generally, you'll set the load behavior to one of the values listed in the following table, which also gives examples of when you would use a specific value:

Load behavior	Registry value	Example
None	0	Helper add-in or library of functions needed by other add-ins only at certain times. You don't have to register the helper add-in because you can always call it in Visual Basic code using *CreateObject*. However, if the helper add-in also has some user interface and custom commands that are shown only when the helper add-in is needed, you should register the add-in for Office.
Startup	3	Always load the add-in. See the following section, "Boot-Load versus Demand-Load COM Add-Ins."
Load on demand	9	Loaded when needed. See the following section, "Boot-Load versus Demand-Load COM Add-Ins."
Load at next startup only	10 (hex) or 16 (decimal)	Use this value so that your add-in has the opportunity to add custom commands at the application's next startup. Office sets this value back to 9 to be demand-loaded later by the custom command.

The load behavior values listed in the table also appear in the Initial Load Behavior drop-down list in the Add-in Designer in Visual Basic, as shown in the following illustration.

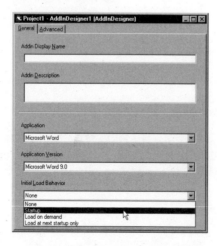

Boot-Load versus Demand-Load COM Add-Ins

Based on the functionality they provide, most add-ins can be categorized as one of either two types (or a combination of both). The first type provides functionality when the user clicks a menu item, a toolbar button, or some other command bar customization. An add-in that needs to be loaded only when a menu item or toolbar button is clicked is called a *demand-loaded* add-in.

The second type is loaded all of the time and just handles document events such as opening, closing, or saving. This kind of add-in can also handle events like selection change or double-clicking in a Word, Excel, or PowerPoint document. An add-in that needs to be loaded all of the time to respond to application events is called a *boot-loaded* add-in. This add-in loads when the Office application starts, or *boots*, and so once your users are ready to use the application, your add-in will be available.

When your add-in monitors events such as saving a document, your add-in may want to determine the file location where the document will be saved. If the document is to be saved to a specific folder, your COM add-in may then determine if specific document properties, such as Title or Comments, are set. Chapter 5, "Managing Documents with Events," describes how to handle the document Save event and determine where the user wants to save a document.

If your add-in monitors the *Selection Change* event for the active window in Word, Excel, or PowerPoint, see Chapter 10, "Handling Window and Content Interaction Events," for information on how to update a command bar customization based on the selection.

You can also write add-ins that both monitor application events and respond when the user clicks a command bar customization.

How Office Loads a COM Add-In

At startup of an Office application, Office reads the \Software\Microsoft\Office \<app>\AddIns key for the application (<app> represents the name of the application being started). Office builds the list of available COM add-ins first from the key HKEY_LOCAL_MACHINE (HKLM) and then from the key HKEY_CURRENT_USER (HKCU). Office first reads from HKLM because if a duplicate COM add-in entry exists under both keys of the registry, the add-in registered under HKLM takes precedence and the HKCU key is ignored. This feature ensures that if an administrator registers an add-in under HKLM, it's always guaranteed to load for all of the machine's users.

Once the list of add-ins is built during the initialization sequence of the Office application, Office starts loading each add-in (at the end of the initialization sequence) whose load behavior is set in the registry to be loaded at startup. In the Windows Registry, the LoadBehavior value would be set to 3.

How Do I...

Office COM add-ins tend to share common elements. It's safe to say that every add-in will have at least some combination of the more common elements listed and described here. Depending on what functionality your add-in provides, you might even consider these elements basic. The previous chapter also describes examples of common elements, such as setting up and handling events in an Office application when the add-in is loaded.

...Set the Programmatic Identifier of a COM Add-In?

Every COM add-in must have a programmatic identifier (ProgID). This is a string that uniquely identifies a given COM add-in. A ProgID, which isn't considered something that an end user should see, is a text string without spaces. ProgIDs are unique identifiers for COM add-ins. A COM add-in can have more than one class, and hence, more than one ProgID.

Set the ProgID in Visual Basic 5.0 or 6.0

You can set the programmatic identifier, or ProgID, of a COM add-in by changing the project name and the class name. Start Visual Basic 6.0, select ActiveX DLL or ActiveX EXE from the New Project dialog box, and complete the following steps:

1. On the Project menu, click Project1 Properties, and then enter **BasicCOMAddIn** or any other project name in the Project Name box. Click OK.

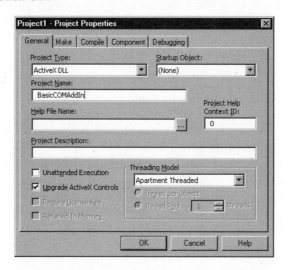

2. In the Project Explorer window, double-click the Add-in Designer to bring it to the front. In the Properties window, set its Name property to any valid string and make sure that its Public property is set to True.

If you're not using the Add-in Designer and you have a class module with the IDTExtensibility2 interface implemented, in the Project Explorer window double-click the Class module Class1 to bring it to the front. In the Properties window, set its Name property to any valid string and make sure that its Instancing property is set to 5 – MultiUse.

...Create a COM Add-In Without Using the Add-In Designer?

To create a COM add-in for Office 2000 without using the Add-in Designer, you need the following programs in addition to Office 2000: Visual Basic 5.0 or 6.0 and Microsoft Notepad (or any application like Microsoft WordPad that allows you to create a text file with the extension .txt). The following example sum-marizes the steps you need to take to create a COM add-in in Visual Basic 6.0 using a .reg file instead of the Add-in Designer. A .reg or REG file is a text file that contains Windows Registry information. The information indicates how you should register the COM add-in for a specific Office 2000 application.

When to Use the Add-In Designer and When to Use a REG File

Each one has its advantages. If you use a REG file, you can create one class that contains the IDTExtensibility2 interface and have this class be used for any Office application the COM add-in is loaded into. This means there is only one ProgID for the COM add-in. This also means there is one *OnConnection* procedure for the COM add-in that is called in every application the add-in is loaded into.

But when you use a REG file you must explicitly register the add-in by importing the contents in the REG file into the Windows Registry each time registration for the add-in changes. (Double-click-ing the REG file in the Windows Explorer imports the contents of the REG file into the Windows Registry.)

For example, if you change the load behavior of an add-in in a specific application, you must change the contents in the REG file and then import the changes to the Windows Registry.

When you use the Add-in Designer, you make the load behavior change in the Initial Load Behavior drop-down list, and the next time you run the project or compile it into a .dll, the changes to the Win-dows Registry are made automatically. This allows you to be a little more efficient in debugging a COM add-in.

The Add-in Designer allows you to register the COM add-in for one application only. If you want to register the add-in for another application, you need to add another Addin Class to your COM add-in project in Visual Basic. The example in the previous chapter under the heading "Adding Another Office Application to the Add-In" shows you how to target your COM add-in for more than one appli-cation. Using multiple Addin classes, however, means that the COM add-in has more than one *OnConnection*, *OnDisconnection*, and any other *IDTExtensibility2* procedure. If you want to have one procedure that is executed every time an add-in is loaded, for example, you must call this procedure from the *OnConnection* procedure in each Addin class module.

Once you have completed the steps in this section that show you how to create a COM add-in using a REG file instead of the Add-in Designer (and have also completed the examples in the previous chap-ter), these differences will be obvious.

> **Important**   If Office attempts to load a registered add-in and the add-in file isn't registered in the Windows system registry, Office automatically removes the add-in's key. Specifically, under the \Office\<app>\AddIns\key, it removes the subkey containing the ProgID of the COM add-in. While debugging your add-in, if you use a REG file rather than the Add-in Designer to register your add-in, you may find its subkey removed. Compile your add-in as a .dll at least once to register your add-in in the Windows system registry. To do this, click Make on the File menu in Visual Basic.

Develop a COM Add-In Without the Add-In Designer

ActiveX DLL

1. Start Visual Basic 6.0 and in the New tab of the New Project dialog box double-click the ActiveX DLL icon to create a new project.

2. On the Project menu, click References to display the References dialog box for the current project, then scroll down the list of Available References and select Microsoft Add-In Designer. Click OK.

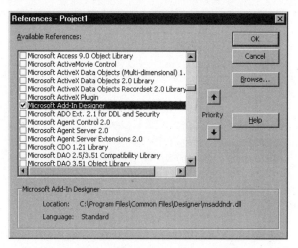

This object library (stored in the file msaddndr.dll) contains the definitions of the IDTExtensibility2 interface, which is what the COM add-in model is centered around and which is described earlier in this chapter in the section "The COM Add-In Model Overview."

3. Add the following line of code to the top of the class module Class1 that's added by default to the ActiveX DLL project:

```
Implements IDTExtensibility2
```

This line of code adds a reference to the *IDTExtensibility2* object to your project. An interface's methods are exposed through the Implements statement. When you enter the above syntax in the class module, IDTExtensibility2's methods become available through the class module's Procedure and Object drop-down lists, as shown in the illustration on the following page.

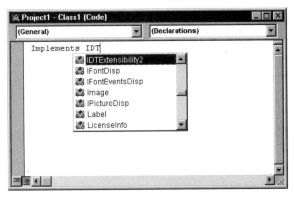

4. Click IDTExtensibility2 in the Object drop-down list of the Class module. The Procedure drop-down list of the class module lists five events for the *IDTExtensibility2* object: OnConnection, OnDisconnection, OnStartupComplete, OnBeginShutdown, and OnAddInsUpdate.

5. Click each of the events in the Procedure drop-down list to add their procedures to the class module Class1. Add a comment in the *OnStartupComplete, OnBeginShutdown*, and *OnAddInsUpdate* procedures and the following two lines in the *OnConnection* and *OnDisconnection* procedures, respectively:

```
MsgBox "Add-in connected"
```

```
MsgBox "Add-in disconnected"
```

The code module should appear as follows:

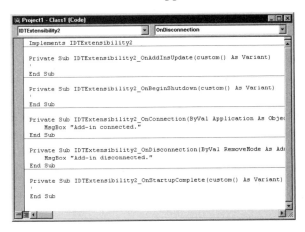

In Visual Basic, you need to add at least a comment to each procedure in order for your code to compile. In the *OnStartupComplete, OnBegin-Shutdown*, and *OnAddInsUpdate* procedures, you add the comment character (an apostrophe) as the one and only line in the procedure.

6. On the Project menu, click Project1 Properties, then enter **BasicCOMAddIn** in the Project Name text box. Click OK.

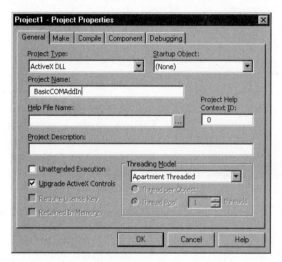

7. In the Project Explorer window, double-click the class module Class1 to make it the active module. In the Properties window, set the Name property of the class module to "Connect" and make sure its Instancing property is set to 5 – MultiUse.

This step and the previous step set the ProgID of the COM add-in. The ProgID allows you to uniquely identify your COM add-in and distinguish it from others.

8. On the File menu, click Save Project to save the project files. Name them as shown in the following table. Visual Basic will provide the indicated extensions automatically.

File	Filename	Extension
Class module	Connect	.cls
Project	BasicCOMAddIn	.vbp

The class module that implements the IDTExtensibility2 interface is the center of every COM add-in. It's the place where the add-in gets called when it's loaded and unloaded in an Office application. In the previous steps, you see a message when you connect and disconnect the add-in. The main class module is where most of the common elements of an add-in are connected, such as adding and removing command bar customizations and responding to events that occur in any of the Office applications.

Test the BasicCOMAddIn Add-In

To make a COM add-in work in Office, you need to make sure that two things happen so that the COM add-in is recognized by an Office application as an available add-in. Both involve registration in the Windows Registry. The first is to register the add-in on the end-user's machine so that the system knows where it's located on the machine. The second is to register the add-in under the Office key so an application knows it's available and can be loaded. Once Office knows the add-in's available, it needs to know when it should load it. This is described in the earlier section of this chapter entitled "COM Add-In Registration."

1. Click the File menu, and then click Make BasicCOMAddIn.dll. In the Make Project dialog box, click OK.

    Doing this will register the COM add-in in the Windows system registry. The act of compiling the .dll registers it in the system registry. However, even though the add-in is registered on the machine, it's yet to be registered where an Office 2000 application will know to load it. This is handled in the following steps.

2. Start Notepad and type the following in the Notepad window:

```
REGEDIT4

[HKEY_CURRENT_USER\Software\Microsoft\Office\
    Word\AddIns\BasicCOMAddIn.Connect]
"LoadBehavior"=dword:00000003
"FriendlyName"="Microsoft Office Basic COM Add-In"

[HKEY_CURRENT_USER\Software\Microsoft\Office\
    Excel\AddIns\BasicCOMAddIn.Connect]
"LoadBehavior"=dword:00000003
"FriendlyName"="Microsoft Office Basic COM Add-In"
```

Important   Make sure that for the text you typed above, the two lines [HKEY_CURRENT_USER\Software\Microsoft\Office\Word\AddIns\BasicCOMAddIn.Connect] are actually concatenated on one line with no space in Notepad. For display purposes in this book, the two lines can't be listed as one. The same holds true for the line beginning with Excel\—make sure that it's typed on the same line that ends with Office\.

---

3. Save the text file as **COMAddin.reg**. You *must* type in the **.reg** extension in the filename text box so that Notepad knows to save the file with the extension .reg rather than .txt.

4. In the Windows Explorer, navigate to the file you saved in the step above and double-click the file COMAddin.reg.

The following message should appear, indicating that the information in the COMAddin.reg file was successfully entered in the registry. If not, you may have typed something incorrectly in step 2. You can also copy the file COMAddin.reg from the Chapter 14 folder on the CD that comes with this book.

5. Switch to the Visual Basic window containing the BasicCOMAddIn project and press F5 to run the project.

6. Start Word or Excel and then switch to the Visual Basic window. The following message box will appear in front of the Visual Basic window:

7. Click OK in the message box and in Word or Excel click Exit on the File menu. Switch to the Visual Basic window.

You'll see the message box in front of the Visual Basic window indicating that the add-in is disconnected. In step 2 on the previous page, the value on the line that lists the text "LoadBehavior" is 3. This means that the add-in is set to be loaded when the Word or the Excel application is started. (Earlier in the chapter, under the section "COM Add-In Load Behavior Settings," the different load behaviors for a COM add-in are described, as are examples to help you decide what the load behavior for your COM add-in should be.)

In the case of the basic COM add-in described here, the add-in is registered and available on your machine. Once your add-in is fully developed, debugged, and ready to go, the next step is to package it and make its functionality available to other users. The previous chapter describes how to deploy your COM add-in so that you can register and install it on any user's machine. The Package and Deployment Wizard also has an option to package a .reg file and have it executed on the user's machine during setup of the COM add-in.

...Distinguish the Office Application Loading the Add-In?

As Office continues to evolve, consistency among the applications becomes more prominent and lasting. More and more Office functionality, like menus, toolbars, and the Office Assistant, is implemented across the applications. The functionality is written once centrally in a .dll and is loaded into each Office application. COM add-ins allow you to develop functionality that can be loaded in any combination of Office applications, including Microsoft FrontPage 2000.

However, there are a few differences among the Office applications, and sometimes you'll have to write code that is application-specific within the shared COM add-in.

To determine what application a shared COM add-in is loaded in, you first retrieve its name. The first argument passed to the *OnConnection* event procedure in the COM add-in is an instance of the *Application* object of the Office application where the add-in is loaded. You can retrieve the application's name by accessing the Name property of the *Application* object. Once you know the application's name, you can use a Select Case statement to distinguish between applications and write application-specific code, as you'll see in the following Select Case statement. Throughout your COM add-in, you'll use a variation of the following Select Case statement when you write application-specific code.

Set Up an Object Variable Assigned to the Host Application

1. In the COM add-in project created in the previous example (in the sections "Develop a COM Add-In Without the Add-In Designer" and "Test the BasicCOMAddIn Add-In"), click Add Module on the Project menu. In the Add Module dialog box, select Module in the New tab and click Open. Add the following declaration:

```
Public HostApp As Object
```

   You define the generic object variable *HostApp* as a public-level variable so you can use it throughout any code module. However, you can declare this variable at any level, depending on how you write your code.

2. Switch to the Connect class module and add the following line as the first line in the procedure *IDTExtensibility2_OnConnection*:

```
Set HostApp = Application
```

   Because the Set statement is the first line in the *OnConnection* procedure, the very first thing that happens when the COM add-in is loaded is the assigning of the variable *HostApp* to the *Application* object of the Office application loading the COM add-in. The first argument passed into the *OnConnection* procedure is named *Application*. The argument is declared as the generic type Object because it could be the application object of any of the Office applications.

3. Below the set statement added in the previous step, add the following Select Case block.

```
Select Case HostApp.Name
    Case "Microsoft Word"
    Case "Microsoft Excel"
    Case "Microsoft PowerPoint"
    Case "Microsoft Access"
    Case "Outlook"
End Select
```

As noted previously, throughout your COM add-in you use variations of the Select Case statement, depending on the differences between applications and how many applications your COM add-in targets; you may not need all the *Case* expressions listed in this step.

4. Add application-specific code within each *Case* expression. The following contains code that writes out the number of items in a specific application collection.

```
Select Case HostApp.Name
    Case "Microsoft Word"
        Debug.Print HostApp.Documents.Count
    Case "Microsoft Excel"
        Debug.Print HostApp.Workbooks.Count
    Case "Microsoft PowerPoint"
        Debug.Print HostApp.Presentations.Count
    Case "Microsoft Access"
        Debug.Print HostApp.CurrentObjectName
    Case "Outlook"
        Debug.Print HostApp.ActiveExplorer _
            .CurrentFolder.Items.Count
End Select
```

5. Repeat steps 1 through 4 in the example in the section "Test the BasicCOMAddIn Add-In" in order to register your COM add-in.

In step 2 of that section, make sure to add the registry information in the Notepad file for each of the applications listed in the Select Case block in the previous step. To do this, copy the follow-ing registry information in the Notepad file for each Office application. You'll also need to change Word in the following registry information to the name of the Office application. Also remember to concatenate in the Notepad file the first two lines below.

```
[HKEY_CURRENT_USER\Software\Microsoft\Office\
Word\AddIns\BasicCOMAddIn.Connect]

"LoadBehavior"=dword:00000003
"FriendlyName"="Microsoft Office Basic COM Add-In"
```

6. Switch to the Visual Basic window containing the *BasicCOMAddIn* project and press F5 to run the project.

7. Start an Office application that the add-in is registered for and switch to the Visual Basic window.

The message box indicating that the add-in is connected will appear in front of the Visual Basic window. After you click OK on the message box, the Immediate window in Visual Basic displays the count of the collection specified in the Select Case block for that application.

Write Code in COM Add-Ins with the Auto List Members Drop-Down List

Unlike what happens when you write code in the Visual Basic Editor in each of the Office applications, when you type in the dot after the object variable *HostApp* in the previous steps, you won't see the Auto List Members drop-down list. This is because you declared the object variable *HostApp* as the generic type Object. Therefore, when you write code, the code editor you're writing in doesn't know which application you're referring to when you hit the dot. You can easily make your code-writing experience take advantage of the Auto List Members drop-down list functionality by declaring more variables that are defined as the application your COM add-in targets.

1. On the Project menu in Visual Basic, click References to display the References dialog box for the current COM add-in project.

2. Scroll down the list of Available References and select each of the object library names listed in the table below.

Microsoft Office 2000 Application	Object Library Name
Office	Microsoft Office 9.0 Object Library
Word	Microsoft Word 9.0 Object Library
Excel	Microsoft Excel 9.0 Object Library
PowerPoint	Microsoft PowerPoint 9.0 Object Library
Access	Microsoft Access 9.0 Object Library
Outlook	Microsoft Outlook 9.0 Object Library

You'll select only the object libraries associated with each of the Office 2000 applications your COM add-in is targeting. The table lists the object library associated with each Office 2000 application. Note that in most cases, you'll also need to reference the shared Office 2000 object library. This object library appears as Microsoft Office 9.0 Object Library in the Available References list.

3. In the standard code module inserted in the previous example, add the following declarations.

```
Public WrdApp As Word.Application
Public XclApp As Excel.Application
Public PptApp As PowerPoint.Application
Public AccApp As Access.Application
Public OlkApp As Outlook.Application
```

You declare each variable as a specific application object. When you made the reference to each application's object library in the previous step, each application became listed in the Auto List Members drop-down list after you typed the word "As" in each declaration.

4. Starting at the first line in the *OnConnection* procedure in the Connect class module, add the following Select Case block.

```
Select Case Application.Name
    Case "Microsoft Word"
        Set WrdApp = Application
    Case "Microsoft Excel"
        Set XclApp = Application
    Case "Microsoft PowerPoint"
        Set PptApp = Application
    Case "Microsoft Access"
        Set AccApp = Application
    Case "Outlook"
        Set OlkApp = Application
End Select
```

Because the Select Case statement is the first line in the *OnConnection* procedure, the very first thing that happens when the COM add-in is loaded is the assessment of the name of the application loading the COM add-in. The appropriate object variable is set, depending on the application.

5. Within each *Case* expression added in the previous example (not the previous step), use the variable for each application object. For example, add the following line to the *Case* expression for Word.

```
MsgBox WrdApp.Documents.Count
```

You'll see the Auto List Members drop-down list when you type in the dot after the variable *WrdApp*.

When the COM add-in is loaded into an application, only one application object variable declared will be set. All others will continue to be set to Nothing by default. This approach means that if you target your COM add-in for multiple Office applications, Visual Basic will define and make space in memory for object variables that are never used. However, this overhead will be small and insignificant. Now you can take advantage of the benefits of the Auto List Members drop-down list functionality.

...Create a Demand-Loaded Add-In?

To create a demand-loaded COM add-in, you need to set the OnAction property on the *CommandBarButton* or *CommandBarComboBox* object. When you click a command bar button, for example, Office parses the string returned by the OnAction property to determine what COM add-in needs to be loaded and to handle the click event. If the syntax of the OnAction string contains a ProgID of a registered COM add-in, the click event is sent to the Click event procedure in the COM add-in. The syntax for the OnAction property string is as follows:

```
!<Prog.ID>
```

In your code that creates a command bar button, the string you assign to the OnAction property would appear similar to the following code:

```
Set cmdBtn = Application.CommandBars("Help") _
    .Controls.Add
With cmdBtn
    .Caption = "&Custom Control"
    .OnAction = "!<Project1.Connect>"
    .Tag = "MyControlTag"
End With
```

Set Up a Demand-Loaded COM Add-In

1. Start Visual Basic 6.0 and double-click the ActiveX DLL icon in the New Project dialog box.

2. On the Project menu in Visual Basic, click References to display the References dialog box for the current COM add-in project, scroll down the list of Available References and select Microsoft Office 9.0 Object Library. Click OK.

3. On the Project menu, click Project1 Properties and in the Properties dialog box, change the Project Name from Project1 to DemandLoad.

4. Click Add Addin Class on the Project menu and on the General tab of the Add-in Designer, select Microsoft Excel from the Application drop-down list and "Load at next startup only" in the Initial Load Behavior drop-down list.

5. In the Properties window, change the Name property from AddinDesigner1 to Connect. Also change the Public property to True. Click OK after you see the message box.

6. Press F7 to display the Addin class module's code window.

7. Add the following lines of code so that the Addin class module appears as follows (and as listed in the DmndLoad.vbp project in the Chapter 14 practice files):

```
Dim HostApp As Object
Dim WithEvents cmdBtn As Office.CommandBarButton
Const m_sProgId As String = "!<DemandLoad.Connect>"

Private Sub AddinInstance_OnConnection( _
    ByVal Application As Object, _
    ByVal ConnectMode As AddInDesignerObjects.ext_ConnectMode, _
    ByVal AddInInst As Object, custom() As Variant)

    Set HostApp = Application
```

```
        Select Case ConnectMode
            Case ext_cm_Startup
                AddCmdBarCustomizations

            Case ext_cm_AfterStartup
                If Not HostApp.CommandBars.FindControls( _
                    Tag:="DemandLoadButton1") Is Nothing Then
                    Set cmdBtn = HostApp.CommandBars _
                        .FindControls(Tag:="DemandLoadButton1") _
                        .Item(1)
                Else
                    AddCmdBarCustomizations
                End If
        End Select
End Sub

Private Sub AddinInstance_OnDisconnection( _
    ByVal RemoveMode As AddInDesignerObjects _
    .ext_DisconnectMode, custom() As Variant)

    If RemoveMode = ext_dm_UserClosed Then
        HostApp.CommandBars.FindControls( _
            Tag:="DemandLoadButton1").Item(1).Delete
    End If
End Sub

Private Sub cmdBtn_Click( _
    ByVal Ctrl As Office.CommandBarButton, _
    CancelDefault As Boolean)

    MsgBox "Demand-loaded add-in is now loaded."
End Sub

Sub AddCmdBarCustomizations()
    Set cmdBtn = HostApp.CommandBars("Tools") _
        .Controls.Add
    With cmdBtn
        .Caption = "&Custom Control"
        .OnAction = m_sProgId
        .Tag = "DemandLoadButton1"
    End With
End Sub
```

8. Add a breakpoint to the first line in the *OnConnection* procedure by placing the cursor in the line `Private Sub AddinInstance_OnConnection` and pressing F9.

9. Press F5 to run the project. Click OK in the project Properties dialog box when it is displayed.

Start Excel and Step Through the COM Add-In

1. On the Windows Start menu, click Programs and then Microsoft Excel. Excel starts and the COM add-in created in the previous example loads. The *OnConnection* procedure is called and execution breaks on the first line.

2. Press F8 to step through the code. The code continues through the Select Case statement and the code in which ConnectMode equals ext_cm_Startup is executed. The procedure *AddCmdBarCustomizations* is called to add a new custom command bar control on the Tools menu. In the *AddCmdBarCustomizations* procedure, the custom control is connected to the Click event procedure.

3. Press F5 to continue execution through the *OnConnection* procedure.

4. Switch to Excel and click Custom Control at the bottom of the Tools menu. The Click event of the command bar button executes and a message box is displayed.

Important   When you debug a COM add-in in Visual Basic, you'll see a message box or a custom dialog box whose parent is the Visual Basic window. The Office application may appear as if it has stopped. However, if you switch back to the Visual Basic window you'll see the message or custom dialog box.

---

5. Switch back to the Visual Basic window and click OK on the message box.

6. Switch to Excel and click Exit on the File menu.

7. Start Excel again. Note that the breakpoint in the *OnConnection* procedure in the running Visual Basic project isn't hit. That's because the *OnConnection* procedure isn't executed. The COM add-in is demand-loaded; therefore, it's not loaded when Excel starts up.

8. Click Custom Control at the bottom of the Tools menu. The COM add-in created in this example loads. The *OnConnection* procedure is called and execution breaks on the first line. By pressing F8, the code continues through the Select Case statement and the code in the case where ConnectMode equals ext_cm_AfterStartup is executed. The existing instance of the custom command bar control is connected to the Click event procedure. Once the *OnConnection* procedure fully executes, the Click event procedure is then executed.

...Delete Command Bar Customizations?

The *OnConnection* procedure is the main place where you should add a call to code that inserts command bar customizations like a menu item, toolbar button, or drop-down control. A couple of important things should happen when this code executes. The first is to determine when the add-in is to be loaded. In other words, is the add-in loaded at the startup of the Office application? Or is it to be demand-loaded by a click of a toolbar button or menu item? In each case your code should search to make sure that the customizations exist.

In the *OnDisconnection* procedure, then, you should add a call to code that removes command bar customizations. However, your code should first determine when the add-in is unloaded. Your code in the *OnDisconnection* procedure will appear similar to the following (similar also to the code in the previous example):

```
If RemoveMode = ext_dm_UserClosed Then
    ' User unloaded add-in through COM
    ' Add-Ins dialog box. Thus, remove commands.

ElseIf RemoveMode = ext_dm_HostShutdown Then
    ' If your add-in is demand loaded,
    ' do not remove commands.
End If
```

The first argument passed to the *OnDisconnection* procedure is the *RemoveMode* value. The two common values passed in are ext_dm_HostShutdown or ext_dm_UserClosed. In the previous example, in the section "Create a Demand-Loaded Add-In," you added code that evaluates the RemoveMode value to the *OnDisconnection* procedure.

...Determine How an Office Application is Started?

Once you register a COM add-in so that it loads when an Office 2000 application starts, your add-in can determine how the Office application starts. Word, Excel, and PowerPoint can be started in one of the following three ways. Outlook and Access can be started in either of the following first two ways.

- **Through the Windows Start menu or the Windows Explorer** A user typically starts an application by clicking Start, Programs, and then the Office application item, like Word, for example. The user can also start an application by double-clicking a file associated with the application in the Windows Explorer.

- **Through Automation** For example, a solution or program creates an instance of Word using the function *CreateObject("Word.Application")* in Visual Basic.

- **Through Embedded Objects** For example, a user inserts a Word document into an Excel spreadsheet. In this case, Word is started through an embedded Word object.

Developers can use the first value passed into the custom() array in the *OnConnection* procedure to determine if an application is started by means of Automation. You can use this information, for example, to not display a message box or custom dialog box until the application is made visible. The following example shows how to evaluate the first value of the custom() array passed into the *OnConnection* procedure and determine how an application is started.

Evaluate the Different Application Start Values

1. Start Visual Basic 6.0 and in the New Project dialog box, double-click the ActiveX DLL icon.

2. Right-click the class module Class1 added by default in the Project Explorer window. Click Remove Class1 on the shortcut menu. Click No in the dialog box that asks if you want to save changes.

3. In the Project menu, click Add Addin Class. If this menu item doesn't appear, click Components on the Project menu. In the Components dialog box, click the Designers tab and select Addin Class in the list box. Click OK. You should see the menu item Add Addin Class on the Project menu.

4. In the General tab of the Add-in Designer, select Microsoft Excel from the Application drop-down list and Startup in the Initial Load Behavior drop-down list.

   You may have to resize the Add-in Designer window in order to see the Initial Load Behavior drop-down list at the bottom of the General tab.

5. Press F7 to display the class module for the Add-in Designer. In the Object drop-down list at the top left of the class module window, select AddinInstance.

6. In the *OnConnection* procedure, add the following Select Case statement:

```
Select Case custom(1)
    Case 1
        Debug.Print "UI"
    Case 2
        Debug.Print "Embedding"
    Case 3
        Debug.Print "Automation"
End Select
```

7. In the Properties window, change the Public property to True. Click OK when you see the message box. Change the name of the Add-in Designer from AddInDesigner1 to AppStart.

8. Add a breakpoint to the first line in the *OnConnection* procedure by placing the cursor in the code `Select Case custom(1)` and pressing F9.

9. Press F5 to run the project. Click OK in the project Properties dialog box when it is displayed.

Start an Application Through the User Interface

1. On the Windows Start menu, click Programs and then Microsoft Excel. Excel is started and the COM add-in created in this example is loaded. The *OnConnection* procedure is called and execution breaks on the first line of the Select Case statement.

2. Press F8 to step through the code. The value of custom(1) is evaluated in the first line of the Select Case statement and code execution continues through to the first Case expression. The string "UI" is printed to the Immediate window in Visual Basic, indicating that Excel has started through the user interface.

3. Press F5 to continue execution through the *OnConnection* procedure.

4. Click Exit on the File menu in Excel.

5. Using the Windows Explorer, navigate to an Excel workbook file. Double-click the file in the Windows Explorer to start Excel and open the workbook. Excel is started and the COM add-in is loaded. The *OnConnection* procedure is called and execution breaks on the first line of the Select Case statement.

6. Press F8 to step through the code. The value of custom(1) is evaluated in the first line of the Select Case statement and code execution continues through to the first Case expression. The string "UI" is printed to the Immediate window in Visual Basic, indicating that Excel has again started through the user interface.

7. Press F5 to continue execution through the *OnConnection* procedure.

8. Click Exit on the File menu in Excel.

Start an Application Through an Embedded Object

The following steps will work only if the security setting in Word (or Excel or PowerPoint) is set to Low. Before completing the following steps, temporarily set the security setting to Low by clicking Macro on the Tools menu and then Security on the submenu. In the Security Level tab, select Low and click OK.

In Word, Excel, and PowerPoint, when the application is started through an embedded object, any COM add-in that isn't digitally signed with a certificate or the certificate is not added to the trusted sources list won't be loaded at startup. To see the list of trusted sources, click the Trusted Sources tab in the Security dialog box. For more information about security and digitally signing your COM add-in before distribution, see the section "Digitally Sign a COM Add-In" later in this chapter.

1. Start PowerPoint and after the default presentation is created, temporarily change the security settings to Low.

2. Click Object on the Insert menu.

3. In the Insert Object dialog box, select Microsoft Excel Worksheet from the Object Type list box in the Create New tab. Click OK.

    Excel is started and the COM add-in is loaded. The *OnConnection* procedure is called and execution breaks on the first line of the Select Case statement.

4. Press F8 to step through the code. The value of custom(1) is evaluated in the first line of the Select Case statement and code execution continues through to the second Case expression. The string "Embedding" is printed to the Immediate window in Visual Basic, indicating that Excel has started through an embedded object.

5. Press F5 to continue execution through the *OnConnection* procedure.

6. Switch to Excel and click Exit on the File menu. Reset the security setting back to Medium or High in PowerPoint by clicking Macro on the Tools menu and then Security on the submenu. In the Security Level tab, select Medium or High and click OK.

Start an Application Through Automation

1. Click ALT+F11 to display the Visual Basic Editor in PowerPoint.

2. Click Module on the Insert menu, and then add the following code:

```
Dim appXL As Object

Sub StartExcelThroughAutomation()
    Set appXL = CreateObject("Excel.Application")
    appXL.Visible = True
End Sub
```

3. Place the cursor in the *StartExcelThroughAutomation* procedure and press F5 to run the procedure.

    Excel is started and the COM add-in is loaded. The *OnConnection* procedure is called and execution breaks on the first line of the Select Case statement.

4. Press F8 to step through the code. The value of custom(1) is evaluated in the first line of the Select Case statement and code execution continues through to the third Case expression. The string "Automation" is printed to the Immediate window in Visual Basic, indicating that Excel has started through Automation.

5. Press F5 to continue execution through the *OnConnection* procedure.

6. Switch to Excel and click Exit on the File menu.

...Communicate Between Two COM Add-Ins?

In Office 97, Word, Excel, PowerPoint, and Access all provide the *Run* method on the *Application* object. However, PowerPoint's method is slightly different than the others. In all cases, the *Run* method doesn't allow you to directly access a class object. The *Run* method allows you to execute a procedure in another add-in file.

With the COM add-in model, you can use the Object property on the *COMAddIn* object (defined in the Microsoft Office 9.0 Object Library) to access a public class exposed by a COM add-in. If two COM add-ins are loaded in one Office application, code in the first COM add-in would expose a class to another add-in by setting the Object property in its *OnConnection* procedure. The code would appear similar to the following:

```
Private Sub IDTExtensibility2_OnConnection( _
    ByVal Application As Object, _
    ByVal ConnectMode As AddInDesignerObjects.ext_ConnectMode, _
    ByVal AddInInst As Object, custom() As Variant)
        '
    ' some code
    AddInInst.Object = MyPublicClass
        '
End Sub
```

Code in the second COM add-in that accesses the public class exposed in the first COM add-in would then use the Object property on the *COMAddIn* object. The code would appear similar to the following:

```
Sub AnyProcedure()
    Dim addinLibrary As Office.COMAddIn
    Dim objFromFirstAddin As Object

    Set addinLibrary = HostApp.COMAddIns("Library.ProgID")
    Set objFromFirstAddin = addinLibrary.Object
    ' use objFromFirstAddin object to access methods
    ' and properties exposed by the public class
End Sub
```

The following example shows how to use this syntax so that one COM add-in can access methods and properties exposed in another.

Set Up a COM Add-In with Public Object

1. Start Visual Basic 6.0 and double-click the ActiveX DLL icon in the New Project dialog box.

2. On the Project menu, click Project1 Properties and in the Properties dialog box change the Project Name from Project1 to Communicate1.

3. Select the class module Class1 added by default in the Project Explorer and in the Properties window, change the Name property to TopLevelObject.

4. Change the Instancing property of the class module to **2 – PublicNot-Createable**.

5. Double-click the TopLevelObject class module to display its code window and add the following code:

```
Public Property Get Name() As String
    Name = "MyCOMAddin"
End Property
```

6. Click Add Addin Class on the Project menu. On the General tab of the Add-in Designer, select Microsoft Excel from the Application drop-down list and Startup from the Initial Load Behavior drop-down list.

7. In the Properties window, change the Public property to True. Click OK when you see the message box. Also change the Name property from AddinDesigner1 to Addin1.

8. Press F7 to display the class module for the Add-in Designer. On the Object drop-down list at the top left of the class module window, select AddinInstance.

9. In the *OnConnection* procedure, add the following line of code so that the procedure appears as follows:

```
Private Sub AddinInstance_OnConnection( _
    ByVal Application As Object, _
    ByVal ConnectMode As AddInDesignerObjects.ext_ConnectMode, _
    ByVal AddInInst As Object, custom() As Variant)

    AddInInst.Object = New TopLevelObject
End Sub
```

10. Add a breakpoint to the first line in the *OnConnection* procedure by placing the cursor in the code `AddinInstance_OnConnection` and pressing F9.

11. Press F5 to run the project. Click OK in the project Properties dialog box when it is displayed.

Set Up a Second COM Add-In That Retrieves a Property Value from the First

1. Start a second session of Visual Basic 6.0 through the Window Start menu. Double-click the ActiveX DLL icon in the New Project dialog box.

2. On the Project menu, click Project1 Properties and in the Properties dialog box, change the Project Name from Project1 to Communicate2.

3. Click Add Addin Class on the Project menu and on the General tab of the Add-in Designer, select Microsoft Excel from the Application drop-down list and Startup from the Initial Load Behavior drop-down list.

4. In the Properties window, change the Public property to True. Click OK when you see the message box. Also change the Name property from AddinDesigner1 to Addin2.

5. Press F7 to display the class module for the Add-in Designer. In the Object drop-down list at the top left of the class module window, select AddinInstance. In the *OnConnection* and *OnStartupComplete* procedures, add the following line of code so that the module appears as follows:

```
Dim HostApp As Object

Private Sub AddinInstance_OnConnection( _
    ByVal Application As Object, _
    ByVal ConnectMode As AddInDesignerObjects.ext_ConnectMode, _
    ByVal AddInInst As Object, custom() As Variant)

    Set HostApp = Application
End Sub

Private Sub AddinInstance_OnStartupComplete(custom() As
Variant)
    Debug.Print _
        HostApp.COMAddIns("Communicate1.Addin1").Object.Name
    Debug.Print _
        TypeName(HostApp.COMAddIns("Communicate1.Addin1").Object)
End Sub
```

6. Add a breakpoint to the first line in the *OnConnection* procedure by placing the cursor in the code `AddinInstance_OnConnection` and pressing F9.

7. Press F5 to run the project. Click OK in the project Properties dialog box when it is displayed.

Start Excel and Step Through the COM Add-Ins

1. On the Windows Start menu, click Programs and then Microsoft Excel. Excel is started and the first COM add-in created in this example is loaded. The *OnConnection* procedure is called and execution breaks on the code `AddInInst.Object = New TopLevelObject`.

2. Press F8 to step through the code. Once the *OnConnection* procedure of the first COM add-in, Communicate1, is executed, the Visual Basic window containing the Communicate2 add-in project is activated and the *OnConnection* procedure of the second COM add-in, Communicate2, is called.

The code in the *OnConnection* procedure of Communicate2 sets the public-level *HostApp* object variable to the Excel *Application* object. As you continue to step through the code, the *OnStartupComplete* procedure in the Communicate2 add-in is called.

The code in the *OnStartupComplete* procedure accesses the *COMAddIns* collection object through the Excel *Application* object. The ProgID of the first COM add-in, "Communicate1.Addin1," is used in the index argument of the COMAddIns property to retrieve the *COMAddIn* object representing the first add-in. The Object property of the *COMAddIn* object is then used to access the class TopLevelObject.

As you continue to step through the code, the Name property, defined in the TopLevelObject class, is accessed. The Visual Basic window containing the Communicate1 add-in project is activated and the value of the Name property is retrieved. The Visual Basic window containing the Communicate2 add-in project is activated and the value of the Name property is printed to the Immediate window.

Note also that the second line of code in the *OnStartupComplete* procedure prints to the Immediate window the name of the type of object returned by the Object property. In this case, the string "TopLevelObject" is returned.

3. Switch to Excel and click Exit on the File menu.

...Digitally Sign a COM Add-In?

Before distributing your COM add-in, you should digitally sign the add-in file. Office 2000 introduces a new security model similar to Microsoft Internet Explorer's default (Low, Medium, High) security settings. You can view the security setting for Word, Excel, and PowerPoint by clicking Macro on the Tools menu and then Security on the submenu.

If the security setting in an Office application is Medium or High, Office requires you to give a digital signature to a COM add-in available before the add-in can be loaded. A digital signature gives Office a way to verify two things: that the contents of a file haven't been altered since it was installed on the user's machine and that the file comes from a responsible source (the author or company that developed and distributed the COM add-in).

To digitally sign your COM add-in, you need a certificate and the file SignCode.exe (along with supporting files) that are part of the Microsoft Platform Software Development Kit. You can buy a certificate from a certificate authority, which is a company that validates your identity and issues you a certificate. The certificate authority not only issues certificates but also manages and revokes them when necessary. Once issued, a unique certificate contains your digital signature and verifies your credentials.

Resources To Digitally Sign Your COM Add-Ins

- In the latest Microsoft Developer Network (MSDN) CD or at *http://msdn.microsoft.com,* search on the words "signing code."

- For information about Microsoft security technologies, the Microsoft CryptoAPI, and other Microsoft technologies, see the Microsoft Security Advisor Web site (*http://www.microsoft.com/security/*).

FAQs

Because this chapter and the previous one should have answered most of your questions about COM add-ins, the following list of frequently asked questions is not complete. It does, however, provide further insight based on the examples and information given in this chapter.

Q: Can a COM add-in be loaded at startup in one Office application and loaded on demand or no-load behavior in another?

A: COM add-ins are registered for each application. When you register a COM add-in for each application, you specify the LoadBehavior value in the registry. For one application, you can set the LoadBehavior value under the application's AddIns key in the Windows registry to boot-loaded (or a value of 3), while you can set the LoadBehavior value under another application's AddIns key to load on demand (or a value of 9).

Q: If a COM add-in targets more than one Office application, can you add a menu item to one application but not another?

A: When the *OnConnection* procedure is called after Office loads an add-in, the code in the *OnConnection* procedure can distinguish the application into which the COM add-in is loaded. Using the *Application* object passed into the *OnConnection* procedure, you can use the Name property to distinguish the application and determine if command bar customizations should be added. The *OnConnection* procedure in the COM add-in may appear as follows:

```
Private Sub IDTExtensibility2_OnConnection( _
    ByVal Application As Object, _
    ByVal ConnectMode As AddInDesignerObjects.ext_ConnectMode, _
    ByVal AddInInst As Object, custom() As Variant)

    Select Case Application.Name
        Case "Microsoft Word"
            ' Do not add custom menu item
        Case "Microsoft Excel"
            ' Add custom menu item
    End Select
End Sub
```

Q: Can I use the add-ins I created in Office 97 in Office 2000, or should I migrate my Office 97 add-ins to COM add-ins in Office 2000?

A: The COM add-in model coexists with the add-in models provided by each individual Office 97 application. You don't need to rewrite your Office 97 add-ins. They should run without modification in Office 2000. If you want to create an add-in that works in both Office 97 and Office 2000, the only way to do it is to create your add-in in Office 97 and install it in Office 2000. If your add-in is specific to Office 2000, it's recommended that you use the COM add-in model based on the table in the section "Why Should You Develop COM Add-Ins?" earlier in this chapter.

Q: How does Office know that a COM add-in works in multiple applications?

A: A COM add-in registers itself for the applications it can be connected to. This is done through the registry key HKEY_CURRENT_USER \Software\Microsoft\Office\<app>\Addins, where <app> represents any one of the Office 2000 applications, including FrontPage.

Q: Why isn't the registry key for COM add-ins located under the Office\9.0 key?

A: The majority of add-ins are written to be version independent. When you install an add-in for Office 97, you expect it to run without modification if you upgrade to Office 2000. When add-ins are installed under a specific version of Office, Office has to transfer these keys when a newer version of Office is installed. In addition, because an add-in from a previous version can be installed after Office 2000 is installed, the add-in will register itself under the specific Office version key. Therefore, Office always needs to read the previous version's key as well as the current version's key.

This introduces a performance impact, because Office has to read several keys to build its list of available add-ins for a particular application. The version-independent COM add-in keys leave it up to the developer to add code in the *OnConnection* procedure of the COM add-in to determine the version of the application—if the add-in is written for a specific version of Office. You can use the Version property on the *Application* object in each Office application. If the add-in should not be loaded in a specific version, you can add the line `AddInInst.Connect = False` in the *OnConnection* procedure.

Q: In Word, the command bar customizations that were modified or removed in the *OnDisconnection* procedure reappear unmodified the next time Word is started. Why aren't the customizations removed?

A: When Word shuts down, the *OnDisconnection* procedure is called after Word has saved changes to the Normal template and any other templates that contain command bar customizations. In the *OnDisconnection* procedure, you need to explicitly save the template that contains the command bar customizations. To save changes to the Normal.dot template, add the line `appWord.NormalTemplate.Save` (where `appWord` represents a variable assigned to the Word *Application* object) to ensure that the modification or removal of command bar customizations persist before Word quits.

Chapter Summary

These final two chapters introduce the COM add-in model in Office 2000 as Office's first consistent add-in model. This model allows you to create a single add-in file targeted for more than one Office application. It also gives you the ability to create add-ins in any Microsoft development environment (although only the use of Visual Basic 6.0 is discussed). Chapter 13 provides step-by-step instructions on how to create a COM add-in. This chapter describes the COM add-in model more thoroughly. Together, the two chapters allow you to build a COM add-in from start to finish.

Index

' (apostrophe), code and, 43

. (dot oper ator), navigating in Object model, 14

(...) (ellipsis), displaying a dialog box, 360

= (equal sign), setting property values, 241

A

accelerator keys
  MultiPage control and, 99
  setting with Caption property, 359–360

Access
  adding code in, 265–266
  creating forms in, 263–265
  creating an Office document from data, 266–269
  creating wizards in, 93
  database properties in, 146
  importing data into, 258–259
  inaccessibility of File dialog box in, 122
  opening databases in, 131
  preventing alert displays in, 139
  producing a Word report from data, 271–276
  retrieving data from, 269–271
  Run method in, 488

active window
  definition of, 289
  using color to indicate, 346
  using custom menu to track, 352

active worksheet, 306

ActiveDocument
  definition of, 289
  overview of, 290–291

ActiveWindow, 290–291

ActiveX controls
  adding to Toolbox, 71–72
  assigning unique names to, 69
  double-click content of, 334
  gathering user input with, 70–71
  inserting into a document, 23
  prefixes of, 74
  setting properties of, 68–70
  using with UserForm, 65, 67

Add method
  compared with CreateItem, 151
  compared with New event, 157
  compared with Open method, 130
  creating new documents with, 132
  in Excel, 134, 203
  functions of, 132
  in PowerPoint, 135, 218
  in Word, 133–134

The manuscript for this book was prepared and galleyed using Microsoft Word 97. Pages were composed by nSight, Inc. using Adobe PageMaker 6.52 for Windows, with text in Stone Serif and display type in ITC Franklin Gothic. Composed pages were delivered to the printer as electronic prepress files.

Cover Designer: Leonhardt Group
Interior Graphic Designer: James D. Kramer
Interior Graphic Artist: Samantha Stanko
Principal Compositors: Angela Montoya, Tara Murray
Principal Proofreaders: Linda Griset, William Oppenheimer
Indexer: Jack Lewis

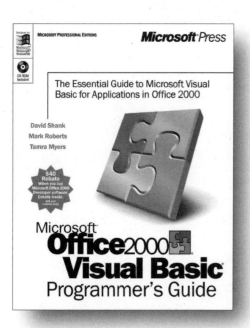

Teach yourself VBA

programming fundamentals step by step!

Take command of Microsoft Office 2000 applications with these teach-yourself guides to Microsoft Visual Basic for Applications (VBA). Each is full of easy-to-follow lessons and real-world examples to help you learn exactly what you need to know at your own pace. Discover how to automate content creation, handle events, write your own functions and procedures, customize menus and toolbars, create component add-ins for all Office applications, save documents to an intranet, connect applications to the Web, and more. Prepared by authors with vast knowledge of VBA and Office design and programming, these new editions of top-selling tutorials have each been expanded to include more than 15 hours of instruction, with numerous screen shots and illustrations.

mspress.microsoft.com

MICROSOFT LICENSE AGREEMENT
Book Companion CD

IMPORTANT—READ CAREFULLY: This Microsoft End-User License Agreement ("EULA") is a legal agreement between you (either an individual or an entity) and Microsoft Corporation for the Microsoft product identified above, which includes computer software and may include associated media, printed materials, and "online" or electronic documentation ("SOFTWARE PRODUCT"). Any component included within the SOFTWARE PRODUCT that is accompanied by a separate End-User License Agreement shall be governed by such agreement and not the terms set forth below. By installing, copying, or otherwise using the SOFTWARE PRODUCT, you agree to be bound by the terms of this EULA. If you do not agree to the terms of this EULA, you are not authorized to install, copy, or otherwise use the SOFTWARE PRODUCT; you may, however, return the SOFTWARE PRODUCT, along with all printed materials and other items that form a part of the Microsoft product that includes the SOFTWARE PRODUCT, to the place you obtained them for a full refund.

SOFTWARE PRODUCT LICENSE

The SOFTWARE PRODUCT is protected by United States copyright laws and international copyright treaties, as well as other intellectual property laws and treaties. The SOFTWARE PRODUCT is licensed, not sold.

1. **GRANT OF LICENSE.** This EULA grants you the following rights:

   a. **Software Product.** You may install and use one copy of the SOFTWARE PRODUCT on a single computer. The primary user of the computer on which the SOFTWARE PRODUCT is installed may make a second copy for his or her exclusive use on a portable computer.

   b. **Storage/Network Use.** You may also store or install a copy of the SOFTWARE PRODUCT on a storage device, such as a network server, used only to install or run the SOFTWARE PRODUCT on your other computers over an internal network; however, you must acquire and dedicate a license for each separate computer on which the SOFTWARE PRODUCT is installed or run from the storage device. A license for the SOFTWARE PRODUCT may not be shared or used concurrently on different computers.

   c. **License Pak.** If you have acquired this EULA in a Microsoft License Pak, you may make the number of additional copies of the computer software portion of the SOFTWARE PRODUCT authorized on the printed copy of this EULA, and you may use each copy in the manner specified above. You are also entitled to make a corresponding number of secondary copies for portable computer use as specified above.

   d. **Sample Code.** Solely with respect to portions, if any, of the SOFTWARE PRODUCT that are identified within the SOFTWARE PRODUCT as sample code (the "SAMPLE CODE"):

      i. **Use and Modification.** Microsoft grants you the right to use and modify the source code version of the SAMPLE CODE, *provided* you comply with subsection (d)(iii) below. You may not distribute the SAMPLE CODE, or any modified version of the SAMPLE CODE, in source code form.

      ii. **Redistributable Files.** Provided you comply with subsection (d)(iii) below, Microsoft grants you a nonexclusive, royalty-free right to reproduce and distribute the object code version of the SAMPLE CODE and of any modified SAMPLE CODE, other than SAMPLE CODE, or any modified version thereof, designated as not redistributable in the Readme file that forms a part of the SOFTWARE PRODUCT (the "Non-Redistributable Sample Code"). All SAMPLE CODE other than the Non-Redistributable Sample Code is collectively referred to as the "REDISTRIBUTABLES."

      iii. **Redistribution Requirements.** If you redistribute the REDISTRIBUTABLES, you agree to: (i) distribute the REDISTRIBUTABLES in object code form only in conjunction with and as a part of your software application product; (ii) not use Microsoft's name, logo, or trademarks to market your software application product; (iii) include a valid copyright notice on your software application product; (iv) indemnify, hold harmless, and defend Microsoft from and against any claims or lawsuits, including attorney's fees, that arise or result from the use or distribution of your software application product; and (v) not permit further distribution of the REDISTRIBUTABLES by your end user. Contact Microsoft for the applicable royalties due and other licensing terms for all other uses and/or distribution of the REDISTRIBUTABLES.

2. **DESCRIPTION OF OTHER RIGHTS AND LIMITATIONS.**

   - **Limitations on Reverse Engineering, Decompilation, and Disassembly.** You may not reverse engineer, decompile, or disassemble the SOFTWARE PRODUCT, except and only to the extent that such activity is expressly permitted by applicable law notwithstanding this limitation.

   - **Separation of Components.** The SOFTWARE PRODUCT is licensed as a single product. Its component parts may not be separated for use on more than one computer.

   - **Rental.** You may not rent, lease, or lend the SOFTWARE PRODUCT.

   - **Support Services.** Microsoft may, but is not obligated to, provide you with support services related to the SOFTWARE PRODUCT ("Support Services"). Use of Support Services is governed by the Microsoft policies and programs described in the user manual, in "online" documentation, and/or in other Microsoft-provided materials. Any supplemental software code provided to you as part of the Support Services shall be considered part of the SOFTWARE PRODUCT and subject to the terms and conditions of this EULA. With respect to technical information you provide to Microsoft as part of the Support Services, Microsoft may use such information for its business purposes, including for product support and development. Microsoft will not utilize such technical information in a form that personally identifies you.

- **Software Transfer.** You may permanently transfer all of your rights under this EULA, provided you retain no copies, you transfer all of the SOFTWARE PRODUCT (including all component parts, the media and printed materials, any upgrades, this EULA, and, if applicable, the Certificate of Authenticity), **and** the recipient agrees to the terms of this EULA.

- **Termination.** Without prejudice to any other rights, Microsoft may terminate this EULA if you fail to comply with the terms and conditions of this EULA. In such event, you must destroy all copies of the SOFTWARE PRODUCT and all of its component parts.

3. **COPYRIGHT.** All title and copyrights in and to the SOFTWARE PRODUCT (including but not limited to any images, photographs, animations, video, audio, music, text, SAMPLE CODE, REDISTRIBUTABLES, and "applets" incorporated into the SOFTWARE PRODUCT) and any copies of the SOFTWARE PRODUCT are owned by Microsoft or its suppliers. The SOFTWARE PRODUCT is protected by copyright laws and international treaty provisions. Therefore, you must treat the SOFTWARE PRODUCT like any other copyrighted material **except** that you may install the SOFTWARE PRODUCT on a single computer provided you keep the original solely for backup or archival purposes. You may not copy the printed materials accompanying the SOFTWARE PRODUCT.

4. **U.S. GOVERNMENT RESTRICTED RIGHTS.** The SOFTWARE PRODUCT and documentation are provided with RESTRICTED RIGHTS. Use, duplication, or disclosure by the Government is subject to restrictions as set forth in subparagraph (c)(1)(ii) of the Rights in Technical Data and Computer Software clause at DFARS 252.227-7013 or subparagraphs (c)(1) and (2) of the Commercial Computer Software—Restricted Rights at 48 CFR 52.227-19, as applicable. Manufacturer is Microsoft Corporation/One Microsoft Way/Redmond, WA 98052-6399.

5. **EXPORT RESTRICTIONS.** You agree that you will not export or re-export the SOFTWARE PRODUCT, any part thereof, or any process or service that is the direct product of the SOFTWARE PRODUCT (the foregoing collectively referred to as the "Restricted Components"), to any country, person, entity, or end user subject to U.S. export restrictions. You specifically agree not to export or re-export any of the Restricted Components (i) to any country to which the U.S. has embargoed or restricted the export of goods or services, which currently include, but are not necessarily limited to, Cuba, Iran, Iraq, Libya, North Korea, Sudan, and Syria, or to any national of any such country, wherever located, who intends to transmit or transport the Restricted Components back to such country; (ii) to any end user who you know or have reason to know will utilize the Restricted Components in the design, development, or production of nuclear, chemical, or biological weapons; or (iii) to any end user who has been prohibited from participating in U.S. export transactions by any federal agency of the U.S. government. You warrant and represent that neither the BXA nor any other U.S. federal agency has suspended, revoked, or denied your export privileges.

DISCLAIMER OF WARRANTY

NO WARRANTIES OR CONDITIONS. MICROSOFT EXPRESSLY DISCLAIMS ANY WARRANTY OR CONDITION FOR THE SOFTWARE PRODUCT. THE SOFTWARE PRODUCT AND ANY RELATED DOCUMENTATION ARE PROVIDED "AS IS" WITHOUT WARRANTY OR CONDITION OF ANY KIND, EITHER EXPRESS OR IMPLIED, INCLUDING, WITHOUT LIMITATION, THE IMPLIED WARRANTIES OF MERCHANTABILITY, FITNESS FOR A PARTICULAR PURPOSE, OR NONINFRINGEMENT. THE ENTIRE RISK ARISING OUT OF USE OR PERFORMANCE OF THE SOFTWARE PRODUCT REMAINS WITH YOU.

LIMITATION OF LIABILITY. TO THE MAXIMUM EXTENT PERMITTED BY APPLICABLE LAW, IN NO EVENT SHALL MICROSOFT OR ITS SUPPLIERS BE LIABLE FOR ANY SPECIAL, INCIDENTAL, INDIRECT, OR CONSEQUENTIAL DAMAGES WHATSOEVER (INCLUDING, WITHOUT LIMITATION, DAMAGES FOR LOSS OF BUSINESS PROFITS, BUSINESS INTERRUPTION, LOSS OF BUSINESS INFORMATION, OR ANY OTHER PECUNIARY LOSS) ARISING OUT OF THE USE OF OR INABILITY TO USE THE SOFTWARE PRODUCT OR THE PROVISION OF OR FAILURE TO PROVIDE SUPPORT SERVICES, EVEN IF MICROSOFT HAS BEEN ADVISED OF THE POSSIBILITY OF SUCH DAMAGES. IN ANY CASE, MICROSOFT'S ENTIRE LIABILITY UNDER ANY PROVISION OF THIS EULA SHALL BE LIMITED TO THE GREATER OF THE AMOUNT ACTUALLY PAID BY YOU FOR THE SOFTWARE PRODUCT OR US$5.00; PROVIDED, HOWEVER, IF YOU HAVE ENTERED INTO A MICROSOFT SUPPORT SERVICES AGREEMENT, MICROSOFT'S ENTIRE LIABILITY REGARDING SUPPORT SERVICES SHALL BE GOVERNED BY THE TERMS OF THAT AGREEMENT. BECAUSE SOME STATES AND JURISDICTIONS DO NOT ALLOW THE EXCLUSION OR LIMITATION OF LIABILITY, THE ABOVE LIMITATION MAY NOT APPLY TO YOU.

MISCELLANEOUS

This EULA is governed by the laws of the State of Washington USA, except and only to the extent that applicable law mandates governing law of a different jurisdiction.

Should you have any questions concerning this EULA, or if you desire to contact Microsoft for any reason, please contact the Microsoft subsidiary serving your country, or write: Microsoft Sales Information Center/One Microsoft Way/Redmond, WA 98052-6399.

Register Today!

Return this
*Microsoft® Office 2000/Visual Basic® for
Applications Fundamentals*
registration card today

Microsoft® Press
mspress.microsoft.com

0-7356-0594-7

Microsoft® Office 2000/Visual Basic® for Applications Fundamentals

FIRST NAME   MIDDLE INITIAL   LAST NAME

INSTITUTION OR COMPANY NAME

ADDRESS

CITY   STATE   ZIP

(   )

E-MAIL ADDRESS   PHONE NUMBER

U.S. and Canada addresses only. Fill in information above and mail postage-free.
Please mail only the bottom half of this page.

start faster go farther

For information about Microsoft Press®
products, visit our Web site at
mspress.microsoft.com

Microsoft®*Press*